Continuous Sedation at the End of Life

Continuous sedation until death (sometimes referred to as terminal sedation or palliative sedation) is an increasingly common practice in end-of-life care. However, it raises numerous medical, ethical, emotional and legal concerns, such as reducing or removing of consciousness (and thus potentially causing 'subjective death'), the withholding of artificial nutrition and hydration, the proportionality of the sedation to the symptoms, its adequacy in actually relieving symptoms rather than simply giving onlookers the impression that the patient is undergoing a painless 'natural' death, and the perception that it may be functionally equivalent to euthanasia.

This book brings together contributions from clinicians, ethicists, lawyers and social scientists, and discusses guidelines as well as clinical, emotional and legal aspects of the practice. The chapters shine a critical spotlight on areas of concern and on the validity of the justifications given for the practice, including in particular the doctrine of double effect.

SIGRID STERCKX is a professor of ethics at Ghent University and at the Vrije Universiteit Brussel (VUB) in Belgium.

KASPER RAUS is a postdoctoral researcher at Ghent University, Belgium.

FREDDY MORTIER is a professor of ethics at Ghent University, Belgium.

Cambridge Bioethics and Law

This series of books was founded by Cambridge University Press with Alexander McCall Smith as its first editor in 2003. It focuses on the law's complex and troubled relationship with medicine across both the developed and the developing world. Since the early 1990s, we have seen in many countries increasing resort to the courts by dissatisfied patients and a growing use of the courts to attempt to resolve intractable ethical dilemmas. At the same time, legislatures across the world have struggled to address the questions posed by both the successes and the failures of modern medicine, while international organisations such as the WHO and UNESCO now regularly address issues of medical law.

It follows that we would expect ethical and policy questions to be integral to the analysis of the legal issues discussed in this series. The series responds to the high profile of medical law in universities, in legal and medical practice, as well as in public and political affairs. We seek to reflect the evidence that many major health-related policy debates in the UK, Europe and the international community involve a strong medical law dimension. With that in mind, we seek to address how legal analysis might have a trans-jurisdictional and international relevance. Organ retention, embryonic stem cell research, physician assisted suicide and the allocation of resources to fund health care are but a few examples among many. The emphasis of this series is thus on matters of public concern and/or practical significance. We look for books that could make a difference to the development of medical law and enhance the role of medico-legal debate in policy circles. That is not to say that we lack interest in the important theoretical dimensions of the subject, but we aim to ensure that theoretical debate is grounded in the realities of how the law does and should interact with medicine and health care.

Series Editors

Professor Margaret Brazier,
University of Manchester

Professor Graeme Laurie,
University of Edinburgh

Professor Richard Ashcroft,
Queen Mary, University of London

Professor Eric M. Meslin,
Indiana University

A list of books in the series can be found at the end of this volume.

This book is due for return on or before the last date shown below.

Continuous Sedation at the End of Life

Ethical, Clinical and Legal Perspectives

Edited by

Sigrid Sterckx, Kasper Raus and Freddy Mortier

CAMBRIDGE
UNIVERSITY PRESS

CAMBRIDGE
UNIVERSITY PRESS

University Printing House, Cambridge CB2 8BS, United Kingdom

Published in the United States of America by Cambridge University Press, New York

Cambridge University Press is part of the University of Cambridge.

It furthers the University's mission by disseminating knowledge in the pursuit of education, learning and research at the highest international levels of excellence.

www.cambridge.org
Information on this title: www.cambridge.org/9781107039216

© Cambridge University Press 2013

First published 2013

Printed in the United Kingdom by the CPI Group Ltd, Croydon CR0 4YY

A catalogue record for this publication is available from the British Library

Library of Congress Cataloguing in Publication data
Continuous sedation at the end of life : ethical, clinical, and legal perspectives / edited by Sigrid Sterckx, Kasper Raus, Freddy Mortier.
 pages cm. – (Cambridge bioethics and law)
Includes bibliographical references and index.
ISBN 978-1-107-03921-6 (hardback)
1. Terminal sedation. 2. Terminal care – Law and legislation.
3. Terminally ill – Psychology. I. Sterckx, Sigrid, editor of compilation. II. Raus, Kasper, editor of compilation.
III. Mortier, Freddy, editor of compilation.
R726.C6725 2013
616.02′9–dc23   2013009518

ISBN 978-1-107-03921-6 Hardback

Contents

Figures

Contributors

MARGARET P. BATTIN is a professor of philosophy and medical ethics at the University of Utah, USA. She has authored, co-authored, edited, or co-edited some twenty books, including works on philosophical issues in suicide, case-puzzles in aesthetics, ethical issues in organised religion and various topics in bioethics. She has published two collections of essays on end of life issues, *The Least Worst Death* and *Ending Life*, and has been the lead for two multi-authored projects, *Drugs and Justice* and *The Patient as Victim and Vector: Ethics and Infectious Disease*. In 1997, Professor Battin won the University of Utah's Distinguished Research award, and in 2000, she received the Rosenblatt Prize, the University's most prestigious award. Her current projects include a comprehensive historical sourcebook on ethical issues in suicide, a volume of puzzle cases about issues in disability and a book on large-scale reproductive problems of the globe, including population growth and decline, teen pregnancy, abortion and male roles in contraception.

SOPHIE M. BRUINSMA works as a doctoral researcher at the Department of Public Health of Erasmus Medical Centre, Erasmus University Rotterdam, The Netherlands. She is a sociologist and epidemiologist by training. She is involved in an international study (the UNBIASED study) that explores the perspectives of clinical staff and bereaved informal caregivers on the use of continuous sedation until death for cancer patients. Her Ph.D. research specifically focuses on the experiences of relatives with continuous sedation at the end of life.

THOMAS CARROLL, MD, Ph.D., was educated at: Nazareth College, Rochester, New York (BS in Biochemistry); the University of Connecticut, Farmington, Connecticut (MD/Ph.D. Medical-Scientist Training Program); and the University of Rochester, Rochester, New York (Internal Medicine Internship and Residency, Chief Resident Internal Medicine and Fellow in Hospice and Palliative Medicine).

He will be staying on at the University of Rochester as faculty with appointments in the divisions of General Medicine and Palliative Care.

EVELIEN DELBEKE specialises in healthcare law in the broad sense of the word (e.g. medical liability, medical disciplinary rules, professional legal advice, bioethical regulations, patient rights, and the like). From 2006 to 2011, she worked as a doctoral researcher in the field of health law at the Faculty of Law of the University of Antwerp, Belgium. In 2011, she obtained the degree of Doctor of Law with a dissertation on the legal aspects of end-of-life care, in which she examined the legal aspects of the various medical end-of-life decisions (euthanasia, ending of life without request, assisted suicide, alleviation of pain and symptoms with a possible life-shortening effect, continuous deep sedation at the end of life, and the withholding or withdrawing of life-sustaining treatment). She compared Belgian law with the laws of The Netherlands, France, Luxembourg, Switzerland, the USA and the UK. She was awarded the prize André Prims for her work. Dr Delbeke is a frequently invited lecturer on these topics. Since 2012, she has been an attorney-at-law with Monard-D'Hulst, a law firm specialising in health law.

CLAUDIA GONZALEZ was born in Mexico City. She received her medical degree from the Universidad Autonoma de Gaudalaja and completed her Internal Medicine residency at Unity Health System, Rochester, New York. Currently she is doing her Hospice and Palliative Care fellowship at the University of Rochester in Rochester, New York.

TIMOTHY HOLAHAN attended medical school at the Lake Erie College of Osteopathic Medicine in Erie, Pennsylvania and graduated with a Doctor of Osteopathic Medicine degree in 2009. He then completed his residency in Internal Medicine at the University at Buffalo in Buffalo, New York in 2012. Currently he is completing a combined fellowship in palliative care and geriatrics at the University of Rochester in Rochester, New York. During his residency training, he developed a strong interest in the field of palliative care. He was a co-author for a case series with Dr Kerr and Dr Robert Milch that was published in the *Journal of Palliative Medicine* in 2011, entitled 'The use of ketamine in severe cases of refractory pain syndromes in the palliative care setting'. Another case series he has contributed to, together with Dr Kerr and Dr Debra Luczkiewcz, describes the use of pentobarbital in the restoration of sleep-wake cycles in refractory delirium. This study is pending publication. He has also spent six months as Chief Medical Resident in the University at Buffalo Internal Medicine program.

SØREN HOLM is a medical doctor and philosopher who generally holds conservative views in relation to euthanasia, physician-assisted suicide and other forms of assisted dying. He is a professor of bioethics and medical ethics. Professor Holm directs the Centre for Social Ethics and Policy at the University of Manchester, UK, and holds permanent visiting chairs at the University of Oslo, Norway and the University of Aalborg, Denmark. He is the former Editor in Chief of the *Journal of Medical Ethics* and the current Editor in Chief of the journal *Clinical Ethics*.

RUTH HORN is an Ethics and Society Wellcome Trust Fellow at the Ethox Centre, University of Oxford, UK. She was awarded a BA in Sociology from Ludwig-Maximilian University Munich (2002), an MA in Sociology from Paris Diderot University (2003) and a Master of Research (2004) and Ph.D. (2009) from the Ecole des Hautes Etudes en Sciences Sociales, Paris. Her doctoral thesis examined the euthanasia debates and end-of-life practices in France and Germany. After conducting postdoctoral research about advance decision-making and discontinuation of life-sustaining treatments in France (funded by the French National Cancer League) at the Ecole Nationale Supérieure in Paris, Dr Horn completed a postdoctoral research project on advance directives in England and France (funded by the European Commission) at the University of Bristol. Her general research interest lies in exploring ethical questions raised by medical practices at the end of life, particularly regarding the tensions between respect for patient autonomy and physicians' duty to protect life. She is interested in understanding in which contexts (legal, cultural, socio-historical) these questions emerge in the public space, and how they are treated in the debates in specific countries (UK, France, Germany).

RICHARD HUXTABLE is Reader in Medical Ethics & Law and Deputy Director of the Centre for Ethics in Medicine, in the School of Social and Community Medicine at the University of Bristol. Qualified in law and socio-legal studies, his research primarily concerns end-of-life decision-making and surgical ethics, and he has published widely in medical, legal and bioethical journals, as well as engaging with the international media. Richard is the author of *Euthanasia, Ethics and the Law: From Conflict to Compromise* (2007) and *Law, Ethics and Compromise at the Limits of Life: To Treat or Not to Treat?* (2012). He is also co-author, with Dickenson and Parker, of *The Cambridge Medical*

Ethics Workbook (2010, Cambridge University Press). He is currently
working on *All That Matters: Euthanasia*, which is due to be published in 2013. A long-standing participant in clinical ethics support,
Richard is also a trustee of the National Council for Palliative Care,
and Chair of its Ethics Forum.

DAVID ALBERT JONES is Director of the Anscombe Bioethics Centre
in Oxford. He is also Research Fellow in Bioethics at Blackfriars
Hall, Oxford and Visiting Professor in the Centre for Bioethics and
Emerging Technologies, St Mary's University College, Twickenham.
Professor Jones read Natural Sciences and Philosophy at Cambridge
(1984–7), and Theology at Oxford (1992–2000). His book *The Soul
of the Embryo* was short-listed for the Michael Ramsey Prize 2007.
His doctorate was published in 2007 as *Approaching the End: a theological exploration of death and dying*. Professor Jones also contributed
to *The Mental Capacity Act: A practical guide* and *A Practical Guide to
The Spiritual Care of the Dying Person*. He is Vice-chair of the Ministry
of Defence Research Ethics Committee, examiner for the Diploma
in the Philosophy of Medicine run by the Society of Apothecaries, is
on the National Reference Group of the Liverpool Care Pathway for
the Dying Patient and was on a working party of the General Medical
Council which helped draft its 2010 guidance on *Treatment and Care
towards the End of Life*. His most recent book, co-edited with Calum
MacKellar, is *Chimera's Children: Ethical, Philosophical and Religious
Perspectives on Human-Nonhuman Experimentation*.

JOHAN LEGEMAATE is a professor of health law at the Academic Medical
Centre at the University of Amsterdam. Over the past twenty years he
has been closely involved with legislation and policy concerning medical decisions at the end of life. He has published several national and
international papers concerning euthanasia and related topics. Until
2010 he was the Chief Legal Counsel for the Royal Dutch Medical
Association. In 2011–12 he was a member of the research team that
carried out the evaluation of the Dutch Euthanasia Act.

FREDDY MORTIER is a professor of ethics at Ghent University. He lectures on courses in Bioethics, Philosophy of Religion, and Moral and
Faith Education. His current research focuses on the ethics of medical decision-making surrounding the end of life and on the epis-
temology of religious thought. He has (co-)authored numerous book
chapters as well as journal articles. He is also a member of several
advisory boards and commissions, including the Belgian Advisory
Committee on Bioethics and the Ethics Committee of Ghent
University Hospital.

DAVID ORENTLICHER is a professor of bioethics and law at Indiana University Robert H. McKinney School of Law and Indiana University School of Medicine. A graduate of Harvard Medical School and Harvard Law School, he has authored *Matters of Life and Death* (2001), and he is co-author of *Bioethics and Public Health Law* (3rd edn. 2013). Before coming to Indiana University, he directed the American Medical Association's division of medical ethics and helped draft the Association's policies on end of life decisions. Between 2002 and 2008, he served in the Indiana House of Representatives.

JOSEP PORTA-SALES studied medicine at the University of Barcelona (1975–82). He specialised in Internal Medicine and trained in Palliative Care at St Christopher's Hospice (London). He obtained an MA in Palliative Care from the University of Barcelona (1998) and an MA in Bioethics from the Autonomous University of Barcelona (1999). Since 1987 he has been working as a palliative care consultant in various hospitals. Dr Porta-Sales is currently Head of Research and Teaching at the Palliative Care Service of the Catalan Institute of Oncology, and Senior Lecturer in Palliative Medicine at the International University of Catalonia. He has authored many national and international articles and textbooks. His main areas of interest and research are palliative sedation, opioids in cancer pain and the organisation of palliative care in acute hospitals.

TIMOTHY E. QUILL is a professor of medicine, psychiatry and medical humanities at the University of Rochester School of Medicine and Dentistry. He is also Director of the Palliative Care Program in the Department of Medicine. Dr Quill has published and lectured widely about various aspects of the doctor–patient relationship, with special focus on end-of-life decision-making, including delivering bad news, non-abandonment, discussing palliative care earlier and exploring last-resort options. He is the author of several books on end of life, including *Physician-Assisted Dying: The Case for Palliative Care and Patient Choice* (2004), *Caring for Patients at the End of Life: Facing an Uncertain Future Together* (2001) and *A Midwife Through the Dying Process: Stories of Healing and Hard Choices at the End of Life* (1996), as well as numerous articles published in major medical journals. Dr Quill was the lead physician plaintiff in the New York State legal case challenging the law prohibiting physician-assisted death that was heard in 1997 by the US Supreme Court (*Vacco v. Quill*). Dr Quill received his undergraduate degree from Amherst College (1971), and his MD from the University of Rochester (1976). He completed his Internal Medicine residency in 1979 and a Fellowship

in Medicine/Psychiatry Liaison in 1981, both from the University of
Rochester School of Medicine and Dentistry. Dr Quill is a Fellow in
the American College of Physicians, an ABMS certified palliative
care consultant, and the immediate past-President of the American
Academy of Hospice and Palliative Medicine.

KASPER RAUS holds an MA in Philosophy (Ghent University, 2008)
and a Ph.D. in Philosophy (Ghent University, 2013). His current research focuses on the ethical issues surrounding end-of-life
decisions in general, and continuous sedation at the end of life in
particular. He has published various articles on this topic in international journals. Together with researchers from the End-of-Life
Care Research Group of the Vrije Universiteit Brussel he is involved
in an international qualitative research study on the experiences
and attitudes of physicians, nurses and relatives concerning continuous sedation at the end of life. Broader aspects, for example the
possible justifications of sedation in end-of-life care, are also being
addressed by this study. This research is being conducted by a
multidisciplinary team of researchers in Belgium, The Netherlands
and the UK.

JUDITH A.C. RIETJENS works as an assistant professor at the
Department of Public Health of Erasmus Medical Centre, Erasmus
University Rotterdam, The Netherlands, and as a part-time professor at the End-of-Life Care Research Group of Ghent University and
Vrije Universiteit Brussel, Belgium. She is a health scientist by training and completed her Ph.D. on end-of-life decision-making in 2006.
She is involved in several local, national and international studies
concerning end-of-life decision-making. She was awarded a VENI
grant (Innovative Research Incentives for Academic Excellence)
and an EUR fellowship. She coordinates the UNBIASED study, an
empirical and ethical evaluation of the practice of continuous sedation at the end of life in The Netherlands, Belgium and the UK.
Her other research interests include different perspectives on end-of-
life decision-making (e.g. international comparisons; comparisons of
perspectives of patients, relatives and healthcare professionals) and
media representations of end-of-life decisions. In 2010 she was a visiting researcher at the Department of Geriatrics of Yale School of
Medicine, New Haven, USA. Judith was selected to participate in the
Erasmus MC Female Career Development Program. In 2010, she was
granted the Young Investigator Award (2nd prize) of the European
Association of Palliative Care, and in 2012 the UNESCO/L'Oréal
For Women in Science Fellowship.

JANE SEYMOUR is head of the Sue Ryder Care Centre for Palliative and End of Life Studies and Director of Research at the School of Nursing, Midwifery and Physiotherapy, the University of Nottingham. The Centre's programme of research has particular focus on older people's needs for palliative and end-of-life care and the improvement of care in resource-poor contexts. It collaborates with a wide range of partners in the UK and internationally and has had graduates from its Ph.D. programme from Jordan, Kenya, India, Thailand and Saudi Arabia, as well as the UK. Jane is a nurse and a social scientist, and has been involved in palliative care research and education since the early 1990s. She has published widely in the palliative care, social science and nursing press. She co-led (with Dr. Katherine Froggatt, Lancaster University) a programme of research related to older people and end-of-life care within one of the UK's two national supportive and palliative care collaboratives: the 'Cancer Experiences Collaborative'. Professor Seymour was the principal investigator in a project examining the use of sedation in end-of-life care in the UK, funded by the Economic and Social Research Council. This study was run in parallel with studies in Belgium and The Netherlands.

SIGRID STERCKX is a professor of ethics at Ghent University and at the Vrije Universiteit Brussel (VUB) in Belgium. She lectures on courses in Theoretical Ethics, Methods in Ethics, Contemporary Continental Ethics, Global Ethics and Environmental Ethics. Her current research focuses on: ethical aspects of medical decisions at the end of life; ethical aspects of biobanking, organ transplantation and patenting of human body material (particularly genes and stem cells); ethical issues regarding human enhancement; patent law (especially in Europe and the USA); and environmental ethics and governance, focusing inter alia on climate change, global and intertemporal justice. Sigrid has (co-)authored numerous book chapters as well as journal articles. She serves on various advisory boards and commissions, including the Belgian Advisory Committee on Bioethics, and works as an ethics consultant for several EU research projects. She is also a member of the Steering Group for the UNBIASED study, an interview study exploring the perspectives of physicians, nurses and bereaved informal caregivers on the use of continuous sedation until death for cancer patients in the UK, The Netherlands and Belgium.

NIGEL P. SYKES is Medical Director and Consultant in Palliative Medicine at St Christopher's Hospice in London, UK, where he has been since 1991. St Christopher's, founded in 1967 by Dame Cicely

Saunders, is often regarded as the birthplace of the hospice movement and the specialty of palliative care. It has both inpatient and community palliative care services and looks after about 2,000 terminally ill people each year. Dr. Sykes' principal research interests concern gastrointestinal and end-of-life symptom management in palliative care, subjects on which he has written extensively. He is a past winner of the Evans Prize for Research in Palliative Medicine. He also teaches widely both in the UK and abroad. Previously a member of the Executive and Ethics committees of the Association of Palliative Medicine of Great Britain and Ireland, Dr. Sykes is currently a member of the Neurological Diseases Strategy Group of the UK National Council for Palliative Care. He set up the first clinical ethics committee to be located in a hospice and has spoken on television and radio, and made presentations to British parliamentary committees, on ethical issues relating to palliative care.

JOHANNES J.M. VAN DELDEN is a professor of medical ethics at the Julius Centre for Health Sciences of the medical school of Utrecht University, The Netherlands. Ever since he worked as a house officer on an intensive care ward, he has been highly interested in medical ethics. He wrote his doctoral thesis on the medical and ethical aspects of 'do not resuscitate' orders. He served as one of the principal researchers for the study of medical decisions concerning the end of life for the Remmelink committee in The Netherlands. Following his education as a nursing home physician, he has worked in several nursing homes for 15 years (until May 2011). His particular areas of interest are: research ethics, ethical problems concerning the end of life and ethical problems in the care of the elderly.

AGNES VAN DER HEIDE, MD, Ph.D., is a professor of medical care and decision-making in the last stage of life, at the Department of Public Health of Erasmus Medical Centre, Erasmus University Rotterdam, The Netherlands. She has coordinated many collaborative research projects on a national and international scale. Her research focuses on epidemiological, clinical and ethical aspects of euthanasia and other end-of-life decisions. She has conducted quantitative and qualitative studies on continuous sedation in the last phase of life. Her research group was the first to demonstrate that the Liverpool Care Pathway for the Dying Patient improves the quality of care in the last days of life.

ELEANOR WILSON is a research fellow with a background in social science and an MSc in Medical Social Anthropology. She is an experienced qualitative researcher working in the Division of Nursing at the Sue Ryder Care Centre for the Study of Supportive, Palliative and End of Life Care of the University of Nottingham since 2000. In that time she has worked on a range of projects focusing on palliative and end-of-life care by investigating patient and family experiences of illness, staff roles and service evaluations. Eleanor is the lead researcher at the Nottingham site for work funded by Marie Curie Cancer Care on 'Nurses' roles in the use of anticipatory prescriptions'. This study is ongoing and is due to be completed by September 2013. Another element of Eleanor's work particularly focuses on the provision of care for those affected by neurological conditions. Her work can be found in several journals and as a chapter in *Palliative Care in Neurological Disease: A Team Approach* (2009) by Byrne et al. This is linked to her doctoral study exploring the needs of those affected by Huntington's disease and the healthcare staff who provide their care.

Acknowledgements

First and foremost, the editors would like to express their heartfelt gratitude to Julian Cockbain, who has not only done a superb job regarding the language editing of the entire manuscript, but has also spent enormous amounts of time double checking and completing literature references, compiling a single reference list for all the chapters, sharing comments and ideas on many of the topics discussed in the book, and lots of other little and big things. Julian, this book owes so much to you that we cannot possibly thank you enough!

Obviously, we also want to thank all the contributors to this volume for writing their insightful chapters, for the positive and constructive attitude they have shown throughout the editorial process, and for never complaining about the tight deadlines that we sometimes imposed on them. Being able to bring together so many fascinating analyses and ideas from so many reputable experts on the topic, from so many different disciplinary and geographical backgrounds, has been a truly exciting intellectual adventure for us.

Sigrid Sterckx would like to thank her parents Marie-Louise and Wilfried, as well as her twin brother Wouter and his partner Fabienne, for their continuous encouragement and moral support.

Kasper Raus is grateful to his family, especially to his wife Leonie Krekels, for providing loving support and understanding for all the days and nights he spent working on this volume. He also owes a great debt of gratitude to his daughter, Martha. Though she may not yet realise it, she has helped him greatly by providing a smile whenever he needed one.

Freddy Mortier especially wishes to thank his wife Annemie Schotanus for enduring his seemingly endless periods of absence and nevertheless continuing to surround him with TLC.

The editors would also like to express their gratitude to Finola O'Sullivan, Juliet Binns and Richard Woodham from Cambridge

University Press, for their skilful assistance, advice and encouragement throughout the journey that led to this manuscript. We are also very grateful to the anonymous referees who provided helpful comments on the initial book proposal.

1   Introduction

Sigrid Sterckx, Kasper Raus and Freddy Mortier

1.   The language of human suffering

Most people's conception of what constitutes a good death is something like the following: at an advanced age, one falls asleep peacefully in one's bed, preferably at home, more or less free from pain, if possible surrounded by one's relatives and close friends, accepting the fact that death is inevitable, in a clear state of mind, after having had the opportunity to balance one's life and to prepare thoroughly for the long goodbye, all in all satisfied with the life one has led, and while regretting some of the mistakes one has committed, hoping to leave behind a positive reputation.

Unfortunately, although palliative care and palliative medicine appear to be committed to this picture of a good death, and, through the benefits of pharmacology and proper care, do contribute a lot to bringing dying patients closer to that ideal, in many cases dying remains a hard and ugly thing. The classic (fictionalised) expression of this harsh reality is, of course, *The Death of Ivan Ilych* (1886) by Leo Tolstoy. At one point he describes Ivan Ilych's predicament as follows:

From that moment the screaming began that continued for three days, and was so terrible that one could not hear it through two closed doors without horror. At the moment he answered his wife realized that he was lost, that there was no return, that the end had come, the very end, and his doubts were still unsolved and remained doubts. 'Oh! Oh! Oh!' he cried in various intonations. He had begun by screaming 'I won't!' and continued screaming on the letter 'O'. For three whole days, during which time did not exist for him, he struggled in that black sack into which he was being thrust by an invisible, resistless force. He struggled as a man condemned to death struggles in the hands of the executioner, knowing that he cannot save himself. And every moment he felt that despite all his efforts he was drawing nearer and nearer to what terrified him. He felt that his agony was due to his being thrust into that black hole and still more to his not being able to get right into it. He was hindered from getting into it by his conviction that his life had been a good one. That very justification of his life held him fast and prevented his moving forward, and it caused him most torment of all. (Tolstoy 1886: 12)

1

We have left out Tolstoy's evocation of the physical torments Ivan Ilych went through, and instead focused on part of the description of Ivan's existential suffering. For Tolstoy, the description fits into the picture he draws of a man who during his lifetime has failed to address the inescapable fact that he had to die.

In the medical context, however, as well as in the medical-professional literature, the features of Ivan's suffering to which Tolstoy draws our attention are termed 'symptoms'. 'Symptoms of what?', one may ask. Lack of reflection, unlike pain caused by cancer, cannot plausibly be conceptualised as a 'symptom' of an underlying disease. Yet this is how modern medicine, and more particularly palliative medicine, has to translate part of the distress of today's Ivan Ilyches. We would submit that the 'symptoms' that palliative medicine seeks to alleviate or eliminate are in fact not defined in a strictly medical way, but rather in a *normative* way, i.e. starting from a particular conception of what a 'good death' implies. Indeed, what counts as a 'symptom' for palliative medicine is a deviation from our culturally ingrained conception of what constitutes a 'good death'.

To be clear, we do not believe there is something inherently wrong with this. The tasks of contemporary medicine clearly go beyond the curing of diseases and in many ways incorporate normative ideals (e.g. preventative medicine, aesthetic surgery, etc.). However, we do believe it is important to remember that palliative medicine and palliative care are *also* guided by normative ideals. Yet the way in which they process those moral values is inevitably coloured by a medical viewpoint, by a language that makes human suffering accessible to medical procedures and treatments.

In the context of today's palliative medicine, Ivan Ilych's existential suffering would be seen as a set of 'refractory symptoms'. In Tolstoy's view, this would be absurd, since the only person who might have lessened Ivan's terminal suffering, was Ivan himself, at a moment earlier in his life when he was still capable of choosing a life of reflection instead of a life of base self-contentment.

In the context of contemporary medicine, then, the problem of the Ivans presents itself roughly as follows: although medication may help many or most of the dying to achieve a state of relative painlessness or serenity, sometimes very distressing symptoms do not respond (quickly enough) to any treatment. Even high and correctly administered doses of pain medication may not sufficiently control excruciating pain. Other symptoms may threaten to render a good death practically unattainable: uncontrollable seizures, severe nausea and frequent vomiting, lasting anxiety and disturbing hallucinations, continuing breathlessness, and so on. In the medical literature, such symptoms are labelled 'refractory'. They cannot be treated by the available medical means within a sufficiently short time span to make what remains of life bearable to the patient and/or her caregivers and loved ones. And of course making the end of life bearable is exactly what palliative care is devoted to.

On the Internet, many stories of terminal illness can be found that illustrate how personal biography at the end of life gets interwoven with medical intervention. One of these is Serge's story, whose struggle with illness took about four and a half years.[1] It would take too much space to reproduce the 'case' of Serge. Suffice it to say that in 2004 Serge suffered a 'grand mal' (type of epilepsy) seizure that was caused by a frontal brain lesion and by lung lesions which were treated by craniotomy and chemotherapy. In 2007 a switch was made from curative treatment to comfort care. The palliative phase eventually lasted one and a half years. In the course of that period, Serge experienced severe seizures, deliria, extreme headaches, and so on, that were controlled in highly complex ways by medication and controlled sedation, until, a few days before dying, he stopped eating and in his very last days he died under continuous sedation.

This book is about continuous sedation at the end of life. It is absolutely certain that, without the benefits of this end-of-life practice, Serge would have died a horrible death. That he was able to say the long goodbye to his loved ones, that he got the time and opportunity to reconcile himself with both life and death, that he did not have to go through excruciating pain, all this and more was only possible thanks to the use of palliative care techniques, of which continuous sedation until death was the ultimate one. Palliative care allowed Serge a good death, or at least one as good and as dignified as possible under the circumstances.

2.   Continuous sedation at the end of life: consensus and criticism

There seems to be some degree of consensus that continuous sedation at the end of life is an ethically acceptable way to relieve otherwise intractable suffering, although reducing or even completely taking away a patient's consciousness is a far-reaching procedure, which reduces not only the experience of suffering, but *all* experiences. The results of a study by Simon et al. illustrate this consensus. In this study, 477 members of the German Academy for Ethics in Medicine were asked

[1] See www.docstoc.com/docs/72215262/Palliative_Sedation_2.

about their opinions regarding continuous sedation. Ninety-eight per cent of them 'regarded terminal sedation in dying patients with treatment-refractory physical symptoms as acceptable' (Simon et al. 2007: 1). Moreover, some of the currently used sedation guidelines state that the practice is ethically acceptable (American Medical Association 2008) and is to be considered as 'normal medical practice' (KNMG 2009b).

However, continuous sedation until death has recently become subject to criticism, for various reasons. One reason has to do with the increase in its frequency: dying after having been continuously sedated for some time is fast becoming one of the standard ways of dying. This book represents an attempt to understand why this is happening and asks whether it is a desirable evolution.

Most people now die expectedly, after some medical decision has been taken that might influence the exact moment of death. Moreover, the trajectories that most patients follow until death call for the alleviation of distressing symptoms. For example, research from Belgium indicates that in Flanders (the Dutch-speaking region of Belgium) in 2007, only 31.9 per cent of all deaths were sudden (Bilsen et al. 2009). This implies that more than two-thirds of all people dying that year had a longer dying trajectory, which was somehow medically assisted, first with a curative approach and later on – probably and hopefully – by means of comfort care. Medical care at the end of life also includes, as a standard component, the making of decisions that may shorten survival. A recent study in The Netherlands, for example, showed that in 2010, an end-of-life decision[2] was taken in 57.8 per cent of all deaths (Onwuteaka-Philipsen et al. 2012).

There is thus reason to believe that a great need exists for effective medical interventions at the end of life. For example, Fainsinger et al. (2000) studied four palliative care programmes (in Israel, Durban, Cape Town and Madrid), showing that more than 90 per cent of all palliative care patients in the inpatient setting required symptom control or management. Although this study looked only at patients in a palliative care unit – who perhaps had a greater likelihood of experiencing severe suffering – it nevertheless indicates that the need for good symptom control remains overwhelming. This need is becoming more widely acknowledged and has led many commentators to conclude that being

---

[2] Understood here as a medical decision (i.e. a decision by a physician or a nurse) that affects or is believed to affect the timing of death of the patient and/or the possibility of meaningful experiences by the patient.

free from pain is nothing less than a fundamental right. As bioethicist Margaret Somerville phrases it:

Leaving people in pain is both a human tragedy and a breach of the most fundamental concepts of human rights and human ethics. (Somerville 2001: 33)

Somerville further argues that leaving people in pain 'should be treated as legally actionable medical malpractice' (Somerville 2001: 33), and this too is increasingly being recognised. In Belgium, for example, the 2002 Act on Palliative Care has made access to palliative care a legal right for every patient who requests it. Advances in palliative care and pain management have indeed made a pain-free end of life an achievable aim for many patients. In some cases, however, a patient's suffering is so severe that 'standard' palliative care is no longer able to relieve the suffering, leading physicians to make more far-reaching decisions, such as increasing medication to a potentially life-shortening dosage and, in countries where this is legal, carrying out euthanasia or physician-assisted suicide.

The end-of-life practice that is the focus of this book is the administration of sedatives resulting in the reduction or removal of a patient's consciousness, thereby ensuring that she no longer experiences any suffering. This is one option (often the only one available that is legally allowed) when suffering at the end of life becomes very severe and symptoms are no longer responsive to standard pain management.

We will come back to epidemiological findings on the frequency of continuous sedation until death. But apart from its sheer frequency, the practice raises ethical, clinical and legal questions (see, for example, Gillick 2004; Tännsjö 2004b). Many of these issues lie at the very heart of continuous sedation, such as, for example, the way in which this practice should be labelled and defined. Some commentators question whether continuous sedation is a proper end-of-life practice within the context of palliative care or whether it is instead just a specific type of euthanasia, a so-called 'slow euthanasia' (Billings & Block 1996). Furthermore, it is not only the ethical acceptability of continuous sedation at the end of life that is under discussion, so too is its legality (see, for example, Gevers 2004 and Chapter 8 in this volume by Delbeke).

In the absence of a single framework or procedure, there is no widely agreed way to perform continuous sedation at the end of life. Research has shown that considerable differences exist *between* countries, for example between Belgium, The Netherlands and the UK (Anquinet et al. 2012), as well as *within* the same country (e.g. Chambaere et al. 2010; Seale 2010). This shows that although there might appear to be some degree of consensus, there is hardly any single aspect of continuous sedation at the end of life that is not up for debate. Many of the debates are scattered across the literature of several different disciplines. Thus, for this volume, we have endeavoured to bring together experts from the various disciplines in which continuous sedation is debated. Before outlining the different chapters, we provide some comments on topics in the 'sedation debates' that are so recurrent that they merit specific attention in this introductory chapter.

3.   Defining sedation at the end of life

The starting point for many of the chapters in this book is that there is no consensus on a definition of sedation at the end of life, and not even on a term to refer to the practice. Terms that have been proposed include: continuous (deep) sedation (e.g. Murray et al. 2008; Rietjens et al. 2008a), sedation to unconsciousness in end-of-life care (American Medical Association 2008), palliative sedation (e.g. Rousseau 2005b; Materstvedt 2012), terminal sedation (e.g. van Delden 2007; Battin 2008), proportionate palliative sedation versus palliative sedation to unconsciousness (Quill et al. 2009), etc.

The terminological issue is closely related to the definition issue, which in turn is closely related to the ethical and normative issues. As for a definition, various propositions have been made in the literature (Morita et al. 2001c; de Graeff & Dean 2007; Cherny & Radbruch 2009), but currently no consensus exists on any of the proposed definitions. Nor is it likely that a consensus will ever evolve. The expression 'continuous sedation until death' covers different and yet closely related clinical practices and realities. Some of these practices are ethically contested. An example is inducing a continuous coma, say about four weeks prior to death, in a patient who requested a life-shortening intervention from her physician, who complied by taking away artificial nutrition and hydration (ANH). This patient is likely to die from dehydration and starvation rather than from the underlying disease. Let us call this the Slow Euthanasia Case (SEC). Under a broad 'descriptive' definition (i.e. one only taking into account whether or not the patient was sedated until death), SEC would be a genuine instance of 'continuous sedation until death'.

As van Delden argues (van Delden 2007; and van Delden, Chapter 13 this volume), a definition of an end-of-life practice should be neutral, and whether the practice was ethically justifiable in a given set of circumstances should be evaluated separately. Others, however, might not be prepared to consider SEC as an instance of whatever their preferred expression for continuous sedation until death is (palliative sedation, controlled sedation, etc.). De Graeff and Dean, for example, state that: '[p]alliative sedation therapy (PST) is the use of specific sedative medications to relieve intolerable suffering from refractory symptoms by a reduction in patient consciousness' (de Graeff & Dean 2007: 68). This definition adds a descriptive qualifier ('to relieve intolerable suffering from refractory symptoms') which happens to play a major role in judging the ethical justifiability of continuous sedation at the end of life (labelled 'palliative sedation' by de Graeff and Dean and many others). It is clear that whether or not the intention of the physician was to relieve refractory symptoms is ultimately an empirical question. Yet, by including this particular requirement in the very definition of the practice, other types of continuous sedation (e.g. for non-refractory symptoms) are excluded.

The ethical issues are further obfuscated when, as is bound to happen, definitions function as what philosopher C.L. Stevenson has called 'persuasive definitions'. The latter typically restrict and specify the usually vague descriptive meaning of a word (e.g. 'democracy'), but leave its (positive or negative) emotive meaning unchanged and thereby (intentionally or not) influence the attitude of the addressee to the issue ('Democracy really is ...') (Stevenson 1944: 210). Including specifying conditions in a definition (e.g. 'Palliative sedation is not life-shortening'), even if they have *descriptive* content, may prejudge the *ethical* evaluation ('Real palliative sedation is not life-shortening', i.e. 'hurrah for palliative sedation!' and, by implication, 'Boo to life-shortening!').

This is not to say that vague descriptive definitions are better than precise ones, or that definitions are better when they cannot possibly be suspected of prejudging the ethical issues. There is no real problem in *defining* continuous sedation at the end of life as 'not life-shortening'. Yet there *is* a problem if such a definition is used in a persuasive way, to settle disagreements in attitude towards end-of-life decision-making.

Moreover, in the context of clinical practice, the emotive loading of terms and definitions appears to carry a special weight. For example, Wilson and Seymour (this volume, Chapter 6) explain that confusion over what constitutes continuous sedation can lead to concerns and emotional burdens for nurses. Not knowing, in end-of-life situations, what one is involved in and contributing to, because of lack of clarity regarding what is being done, can indeed be very distressing. Some people object to the label 'terminal sedation' because the expression suggests intentional life-shortening. Others object to expressions like 'palliative sedation' because they are perceived as euphemisms. Thus, another important aspect of the 'definition issue' appears to be its role in coping on the part of healthcare personnel. This issue is not addressed in this volume, but it deserves mentioning here.

4.   Artificial nutrition and hydration

Continuous sedation at the end of life can occur either *with* or *without* ANH. The main issue regarding withholding or withdrawing ANH, from both an ethical and a legal perspective,[3] seems to be that it makes life-shortening either probable or likely. Thus, in sedation without ANH, what causes the death of the patient may be the withholding or withdrawing of ANH, rather than the underlying disease or the sedation. The frequently cited Dutch national guideline on sedation maintains that, if sedation is *only* used for patients with a life expectancy of two weeks or less (as this guideline recommends), the patient will die of her disease before dehydration or starvation can have any effect. However, some commentators (e.g. van Delden, Chapter 13 in this volume, and Holm, Chapter 14) point out that accurately determining life expectancy is nearly impossible, and that life-shortening thus frequently cannot be ruled out.

Although the relevance of withholding ANH is recognised by many commentators, there is some debate on whether initiating continuous

---

[3] As to the ethical debate regarding ANH, this is related to the debate regarding the distinction between ordinary and extraordinary means of preserving life. The latter has its roots in Thomas Aquinas' comments on suicide and bodily mutilation: 'A man has the obligation to sustain his body, otherwise he would be a killer of himself … by precept, therefore, he is bound to nourish his body and likewise, we are bound to all the other items without which the body cannot live' (quoted in Cronin 1958: 48). In the seventeenth century, Juan Cardinal de Lugo, a Catholic moral theologian, refined the Catholic viewpoint by clarifying the distinction between ordinary and extraordinary means of preserving life (i.e. actions that are obligatory versus actions one is not required to perform in order to preserve life). As explained by de Lugo: '[A] man must guard his life by ordinary means against dangers and death coming from natural causes … because the one who neglects the ordinary means seems to neglect his life and therefore to act negligently in the administration of it, and he who does not employ the ordinary means which nature has provided for the ordinary conservation of life is considered morally to will his death' (quoted in Henke 2007: 57). According to Henke, another important contribution de Lugo made to the Catholic moral tradition was the introduction of the concept of 'proportional benefit', implying that: '[W]ithin the domain of an ordinary means of preserving life, circumstances could exist which effectively rendered such a means extraordinary. Using the example of a man surrounded by fire and facing certain death by that fire, de Lugo illustrated the concept of proportional benefit. The man in the fire has at hand, in de Lugo's scenario, enough water to extinguish part of the fire, but not all of it, and if he used the water to quench some of the fire, his certain death would be delayed only a short time. In this case, the crucial element that determines proportional benefit is whether there exists a reasonable hope of recovery or continued life for an extended period of time, not simply a few extra moments' (Henke 2007: 58, footnote omitted).

sedation without ANH should be considered as a single decision, or as the combination of two decisions. The initiation of sedation might be justified, for example, by demonstrating the presence of severe refractory symptoms. However, justifying the withholding or withdrawing of ANH with an argument that, since the patient is unconscious (as a result of sedation), ANH is 'futile', has been labelled as a fallacious 'salami-slicing technique' (van Delden 2007 and Chapter 13 in this volume). Withdrawing cr withholding ANH might be justified by demonstrating that the patient has requested just that, or by making a convincing case for the futility of ANH. However, some commentators (e.g. Holm, Chapter 14 in this volume) point out that the concept of 'futility' is often misused in this context.

Sykes (Chapter 5, this volume), however, argues that, when properly performed, no life-shortening is involved in withholding ANH. His main argument is that the patients receiving continuous sedation have already stopped eating and drinking as a result of the dying process, so that withholding ANH does not add a life-shortening effect. He notes that administering ANH, on the contrary, may cause discomforting symptoms in the patient. At the same time, he warns that, if professional guidelines on sedation are to avoid giving the impression of sedation being 'euthanasia by stealth', they should not include a blanket prohibition on the use cf ANH.

Gillian Craig, a geriatrician, in an article published almost two decades ago, wondered whether palliative medicine 'has gone too far' as regards its attitude towards ANH. In this article, which sparked a fierce debate in the literature, Craig expressed the following view:

If death is imminent few people would feel it essential to put up a drip but ethical problems arise if sedation is continued for more than one or two days, without hydration, as the patient will become dehydrated ... The only way to ensure that life will not be shortened is to maintain hydration during sedation in all cases where inability to eat and drink is a direct consequence of sedation, unless the relatives request no further intervention, or the patient has made his/her wishes known to this effect. (Craig 1994: 140)

Craig appears to suggest that, in the context of palliative medicine, a generally negative attitude towards ANH seems to exist, which may result in the wishes and emotional and ethical sensitivities of patients and their relatives being insufficiently taken into account. Since this, arguably important, aspect of the debate is not addressed further in this volume, Craig's comments deserve mentioning here:

The consensus in the hospice movement seems to be that rehydration and intravenous fluids are inappropriate in terminal care ... Some say that a patient

should be comatose, so as not to experience thirst, before it is morally acceptable to withhold or withdraw intravenous fluids ... Thirst may or may not
bother the patient. Concern about thirst undoubtedly bothers relatives. They
will long to give their loved one a drink. They may sit by the bed furtively
drinking cups of tea, taking care to make no sound lest the clink of china is
torture to the patient. Anyone who has starved for hours before an anaesthetic
will sympathise with dying patients who seem to thirst and starve for days.
Nurses are taught that moistening the patient's mouth with a damp sponge
is all that is necessary to prevent thirst. Relatives may not be convinced ...
Staff who believe strongly that intravenous fluids are inappropriate should not
impose their views on ... relatives who request that a dying patient be given
intravenous fluids to prevent dehydration or thirst. To overrule such a request
is, in my view, ethically wrong. The only proviso would be if the patient had,
when *compos mentis*, specifically said that he/she did not want a drip under any
circumstances. No relatives should be forced to watch a loved one die while
medical staff insist on withholding hydration ... Such an experience is deeply
disturbing and could haunt a person forever. Is all this agony worth it for the
sake of avoiding a drip? ... The converse also applies. There will be occasions
when the medical staff who are professionally involved would like to use a drip,
but a knowledgeable relative requests no intervention. In this situation, the
medical team will need to make a carefully balanced judgement as to whether
intervention is essential or not ... A doctor cannot be obliged to act contrary
to his or her own conscience but equally doctors should bear in mind that relatives also have consciences ... Care must be taken to ensure that the burden of
bereavement is not loaded heavily by distress about patient management in the
terminal phase. (Craig 1994: 142–3, references omitted)

Clearly, the controversy surrounding ANH in end-of-life care, and
especially with regard to continuous sedation, continues.

5.   The doctrine of double effect

The doctrine of double effect (DDE) is one of the most commonly
cited justifications for continuous sedation at the end of life. Indeed,
it is mentioned in most of the chapters in this volume. For DDE (in
its most common interpretation, viz. the natural law interpretation, as
explained in Chapter 11 by Raus, Sterckx and Mortier) to be an adequate justification for continuous sedation, some conditions need to be
met. First, there must be some good effect as well as some sort of harm
associated with sedation, and, second, the harm must not be intended
and must not be the means to obtain the good effect.

As regards the possible harm done by sedation, as noted earlier, the
'classic candidate' is life-shortening. Different views are expressed in
this volume as to whether this indeed forms a problematic aspect of
continuous sedation at the end of life and, if so, whether and how it

can be avoided by, for example, including specific recommendations in professional guidelines on sedation. However, some commentators note that, even when no life-shortening is at issue, the permanent reduction or removal of consciousness itself constitutes a harm (e.g. Holahan et al.; Raus et al.; van Delden; and Delbeke, in this volume).

The requirement for the applicability of DDE to justify continuous sedation is that the harm (whether life-shortening or consciousness-reduction or both) must be brought about unintentionally. The 'intention issue' is obviously a complex one. However, in this regard, it would seem instructive to take into account empirical studies of the practice of continuous sedation. As is clear from the literature review provided by Bruinsma et al. in Chapter 2, it is not uncommon for physicians performing continuous sedation at the end of life to report that, when initiating the sedation, they *did* have an intention to shorten life. Moreover, the overview of clinical, pharmacological and practical aspects of sedation, provided by Porta-Sales in Chapter 4, shows that some drugs have consciousness loss as a *primary function*, which raises the question how those can be said to be administered without an intent to reduce consciousness.

In view of these and other complications, some of the contributors to this volume argue that invoking DDE to justify continuous sedation at the end of life is, at best, problematic and, at worst, unconvincing. Delbeke (Chapter 8) rejects DDE as a *legal* justification for continuous *deep* sedation, while Raus et al. (Chapter 11) reject it as an *ethical* justification for this type of sedation. In contrast, Huxtable and Horn (Chapter 10) acknowledge that DDE involves problems but nevertheless propose to hold on to it as a sort of compromise position.

6.   Other parties involved

Another issue that is mentioned in various chapters is that sedation is a process rather than a decision. It is not only the physician and the patient who play a role in this process, the patient's relatives as well as other carers are usually involved as well. From a *legal* perspective (see, for example, Chapter 8 by Delbeke) as well as from an *ethical* perspective (see, for example, Chapter 4 by Porta-Sales and Chapter 12 by Holahan et al.), relatives can be important in decision-making when the patient has become incompetent. They then have a formal and legally recognised role as the representative of the patient, and should be involved in deciding what the patient would have wanted had she been competent or, if that is impossible to determine, which course of action would be in her best interests.

Indeed, several professional guidelines on continuous sedation at the end of life mention the important role of relatives or other representatives of the patient. However, research cited by Bruinsma et al. in Chapter 2 indicates that the degree to which relatives are involved in the decision-making process varies significantly. Relatives often also have a role to play once sedation has been initiated. They often care for the patient, and the emotional impact on relatives of seeing their loved one, for example, in a state of continuous deep sedation, should not be underestimated (e.g. Raus et al. 2012).

The role of nurses is also crucial, as is clearly shown by the literature review conducted by Wilson and Seymour (Chapter 6). Nurses often struggle with their (perceived) lack of involvement in decision-making at the end of life and, in the case of continuous sedation at the end of life, this may cause particular emotional and moral distress.

7.   Determining depth of sedation/unconsciousness

A large degree of consensus seems to exist that sedation should be used *proportionally to the severity of the symptoms* the patient is suffering from. Indeed, this is emphasised in *all* the published sedation guidelines that we are aware of (e.g. Cherny & Radbruch 2009; KNMG 2009b). This implies that physicians and/or nurses need to ensure that a patient is not sedated too lightly (the patient's experience of suffering must be taken away), or too heavily (as warranted by the degree of severity of the symptoms). It would therefore seem to be very important to assess, as accurately as possible, how deeply the patient is sedated, so that sedation can be increased if it turns out to be too light, and decreased if too heavy.

The view that consciousness is morally significant has been argued for by various commentators, on the basis of different moral frameworks (e.g. Kamm 1999; Singer 2003). Thus, if consciousness is permanently reduced or taken away, this may be problematic from an ethical perspective (e.g. Janssens et al. 2012). Hence proportionality is important, yet 'obtaining' the 'proper' level of consciousness is difficult in practice for a number of reasons. Accurately assessing depth of sedation is difficult enough for anaesthesiologists in cases where patients are temporarily sedated to undergo surgery (Shafer & Stanski 2008), yet even more so for patients who are in poor physical condition and in their last stages of life. While the problem of *potentially undetected awareness* has been widely researched for patients undergoing anaesthesia (e.g. Mashour 2010), hardly any research on this topic exists for patients who are continuously sedated until death, implying the possibility that at least some *seemingly* sedated patients are actually experiencing (some degree of) suffering.

Probably the most commonly used tool to assess depth of sedation in cases of continuous sedation is *basic clinical assessment*, where a physician observes whether the sedated patient is comfortably asleep. If the patient shows signs of being awake (e.g. groaning while being washed or handled), dosages can be adjusted. However, various studies have shown that this approach is problematic since it reduces 'consciousness' to 'responsiveness to certain stimuli', whereas recent research has shown that patients can be *unresponsive and yet aware* (Noreika et al. 2011). Moreover, the accuracy of clinical assessment is likely to depend on how often the physician doing the assessment has come into contact with continuously sedated patients at the end of life.

In some professional guidelines, the use of sedation scales has been proposed (e.g. Cherny & Radbruch 2009). Indeed, using such scales has several advantages (Rinaldi & De Gaudio 2006), as it allows for scores to be checked by colleagues or for measuring over time to monitor fluctuations in depth of sedation. However, only a few sedation scales have been validated for palliative care patients, and questions remain concerning both the effectiveness and the invasiveness of sedation scales. With regard to *effectiveness*, the concern is voiced that sedation scales, like basic clinical assessment, measure response to stimuli, which is not the same as consciousness and thus raises doubts on the effectiveness of such scales (Alkire et al. 2008). As regards *invasiveness*, admittedly, the use of scales does not require putting patients on machines, yet in an important sense their use *is* invasive, for the physician or nurse needs to stimulate the patient, for example by calling out her name, prodding, shaking or even providing painful stimuli.

Instead of using clinical assessment or scales, one could look directly at brain activity, by, for example, analysing a patient's electroencephalogram (EEG). However, a raw EEG produces a great amount of information that is not relevant for measuring consciousness, and interpreting this information requires a lot of expertise. Techniques have been developed that process the EEG signal to generate a more readily usable value. An example of such techniques is the so-called 'BIS monitor' (for 'bispectral analysis'), which analyses a single EEG to produce a number on a scale ranging from 0 (inert) to 100 (awake state), making it a highly practical and easily interpretable tool. This technique merely requires placing an electrode patch on a patient's forehead, and so does not require patient stimulation. Another advantage is that the BIS monitor allows continuous measurement. Some research exists that indicates the applicability of this technique to patients who are continuously sedated at the end of life (Liu et al. 1996); however, more research is urgently needed if the requirement of proportionality is to have real substance.

8.   Refractory symptoms and existential suffering

Continuous sedation at the end of life is usually thought of as a last resort measure, to be applied when symptoms have become refractory. As explained earlier, a symptom is refractory when there is no other method than continuous sedation that can be used for palliation within an acceptable time frame and/or without unacceptable adverse effects (Cherny & Radbruch 2009).

Sometimes it is observed, also by some of the contributors to this volume, that the high frequency of continuous sedation in Belgium, The Netherlands, and the UK indicates that this practice is de facto also being used in patients with *non*-refractory symptoms. There is a lot of debate as to whether the studies in these different countries really consider the *same* phenomenon, and thus whether the numbers can be compared. Yet, even if the responding physicians in different countries may have had different understandings of the questions they were asked, one might wonder whether frequencies of continuous sedation of up to 12.3 per cent (of all patients who died in The Netherlands in 2010, see Onwuteaka-Philipsen et al. 2012) or up to 14.5 per cent (Belgium in 2007, see Chambaere et al. 2010) are compatible with a 'last resort' option.

Some of the contributions to this volume shed light on this matter (e.g. Chapter 13 by van Delden; Chapter 7 by Orentlicher). In sum, what defines refractoriness is not the nature of a symptom, but *how* one may fail to treat it. Failure can have many faces in this context: a treatment method may be available, but it may take too long to become effective in order for it to be of any use to a dying person; there may be no treatment at all; a treatment may be available, yet not adapted to the setting in which the patient finds herself (e.g. home versus hospital); a treatment may exist, yet not be known or sufficiently mastered by the patient's physician; the available treatment may be one that alleviates the initial problem (e.g. severe pain) in time, but at the cost of other equally or even more distressing symptoms (e.g. hallucinations). Thus, in fact 'refractoriness' is an outcome of the patient's disease symptoms and the available medical resources, including the physician's abilities. This has a bearing on the frequency question: the fewer palliative care resources available (*ceteris paribus*), the higher the number of refractory symptoms. Thus, setting a baseline of what might be a 'normal' frequency of refractoriness is a very tricky matter.

Last resort considerations are particularly complicated in cases of so-called 'existential' or 'spiritual' suffering in the patient. We argued earlier (in section 1 of this Introduction) that the term 'symptom' is vague and may cover a range of problems that do not properly fall under the 'action radius' of medicine (the 'Ivan Ilych cases'). Yet, allowing a patient to die a good death may require bringing existential suffering within the reach of medical action. The extension of permissible indications for continuous sedation to existential suffering, however, is highly controversial. Existing professional guidelines contradict each other in this respect, in that some include existential suffering as an indication for continuous sedation at the end of life, while others do not.

9.   Patient requests for continuous deep sedation; the non-imminently dying

Another issue that is addressed by several contributors to this volume (e.g. Orentlicher; Delbeke; and Holm) is the meaning of a patient request or of patient consent for a decision to initiate continuous sedation at the end of life. Professional guidelines emphasise that continuous sedation should be preceded by patient consent (or a surrogate for it). Epidemiological findings show, however, that patient consent is not always sought and obtained by the physician (see Chapter 2 by Bruinsma et al.). How much of a problem is this?

Last resort considerations as well as double effect considerations can survive perfectly in the absence of consent. Autonomy-based considerations (which emphasise the need for consent) are independent from, and supplementary to, the lines of reasoning implied in last resort and double effect considerations. Moreover, some commentators (e.g. Battin, this volume) argue that, even when consent to continuous sedation at the end of life is obtained, the patient may not have been well informed, or may even have been misled with respect to what she is consenting to.

It has also been observed (e.g. Orentlicher, this volume) that the restriction of continuous sedation to patients expected to die within no more than two weeks leaves a segment of the patient population without 'arms' in the face of refractory symptoms. Indeed, if this restriction, which is typically mentioned in professional guidelines on sedation, is observed in practice, non-imminently dying patients have no access to the benefits of continuous sedation, even if they ask for it, and even if potential alternatives like euthanasia or physician-assisted suicide are legally unavailable.

Holm and Battin, in their contributions, also draw attention to the implications of the increased frequency of continuous sedation for our *ars moriendi* (the way people think of and go about dying). Although there are obvious benefits to this end-of-life practice, alleviating and controlling pain is at risk of becoming the *sole overriding value* served by medicine at the end of life. This value, albeit a very important one, risks systematically overriding the value of life and the value of patient autonomy. This may result in a 'new wave' of paternalism.

Understandably, the devotion to eliminating suffering is perfectly in line with the physician's ethos: it allows her to focus on the technical problems of titrating drugs, monitoring side-effects and administering drugs to diminish their impact. In other words, the ground that is familiar to physicians in any specialty. In The Netherlands, there has been a shift from euthanasia to continuous sedation, and this has been attributed to the psychological and administrative burdens – for the physician – of performing euthanasia (van der Heide et al. 2007). Although it may be understandable from both a practical and ethical perspective, this shift indirectly also implies a choice for technicality over going through difficult discussions with patients and their relatives. The speed at which continuous sedation is spreading in end-of-life care is perhaps an indication that the habits of high tech medicine are gaining ground in end-of-life care.

10.   Safeguards and 'normal medical practice'

In the opinion of most of the contributors to this volume, continuous sedation at the end of life is an example of 'normal medical practice'. We do not have the space here for an in-depth analysis of the question what 'normal medical practice' might be. The main idea, however, appears to be that if the medical profession has internally regulated, either by practical consensus or by guidelines, what practice to use in order to address certain problems, then the practice is 'normal'. For example, when Australian physicians regularly refer their patients to chiropractors and osteopaths for complementary treatments, this constitutes 'normal medical practice', because it is sufficiently widespread and accepted (Easthope et al. 2000). When physicians shorten their patients' lives by withholding treatment, according to the internal norms of the medical profession regarding good practice in this context, this constitutes 'normal medical practice'.

What makes a medical practice 'normal' is thus that internal regulations (e.g. deontological codes or professional guidelines) are deemed sufficient for containing possible abuses. Yet when physicians seek to obtain the same result, at the patient's request, by using lethal means, the practice is *not* normal (Ten Have & Welie 1992). We would submit that what makes such practices 'non-normal' is the idea that, in order to contain the dangers inherent in deliberate killing, a stronger form of regulation is needed, one that is laid down in special laws. In countries where euthanasia and physician-assisted suicide are legalised, the non-normal character of deliberate life-shortening is signalled by the obligation on physicians to report these practices to a (quasi-)government body that controls whether the safeguards for good medical practice have been observed. The scrutiny of these practices is thus more thorough, and more external, than for 'normal' medical practices.

How is this relevant to continuous sedation at the end of life? It is frequently argued that this constitutes normal medical practice, because its aim is not to shorten life and because the regulations governing it have been laid down in professional guidelines (i.e. 'lesser' regulation). However, some commentators (e.g. Janssens et al. 2012; Orentlicher; Delbeke; and Holm in this volume) state, or at least imply, that continuous sedation at the end of life is not so normal. First, as mentioned earlier, its non-life-shortening nature is contested. Second, some argue that a patient who has permanently lost consciousness, while remaining alive, has lost just as much as a patient who has lost both consciousness and life: the possibility of having meaningful experiences. Society has a stake, according to these commentators (e.g. Battin in this volume), in controlling the tendency of indications of refractoriness to expand into existential and psychological suffering, and in questioning the 'standard way of dying' that is being imposed on terminally ill patients.

An important practical question that arises from all the above considerations is whether (certain types of) continuous sedation at the end of life should be reported to an official body, as is the case for physician-assisted suicide and euthanasia in the jurisdictions where these practices have been legalised.

11.   Overview of chapters

In Chapter 2, *Continuous sedation until death: state of the art*, the stage is set by Sophie Bruinsma, Judith Rietjens and Agnes van der Heide, who give an overview of the state of the art of current published research on continuous sedation. Bruinsma, Rietjens and van der Heide point out that there is no agreement on what constitutes continuous sedation until death. Recognising this is crucial if one wants to understand and interpret the existing research, because the definition the researcher uses influences her results. Studies have found different incidences of continuous sedation and its complications, but comparing these is difficult due to a lack of clear definitions. This problem is further elaborated upon by David Albert Jones in Chapter 3, who shows that the lack of a consistent definition complicates not only the interpretation of empirical research but also the moral evaluation of sedation.

After showing that existing research indicates that continuous sedation is used frequently, Bruinsma, Rietjens and van der Heide discuss two frequently cited guidelines on sedation to show the degree to which their recommendations are followed in practice. The guidelines they focus on are the framework issued by the European Association for Palliative Care (EAPC) and the Dutch national guideline. In Chapter 9, Johan Legemaate, who was involved in the drafting of the Dutch national sedation guideline, will discuss that guideline in more detail.

Many of the issues that are discussed by Bruinsma et al. play an important role in further chapters. They touch upon clinical aspects of continuous sedation such as the indications for its use and the drugs that are used. This links this chapter nicely to the contribution of Josep Porta-Sales (Chapter 4), who deals with these clinical issues in depth. Also discussed by Bruinsma et al. is the question of the intention that physicians claim to have when starting sedation, which can and sometimes does include hastening the patient's death. The importance of intentions plays a central role in some of the other chapters, for example the contribution by Kasper Raus, Sigrid Sterckx and Freddy Mortier on the doctrine of double effect (Chapter 11). A third aspect that is touched upon by Bruinsma et al. is the issue of decision-making. Who decides on continuous sedation, who is involved in the decision and what are the different actors' degrees of involvement? Bruinsma et al. show that involvement may vary widely in different countries and different settings. In Chapter 6, by Eleanor Wilson and Jane Seymour, the role and involvement of nurses in decision-making at the end of life in general, and in continuous sedation in particular, is discussed in more detail. Importantly, Bruinsma et al. show that the administration of artificial nutrition and hydration (ANH) is a point of contention. Between various countries and settings, research has shown that the incidence of continuous sedation without ANH varies greatly. The importance of this issue is confirmed by several of the other chapters. Evelien Delbeke (Chapter 8) and Richard Huxtable and Ruth Horn (Chapter 10) show that whether ANH is administered matters from a legal perspective, while Søren Holm (Chapter 14) and Margaret Battin

(Chapter 15) argue that it matters for the ethical evaluation of continuous sedation.

In Chapter 3, *Death by equivocation: a manifold definition of terminal sedation*, David Albert Jones looks at the diversity of terms and definitions used for continuous sedation. Although 'continuous sedation' is increasingly being used as the label (as shown by Bruinsma et al.), Jones argues that the use of multiple definitions has complicated the debate by making it nearly impossible to compare practices.

Jones takes this even further and argues that the multitude of definitions has also clouded the moral debate surrounding continuous sedation (something that, for example, is also argued by Johannes van Delden in Chapter 13). Continuous sedation, Jones argues, can refer to a practice that is closely related to euthanasia (because of an intention to shorten life) or to a practice that is closely related to palliative care (because of an intention to palliate). Distinguishing these is central, according to Jones, as the ethical questions are entirely different for the two practices, and bundling them together muddles the debate. A principle that is often invoked to make this distinction is the doctrine of double effect. The application of this doctrine to sedation at the end of life is one of the threads throughout this entire volume; it is mentioned in nearly every chapter and Chapter 11 by Raus, Sterckx and Mortier investigates whether this doctrine can be applied to justify *deep* continuous sedation.

Jones argues that in order to bring ethical nuance into the debate on continuous sedation, we need a manifold definition that includes every aspect of the practice. That manifold definition, Jones finds, involves no less than seventeen different elements (not including the nature of the drugs used), each of which must be determined to know just where on the ethical spectrum a particular example of the practice might lie.

Many of these variables are also discussed in the other chapters. For example, the issues of whether sedation is a primary or secondary pharmacological effect and whether there is an intention to hasten death are dealt with in the chapters by Raus, Sterckx and Mortier (Chapter 11) and Holm (Chapter 14). The issue of existential versus physical distress is discussed in depth by Delbeke (Chapter 8). The legal difference between sedating an imminently dying patient and sedating a patient with a somewhat longer life expectancy is discussed by Huxtable and Horn (Chapter 10).

Chapter 4, *Palliative sedation: clinical, pharmacological and practical aspects*, is a clinical contribution in which Josep Porta-Sales discusses the main pharmacological and practical issues regarding continuous sedation. He emphasises that it is important to remember that sedation is a common technique in medicine that can be indicated for a broad variety of reasons. Continuous sedation until death is thus only one of the possible types. In this chapter, Porta-Sales discusses in which respects continuous sedation until death can be distinguished from other types of sedation. He expands on the discussion, in Chapter 2, of the most common indications for continuous sedation, as well as of the most frequently used drugs. He provides an in-depth overview of the properties of the drugs used for sedation. Porta-Sales is attentive to practical issues that are relevant for physicians performing sedation, such as dosage, routes of administration and side-effects. This discussion reveals the complexity of continuous sedation practice. He shows that 'sedative' is actually an umbrella term for a wide variety of different drugs with different properties. Some of these drugs have strong sedative effects, while others may have a lower sedative effect but a stronger anxiolytic or antipsychotic action.

After discussing the most commonly used drugs, Porta-Sales addresses other practical issues such as guidelines and the use of sedation scales. In this way, his chapter ties in with the chapter by Timothy Holahan, Thomas Carroll, Claudia Gonzalez and Timothy Quill (Chapter 12), which also offers practical recommendations for clinicians faced with an indication or request for continuous sedation.

A final important aspect of Porta-Sales' contribution is that he pays significant attention to the concerns of the relatives and the care team, thereby reminding us that continuous sedation is about more than just the patient and physician.

In Chapter 5, *Clinical aspects of continuous sedation*, Nigel Sykes notices that the use of sedation at the end of life is a technique that is as old as palliative care, but one that seems to have been stirring up an ethical debate in recent years. Sykes argues that there is a profound confusion over what the practice involves and that, as a result, the practice is often portrayed as more problematic than it is.

Like most of the other contributors (and in particular Jones in Chapter 3), Sykes observes that there are various definitions of 'sedation'. For some, the concept conjures up images of patients being rendered comatose or even of patients having their life shortened. The practice then becomes tainted by association, even though, according to Sykes, sedation is a normal practice that can be used for various indications. Often, Sykes argues, sedation is discussed in an unnuanced way, as if it always involves inducing a coma, whereas in fact many levels of sedation exist. He notes that the intention is always to relieve distressful symptoms by lowering consciousness as little as possible, but as much as needed.

Moreover, research indicates that losing consciousness at the end of life is common in all patients, including those who receive no sedatives. Sykes further argues that sedation is also only administered continuously if this is indicated by the symptoms (e.g. symptoms causing continuous distress), so continuous sedation is not necessarily sinister or problematic.

Continuous sedation at the end of life is also seen as problematic because it supposedly shortens life, especially if combined with the withdrawal of ANH. In this chapter, Sykes argues that, on the basis of current research, there is no reason to believe that sedation actually has a life-shortening effect. Some of the other contributors, for example Holm (Chapter 14) and Battin (Chapter 15), disagree, noting that – if combined with withholding or withdrawing ANH – continuous sedation may well be life-shortening. Sykes concludes that properly applied sedation is not a problematic practice.

In end-of-life decisions, usually more actors are involved than just the physician and the patient. Chapter 6, *Understanding the role of nurses in the management of symptoms and distress in the last days of life* by Eleanor Wilson and Jane Seymour, looks closely at the role of nurses. As it is impossible to isolate nurses involvement in continuous sedation from their involvement in other end-of-life practices, this chapter first discusses the results of general studies of the role of nurses in end-of-life care, before focusing on their experiences with and attitudes towards continuous sedation at the end of life.

Wilson and Seymour have conducted a systematic review of published research from all over the world. On the basis of this literature review, they identified several key themes: nurses' relationships with the patient (anticipating the patient's care needs), with the family (informing and supporting) and with other professionals (communicating and guaranteeing the smooth functioning of care). This discussion highlights how central a role nurses play.

Wilson and Seymour then focus on two specific situations, namely nurses' involvement in non-treatment decisions and in decisions to start continuous sedation. In both cases, research clearly shows that nurses often encounter challenges relating to their position as nurses. They frequently want to be involved and make decisions, but may lack the necessary authority due to their professional status. This becomes especially clear with regard to continuous sedation at the end of life. Studies indicate that nurses are often involved in the administration of sedation and that they report a certain degree of distress. They often perceive sedation as involving an intention to shorten life, and sometimes they even refuse to carry out a GP's orders. Research also shows that nurses believe it would benefit practice and relieve distress if there was a clear definition of sedation and if there were clear guidelines on how to perform it.

In Chapter 7, *Principle and practice for palliative sedation: gaps between the two*, David Orentlicher deals with the gap between the way in which continuous sedation *should* be performed (according to guidelines by professional associations or laws) and the way in which it *is* performed in practice. Orentlicher identifies some of the specific gaps where what *should* happen differs greatly from what actually happens. For example, he observes that continuous sedation is often said to be a 'last resort' measure, yet available research sometimes shows a very different picture. Furthermore, various professional guidelines recommend that sedation only be initiated for physical suffering, that patient or surrogate consent should always be obtained, and that there must not be any intent to hasten death. Again, available research indicates that, often, these recommendations are not followed in practice.

The question then arises as to why these gaps exist. According to Orentlicher, they might indicate a deficiency in principle (i.e. the principles under which physicians are asked to act are not fully or properly thought out) or in practice (e.g. physicians sometimes fail to follow the guidelines). It might also be the case that existing laws and/or guidelines are too restrictive. Orentlicher reminds us that continuous sedation at the end of life is practised by physicians who are influenced by their personal beliefs as well as by societal values, which can explain differences in practice among physicians and deviations from the recommended way to perform sedation. The healthcare needs of patients who do not share these values might remain unmet as a result.

With regard to the solution to addressing the gaps, Orentlicher suggests that, on the one hand, it might be a good idea to monitor more tightly whether guidelines are in fact followed. On the other hand, he emphasises that professional medical guidelines should always be tailored to take into account practical issues, and that we may have to adjust guidelines if they fail to function properly.

Surprisingly little attention has been paid in the international sedation literature to the question of whether continuous sedation at the end of life is in fact legal. In view of the fact that (as shown in Chapter 2) the practice occurs frequently, its legality would seem to be a particularly relevant question. In Chapter 8, *The legal permissibility of continuous deep sedation at the end of life: a comparison of laws and a proposal*, Evelien Delbeke tackles this question as regards *deep* continuous sedation. She divides her argument into two parts. In the first part, she considers the possible avenues for legally justifying continuous sedation. In the second part, she tackles the question of the conditions that would have to be fulfilled for continuous deep sedation until death to be justified.

Delbeke argues that there are reasons for considering continuous deep sedation to be a criminal offence, even in cases where life is not shortened by it. This is due to the fact that continuous deep sedation permanently takes away consciousness, and thus constitutes a harm. That permanently taking away consciousness is a problematic feature of continuous deep sedation is a topic that is also discussed, for example, by Huxtable and Horn (Chapter 10), Raus, Sterckx and Mortier (Chapter 11), Holahan, Carroll, Gonzalez and Quill (Chapter 12), van Delden (Chapter 13), Holm (Chapter 14) and Battin (Chapter 15). Delbeke argues that double effect, necessity and the availability of a professional guideline cannot justify continuous deep sedation, and that an explicit legitimisation by the law is required.

The next question that arises is then, obviously, which specific conditions would need to be fulfilled for this practice to be legal. Delbeke argues that, from a legal perspective, it is important to distinguish between sedation *without* ANH and sedation *with* ANH. It is mostly the former type that raises ethical and legal issues, since it is this form that implies the highest likelihood of life-shortening. However, according to Delbeke, continuous deep sedation without ANH should be legally permitted, even for patients who are not in their last days of life. Withholding or withdrawing ANH is a decision that is distinct from the decision to initiate sedation and should therefore be justified separately, she argues. If there are proper indications to sedate *and* good reasons to withdraw or withhold ANH, there is no legal problem in combining them. In this regard, an interesting contrast can be observed with the chapters by van Delden (Chapter 13), who argues that when both practices occur together, one should evaluate this as a single decision, and Holm (Chapter 14) who argues that withdrawing ANH after initiating sedation often *is* problematic.

Of the existing guidelines that deal with continuous sedation at the end of life, one of the most often cited is the Dutch national guideline, issued by the Royal Dutch Medical Association (RDMA) in 2005 and amended in 2009. Indeed, several of the chapters in this volume (e.g. Chapter 2 by Bruinsma et al., and Chapter 8 by Delbeke) mention various aspects of this guideline. In Chapter 9, *The Dutch national guideline on palliative sedation*, this guideline is discussed in great detail by Johan Legemaate, who oversaw the drafting of the guideline as the then chief legal counsel of the RDMA. Importantly, this guideline has legal ramifications in The Netherlands; when it was published, the public prosecutor officially stated that he saw no reason to prosecute a physician who performed sedation in accordance with the guideline. This chapter therefore contrasts with the previous chapter by Evelien Delbeke who, just like Johan Legemaate, is an expert in medical law, but who makes a case for adopting statutory legalisation on sedation rather than (merely) a professional guideline.

In his chapter, Legemaate first sketches the context in which the guideline was drafted. Next, he discusses the structure and content of the guideline, thereby giving attention to all its recommendations. Interesting to note here is that the guideline is concerned with: *legal* issues (as it considers sedation to be 'normal medical practice'); *theoretical* issues (e.g. it provides a definition of sedation and discusses the similarity with euthanasia); and *practical* issues (such as the procedural requirements for performing continuous sedation). This chapter thus has interesting parallels with the other legal chapters in this volume (Chapter 8 by Delbeke, and Chapter 10 by Huxtable & Horn), as well as with the more theoretical chapters (e.g. Chapter 3 by Jones, Chapter 13 by van Delden and Chapter 14 by Holm), and also with the clinical chapters (e.g. Chapter 4 by Porta-Sales and Chapter 5 by Sykes).

Continuing with the legal issues raised in the two previous chapters, in Chapter 10, *Continuous deep sedation at the end of life: balancing benefits and harms in England, Germany and France*, Richard Huxtable and Ruth Horn explain the legal situation regarding continuous deep sedation in England, Germany and France. Their analysis reveals that, although there are differences between these three jurisdictions, they share a commitment to the doctrine of double effect (DDE) as a means of balancing benefits and harms at the end of life. Consequently, these jurisdictions also share several problems associated with DDE and its (supposed) place in palliative care. Huxtable and Horn discuss various clinical, ethical and legal difficulties with DDE, as it pertains to continuous deep sedation. This issue is further developed by Raus, Sterckx and Mortier in Chapter 11.

Huxtable and Horn conclude that, despite the problems with DDE, a case can be made for continuing to use it, with reference to three different accounts of the value of life. These three accounts, they argue, respectively see life as having a self-determined value (emphasising respect for autonomy – the approach that is predominant in Germany), an instrumental value (emphasising the promotion of welfare and the eradication of suffering, as can be observed in England), or an intrinsic value (emphasising the protection of life without disproportionately requiring its extension, an account that underlies the legal approach in France). According to Huxtable and Horn, DDE should be retained since it may represent a point of consensus and since it at least captures a compromise position, thus occupying the middle ground between the different accounts of the value of life. They nevertheless acknowledge that further debate is needed in order to clarify and monitor the relevant boundaries of DDE.

Many of the chapters in this volume refer to DDE. This doctrine is indeed frequently referred to as the main justification for continuous sedation. Nevertheless, as discussed in some detail in Chapter 8 by Delbeke and Chapter 10 by Huxtable and Horn, DDE has problematic aspects. In Chapter 11, *Can the doctrine of double effect justify continuous deep sedation at the end of life?*, Kasper Raus, Sigrid Sterckx and Freddy Mortier argue that references to 'the' doctrine of double effect are problematic since various interpretations of this doctrine exist. However, looking at the most commonly used form of the doctrine, the natural law interpretation, it becomes clear that DDE cannot justify continuous *deep* sedation at the end of life, and, if properly applied, even forbids sedation. The foremost reason is that in continuous deep sedation, one deliberately and permanently takes away consciousness, even if in many cases one may not shorten life. This point is also highlighted in Chapter 8 by Delbeke, Chapter 12 by Holahan, Carroll, Gonzalez and Quill and Chapter 13 by van Delden.

However, Raus, Sterckx and Mortier also note that in fact the most commonly invoked justification for continuous deep sedation is not a double effect argument, but rather a *last resort* argument, according to which in last resort cases, taking away consciousness may be bad, but it is the least of two evils. However, if this is the real justification for continuous deep sedation, it seems misleading to keep saying one is invoking double effect.

An important question discussed in Chapter 11 on double effect is what it means to permanently and deeply sedate someone. This issue is also taken up in Chapter 12, *Palliative sedation, consciousness and personhood*, by Timothy Holahan, Thomas Carroll, Claudia Gonzalez and Timothy Quill. In this chapter the authors distinguish between different types of sedation according to their aim. This results in a key distinction between proportionate palliative sedation (PPS) and palliative sedation to unconsciousness (PSU).

In PPS, by definition, sedation is increased proportionally as necessary. PSU, by contrast, results in immediate unconsciousness. However, *both* practices can result in the patient becoming totally unconscious, so the crucial question is how the reduction or even complete taking away of consciousness affects the patient's personhood. If one views personhood as involving consciousness, both PPS and PSU can result in a loss of personhood. Others might disagree on the basis of a different conception of personhood, but few will dispute that total loss of consciousness is a radical event with significant ethical ramifications. According to Holahan, Carroll, Gonzalez and Quill, in view of the link between personhood and consciousness, care must be taken not to lower consciousness any more than necessary. Furthermore, they argue that, since extreme suffering can result in the disintegration of the person, in extreme cases, PPS or PSU can help preserve what remains of personhood when it is being assaulted by the ravages of advanced disease.

The issue of lowering consciousness and its effects on personhood is also central to Chapter 13, *The ethical evaluation of continuous sedation at the end of life*, by Johannes van Delden. In this chapter, van Delden observes that the ethical evaluation of sedation is complicated by the fact that many definitions of continuous sedation already contain normative claims (which is also one of the main points made by David Albert Jones in Chapter 3). Only a descriptive definition, van Delden argues, will allow for a proper ethical evaluation of continuous sedation at the end of life.

Subsequently, he notes that two issues are particularly relevant to such an evaluation. The first is the most commonly debated, namely whether sedation shortens life (also a key focus of Chapter 14 by Søren Holm). A possible life-shortening effect of sedation must be avoided in order to make continuous sedation until death appear to be a 'normal medical practice' (and thus legally permissible), and as such distinct from euthanasia (and thus ethically permissible). Some guidelines address this issue by stating that sedation should only be administered to patients with a short life expectancy (e.g. less than two weeks in the Dutch national guideline). However, according to van Delden, this time limit is not supported by the ethical principles most often invoked to justify continuous sedation until death.

The second issue, which van Delden calls 'the other issue', is often missed in the literature, namely that sedation in its most extreme form takes away *all* experiences, thereby ending a patient's biographical life (see also Chapter 11 by Raus et al. and Chapter 12 by Holahan et al.). Even in the absence of life-shortening, taking away consciousness is a drastic measure since it deprives patients of all capacity to communicate. As van Delden explains, remaining able to communicate is often considered important by both patients and relatives, thus he advocates that sedation to unconsciousness *only* be practised in real last resort cases.

In Chapter 14, *Terminal sedation and euthanasia – the virtue in calling a spade what it is*, by Søren Holm, he notices that continuous sedation is often portrayed in very different ways, and that a proper and intellectually honest portrayal of the practice is necessary. When it comes to ethically evaluating the practice, Holm argues that a distinction is needed between continuous sedation *with* and *without* ANH, as this aspect fundamentally affects the ethical nature of the practice. Regarding continuous sedation *without* ANH, it is clear for Holm that this practice is very similar to euthanasia. Like van Delden, he points out that physicians are notoriously bad at estimating life expectancy, so that a life-shortening effect of withdrawing or withholding ANH cannot be excluded. Separating the evaluation of the decision to stop food and fluids from the evaluation of the decision to sedate (as suggested, for example, by Delbeke in Chapter 8) does not solve the issue according to Holm, since it presupposes that the patient is competent, and as the literature review by Bruinsma et al. in Chapter 2 has demonstrated, this is often not the case.

For Holm, matters are different if ANH is continued. In these cases there can be no life-shortening and the practice of continuous sedation can be distinguished from euthanasia on the basis of intention and/or a functional difference between the two (since permanent unconsciousness is different from death). Holm acknowledges that there might be good reasons why people prefer sedation, as it is often believed to be associated with positive things, such as dying peacefully, living a long life, and the possibility of preparing oneself for death. However, Holm argues that these links are contingent and do not absolve us from the responsibility to scrutinise the practice of continuous sedation at the end of life.

In the final chapter, Chapter 15, *Terminal sedation: recasting a metaphor as the* ars moriendi *changes*, Margaret Battin investigates whether an argument that she developed half a decade ago, namely that sedation may be 'pulling the sheet over our eyes', is still valid today. In 2008 she argued that sedation was being proposed as a sort of compromise in the controversy over physician-assisted dying, but that it is a bad compromise.

It is clear for Battin that sedation is not in itself better than other practices at the end of life, so this cannot be the reason why its popularity is increasing so quickly. The real reason, Battin argues, lies in the perception of terminal sedation. It *feels* natural, safe and something which a patient can autonomously request, yet this is mere perception. According to Battin, we should embrace this practice with caution and be sceptical about efforts to promote it.

Today, the question of whether a sheet is being pulled over our eyes (i.e. whether sedation is concealing something that we should be seeing) can be framed in a different way and remains a relevant question. However, equally important is the *societal background* against which questions about sedation are framed. In this regard, Battin refers to the remark made by Holm (in Chapter 14) that terminal sedation will become more and more attractive as our *ars moriendi* shifts to a managed death process that is free from suffering. Like Holm in Chapter 14, Battin notes that the increasing frequency of sedation at the end of life might be a symptom of a shifting *ars moriendi* (i.e. the way people think of and go about dying). Requiring that a physician may not let a patient suffer makes a trade-off between pain relief and other values that are potentially important for a patient, impossible. The new *ars moriendi* might seem patient centred; however, according to Battin it may well herald a new wave of paternalism.

12.   Conclusion

The contributions to this volume on continuous sedation at the end of life show that there are still many legal, clinical and ethical issues that require further analysis and debate, and that an attitude of openness, transparency and intellectual honesty is vital for those issues to be resolved. We strongly hope that this book will help to achieve that goal.

2 Continuous sedation until death: state of the art

Sophie M. Bruinsma, Judith A.C. Rietjens and Agnes van der Heide

> To be, or not to be: that is the question:
> Whether 'tis nobler in the mind to suffer
> The slings and arrows of outrageous fortune,
> Or to take arms against a sea of troubles,
> And by opposing end them? To die: to sleep;
> No more; and by a sleep to say we end
> The heart-ache and the thousand natural shocks
> That flesh is heir to
> (William Shakespeare, *Hamlet* Act 3, Scene 1)

1. Introduction

In this chapter, the state of the art of continuous sedation until death is discussed with respect to terminology, empirical research, guidelines and regulations. Terms such as 'palliative sedation' and 'terminal sedation' are explained, critically discussed and subsequently placed in a research framework. An overview is given of research reporting the frequency of use of continuous sedation until death, with special attention to differences and similarities between countries and developments over time. Guidelines about continuous sedation are addressed, in particular the framework recently launched by the European Association for Palliative Care and the Dutch national guideline. Also, findings regarding clinical characteristics of the practice of continuous sedation will be summarised, for example the indications for sedation, and aspects of decision-making (such as involvement of patients, relatives and palliative care experts) and the performance of sedation (such as the type of drugs).

2. What is continuous sedation until death?

During the past century, the circumstances in which people die have changed substantially. Acute deaths due to infectious diseases have been gradually replaced by more prolonged dying trajectories (Seale 2000). One-third of all deaths in The Netherlands occur suddenly and unexpectedly (van der Heide et al. 2003; van der Wal et al. 2003). The increasing importance of chronic diseases as a cause of death and the attention currently being paid to patient-centred care at the end of life have created interest in the role of medicine in the timing and mode of death and dying (Seale 2000). In many instances, death is not merely the result of the natural course of a lethal disease: medical decision-making often contributes (Drazen 2003; van der Heide et al. 2003; Quill 2004; Murray et al. 2005). Such decision-making may concern the use of medical treatment to prolong the life of seriously ill patients (Rietjens 2006). However, prolonging life is not always the most appropriate goal of medicine at this stage in life, and preserving quality of life and alleviating suffering are increasingly recognised as important (Sepulveda et al. 2002).

Sometimes, patients who are nearing death have symptoms that cannot be relieved with conventional medical care, such as intractable pain, dyspnoea and delirium. One option to relieve such suffering entails the continuous use of sedating drugs to induce a state of unconsciousness until death, so that the patient's perception of symptoms is taken away. Continuous sedation until death is mostly used for patients whose death will ensue in the reasonably near future – that is, within one to two weeks (de Graeff & Dean 2007; Verkerk et al. 2007; Rietjens et al. 2009c). Continuous sedation until death occurs in all settings where patients die, but most often in hospitals and for patients with cancer (Rietjens et al. 2004; Miccinesi et al. 2006).

While it is commonly argued that the adoption of a single, clear-cut and well-defined term for the use of continuous sedation until death, and a clear definition for the practice, would greatly improve the quality and comparability of studies that investigate the practice of sedation (Rietjens et al. 2009b), there are large variations in the terms and definitions currently used. 'Palliative sedation' is the term most commonly used in guidelines and research papers (Morita et al. 2005a; Claessens et al. 2008; KNMG 2009b; Cherny & Radbruch 2009). However, several other terms with different connotations are also being used, for example 'terminal sedation' (Chater et al. 1998; Quill & Byock 2000; Cowan & Walsh 2001), 'sedation for intractable distress in the imminently dying' (Krakauer et al. 2000), 'end of life sedation' (Furst & Hagenfeldt 2002), 'total sedation' (Peruselli et al. 1999), 'controlled sedation' (Salacz & Weissman 2005; Taylor & McCann 2005), 'palliative sedation therapy' and 'proportionate sedation'. Furthermore, there is wide variety in how these terms are defined. Broadly speaking, the definitions fall into two types: those which include criteria of due care and those which are predominantly descriptive. For instance, Claessens et al. defined 'palliative sedation' as: 'The intentional administration of sedative drugs in dosages and combinations required to reduce the consciousness of a terminal patient as much as necessary to adequately relieve one or more refractory symptoms' (Claessens et al. 2008: 329). It is clear that this definition mixes descriptive language with criteria of due care: the use of sedating medications, proportionality, the patient being terminally ill and the presence of refractory symptoms (Rietjens et al. 2009b). However, by incorporating normative elements within a definition, moral discussions become obfuscated and the question is raised as to what to call cases in which the same acts were performed but in which other medications, indications or patients were involved. Generally speaking, the definition of an intervention should be purely descriptive, allowing for a separate discussion about the conditions under which this intervention would be morally acceptable (van Delden 2007). Only with a descriptive definition can valid comparable research be conducted in a methodologically sound manner. Therefore, in this chapter the authors will use the descriptive term 'continuous sedation until death', occasionally abbreviated to 'continuous sedation', but in those instances too we refer to the use of the practice until death.

3.   The debate about continuous sedation until death

The benefits and drawbacks of continuous sedation until death are frequently discussed by patients, relatives, caregivers and legal and ethical experts. On the one hand, it is often praised as an easy, innovative and indispensable technique to alleviate suffering, which is one of the most important goals of end-of-life care. On the other hand, it may be used too easily (Murray et al. 2008). Lowering a patient's consciousness until death is a far-reaching intervention that has an important impact on the patient, the relatives and the caregivers. It deprives patients in their very last days of the possibility to communicate and to say goodbye, and many patients consider being conscious until death as extremely important (Steinhauser et al. 2000). Relatives and caregivers also consider this procedure to be distressing (Morita et al. 2004a, 2004b; Rietjens et al. 2007). For instance, some Dutch nurses found it hard to use continuous sedation with patients who suffered from non-physical symptoms (Rietjens et al. 2007). In a Japanese study, relatives reported guilt, helplessness and physical and emotional exhaustion when patients received continuous sedation. They were concerned about whether sedated patients experienced distress, wished to know that the maximum efforts had been made, wished to prepare for patient death, wished to tell important things to patients before sedation, wished to understand patients' suffering, and wanted medical professionals to treat patients with dignity (Morita et al. 2004a). Further, some studies show that continuous sedation is not always performed in accordance with the relevant guidelines or recommendations, for example the sedative drugs recommended – benzodiazepines – are not always used (Miccinesi et al. 2006; Bilsen et al. 2007; Rietjens et al. 2008a; Seale 2009). Another issue that is often debated is whether the use of continuous sedation until death may shorten life. While some argue that it should be clearly distinguished from euthanasia (van Delden 2004, 2007), others argue that it may resemble euthanasia without the legal supervision or even consider it to be 'slow euthanasia' (Billings & Block 1996). Some others consider it to be a 'third way' between pro- and anti-euthanasia stances (Seymour et al. 2007). There are also indications that, in countries where euthanasia is legal, continuous sedation is sometimes used as an alternative to euthanasia by physicians who struggle with euthanasia, for example because of religious objections, or wish to avoid the legal procedures involved with euthanasia in jurisdictions in which it is permitted (Rietjens et al. 2009a).

4.   How often is continuous sedation until death used?

Despite its potential drawbacks, findings from surveys of physicians suggest that continuous sedation until death has a rather high frequency of use (Miccinesi et al. 2006). Within palliative care settings, estimates of the frequency of use of sedatives range from 15% to more than 60% (Stone et al. 1997; Fainsinger et al. 1998, 2000; Chiu et al. 2001; Muller-Busch et al. 2003; Sykes & Thorns 2003a, 2003b). Furthermore, a survey among palliative care specialists in North America and the UK showed that 77% of respondents had at one time applied deep sedation in patients close to death and a study from Japan showed that 64–70% of a sample of palliative care physicians and oncologists reported having used some form of deep sedation for severe physical distress (Morita et al. 2002a). However, these estimates are difficult to compare due to differences in the settings studied and the definitions used.

One group of studies exists that has enabled comparisons to be made; these focus on quantifying types of medical end-of-life decisions, looking at representative samples of death certificates, and using questionnaires to ask physicians to describe the decision-making and care for recent deaths they attended (Sepulveda et al. 2002; van der Heide et al.

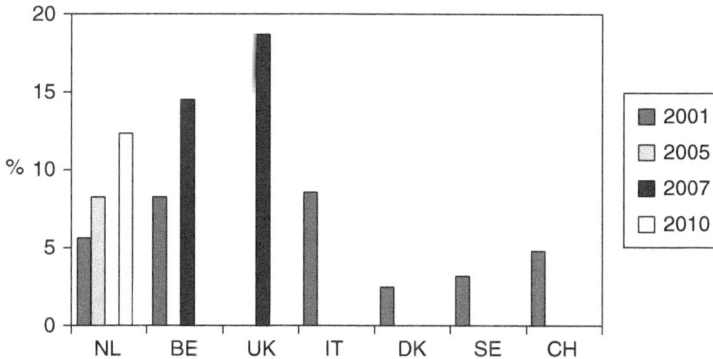

Figure 2.1 Frequency of continuous deep sedation until death in different European countries. NL, The Netherlands; BE, Belgium; UK, United Kingdom; IT, Italy; DK, Denmark; SE, Sweden; CH, Switzerland.

2003; Rietjens 2006; Bilsen et al. 2007; Chambaere et al. 2010). In these studies, the narrow definition 'continuous deep sedation until death' was employed to compare physicians' reports. Figure 2.1 compares and summarises the findings of these studies. In 2001, in six European countries with comparable epidemiology of terminal diseases, there was a variation in prevalence of continuous deep sedation until death of between 2.5% and 8.5% of deaths (Miccinesi et al. 2006). Italy and Belgium reported the highest percentages of continuous deep sedation: 8.5% and 8.2% of all deaths, respectively, were preceded by the use of continuous deep sedation. Denmark and Sweden reported the lowest frequencies: 2.5% and 3.2%, respectively. Switzerland was somewhere in between (4.8% of all deaths) (Miccinesi et al. 2006). A survey in the UK conducted in 2007 employing the same definition found a frequency of 16.5% of continuous deep sedation until death, although study limitations may have led to overestimation of prevalence (Seale 2009). A detailed analysis of the practice of continuous deep sedation until death in these countries suggests that these differences reflect complex legal, cultural and organisational factors more than differences in patients' characteristics or clinical profiles (Anquinet et al. 2012) (Figure 2.1).

In a more recent study, using the same definition and methodology, it was estimated that in The Netherlands in 2010, 12.3% of all patients received continuous deep sedation until death (Onwuteaka-Philipsen et al. 2012). This showed an increase compared to the figures of 5.6% for 2001 and 8.2% for 2005 (Rietjens et al. 2008a; Onwuteaka-Philipsen et al. 2012). In Flanders (Belgium), a similar increase in the use of continuous deep sedation was demonstrated, from 8.2% in 2001 to 14.5% in 2007 (Bilsen et al. 2007). The increase occurred in almost all care settings, among both sexes, in all age groups, and in patients with various causes of death (Chambaere et al. 2010), which indicates its generally rising acceptance as a medical end-of-life practice. This trend may be related to the increased attention given to its use and to the importance of relieving suffering in general: guidelines have been published and continuous deep sedation has received increasing societal and media attention. In Belgium, this is also likely to be related to recent developments in the implementation and organisation of palliative care, partly instigated by the Act on Palliative Care of 14 June 2002.

However, other factors have presumably also influenced the increase. Although euthanasia is legal in Belgium and The Netherlands, it is possible that some physicians and patients view continuous deep sedation as a psychologically, ethically and medically preferable alternative to euthanasia. Institutional policy may also have had an effect, for example many Belgian hospitals have introduced additional safeguards beyond the legal requirements for euthanasia (Lemiengre et al. 2007), possibly causing continuous deep sedation to be favoured over euthanasia as a last resort decision. Alternatively, perhaps, physicians may currently be increasingly more willing to report the use of continuous deep sedation. Lastly, it could also be the case that physicians find it more appropriate to use continuous sedation than to deal with a multitude of persistent symptoms that are difficult to treat (Chambaere et al. 2010).

5.   Guidelines

In a few countries, national or local guidelines have been developed for the use of sedatives in the last phase of life. Procedural guidelines are helpful for educating medical practitioners, setting standards for best practice and promoting optimal care (Cherny & Radbruch 2009). In 2009, the European Association for Palliative Care (EAPC) published a framework of recommendations for the use of sedation in palliative care comparable with earlier published international recommendations (Cherny & Radbruch 2009). In 2005, in The Netherlands, the Royal Dutch Medical Association launched a national guideline, which was revised in 2009 (KNMG 2009b). Guidelines have been published in other countries, for example, in 2005, a clinical guideline for continuous sedation was prepared in Japan (Morita et al. 2005a), and, in 2010 in Flanders (Belgium), a guideline was presented by the Federation for Palliative Care Flanders (Broeckaert et al. 2010). In this section, we will present the main recommendations of these guidelines, and in the subsequent section we will discuss current practice.

5.1.   EAPC framework

The European Association for Palliative Care (EAPC) considers sedation to be an important and necessary intervention in the care of patients with otherwise refractory distress (Cherny & Radbruch 2009). It states that prudent application of this approach requires due caution and good clinical practice and that problematic practices and inattention to potential risks can lead to harmful and unethical practice. The EAPC aims to facilitate the development of guidelines on the use of sedation by presenting a 10-point framework (see Box 2.1) that is based on the existing guidelines and literature and extensive peer review (Cherny & Radbruch 2009).

5.2.   The Dutch national guideline

In 2005, drawing on previous local Dutch guidelines, the Royal Dutch Medical Association published a national guideline for 'palliative sedation' (KNMG 2009b). This guideline sought to define 'palliative sedation' (including continuous sedation), to set rules for indications and contraindications, and to give recommendations for medication and

---

Box 2.1 Ten-item framework EAPC

- Recommend pre-emptive discussion of the potential role of sedation in end-of-life care and contingency planning.
- Describe the indications in which sedation may or should be considered.
- Describe the necessary evaluation and consultation procedures.
- Specify consent requirements.
- Indicate the need to discuss the decision-making process with the patient's relative.
- Present direction for selection of the sedation method.
- Present direction for dose titration, patient monitoring and care.
- Guidance for decisions regarding hydration and nutrition and concomitant medications.
- The care and informational needs of the patient's relatives.
- Care for the medical professionals.

practical procedures. The guideline defines 'palliative sedation' as 'the deliberate lowering of a patient's level of consciousness in the last stages of life'. It distinguishes between two types of sedation: continuous sedation until death; and temporary or intermittent sedation. The main premise of the guideline is that, unlike euthanasia, continuous sedation is normal medical practice. A summary of the main recommendations of the guideline is presented in Box 2.2.

6.   Description of clinical practice

In this section, the key concepts that are shared by most of the guidelines on continuous sedation will be discussed in the light of clinical practice.

6.1.   Indications

The guidelines state that indications for continuous sedation are present when one or more intractable or 'refractory' symptoms are causing the patient unbearable suffering (Morita et al. 2005a; Cherny & Radbruch 2009; KNMG 2009b). A symptom is, or becomes, 'refractory' if none of the conventional modes of treatment is effective or fast-acting enough, or if these modes of treatment are accompanied by unacceptable side-effects. The physician will have to decide whether a symptom is treatable or not on the basis of accepted good medical practice, bearing in mind the specific circumstances of a patient in the last stages of life (KNMG 2009b). The indications for continuous sedation are therefore considered to be medical in nature. Nevertheless, the perspectives of the patient and of the relative are very important, especially as regards the discomfort and side-effects of any possible mode of treatment (Swart et al. 2012b).

The symptoms most commonly experienced by patients in the last stages or final week of life are fatigue (83%), dyspnoea (50%), pain (48%), confusion (36%), anxiety (31%), depression (28%) and nausea and vomiting (25%) (KNMG 2009b). Fatigue is perceived as the greatest burden, followed by pain, anxiety, dyspnoea, depression, nausea and vomiting, and confusion, in that order (KNMG 2009b). Pain, dyspnoea and delirium are the refractory symptoms that lead most frequently to the use of continuous sedation. Severe forms of nausea and vomiting also motivate its use, but do so less frequently (KNMG 2009b).

Box 2.2 Main recommendations of the Dutch guideline

- Continuous sedation should always be administered in the final stages of life to patients who are dying and are experiencing unbearable suffering.
- Indications for sedation are present when one or more intractable or 'refractory' symptoms are causing the patient unbearable suffering. The physician will have to decide whether a symptom is treatable or not on the basis of accepted good medical practice, bearing in mind the specific circumstances of a patient in the last stages of life.
- The patient's life expectancy should not exceed one to two weeks.
- If the patient is capable of making a conscious decision, the patient must agree with sedation; if the patient is no longer competent to make an informed decision, the physician must consult the patient's representative
- The advice of a consultant is mandatory if the attending physician possesses insufficient expertise and/or is in doubt about key issues such as medical indications and life expectancy.
- The sedation is aimed at the relief of the patient's suffering and not at hastening or postponing death.
- The attending physician must be present at the initiation of the sedation.
- Midazolam is the drug of choice. The use of morphine as a sedative is regarded as bad practice; morphine should only be given or continued (alongside sedatives) to relieve pain and/or dyspnoea.
- In cases of continuous, deep sedation until the moment of death, there should be no artificial administration of fluids.
- Accurate records must be kept of the decision-making process, the way sedation is being administered and the effect of the intervention.
- Relatives play an important role, both when sedation is being considered and while it is being carried out and should be involved in the decision-making process. They can assist in monitoring and caring for the patient, and they should be clearly informed and supported. Further, it is important not only to provide the best possible information and emotional support for the patient and her family, but also to care for the various professionals involved in the case.

A systematic review of the literature showed that the majority of papers listed only physical symptoms as the reason for sedating a patient, the most important being delirium, dyspnoea and pain (Claessens et al. 2008). Other physical symptoms listed included fatigue, agitation, physical restlessness, insomnia, and nausea and vomiting. A minority of studies mentioned psycho-existential suffering as well as physical suffering as being a reason for sedating a patient, even though this was only true for a minority of patients. Most frequently mentioned were anxiety, mental anguish and psycho-existential suffering (without elaboration) (Claessens et al. 2008). A Dutch study showed that the indication for sedation typically originates from physical symptoms and non-physical factors 'adding up' to a situation in which a patient in the last phase of life suffers unbearably (Swart et al. 2012b).

6.2.   Life expectancy

Besides the requirement for an appropriate medical indication, a precondition for the use of continuous sedation is the expectation that death will ensue in the reasonably near future – that is, within one to two weeks (KNMG 2009b).

Studies have shown that continuous sedation is rarely performed when life expectancy is more than two weeks at the start of sedation (Swart et al. 2011). A Dutch study showed that the life expectancy at the start of continuous sedation was estimated to be less than two weeks in 97% of cases: 4% of the included physicians estimated a life expectancy of less than one day; 32% between one and two days; 38% between three and six days; and 23% between one and two weeks (Swart et al. 2011). Other research showed that, in The Netherlands, in most cases, life expectancy at the start of continuous sedation was estimated to be less than two weeks (Swart et al. 2010).

Based on retrospective reports from Dutch physicians, Rietjens et al. found that 38% of patients died within 24 hours, whereas 96% of patients died within one week (Rietjens et al. 2004, 2006). Morita et al. reported a survival time of less than three weeks in 94% of patients receiving continuous sedation in Japan. A systematic review showed that the mean survival time of patients after the onset of continuous sedation ranged from one to six days (Claessens et al. 2008).

It should be noted here that it may be difficult to estimate life expectancy accurately (Glare et al. 2003; Brandt et al. 2006b; Rietjens et al. 2009a). Clinicians have a tendency to overestimate life expectancy: it has been shown that survival time of patients is typically 30% shorter than predicted by physicians, but that the accuracy of prediction increases as death approaches (Glare et al. 2003).

6.3. Aim of continuous sedation

Guidelines, such as the Dutch national guideline, state that the aim of continuous sedation until death should be to relieve suffering, and that lowering the level of consciousness should be the means to that end (KNMG 2009b). The aim (and therefore the intention of the physician) should not be to lengthen or shorten the patient's life. The concept of intention is often regarded as difficult. Intentions, to a large extent, are highly personal and dependent on how one views one's own actions. Critics might say that they depend on how one wants one's actions to be viewed (Rietjens et al. 2012).

In a study that described the practice of continuous sedation in The Netherlands before the introduction of the national guideline, 36% of physicians reported having made their most recent decision to perform continuous sedation without the intention of hastening death (Rietjens et al. 2004). The physicians partly had the intention to hasten death in 47% of cases and had the explicit intention to hasten death in 17%. In most reported cases, this explicit intention concerned the decision not to give artificial nutrition or hydration (Rietjens et al. 2004). A study conducted a few years later by Swart et al. on physicians' and nurses' experiences with continuous sedation in The Netherlands showed that physicians had no intention to hasten death in 85% of cases, partly the intention to hasten death in 14% and had the explicit intention to hasten death in 1% (Swart et al. 2010).

A qualitative study performed by Rietjens et al. in 2007–8 among physicians from The Netherlands and the USA showed that respondents mentioned different and sometimes multiple intentions for their use of sedation (Rietjens et al. 2012). Besides alleviating severe suffering, most Dutch respondents justified its use by stating that it does not hasten death, while most American respondents indicated that it might hasten death but that this was justifiable as long as that was not their primary intention.

6.4. Decision-making process

The physician has to decide whether a symptom is treatable or not on the basis of accepted good medical practice, bearing in mind the specific circumstances of a patient in the last stages of life (KNMG 2009b). Continuous sedation is a medical procedure, and the responsibility for assessing medical indications, decision-making and implementation therefore lies with the attending physician (KNMG 2009b). Wherever possible, sedation should only be initiated with the consent of the patient. However, caregivers must provide the relatives with information, support them, help them understand the situation and the procedure to be adopted, and help them to cope with the experience. If the patient is no longer competent to take an informed decision, the physician must consult the patient's representative. The patient's right of informed consent is then transferred to her representative (KNMG 2009b).

A systematic review on continuous sedation showed that 15 papers provided information about the decision-making process (Claessens et al. 2008). All of these reported that consent was obtained from almost all patients who were not cognitively impaired. The most important reason for not discussing the decision with competent patients was to protect them from anxiety and/or sudden onset of refractory suffering. In 50–99% of cases, a relative was involved in the decision-making process (Claessens et al. 2008).

A recent study that described the practice of continuous deep sedation until death at home in Belgium in 2005–6 from the perspective of the general practitioner (GP) showed that a minority of the GPs had not consulted a competent patient but had consulted a relative of the patient. GPs provided various explanations for this. For instance, some thought that it was better for the patient, while others indicated that they thought that the patient preferred to leave the decisions up to the physician (Anquinet et al. 2011). A study performed in The Netherlands and the USA showed that, while many Dutch respondents indicated that they initiated open discussions about sedation proactively to inform patients about their options and to allow planning, the accounts of American respondents contained fewer and less open discussions, mostly late in the dying process and with the patient's relatives (Rietjens et al. 2012).

A study performed by Inghelbrecht et al. showed that nurses in different healthcare settings in Belgium are often involved in communication about continuous deep sedation until death (Inghelbrecht et al. 2011). The patient and relatives had communicated with the nurse about the continuous deep sedation in approximately 25% and 75% of cases, respectively. In 17.6% of cases, there was no communication between the nurse and the physician about the continuous deep sedation; in 29.1%, the physician and nurse only exchanged information; and in 23.4%, they made the decision jointly; in the other 30% of cases, nurses' personal opinion about the continuous deep sedation was asked or given (11.1%), the nurse advocated for the patient's or relatives' wishes (10.7%) or the physician communicated the continuous deep sedation decision after it was made (8.2%). Other studies also show figures on the involvement of nurses in the decision-making process. In a Dutch study 72% of nurses reported having been involved with a case of continuous sedation (Arevalo et al. 2013). In 96% of the cases, nurses were in agreement with the physician's indication of sedation, and in 84% they or a colleague were involved in the decision to use sedation. In 96% of the cases, nurses felt no pressure to perform procedures related to sedation. Sedation was proposed most often by physicians (33%), patients (17%), nurses (16%) and relatives (6%). In 3% of the cases, others were involved; in 10% it was unknown who was involved in the decision to start sedation and in 15% more than one person was involved (most often a physician, either in combination with a nurse or a patient).

Another review focused specifically on the involvement of relatives in the decision-making process of continuous sedation (Bruinsma et al. 2012). The (degree of) involvement was described in various ways in the literature. The results showed that caregivers involved relatives in the overall decision-making process in 69–100% of all cases. Relatives were involved in the decision-making process in 81–100% of all cases of continuous sedation; specific aspects of the use of continuous sedation were discussed with the relatives in 90–93% of cases; relatives gave their consent to use sedation in 69–100% of cases; and the relatives were informed about the decision in 95–100% of cases (Bruinsma et al. 2012).

6.5.   Consultation

The Dutch guideline states that where a physician has doubts regarding her own expertise, or has difficulty balancing the different considerations involved in deciding whether to start continuous sedation (e.g. indications, life expectancy and the importance of exercising due care), it is standard professional practice to consult an appropriate expert in good time (KNMG 2009b). According to the European Association for Palliative Care (EAPC) framework for the use of sedation in palliative care, injudicious use of sedation occurs in 'situations in which before resorting to sedation, there is a failure to engage with clinicians who are experts in the relief of symptoms despite their availability' (Cherny & Radbruch 2009; Janssens et al. 2012). The American Medical Association's Code of Medical Ethics states that a physician considering sedation should consult with a multidisciplinary team, if available, including a physician with expertise in palliative care (Raus et al. 2011).

Consultation with a further expert or team prior to continuous sedation ('palliative consultation') is rather rare in The Netherlands. Rietjens' 2008 study revealed that palliative consultation was requested in the last month before death in only 9% of cases of continuous sedation (Rietjens et al. 2008a), and was most often requested by GPs. A study among Dutch physicians performed by Swart et al. showed that consultation with a palliative care team before the start of sedation occurred significantly less often for non-cancer patients than for cancer patients (10% as opposed to 27% of cases) (Swart et al. 2012a). This consultation was considered helpful in 89% of the cases, for both cancer and non-cancer patients. Research reveals that in 41% (47 out of 113) of cases where the palliative consultation team of the Comprehensive Cancer Centre Netherlands was consulted on continuous sedation, a negative advice was given (de Graeff 2008; Janssens et al. 2012). The consultants' impressions were that some physicians had agreed to continuous sedation too early. The authors concluded that the high percentage of negative advice indicates the necessity for consultation.

6.6.   *Drugs*

It is considered crucial for continuous sedation to be applied proportionately and adequately, in response to the appropriate medical indications. Guidelines state that it is the degree of symptom control, rather than the degree to which consciousness must be reduced, that determines the drug or drug combinations to be used as well as the dose and duration of dosage (KNMG 2009b). According to the EAPC framework, benzodiazepines, in particular midazolam, are the preferred drugs for continuous sedation until death (Cherny & Radbruch 2009). Arguments in favour of midazolam include its short half-life, which means that treatment can be rapidly adjusted, and the considerable experience already gained with it in cases of continuous sedation. If the patient fails to respond adequately to midazolam, checks should be made to see whether the mode of administration and the medication are in order, and whether any disruptive and remediable factors (e.g. a full bladder or constipation) are playing a role. Only then can consideration be given to the use of a different sedative, such as levomepromazine or propofol (KNMG 2009b). In situations where continuous deep sedation until death is being considered, morphine is often already being given to treat pain or dyspnoea. The Dutch guideline regards the use of morphine as a sedative as bad practice. Morphine should only be given or continued (alongside sedatives) to relieve pain and/or dyspnoea; the dose should be calculated to relieve the actual or assumed extent of the pain and/or dyspnoea (KNMG 2009b).

A systematic review performed in 2008 showed that 32 per cent of the studies mentioned midazolam as the main drug used for continuous sedation (Claessens et al. 2008). Other drugs used either alone or in combination with midazolam included haloperidol, phenobarbital and opioids.

A study conducted in Flanders (Belgium), The Netherlands and the UK and published in 2012 showed that benzodiazepines (sometimes combined with opioids and/or other drugs) were more frequently used than opioids alone to induce continuous deep sedation, especially in the home setting. In The Netherlands, the proportion of cases in which continuous deep sedation was induced with benzodiazepines (sometimes combined with opioids and/or other drugs) was higher than in Flanders and in the UK (Anquinet et al. 2012).

A study performed by Swart et al. investigated Dutch physicians' considerations about the depth of continuous sedation. They found two approaches towards the depth of continuous sedation: starting with mild sedation and only increasing the depth if necessary; and deep sedation right from the start. Physicians who choose either mild or deep sedation appear to be guided by the same objective of delivering sedation in proportion to the relief of refractory symptoms, as well as other needs of patients and their families (Swart et al. 2012c).

6.7. *Artificial hydration*

In most cases, continuous sedation until death is used for patients who are no longer able or willing to take any fluids, because they are actively dying (AVVV et al. 2006). In such situations, the Dutch guideline advises that artificial administration of fluids during sedation is not beneficial and could even result in unwanted side-effects, such as oedema, ascites and bronchial secretions (KNMG 2009b).

A systematic review performed in 2008 showed that figures on artificial fluid intake in relation to continuous sedation varied significantly between countries and settings (Claessens et al. 2008). Miccinesi et al. and Menten reported that in 35% of cases in Italy and 64% in Denmark and The Netherlands continuous sedation was performed without administering artificial fluids (Miccinesi et al. 2006; Menten 2010). Italy and Belgium had the highest estimates for continuous deep sedation until death with artificial nutrition or hydration (Miccinesi et al. 2006). Other studies describe the situation before and during continuous sedation (Morita et al. 1999, 2005b; Cameron et al. 2004). Studies performed in South Africa and Japan showed that where patients had received artificial fluids before sedation, in 20–69% of cases fluid intake continued during sedation (Cameron et al. 2004; Morita et al. 2005b). In 24–44% of patients in two Japanese studies, fluid administration was reduced (Morita et al. 1999, 2005b). One South African study reported that no sedated patients received artificial fluid (Fainsinger et al. 1998). Some studies reported that mildly sedated patients were able to take fluids and/or food orally (Muller-Busch et al. 2003; Cameron et al. 2004; Morita et al. 2005b). These differences were partly due to differences in setting.

Artificial hydration is a controversial issue. Generally, there are few medical arguments for giving parenteral hydration when sedation is initiated in the imminently dying patient who is already unable to take fluids herself; however, other (e.g. emotional or cultural) considerations may play a role (de Graeff & Dean 2007) as may ethical considerations.

6.8.   The start of the sedation

A multidisciplinary approach is a characteristic feature of palliative care (KNMG 2009b). Nursing staff may provide important input in helping to decide what procedure is indicated, in assessing whether the prerequisites are met, and in carrying out continuous sedation. However, the physician is responsible for the administration of continuous sedation. Because the start of sedation is an emotionally charged event, and situations may arise in which the physician must be able to intervene, guidelines recommend that the physician should be present when continuous sedation is initiated. Guidelines further state that if, due to unforeseen circumstances, the attending physician is unable to be present at the initiation of continuous sedation then, in acute situations, experienced nursing staff may initiate the sedation. However, this is only permissible in cases where the physician has already discussed the possibility of acute sedation with the patient, a relative and nursing staff (KNMG 2009b).

It has become clear that, before the introduction of the national guideline, Dutch physicians were not always present when continuous sedation is initiated (Klinkenberg et al. 2004; Boorsma et al. 2005). In 2008, i.e. after the adoption of the guideline, Dutch physicians were present in 81 per cent of cases (Swart et al. 2011). A nationwide study conducted in The Netherlands to assess experiences of nurses involved in continuous sedation at home after the introduction of the Dutch guideline found that in a third of cases continuous sedation was started without the presence of the GP (Brinkkemper et al. 2011). Moreover, the majority of the 211 respondents (71 per cent) reported that the GP did not stay present until the desired level of sedation had been reached. However, in most of these cases, the respondents reported that the GP was available if necessary.

6.9. *Caring for the professional caregivers and relatives*

According to the guidelines, it is important not only to provide the best possible information and emotional support to the patient, but also to care for the professional caregivers involved in the case and for the patient's relatives (KNMG 2009b).

With a few exceptions, there has been little research exploring the experiences of physicians, nurses and relatives regarding the use of continuous sedation until death (Seymour et al. 2011). Those studies which do exist suggest that some physicians and nurses struggle with the meaning and significance of sedation use in end-of-life care (Beel et al. 2006), are concerned about its possible link to practices which may end life prematurely (Morita et al. 2004c), or have objections to the practice on the grounds of religious belief or moral conviction (Curlin et al. 2008) or because of ideas about the appropriateness of the practice for certain 'types' of suffering (Blondeau et al. 2005; Rietjens et al. 2007; Curlin et al. 2008).

The results from a systematic review by Bruinsma et al. suggest that, despite the fact that the majority of relatives reported that they were comfortable with the use of continuous sedation, some relatives may express distress before or during the application of sedation (Bruinsma et al. 2012). On the one hand, the relatives wanted the patients' suffering to end; on the other hand, they expressed concerns regarding the aim of the sedation, the patients' well-being and their own well-being.

7.   Conclusion

In this chapter, we have shown that different studies use different terms and definitions for the practice of continuous sedation until death. For many years, continuous sedation until death has been a much debated and controversial issue within and outside the field of palliative care, mostly because of its potential life-shortening effect and the lowering of patients' consciousness. Despite its potential drawbacks, studies show that continuous sedation has a rather high frequency of use, and that its use is increasing. In this chapter, the key concepts of guidelines on continuous sedation were discussed in the light of clinical practice. It was shown that reported practice regarding continuous sedation until death largely reflects the recommendations from these guidelines. However, there are still several inconsistencies, for instance with regard to the administration of fluids and palliative consultation. Further research to clarify these issues should be based on multicentre, prospective, longitudinal and international studies using a uniform definition of continuous sedation, as well as valid and reliable methods. Such research would also inform the debate about several important ethical and legal issues surrounding continuous sedation.

3   Death by equivocation: a manifold definition of terminal sedation

David Albert Jones

Knock, knock! Who's there, in the other devil's name? Faith, here's an equivocator, that could swear in both the scales against either scale, who committed treason enough for God's sake, yet could not equivocate to heaven. O, come in, equivocator.

(William Shakespeare, *Macbeth* Act 2, Scene 3)

1.   Introduction

The phrase 'terminal sedation' (TS) was first used in the context of palliative medicine in the early 1990s (see, for example, Enck 1991). However, from the very outset there have been problems created by a lack of agreed terminology and, more significantly, a lack of agreed definition of terms. In this chapter, we seek to establish a richer, multi-dimensional definition of TS, our 'manifold' definition, which captures the critical factors involved in the various forms of TS. We begin, in section 2, by considering the range of definitions and terms that have been used for TS, before considering in section 3 what factors should be included in our definition, and, in section 4, setting out the group of binary factors that constitute our manifold definition of TS.

2.   Diverse terminology and definitions of end-of-life sedation

de Graeff and Dean (2007: 69) list nine different terms used in the literature to describe the use of sedatives in end-of-life care: 'sedation'; 'terminal sedation'; 'sedation for intractable distress in the imminently dying'; 'end of life sedation'; 'total sedation'; 'sedation in the terminal or final stages of life'; 'controlled sedation'; 'palliative sedation'; and 'palliative sedation therapy'. This list overlaps considerably with the nine terms listed by Muller-Busch et al. (2004: 337), although they add the terms: 'slow euthanasia' (Billings & Block 1996); and 'sedation for comfort at end of life' (Walton & Weinstein 2002). To this list could be added: 'sedation of the imminently dying' (Wein 2000); 'sedation towards death' (Jansen & Sulmasy 2002); 'sedation to death' (Sulmasy et al. 2010); 'early terminal sedation' (Cellarius 2011); and the now ubiquitous 'continuous deep sedation' (Seale 2009; and many others).

If these terms were synonymous, then it would be a trivial matter that people referred to the same practice using different terminology. However, some of these terms are explicitly intended to characterise contrasting practices. For example, 'early terminal sedation' is 'early' precisely because it does not refer to 'sedation of the imminently dying'. There are a number of possible sedative practices here, and different definitions will typically capture different ranges of practice.

This is perhaps best seen by way of example. Kelly Taylor, a resident in the UK had Eisenmenger's syndrome, which gave her chest pain and left her short of breath, and also had a spinal condition, Klippel–Feil syndrome, which restricted her mobility. Her condition was terminal, but her death was not imminent. In 2007, she began court proceedings to force her doctors to accede to her request for an increased dose of morphine sufficient to induce a coma and keep her in that state. She had also made a written advance refusal of artificial nutrition and hydration. It was her intention that the combination of sedation to unconsciousness and withdrawal of hydration would bring about her death.

The doctors refused her request and their stance was supported by the British Medical Association, which stated that: '[W]e cannot support her request for doctors to sedate her to a state of unconsciousness with the specific intention of ending her life. In our view this would involve the doctors in assisting her suicide, which is both unlawful and unethical' (Dyer 2007).

From a clinical perspective, it was also problematic that her request was for a higher dose of morphine, which she was already receiving as a painkiller, as this would not be the intervention of choice if sedation was desired for symptom relief:

Evidence over the past 20 years has repeatedly shown that, used correctly, morphine is well tolerated and does not shorten life or hasten death. Its sedative effects wear off quickly (making it useless if you want to stay unconscious), toxic doses can cause distressing agitation (which is why such doses are never used in palliative care), and it has a wide therapeutic range (making death unlikely). The Dutch know this and hardly ever use morphine for euthanasia. (Regnard 2007)

Kelly Taylor later withdrew her court case and sought alternative means of palliative treatment to alleviate her distress, but the case remains significant because it highlighted the tensions between different possible understandings of the use of sedatives at the end of life (Stewart 2007: 170). The British Medical Association was not objecting to the use of sedatives in end-of-life treatment and care per se, but was objecting specifically to the combination of sedation and refusal of treatment with the *intention of ending life*. Depending on how TS is understood, and what intentions are included, the term TS could cover the use of sedatives in palliative care, the use of sedatives as part of a plan to bring about death, or both.

In the face of such terminological confusion, it is common to begin a discussion of TS by choosing some established term or by devising a new term and then defining what is covered by the new term for the purpose of the discussion. However, this approach tends to lead merely to the stipulation of a preferred definition which will either be at variance to some existing uses of that term, or, if it is new, will add to an already overcrowded plethora of competing terms.

Sometimes a new term will be criticised because it seems to beg the ethical question or to obscure what are taken to be important distinctions. For example, Murray, Boyd and Byock objected to the use of the term 'continuous deep sedation' on the basis that it is 'not precise enough to discern the reasoning and motives of clinicians needed to support relevant ethical analyses ... We suggest that subsequent surveys that ask doctors about reported deaths use clear categories that can help us interpret empirical patterns of end of life care' (Murray et al. 2008: 781). Nevertheless, the term 'continuous deep sedation' was subsequently used in the much quoted work of Clive Seale on the prevalence of TS in the UK. The survey conducted by Seale deliberately avoided asking about intention. Seale decided on this approach in order to facilitate international comparisons, as he used the same question that was used in surveys of Dutch and Belgian practice. However, it is highly debatable whether the advantages of a common question outweigh the disadvantages of an ambiguous one. It is noteworthy that on questions relating to 'hastening death' Seale departed from previous approaches precisely in order to avoid 'the conflation of these things in the Dutch-inspired surveys' (Seale 2009: 199).

In other cases, a definition, or a linked pair of definitions, will introduce a distinction only for other commentators to dispute the significance of the purported distinction. For example, after Quill et al. (2009) proposed a distinction between 'proportionate palliative sedation' (PPS) and 'palliative sedation to unconsciousness' (PSU), Cellarius and Henry (2010) disputed the fact of the distinction, suggesting that PSU was best regarded as the extreme case of PPS. On the other hand, Sulmasy et al. (2010) agreed that Quill had identified an important distinction between different sedative practices, but thought that Quill had mischaracterised the nature of the distinction. This kind of qualified acceptance, which is relatively common, is the worst situation from the perspective of agreeing terminology, for it means different people might use the same term to cover different practices.

This can easily be illustrated in relation to the most popular term, 'terminal sedation' (TS). Cellarius (2011) uses TS in contrast to what he calls 'early terminal sedation' (ETS), whereas Battin (2008) and Tännsjö (2004b) and others use TS precisely to *mean* early terminal sedation. Again, another very popular term in the literature is 'palliative sedation' (Claessens et al. 2008; Hauser & Walsh 2009; Quill et al. 2009; Pitre 2009; Cellarius & Henry 2010; and many others), or some variant such as 'palliative sedation therapy' (Morita et al. 2001c; de Graeff & Dean 2007; Maltoni et al. 2009) or 'proportionate palliative sedation' (Quill et al. 2009; Sulmasy et al. 2010). 'Palliative sedation' is often used to characterise sedation where neither the inducement of unconsciousness nor the hastening of death is the intent of the practice, and it is typically contrasted with TS which does, or can, mean intentionally bringing about unconsciousness and early death. However, Rady and Verheijde (2010), while they differ from Battin (2008) on the ethics of euthanasia, agree with her in taking 'palliative sedation' to be a euphemism, and hence a synonym, for TS. It is not enough here to defend the terminology by saying that some people use 'palliative sedation' in contrast to TS. The problem is precisely that different people use the same words to cover different sets of practices, and this is true also for the term 'palliative sedation' and its variants.

In the context of such a confusion of overlapping, contrasting or contradictory terms, definitions and underlying practices, it is unsurprising that it is difficult to establish or compare the prevalence of practices in this area. Studies of the prevalence of TS vary tremendously, so that while Seale (2010: 45) reports a range of 2.5–16.5% among European countries, Miccinesi et al. (2006: 123) report the prevalence of use of sedatives at the end of life as being from 15% to more than 60% in different studies. It is commonly argued that this diversity in part reflects an underlying confusion in the use of terms and definitions. As argued above, even where the same term is used, there may be different definitions of the term, and even where the definition is made explicit and is the same across different studies, it may be that the definition is understood differently so that it is ambiguous between significantly different practices. In this case, similar figures may still stand for very different patterns of practice, especially where the data were gathered in temporally or geographically different contexts (since context will influence interpretation).

In addition to the problems that this situation causes for empirical research, the lack of an agreed definition also complicates the ethical analysis. From the original introduction of the term TS, one central ethical question has shaped discussion of TS, and this is whether or not TS should be regarded as a covert form of euthanasia (this is evident, for example, in the title of the collection edited by Torbjörn Tännsjö (2004a) *Terminal Sedation: Euthanasia in Disguise?*). This was the issue at the heart of the Kelly Taylor case (Dyer 2007; Stewart 2007: 170). There are a number of possible responses to this. Three common responses are:

1. to regard TS as a form of (or equivalent to) euthanasia and distinct from conventional palliative medicine (e.g. Rady & Verheijde 2010);
2. to regard TS, if practised correctly, as a form of (or equivalent to) conventional palliative medicine and distinct from euthanasia (e.g. Maltoni et al. 2009; Cherny & Radbruch 2009);
3. to regard TS as a tertium quid, distinct both from conventional palliative medicine and from euthanasia (e.g. Cellarius 2011; Raus et al. 2011; Bernat et al. 1993)

However, if there is no clarity as to which practices fall under the term TS, then there is a great danger that people will argue at cross purposes; for example, those who assert that TS is equivalent to euthanasia may not be talking about the same set of practices as those who argue that TS is no more than a form of palliative care.

The wish to distinguish euthanasic from palliative *intent* in use of sedatives is common in the literature. This is because many moralists consider intention to play a key role in ethics. According to the principle of the inviolability of human life, as expressed in the mainstream Western moral tradition and in the criminal law of most jurisdictions, it is wrong intentionally to kill an innocent human being. Nevertheless, if sedation were needed to alleviate symptoms, then it might well be ethical to provide it, even if as a side-effect it hastened the death of the patient. This acceptance of side-effects is sometimes termed 'the doctrine of double effect' and the use of sedation in end-of-life situations has been one of the archetypal examples in that tradition (Hawryluck & Harvey 2000; Finnis et al. 2001; Gormally 2004; Boyle 2004), notwithstanding doubts as to whether properly administered sedation does have death-hastening effects (Sykes & Thorns 2003a, 2003b; Maltoni et al. 2009).

There are of course schools of thought that reject the centrality of intention and the doctrine of double effect (Quill et al. 1997a; Kuhse 2004), and there are jurisdictions which have legalised euthanasia (The Netherlands, Belgium and Luxembourg). For someone who rejects the doctrine of double effect, the features that will carry ethical significance will change. Nevertheless, it will remain the case that the ambiguity of the meaning of TS will cause problems. It is striking that a number of proponents of euthanasia have been critical of the practice of TS, regarding it as 'slow euthanasia' (Kuhse 2004) without the regulatory framework or safeguards of legalised euthanasia (on this issue, see also Billings & Block 1996; Orentlicher 1997b; Quill et al. 2004). For example, among supporters of euthanasia it is common to draw a sharp distinction between voluntary and non-voluntary forms (even for those who think non-voluntary euthanasia is acceptable in some cases). However, rarely in surveys or analyses of TS is attention specifically drawn to the presence or absence of a request from the patient.

It is common for ethicists to distinguish two forms of TS: one of which covers a set of TS practices that are equivalent to euthanasia; and the other of which covers a set of practices that are equivalent to palliative therapy. However, while such a distinction can certainly be made, it is by no means clear that this single binary approach is adequate for the analysis of the range of practices which may fall under TS. There is a danger that seeing the ethics of TS only in terms of its relation to euthanasia may narrow the range of ethical questions that are thought to be relevant. For example, concerns about over-sedation or under-sedation may have very little to do with hastening death (and thus euthanasia), but may relate to issues of good practice, symptom control and the importance of maintaining awareness for the sake of personal and spiritual goods (CBCEW 2010: 30–2).

When data from The Netherlands showed a decline in the rate of euthanasia taking place at the same time as a rise in TS, some suggested that this was because TS was being used as a way to bring about death without having the ethical controversy and emotional and regulatory burden of euthanasia: 'continuous deep sedation may enable doctors to evade the procedural requirements for euthanasia' (Murray et al. 2008: 781). The data were taken to imply that TS may well have been used with euthanasic intent. Nevertheless, the reasons behind the increase in TS in The Netherlands need not have involved a relation to euthanasia, for it seems that rates of TS are rising significantly in all countries, whether or not they have legal euthanasia (Raus et al. 2012). When Seale (2009: 201) presented data that showed a rate of TS in the UK roughly twice that of The Netherlands or Belgium (16.5% as compared with

8.2% and 8.3%, respectively), some were incredulous. It was suggested that these figures did not represent intent to produce unconsciousness and to hasten death (as allegedly was happening in The Netherlands), but only the use of sedatives for palliative reasons. Data from a national audit of hospital deaths in the UK in 2009 showed that, when sedatives were used, the actual quantity used was low (median dose 10 mg, given as a continuous subcutaneous infusion over 24 hours) (MCPCIL 2009: 7; Stephenson 2012). Perhaps clinicians were wrongly assuming that when a patient lost consciousness before death, as is relatively common,[1] this was *caused* by the sedatives. Nevertheless, while it is right to question the reported figures for continuous deep sedation in the UK, the same caution must then be applied equally to the data from The Netherlands. Seale deliberately used the same question as was used in surveys in The Netherlands, and if there was ambiguity in the question in the UK, then it may well have been ambiguous also in The Netherlands. In both cases, it seems that the terms and definitions used provide insufficient clarity to resolve the key clinical and ethical issues.

It is clear then that neither empirical research nor ethical analysis of TS can make progress without some agreed definition of what is meant by the term TS.

3.   The elements of a manifold definition

While many writers give only one definition of TS, and others distinguish two forms (a euthanasic form and a palliative form), Morita et al. (2001c) distinguish five different variables: degree of sedation; duration; pharmacological properties; target symptoms; and target populations. This complex fivefold definition, combining different factors, is certainly a step forward, but it is noticeable that even this fivefold definition includes no reference to request or to intention. It would not escape the criticism directed against the term 'continuous deep sedation' that it fails to distinguish the key factors necessary for an adequate ethical analysis (Murray et al. 2008: 781).

What is needed, therefore, is an expansion of Morita's definition so that it includes all those distinctions that are present in the discussions in the literature. To understand the full range of practice covered by TS, it is here proposed to start with a catch-all definition that is wide

---

[1] In a study of nursing home patients in The Netherlands conducted by Hella Brandt and others, 25% of patients had slipped into unconsciousness by 24 hours prior to death and a further 19% slipped into unconsciousness in the last 24 hours (Brandt et al. 2006a: 537).

in scope, and then to distinguish within this the main elements which may or may not be present and which lead to the narrower, more specific definitions. This method produces what is here called a 'manifold definition'. This has the advantage of including all that people mean by the term TS, while at the same time highlighting those variable features that are relevant to the ethical analysis of this set of practices.

To fall under the description 'terminal sedation', it would seem firstly that the practice must involve use prior to and proximate to death ('terminal') of drugs that have a sedative effect ('sedation'). This immediately exposes the first ambiguity, which is about the relation of these terms. Is TS given to someone who is dying or is sedation given so that someone will die? This question leads Hallenbeck to raise a further series of questions:

> A temporal linkage between sedation and a patient's death is implied. However, does a causal relationship exist? Does this matter? Must the patient be terminally ill? If so, is it essential that death be imminent? Must the patient have stopped eating and drinking prior to the initiation of sedation? Does it matter what the nature of suffering is for which sedation is administered? (Hallenbeck 2000: 314)

Each of these questions helps identify an element of a manifold definition, as will become apparent below. The aim of this chapter is to produce a definition that will cover all of these possibilities and their contraries. De facto, the term TS is used both for practices that are part of the palliative care of the dying and for practices intended to bring about death. At the highest level of generality, TS thus refers simply to the use of sedatives prior to death. However, the phrase 'prior to death' would be insufficient as, literally understood, all treatment on living patients is prior to death. Nor is it enough that the sedation occur shortly before death. It is also important that the death be anticipated and be somehow linked to the sedation, in that the sedation was an element of the end-of-life care or in that the sedation hastened or was thought to hasten death. If someone under sedation is a passenger in a car which is involved in a road traffic accident, and the passenger is killed outright, the fact that she was on sedatives immediately prior to death would not mean that this sedation could reasonably be described as 'terminal sedation'. The end-of-life context must be understood when the sedatives were given in order for it to be terminal sedation. Hence a more adequate general description might be the *use of sedatives in an end-of-life context* (if this is understood to cover both cases where death is antecedently anticipated to be imminent and cases where the use of sedatives is thought likely to bring about death, but not cases where death occurs unexpectedly).

The phrase terminal sedation is perhaps most commonly used to refer to sedation given in the period immediately prior to death and still operative up to the moment of death, but this is complicated in that sedatives can be used *intermittently* in an end-of-life context. This highlights perhaps the most well-established distinction among possible forms or subcategories of terminal sedation, the distinction between continuous deep sedation (CDS) and sedation that is either intermittent or mild. Some people use TS and CDS as synonyms (e.g. Tännsjö 2004b; Battin 2008), whereas others take TS also to include intermittent and mild sedation. Patricia Claessens argues that, to get an accurate picture of the use of sedatives in end-of-life treatment and care, we need an approach that includes mild and intermittent sedation as well as continuous deep sedation: 'To be able to give an overall definition that captures all possible forms of palliative sedation occurring in practice, mild and intermittent sedation must be included in the definition of palliative sedation' (Claessens et al. 2008: 328). A manifold definition of TS is precisely one that 'captures all possible forms' of end-of-life sedation. In the definition developed here, TS is therefore used as the most general term which will thus include CDS and other practices.

There has in fact been some useful empirical research that differentiates between CDS and mild or intermittent forms of sedation. This distinction is generally made because it is CDS that is more likely to be the focus of ethical controversy as it seems more like euthanasia. Nevertheless, while most authors take this to be a distinction between just two forms of sedation, CDS over and against sedation that is neither deep nor continuous, there can be sedation that is not deep but is continuous and there can be sedation that is deep but is not continuous. Also it should be noticed that continuous or deep sedation is not the same as continuous or deep unconsciousness, for someone may be unconscious without any use of sedatives whatsoever. In relation to terminal *sedation*, the terms continuous/intermittent and deep/mild thus refer to the way in which the sedatives are given and the effects of these sedatives, not simply to the level of awareness or unconsciousness. There are thus two distinctions here.

To these two distinctions, (1) *continuous* versus *intermittent* and (2) *deep* versus *mild*, Morita (Morita et al. 2001c, 2002b) adds a third: (3) 'primary sedation', when the drug has no beneficial pharmacological effects other than sedation, and 'secondary sedation', where the drug has an effect in treating some underlying symptom but also has a sedative effect. This distinction has been less influential than the deep/mild and continuous/intermittent distinctions, but it is invoked in the literature and has been used to guide empirical research in the area.

For those who are concerned to distinguish sedation in a palliative care context from sedation as a means of euthanasia, a key distinction is proportionality (4). Palliative care uses sedatives in just the quantities that are needed to control symptoms that cannot be controlled in other ways (what are termed 'refractory symptoms') (Cherny & Portenoy 1994). In contrast, the use of sedatives intentionally to bring about unconsciousness and death is not in proportion to symptoms. Hence Claessens states that 'The notion of proportionality is crucial to differentiate palliative sedation from euthanasia' (Claessens et al. 2008: 328). Sometimes proportionate palliative sedation (PPS) is contrasted with CDS as though these were contraries. However, these are in fact independent variables. It may be that for very severe symptoms, in some rare cases, the use of sedation that is both deep and continuous will be the proportionate response (Cellarius & Henry 2010). Concomitantly, sedation might be mild or intermittent but might still be in excess of what is proportionate to the symptoms. Proportionality is an independent fourth element.

There is, however, a further difficulty here and that is how 'refractory symptoms' are defined. In particular, opinion is divided as to whether what is termed 'existential' or 'psycho-existential' distress (Morita 2004a) should be included as a refractory symptom. Some clinicians think that it is a valid indication for sedation, but others strongly resist this, arguing that such distress is more appropriately addressed by other means. The summary of de Graeff and Dean is fair: 'Psychological and existential distress as an indication for Palliative Sedation Therapy is a controversial issue' (de Graeff & Dean 2007: 71). While it is common to include 'refractory symptoms' in definitions of palliative sedation (see, for example, Cherny & Radbruch 2009; Hauser & Walsh 2009), the lack of agreement as to whether (5) *existential distress* should be included renders this definition ambiguous, both as a guide to and as a measure of practice. The inclusion or not of existential distress is thus a further variable feature in our definition.

If existential distress, for example the kind of distress that might be experienced by someone who feels unable to cope with the onset of disability, were counted as an indication for deep sedation, then this could pave the way for the use of TS as covert euthanasia. This is why it is controversial and it is partly in an effort to exclude this that a common element of some definitions of TS is the inclusion of the requirement that (6) the patient is imminently dying (Levy & Cohen 2005; Wein 2000). If the patient is close to death, then the risk of actually hastening death is much less. In contrast, much greater justification is needed before subjecting someone to these risks if she has the potential for a long life:

'For immediately pre-terminal patients, this risk may be judged to be trivial relative to the goal of relieving otherwise intolerable suffering. In other circumstances, such as patients requesting transient respite from overwhelming symptoms, the risk of potentially hastened death may have significant, or even catastrophic, consequences' (Cherny & Radbruch 2009: 582). These cases are sufficiently different that they are often, and quite reasonably, distinguished within the definition of TS. Note, however, that, as with the other features, the imminence of death is a feature that is independent of the continuousness, depth or pharmacology of sedation, and while it affects the weighing of 'proportionality' it can still be that sedation is judged to be proportionate in a patient who is not imminently dying and can be judged disproportionate in a patient who is imminently dying. In this sense it is another independent variable.

Thus far, the elements of our definition have focused on such clinical factors as depth, duration, causation and indications for sedation. They have not included the element of intention. However, as outlined above, many commentators have recognised the relevance of intention and some have included it as part of the definition of TS. For example, Tännsjö defines TS as 'a procedure where through heavy sedation a terminally ill patient is put into a state of coma, where the *intention of the doctor* is that the patient should *stay comatose* until he or she is dead' (Tännsjö 2004b: 15; emphasis added). However, while Tännsjö calls attention to the intentions of the doctor, it is surely also relevant to ask about the intentions of the patient, and of those close to the patient who may be involved in the decision (e.g. carers, relatives or legal representatives), and also whether the sedation has been requested by the patient or by her representative. Just as voluntary euthanasia is rightly distinguished from non-voluntary euthanasia, so too must a distinction be made between terminal sedation at the patient's request and terminal sedation of a patient who could not or did not so request. The question of intention thus leads to five further distinctions: (7) the patient might request sedation or not; (8) a relative, carer or proxy might make this request or not; (9) a request might or might not embody the patient's wish to become unconscious until death; (10) a request might or might not embody the wish of the relative, carer or proxy that the patient become unconscious until death; or (11) a request might or might not embody the wish of the doctor that the patient become unconscious until death. These three actors might not share the same intention. For example, the patient might request sedation wishing to be unconscious, while the doctor might give sedation for the sake of symptom relief and in proportion to symptom relief.

Moreover, a proxy might have a different view to that of either or both the patient and the doctor.

When clinicians or ethicists are writing about TS, they frequently include within the definition the (12) withholding or withdrawing of artificial nutrition and hydration (ANH)[2] (see, for example, Tännsjö 2004b; Rady & Verheijde 2010; Cellarius 2011). Nevertheless, international comparative surveys of continuous deep sedation show that hydration is given in between 36 per cent (Denmark and The Netherlands) and 65 per cent (Italy) of cases (Miccinesi et al. 2006: 122). Hence it is a feature of some, but not all, TS. As sedation might be requested explicitly by the patient, so too might nutrition and hydration be explicitly refused by the patient. In most jurisdictions, this has legal implications, and arguably also ethical implications. Hence the presence or absence of (13) an *advance refusal* of ANH should be specified when defining terminal sedation.

Many of the distinctions so far examined relate to the characterising of TS as 'euthanasia in disguise' (Tännsjö 2004a). This implies that TS does hasten death and so could be used deliberately to hasten death. However, within the context of proportional use of sedatives in palliative care, it is often denied that sedatives do actually hasten death. On the other hand, there are certainly many doctors who believe that their use of sedatives has hastened death by hours or days, and in inexpert hands or in circumstances where the patient is not imminently dying, the small risk that exists (through respiratory depression, aspiration or haemodynamic compromise) may have 'significant, or even catastrophic, consequences' (Cherny & Radbruch 2009: 582). There are also patients who are not imminently dying who wish to use TS in order to hasten death, and it seems that TS could be used for this purpose, especially in cases where it is combined with withholding or withdrawing ANH. To distinguish these cases, it seems relevant to ask whether (14) the protocol does hasten death in this kind of case. This is the first case in which a new distinction is the concomitant of a distinction that has already been made, rather than a new independent variable. For in so far as the overarching definition requires an *end-of-life context* this will only be the case either if the patient is imminently dying antecedent to the use of sedatives (distinction 6) or if the use of sedatives hastens death (distinction 14). Hence this is not an extra distinction but it is nevertheless useful to re-express it in this way in order to draw attention to the fact that sedation may or may not hasten death and may or

---

[2] The term more generally used in the UK is clinically assisted nutrition and hydration (CANH); however, for consistency with the other chapters in this book, the equivalent term ANH is used in this chapter.

may not be intended to. Just as it was relevant to ask whether the doctor and the patient intended to bring about unconsciousness by the use of sedatives, so it is relevant to ask whether by the use of sedatives and (where this occurs) the withdrawal or withholding of artificial nutrition and hydration, (15) the patient, or (16) the relative, carer or proxy, or (17) the doctor intends the protocol to hasten death. This feature might seem to be implicit in all that has gone before, but this may be less clear because of the complex character of TS with the possible withdrawal of ANH and with a possible advance decision. Neither the decision to cause unconsciousness nor the decision to withhold ANH need imply that death is the aim of the exercise.

Consideration of the independent features which may or may not be present in TS therefore produces a manifold definition with 17 elements:

Terminal sedation is the use of sedatives in an end-of-life context that either:

(1) is continuous or intermittent;
(2) is deep or mild;
(3) is the primary or the secondary pharmacological effect;
(4) is proportionate or disproportionate to 'refractory symptoms';
(5) includes or does not include 'existential distress' as a valid indication;
(6) is applied to a patient who is or is not imminently dying;
(7) is or is not at the request of the patient;
(8) is or is not at the request of the relative, carer or proxy;
(9) has the patient intending or not intending that unconsciousness until death be brought about;
(10) has the relative, carer or proxy intending or not intending that the patient's unconsciousness until death be brought about;
(11) has the doctor intending or not intending that the patient's unconsciousness until death be brought about;
(12) is or is not combined with withholding nutrition and hydration;
(13) has or has not an advance refusal of nutrition and hydration;
(14) accordingly involves a protocol that does or does not hasten death;
(15) such protocol is or is not intended by the patient to hasten death;
(16) such protocol is or is not intended by the relative, carer or proxy to hasten the patient's death; and
(17) such protocol is or is not intended by the doctor to hasten the patient's death.

4.   Strong, weak and intermediary forms of terminal sedation

All the terms in this manifold definition are either present in popular definitions of some form of sedative practice at the end of life or they are prominent in the literature around the issue. The only complication added by the definition is a clear distinction between the intentions of the doctor, of the relative, carer or proxy, and of the patient, all of which are taken to be morally relevant.

The manifold definition is in many ways a simplification. It assumes that each variable is binary, whereas there is, for example, a continuum between mild and deep sedation; nor does the definition name particular pharmacological agents or doses which are alleged to produce these effects; nor does the definition consider epistemological problems in relation to diagnosis or prediction. The definition refers to unconsciousness as the effect of sedatives, but where a patient is unconscious at the end of life it may not be apparent whether sedation was a contributory factor. Many patients suffer a period of unconsciousness prior to death. The term 'deep sedation' in the definition is taken to mean coma or unconsciousness that is *caused* by the sedatives. It is in this context that consideration of the specific drugs used and the doses given may help clarify whether unconsciousness was caused by or simply followed after the use of sedatives.

This point leads to a more general one. A number of the distinctions in the definition rely on clinical judgement and there may be a distance between the opinion of the clinician and the actual situation. The physician may be mistaken as to the level of awareness of the patient, the primary and secondary effects of the sedatives, the nature and extent of the symptoms, the question as to whether the symptoms are refractory, and the benefit and risks to the patient of providing ANH. These mistakes may be of great ethical significance, especially if they are due to negligence. The definition does not capture every ethical issue and the ethical importance of good clinical judgement is not to be underestimated.

Moreover, within the manifold definition the relative, carer or proxy is thought of as a single person when there is often more than one, with more than one view, and no distinction is made between the possible differences in legal status of a relative and a proxy. It also assumes that the intentions of the patient, the relative, carer or proxy, and the doctor are independent. However, in reality they influence one another in complex ways, and this also creates ethical problems (e.g. of undue influence, projection or poor communication). Nevertheless, by adverting to the different possible intentions of these three kinds of agents, the definition at least calls attention to the complexity of moral judgements in this area.

The manifold definition set out above shows the range of practices that may be expressed by the phrase terminal sedation. Furthermore, for most factors, one possibility brings TS closer to euthanasia and the other brings TS closer to palliative therapy. This is perhaps most easily illustrated by taking two possibilities as extremes, which may be termed strong TS and weak TS.

Strong (euthanasic) terminal sedation is the use of sedatives in an end-of-life context that:

(1) is continuous;
(2) is deep;
(3) is the primary pharmacological effect;
(4) is disproportionate to 'refractory symptoms';
(5) includes 'existential distress' as a valid indication;
(6) is applied to a patient who is not imminently dying;
(7) is at the request of the patient;
(8) is at the request of the relative, carer or proxy;
(9) has the patient intending that unconsciousness until death be brought about;
(10) has the relative, carer or proxy intending that the patient's unconsciousness until death be brought about;
(11) has the doctor intending that the patient's unconsciousness until death be brought about;
(12) is combined with withholding nutrition and hydration;
(13) has an advance refusal of nutrition and hydration;
(14) accordingly involves a protocol that does hasten death;
(15) such protocol is intended by the patient to hasten death;
(16) such protocol is intended by the relative, carer or proxy to hasten the patient's death; and
(17) such protocol is intended by the doctor to hasten the patient's death.

Weak (palliative) terminal sedation is the use of sedatives in an end-of-life context that:

(1) is intermittent;
(2) is mild;
(3) is the secondary pharmacological effect;
(4) is proportionate to 'refractory symptoms';
(5) does not include 'existential distress' as a valid indication;
(6) is applied to a patient who is imminently dying;
(7) is not at the request of the patient;
(8) is not at the request of the relative, carer or proxy;
(9) has the patient not intending that unconsciousness until death be brought about;
(10) has the relative, carer or proxy not intending that the patient's unconsciousness until death be brought about;
(11) has the doctor not intending that the patient's unconsciousness until death be brought about;
(12) is not combined with withholding nutrition and hydration;

(13) does not have an advance refusal of nutrition and hydration;
(14) accordingly involves a protocol that does not hasten death;
(15) such protocol is not intended by the patient to hasten death;
(16) such protocol is not intended by the relative, carer or proxy to hasten the patient's death; and
(17) such protocol is not intended by the doctor to hasten the patient's death.

It should be apparent that strong TS is ethically distinct from weak TS and that strong TS is reasonably regarded as a form of voluntary euthanasia while weak TS is an example of palliative treatment and care. This echoes the conclusion of a previous section that terminal sedation is ambiguous between euthanasia and palliative therapy. However, what discussions of TS generally fail to bring out is the way that different features of terminal sedation may be present or absent. So, for example, if the patient did not wish sedation but a request was made by a proxy wishing to hasten death and the doctor agreed for that reason, then this would be a form of non-voluntary euthanasia. Again a patient may request sedation in order to become unconscious, whereas a doctor might provide this only for reasons of symptom control. This is clearly a very different kind of case.

There are not just 'two types of practices' (Belgrave & Requena 2012: 268) here, but with 17 independent elements capable of being affirmed, denied or left open there are 3^{17} different possible definitions, a staggering 129,140,163 variations!

For the purpose of ethical analysis, many of these intermediary forms of TS will be easy to assimilate to strong TS or to weak TS, and some, while logically possible, may be regarded as unlikely in reality (if the patient is dying and proportionate sedation is used and if nutrition and hydration is also given, then is it really likely that the intention of the doctor is to hasten death?). However, some intermediary forms will be distinct from each other in important ways and may involve other ethical issues.

The facts that sedation and the withholding of ANH are independent features, and that the intentions of doctor, relative and patient are independent features, lead to some forms of TS being unlike either strong TS or weak TS. The doctor might agree to sedation only as proportional to symptoms and may withhold ANH in order to respect an advance decision (Callahan 2004). In contrast, the patient may request the first and refuse the second out of suicidal motives. In such a case, a practice may be legitimate for a physician in relation to traditional inviolability of life principles even though it is requested by a patient as an alternative means to euthanasia. Thus Cellarius (2011: 54) is correct in holding that there can be a form of TS that represents a 'distinct entity', irreducible either to euthanasia or to conventional palliative care. However, he underestimates the number of possibilities between these two limiting cases. Terminal sedation is not a third reality, but a manifold reality, a large set of possible practices each with its own ethical significance, some being acceptable forms of palliative care, some being forms of euthanasia, and some fitting into neither category.

This variety of possible practice also gives rise to caution about interpreting data. The practice of TS in The Netherlands is not necessarily equivalent to euthanasia, nor is the practice in the UK necessarily innocent. The available data tells us little about intention and little about causation. An early criticism of the Liverpool Pathway for the Care of the Dying (LCP) is that it encouraged over-sedation and under-hydration. Dr Adrian Treloar, a critic of the pathway, later withdrew the charge that it was a 'pathway for continuous deep sedation' (Treloar 2008a): 'I am happy to accept that, properly used, the LCP is not deep sedation and thus in these circumstances my use of the term "deep sedation" for the LCP is misplaced. I apologise for this' (Treloar 2008b). Nevertheless, he maintained that it could lead to over-treatment. Whether or not this hastens death, or is intended to, it raises ethical questions because of the possibility of needlessly compromising the awareness of the patient. If sedation is out of proportion to symptoms, then it is poor care and is wrong for this reason.

The irony of incorporating continuous deep sedation into the practice of palliation is that 96% of terminally ill patients and 65% of treating physicians in the United States consider mental alertness an important attribute at the end of life (Rady & Verheijde 2010: 210; see also CBCEW 2010: 30–2)

5.   Conclusion

The function of the manifold definition developed in this chapter is not to supplant existing definitions of TS or to recommend a new definition. It serves rather to show how existing definitions relate to one another and to remind researchers and ethicists of the variety of features that may characterise sedation in an end-of-life context. The manifold definition is thus a tool for examining the ethical implications of definitions and for highlighting variable possible features of TS practice. While situating TS between euthanasia and palliative care is helpful for some purposes, the ethics of TS are much richer than the simple question as to whether any particular form of TS is equivalent to euthanasia. Different permutations of the manifold definition call attention to different ethical issues. If attention is not given to these distinctions then it will be impossible to distinguish appropriate care from unethical practice and patients will continue to suffer a death by equivocation.

4 Palliative sedation: clinical, pharmacological and practical aspects

Josep Porta-Sales

1.   Introduction

Sedation, understood as lowering a patient's awareness of pain and distress by reducing her consciousness, is a common manoeuvre frequently indicated and used in a great variety of medical contexts. In a general sense, sedation is applied to allow comfort during some diagnostic procedures, such as, for example, colonoscopy or other invasive and/or painful techniques (Dumonceau et al. 2010; Wahidi et al. 2011). Sedation is also used in cases of painful and distressful therapeutic manoeuvres, such as some ocular surgery (Greenhalgh & Kumar 2008; Ursea et al. 2011), electroconvulsive therapy (Hooten & Rasmussen 2008), intubation, and management of severely injured patients in the casualty room or the intensive care unit (McMillian et al. 2011; Patel & Kress 2012). It is also used to allow some control over conditions and situations related to a disease itself; this could be the case for the management of psychotic, agitated patients (Battaglia 2005; Cañas 2007) or of refractory symptoms in the dying.

In some of these circumstances, potential harm and distress can be expected, while in others the harm and distress is already present. In either case, the only aim of sedation is to protect the patient against harm, i.e. physical and mental distress. Depending on the clinical context, the expected evolution of the sedated patient can be very different. For instance, patients undergoing endoscopy, surgery or electroconvulsive therapy are expected to recover fully after sedation, while with some patients in an intensive care unit it can be expected that they will die due to the severity of their injuries or the critical condition of their illness. In the case of sedation at the end of life, usually called palliative sedation, the expected result is that the sedated patient will die from the evolution of her terminal condition.

Sedation is an invasive anaesthetic technique with its own intrinsic benefits and risks. It has certain ethical aspects in common with other invasive procedures, for example in terms of indication, consent, procedure and assessment. It should be acknowledged that palliative sedation has the additional end of life emotional component and is persistently confused with euthanasia (Porta-Sales 2003; Materstvedt et al. 2003; Materstvedt 2012).

Thus palliative sedation is usually understood as a therapeutic manoeuvre whose aim is to relieve intolerable refractory suffering in a patient with an irreversible and advanced disease who has a short life expectancy (from a few hours to a few days) through the administration of sedatives or anaesthetic drugs, reducing the patient's consciousness as much as is needed to alleviate suffering, and using appropriate sedation scales for assessment (Morita et al. 2002b; Porta-Sales et al. 2002; Rousseau 2004; Cherny & Radbruch 2009).

Sedation is identified as being indicated by the care team (Morita et al. 2005a, 2005b). Whenever possible, patients must give consent for the sedation (Porta-Sales et al. 1999; Morita et al. 2005b). However, if that is not possible, it is advisable to seek the agreement of the next of kin (Cherny & Radbruch 2009). The main cause for a patient's inability to participate in the decision-making procedure is delirium (Morita et al. 2003a, 2005b).

The setting in which palliative sedation is indicated must be well understood (Box 4.1). Palliative sedation is only indicated in the presence of a refractory symptom, meaning that palliative sedation is a last resort for symptom alleviation. Consequently it is not uncommon for most patients and families to have been experiencing difficult symptom control and suffering before palliative sedation is indicated and initiated (Morita et al. 2004b). In such situations, some patients and families may feel frustrated and emotionally exhausted after each failed attempt at symptom relief. That death is near is usually obvious to the patient and her relatives. These patients will generally have been on psychotropic drugs, such as opioids, benzodiazepines or neuroleptics, for a long time. This is an important pharmacological difference between palliative care patients and the great majority of patients who need to be sedated in other circumstances such as, for example, surgery or emergencies. Patients who have been using opioids and tranquillisers for long periods of time may have developed tolerance to such drugs (Morita et al. 2003b), and consequently the dose-effect could be quite dissimilar to that in naïve patients. On the other hand, patients at the end of their lives requiring palliative sedation are very frail, both physically and mentally, which is also a key difference with patients who need sedation to undergo surgery or invasive diagnostic procedures. Accordingly, palliative sedation should not only be effective

---

Box 4.1 Characteristics of the setting where palliative sedation is usually indicated

- Patient and family have endured 'hard times'.
- Patient and family are frustrated after the evident failure of each therapeutic attempt to relieve the refractory symptom(s).
- The end of life has become more or less evident for everyone concerned.
- Patient's coping strength is running down.
- Patient has usually been on opioids, benzodiazepines or neuroleptics for a long time.
- Patient's physical condition is extremely frail.
- The selected sedation technique should be safe, since there is not much time for rectification.

---

but also safe, since in a patient close to death there is little room for rectification if side-effects occur (e.g. convulsions or an unexpectedly quick death), usually with a great impact on the relatives' memories. In sum, patients at the end of life cannot be compared either physically or pharmacologically with patients needing sedation under other circumstances, with the possible exception of critically ill patients in intensive care units.

2.   Indications and commonly used drugs

Since the early work of Ventafridda et al. (1990), several studies have provided epidemiological information about the uncontrollable or refractory symptoms that are indications for palliative sedation, as shown in Table 4.1. The methodologies, the operational definitions of palliative sedation and the enrolled populations are so different across these studies that only a general picture of the situation can be drawn. Nevertheless, the overall frequency of palliative sedation is estimated to be about 36 per cent, ranging from 15 to 78 per cent (Table 4.1). Delirium, dyspnoea and pain are the three symptoms most consistently reported as the main reason for administering palliative sedation (Table 4.1).

Although psycho-existential suffering is not reported on in many studies, its mean frequency in those studies where it is reported is around 22 per cent (Table 4.1). The difficulty of assessing refractory psycho-existential suffering as an indication for palliative sedation

Table 4.1 Palliative sedation frequency and main indications for sedation

Authors	Year	Sample	Type study	Sedation frequency (%)	Delirium (%)	Dyspnoea (%)	Pain (%)	N/V (%)	Bleeding (%)	Seizures (%)	Psycho-existential suffering (%)
Ventafridda et al.	1990	Home	P	52.5	17	52	49	8	—	—	—
Fainsinger et al.	1991	InP	R	16	26	—	6	—	—	—	—
Morita et al.	1996	InP	R	48.3	23	49	39	10	—	—	—
Stone et al.	1997	InP	R	38.2	60	20	20	—	—	—	26
Ojeda Martín et al.	1997	Mix	P	19.1	37	74	6	3	8	—	—
Fainsinger	1998	InP	R	30	91	9	—	—	—	—	—
Morita et al.	1999	InP	P	45	42	41	13	2	—	—	2
Porta-Sales et al.	1999	Mix	P	23	21	23	23	6	9	—	36
Peruselli et al.*	1999	Home	P	25							
Fainsinger et al.	2000	InP	P	25	60	25	7	9	3	—	7
Chiu et al.	2001	InP	P	27.9	57	23	10	—	—	—	—
Kohara et al.	2005	InP	R	50.3	21	63	25	—	—	—	40
Rietjens et al.	2008b	InP	R	43	62	47	28	—	—	—	6
Vilà Santasuana et al.*	2008	InP	R	78							
Porzio et al.	2009	Home	R	36.4	81.2	18.3	—	—	—	—	—
Elsayem et al.	2009	InP	R	41	82	6	—	—	—	2	—
Van Dooren et al.	2009	InP	R	—	64	44	33	—	4	—	—
Van Deijck et al.	2010	InP	R	15	24	40	52	—	—	—	34
Alonso-Babarro et al.	2010	Home	R	12	62	14	3	7	—	7	7
Mercadante et al.*	2011	Home	P	35.7							
Caraceni et al.	2012	InP	R	64.3	31	37	—	—	—	—	—
Maltoni et al.	2012a	InP	P	31.9	61.1	29.2	20.8	1.4	1.4	—	37.5
Average				*36*	*48.5*	*34.1*	*22.3*	*5.8*	*5.0*	*4.5*	*21.7*

InP = inpatient; P = prospective; R = retrospective; N/V = nausea and vomiting.

*Refractory symptom frequency not provided.

has been a cause of controversy (Shaiova 1998; Cherny 1998; Morita 2004a; Taylor & McCann 2005). Nowadays a clearer agreement exists about its diagnosis, as well as an acceptance of palliative sedation as an appropriate therapy when existential suffering becomes refractory in patients in the last stages of their lives (Schuman-Olivier et al. 2008; Cassell & Rich 2010).

According to the literature on palliative sedation, the most commonly used drug is midazolam, along with a relatively narrow range of other drugs, mainly other benzodiazepines, neuroleptics and anaesthetics (Table 4.2). One recent study (Caraceni et al. 2012) reports that apart from opioids, 25 per cent of patients were sedated with benzodiazepines, 17 per cent with neuroleptics, and the rest with a combination of drugs, mainly benzodiazepines, neuroleptics and antihistamines. Although opioids are mentioned in the majority of studies, their use as the single sedating drug is not now recommended (Reuzel et al. 2008).

3.   Basic and practical pharmacology

In this section we will review the different classes of drugs that are used in palliative sedation: benzodiazepines, neuroleptics, barbiturates, anaesthetics and other drugs.

3.1.   Benzodiazepines

All benzodiazepines share the same mechanism of action through enhancing the γ-amino-butyric acid (GABA) at the $GABA_A$ receptor, producing a dose-dependent central nervous system (CNS) depression ranging from calmness, drowsiness (sedation), and sleepiness to unconsciousness (Nemeroff 2003). When benzodiazepines are administered together with other CNS depressants, this can result in surgical anaesthesia, coma or even death if the dose is increased. The general indications for their use are anxiety, insomnia, muscle spasm and epilepsy (Greenblatt 1992; Wolf 2011), and in palliative care they can also be used for palliative sedation (McNamara et al. 1991). The different action potencies, common doses and routes of administration are summarised in Table 4.3. Diazepam should not be given subcutaneously (SC) due to the oily solution required, and even intravenous (IV) administration can produce some discomfort (Becker 2012). It is important to be aware that all benzodiazepines induce tolerance after a couple of weeks of administration, and in the case of patients with far-advanced diseases it is not uncommon to use benzodiazepines for longer periods. This should be taken into account when considering the starting doses

Table 4.2 *Drugs described as sedatives used in different studies, and main route of administration*

Authors	Year	Sample	Type study	Midazolam % (mg/day)	Haloperidol % (mg/day)	Levomepromazine % (mg/day)	Phenobarbital % (mg/day)	Propofol % (mg/day)	Opioids % (mg/day)	Main route
Turner et al.	1996	InP	P	88 (25)	—	—	—	—	80 (66)	SC
Morita et al.	1996	InP	R	55	33	—	—	—	55	SC
Stone et al.	1997	InP	R	80 (22)	37 (5)	33 (64)	—	—	—	—
Fainsinger	1998	InP	R	61 (29)	—	—	—	—	100 (79)	—
Morita et al.	1999	InP	P	31 (7)	31 (3)	—	—	—	37 (5)	SC/IV
Porta-Sales et al.	1999	Mix	P	78 (38)	25 (14)	5 (197)	—	—	64 (74)	SC
Fainsinger et al.	2000	InP	P	75 (26)	19	5	—	—	—	—
Chiu et al.	2001	InP	P	24	50	—	—	—	12	PO/ SC
Elsayem et al.	2009	InP	R	89*	—	44†	—	—	—	—
Van Deijck et al.	2010	InP	R	91 (47)	18 (6)	7 (50)	—	—	64 (65)	SC
Alonso-Babarro et al.	2010	Home	R	93 (74)	—	7 (125)	—	—	—	SC
Maltoni et al.	2012a	InP	P	46 (17.5)	35 (4)	32 (68) †	—	—	—	IV

InP = inpatient; P = prospective; R = retrospective; SC, subcutaneous; IV, intravenous; PO, by mouth.
*After having received lorazepam. †After having received chlorpromazine.

Table 4.3 *Characteristics of the common benzodiazepines used for palliative sedation*

	Diazepam	Clonazepam	Lorazepam	Midazolam
Actions				
Anxiolytic	+++	+	+++	++
Hypnotic	++	+++	++	+++
Muscle relaxant	+++	+	+	+
Anti-epileptic	+++	+++	+	+++
Pharmacology				
Starting	Bolus 5–10 mg IV	Bolus 0.5–1 mg SC-IV	Bolus 2–4 mg IV	Bolus 5–10 mg SC-IV
Maintenance (mg/day)	10–30	2–8	2–20	30–120
$t_{\frac{1}{2}}$ (hours)	20–100	20–40	10–20	1–3
Route of administration	IV-PR	SC-IV	IM-SC-IV	SC-IV

+ = Mild; ++ = moderate; +++ = intense; $t_{\frac{1}{2}}$= half-life; SC, subcutaneous; IV, intravenous; IM, intramuscular; PR, per rectum.

of benzodiazepines for palliative sedation, since the effect of the benzodiazepines is dose-dependent (Morita et al. 2003b). Another major worry with the use of benzodiazepines is the existing evidence that they can precipitate delirium, or worsen a pre-existing delirium, which is the most common indication for palliative sedation (Breitbart et al. 1996; Jones & Pisani 2012). It is therefore recommended to avoid benzodiazepines in cases of delirium not related to alcohol abuse (Wilson et al. 2012). If this evidence is not taken into account, a delirium worsened by benzodiazepines in a dying patient can be mistaken for 'normal' or 'expected' agitation and masked with a subsequent rapid increase of the benzodiazepine dose until the patient becomes comatose or dies. The frequency of this problem has not been reported in the case of the dying, but it can easily be prevented by using neuroleptics first.

All benzodiazepines are metabolised through the liver using the P450 enzymatic system (CYP3A4 and CYP2C19). The main differences between the various different benzodiazepines relate to their periods of action. According to their period of action, they are classified as: short acting (less than 6 hours), for example midazolam; intermediate acting (6 to 24 hours), for example lorazepam; and long acting (more than 24 hours), for example diazepam or clonazepam (Becker 2012).

The benzodiazepine family is a large group of drugs, and midazolam is usually the preferred drug for palliative sedation since it can be administered both IV and SC, making it suitable for use in home care or when it is not practical to use an IV line. Other benzodiazepines that have been used for sedation include lorazepam, diazepam, delorazepam and clonazepam.

3.2.   *Neuroleptics*

Neuroleptics are a large family of drugs usually classified as *typical* or *atypical* (e.g. risperidone, olanzapine, quietiapine). In the case of palliative sedation, the *typical* ones are used, more specifically the phenothiazines (chlorpromazine and levomepromazine (methotrimeprazine)) in view of their sedating profile. The other *typical* neuroleptic that is used is a butyrophenone: haloperidol. Haloperidol has been reported as being extensively used in sedation, which could be due to the fact that haloperidol is the drug of first choice in the management of delirium in palliative care. In a revision to the recommendations for the use of haloperidol in palliative care, it is clearly stated that haloperidol is a better antipsychotic than it is a sedative, and it is recommended not to use it as a sedative when a neuroleptic drug is needed (Vella-Brincat & Macleod 2004).

All neuroleptics exert their pharmacological action through antagonising the dopamine subtype 2 receptors, and to a variable extent other receptors, mainly histamine (H_1), α_1-adrenergic, acetylcholine and serotonin ($5HT_2$) (Twycross & Black 1997), which explains the side-effects that are commonly observed with their use, such as sedation, hypotension, urine retention, drying up of exocrine gland secretions and blurred vision (Table 4.4). The neuroleptics are metabolised in the liver by oxidation (P450) and glucuronidation (Haduch et al. 2011).

Neuroleptics are indicated for the management of schizophrenia, paranoia, psychotic depression, agitation and aggressive behaviour, and in delirium and dementia (Lee et al. 2004; Meyer 2007). In the particular case of palliative care, neuroleptics are used as anti-emetics (Twycross & Black 1997; Critchley et al. 2001), in the management of delirium (Vella-Brincat & Macleod 2004) and in palliative sedation. The pharmacological actions of these drugs are very interesting and useful since they reduce the patient's interest and initiative to react to environmental stimuli, reduce the manifestation of emotions, reduce the adverse perception of threats and ameliorate psychotic symptoms, such as hallucinations or disorganised thinking.

Table 4.4 *Characteristics of the common neuroleptics used for palliative sedation*

	Haloperido	Chlorpromazine	Levomepromazine
Actions			
Antipsychotic potency	+++	+	++
Sedative	+	++	+++
Extrapyramidal	+++	+	+
Hypotensive	+	++	+++
Pharmacology			
Starting	Bolus 1.5–10 mg/SC-IV	Bolus 25mg/IV	Bolus 2–4 mg/IV
Maintenance (mg/day)	10–15	100–150	2–20
t$_{1/2}$ (hours)	24 (12–36)	24 (8–35)	24 (15–30)
Route of administration	SC-IV	IV	SC-IV (infusion)

+ = Mild; ++ = moderate; +–+ = intense; t$_{1/2}$ = half-life.

In sum, neuroleptics allow for a reduction of a patient's perception of real or potential threats, permitting a more neutral thinking. Consequently, neuroleptics can be very useful drugs in the particular case of delirium that is refractory to haloperidol, and in cases of extreme anguish in the dying patient (O'Neill & Fountain 1999). The potent anticholinergic action of levomepromazine and chlorpromazine makes them especially useful for patients dying with malignant bowel obstruction due to their ability to reduce bowel secretions (Baines et al. 1985; Kennett et al. 2005). However, at the same time, due also to the anticholinergic action, carers should be aware of the potential risk of urine retention, which can precipitate discomfort and agitation. Regarding administration, apart from oral administration, *typical* neuroleptics can be used parenterally, but it is recommended not to use chlorpromazine subcutaneously due to its acidity (pH 5) and its risk of painful skin irritation (Twycross & Lack 1986).

3.3.   Barbiturates

Nowadays, barbiturates, and more specifically phenobarbital, are reserved for the treatment of epilepsy (Meierkord et al. 2010). In the past barbiturates have been used as hypnotics but, because of their low safety profile, they have now been replaced by benzodiazepines for this use. In palliative care, phenobarbital is used for uncontrollable seizures and in palliative sedation (Stirling et al. 1999). Its mechanism of action, like that of the benzodiazepines, is through promoting the binding of GABA at $GABA_A$ receptors, as well as antagonising glutamate in the non-NMDA receptors. Phenobarbital is metabolised through the liver by oxidation (P450) and glucuronidation, and approximately 25 per cent of the drug is excreted unchanged in the urine (Mattson 1996; Czapiński et al. 2005).

Regarding its administration, a loading dose should be given intramuscularly (100–200 mg) followed by a continuous subcutaneous infusion (120–2400 mg/24 h). Phenobarbital should not be mixed with other drugs, and opioids must be maintained and administered separately. In the context of palliative sedation, phenobarbital can be considered a good choice for patients with a past history of seizures, especially because fever is common in the dying process and it is well known that fever reduces the convulsion threshold. It should also be taken into consideration that, like all barbiturates, phenobarbital can produce cardiorespiratory instability, easily producing bronchial secretion (death-rattle), and so prophylactic administration of scopolamine (hyoscine) is advisable (Greene & Davis 1991; Truog et al. 1992; Stirling et al. 1999).

3.4.   Anaesthetics

Propofol is probably the anaesthetic drug most used in palliative sedation, even though only a few reports of its use in palliative care have been published (McWilliams et al. 2010). Propofol is commonly used for general anaesthesia for short procedures and in intensive care units (McKeage & Perry 2003). In palliative care, it is used in palliative sedation and for the management of intractable nausea and vomiting (Lundström et al. 2005). The main pharmacological actions are anaesthetic, anti-emetic, antipruritic, anxiolytic, muscle relaxing, anticonvulsant, bronchodilating, and reducing intracranial and intraocular pressure. The mechanism of action is to enhance GABA at the $GABA_A$ receptors and to antagonise serotonin at $5HT_3$ receptors. Propofol is metabolised in the liver and excreted in the urine as sulphate and glucuronide (Lundström et al. 2010).

Propofol can only be administered intravenously. It has a rapid onset of action (30 s) and a transient time of action (3–10 min), so it must be given by IV infusion. The starting dose is 1 mg/kg per hour IV, followed by increases of 0.5–1 mg/kg per hour every 5–10 minutes, until the desired level of sedation is reached. Propofol must not be mixed with other drugs except lidocaine and alfentanil, and can be diluted in 5% glucose. Opioids must be maintained and administered separately. Propofol is a very lipophilic drug and tolerance tends to appear very quickly, so it is sometimes necessary to increase the infusion rate during palliative sedation in order to keep the patient comfortable. The pro-convulsant effect of propofol during sedation induction in patients with a past history of seizures should be noted (Sneyd 1999; Walder et al. 2002). This potential adverse effect should be taken into account since in patients with epilepsy and seizures due to brain tumours, phenobarbital could be more advisable. Propofol is currently used safely by non-anaesthesiologists in many medical fields (Cohen et al. 2003; Tan & Irwin 2010), including palliative medicine (Mercadante et al. 1995; Moyle 1995).

Ketamine is another potential drug for use in palliative sedation. It is an NMDA antagonist, and it has been used for anaesthetic procedures for a long time (White et al. 1982). Ketamine in palliative care is mainly used in sub-anaesthetic doses for the management of neuropathic pain (Prommer 2012). Ketamine has the advantage that it barely depresses respiration, so it can be considered to be a relatively save drug. Unfortunately, it can produce psychomimetic side-effects, and cannot be considered a drug of choice for palliative sedation. In fact, there is only one case report in the literature for this indication (Carter et al. 2008).

More recently, the potential usefulness of dexmedetomidine in palliative care has been explored, especially with regard to the management of delirium, but also for palliative sedation (Jackson et al. 2006; Prommer 2011). Dexmedetomidine is a highly potent α_2-adrenergic agonist, with no evidence of clinically significant drug interactions. It has been used in mechanically ventilated patients, there is also evidence of its usefulness for sedation in non-intubated patients (Shukry & Miller 2010).

3.5.   Other drugs

Other drugs used in palliative sedation include the sedating antihistamines (Caraceni et al. 2012). Sedating antihistamines, such as prometazine or chlorphenamine, have a sedative effect, acting as antagonists at histaminergic and cholinergic receptors, counteracting the excitatory effect of histamine and acetylcholine. No action on GABA receptors has been described. Prometazine also exhibits an anti-emetic action through dopaminergic blocking (Becker 2010). Antihistamines are weaker sedating agents than benzodiazepines, and it is usually advised to use them concurrently with other sedating agents (Becker 2012).

4.   Sedation guidelines

The reader can find information regarding guidelines elsewhere, both in the medical literature and on medical societies' websites. The Royal Dutch Medical Association (KNMG) Guideline for Palliative Sedation, first published in 2005, and updated in 2007 and 2009, is one of the best-known guidelines and has inspired many others (KNMG 2009b). This guideline was drafted to help all physicians in The Netherlands to perform palliative sedation. In addition to extensive sections dealing with ethical considerations, the most recent version of the guideline provides a short and easy scheme for pharmacological treatment (Figure 4.1).

The Spanish Society of Palliative Care published a guideline in 2005 (Pinna et al. 2005) which was addressed specifically at palliative care professionals and so provided a more detailed approach (Figure 4.2). This guideline takes into consideration the evidence that benzodiazepines can precipitate and worsen a pre-existing delirium (Breitbart et al. 1996; Jones & Pisani 2012), and the benefits of using neuroleptics in this situation (O'Neill & Fountain 1999; Lee et al. 2004; Meyer 2007). For sedation, it is advised to use a sedating neuroleptic, such as levomepromazine, after the failure of haloperidol, which is the neuroleptic of first choice for delirium. In the case of refractory symptoms other than delirium (e.g. dyspnoea), benzodiazepines, such as midazolam, should be considered first, due to their ability to lessen the respiratory effort and to relieve the feeling of dyspnoea (Navigante et al. 2006, 2010).

Regarding hydration and nutrition during palliative sedation, it is advised that these be managed on an individual basis, as recommended by the Spanish Society of Palliative Care guideline and others. The opinion of other researchers supports this point of view (Dalal et al. 2009; Dev et al. 2012). Nutrition is not recommended at all in continuous deep sedation, but parenteral hydration (at a minimum of about 500 mL/day) should be considered in accordance with the values and wishes of the patients and their families in view of the positive psychological meaning that it has (Mercadante et al. 2005).

The Spanish Society of Palliative Care guideline has had a great influence in the Spanish-speaking world, and was recently endorsed by the Spanish Medical Association (Organización Médica Colegial).

5.   General considerations

Since sedation must be a safe procedure, the prevention of any cause of failure is important as there is so little time for rectification (see Box 4.2).

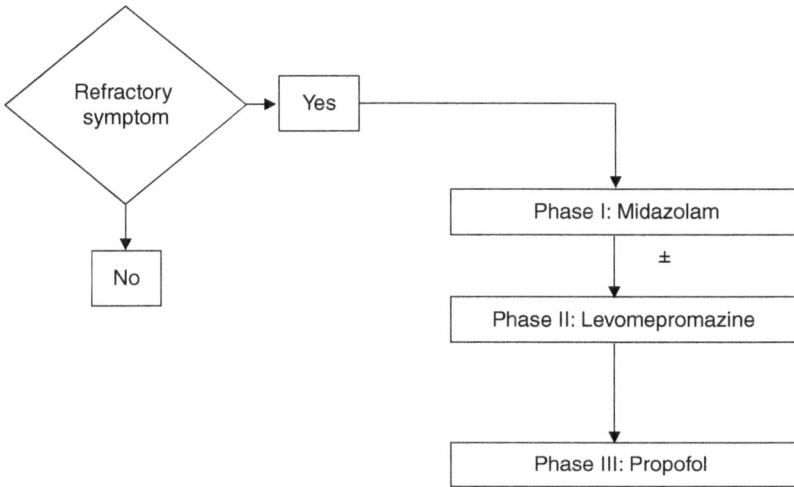

Figure 4.1 Pharmacological flowchart proposed by the Royal Dutch Medical Association Guideline for Palliative Sedation, 2009.

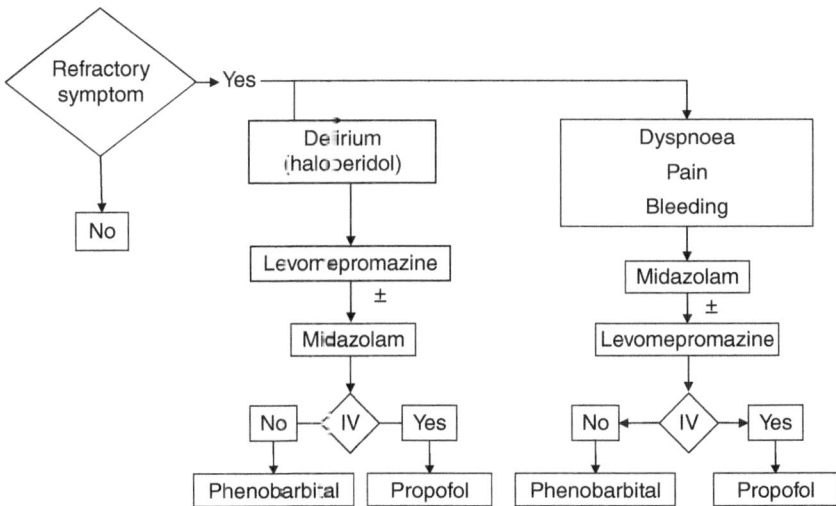

Figure 4.2 Pharmacological flowchart proposed by the Spanish Society for Palliative Care Guideline for Palliative Sedation, 2005.

Box 4.2 Key points for administration of sedative drugs

- Patient's general condition.
- Administration route (consider an eventual inability to administer IV).
- Previous use of benzodiazepines.
- Past history of epilepsy.
- Risk of death-rattle, full bladder or rectum.
- Identify level of sedation (use a sedation scale).
- Dose adjustment after the first 4 hours and thereafter every 8 hours, based on rescue doses needed.

First, the patient's general state must be considered: cachectic patients are more sensitive to sedatives. It is important to select the drug and its route of administration according to its pharmacological properties, for instance by avoiding giving chlorpromazine SC or remembering that propofol can only be given IV, and also according to the patient's condition. For patients with clotting disorders, it may be best to avoid the SC route, due to the risk of bruises with consequent pain and risk of low drug absorption. Patients with benzodiazepine tolerance could need a more rapid drug titration and larger doses than those without previous exposure to benzodiazepines. A past history of epilepsy (primary or secondary) must be taken into account since the appearance of seizures during propofol induction can be experienced as catastrophic, and leave the witnesses with bitter memories. In such circumstances, one might consider the use of barbiturates. For patients with known or potential urine outlet problems (e.g. elderly men, or men with prostate cancer), carers must keep in mind the risk of a full bladder after the administration of anticholinergic drugs. The level of sedation must be defined and checked using the scale agreed by the team, and finally, the doses must be adjusted regularly and promptly, particularly during the first few hours, to provide a proportionate, secure and efficacious sedation. Sedation assessment on only a daily basis bears the risk of under- or over-medication, each with its own drawbacks. For an overview of recommended doses, see Table 4.5.

6.   Sedation scales

All sedation scales, except the Consciousness Scale for Palliative Care (CSPC) (Gonçalves et al. 2008), are derived and adapted from the

Table 4.5 *Common drug doses recommended for use in palliative sedation*

Drug	Dosage			Observations
	Induction	Rescue	Maintenance	
Levomepromazine	12.5–25 mg	12.5–25 mg	5 mg/h SCCI-IV	>300 mg*/ day + MDZL
Midazolam	5–10 mg	5–7.5 mg	1.5–2 mg/h SCCI-IV	>200 mg*/ day + LMPZ
Propofol	1–1.5 mg/kg	50% induction dose	2–3 mg/kg/h IVCI	No mix with other drugs
Phenobarbital	200 mg IM	100 mg	60–100 mg/h SCCI	No mix with other drugs

SCCI = subcutaneous continuous infusion; IVCI = intravenous continuous infusion; MDZL = midazolam; LMPZ = levomepromazine.

*Reduce by 33% the daily dose of the current drug used when adding a second drug.

scales used in intensive medicine (Carrasco 2000). Unfortunately a consensus is lacking in the palliative care field. The scales most commonly used and reported on in the palliative care literature are: the Ramsay scale (Ramsay et al. 1974) and some variations (Porta-Sales 2008); the Richmond Agitation Sedation Scale (RASS) (Sessler et al. 2002; Benitez-Rosario et al. 2012); the Glasgow Coma Scale (Teasdale & Jennett 1974; Claessens et al. 2012); and the bispectral monitoring (BIS) index (Barbato 2001; Gambrell 2005).

The BIS index is the output from an advanced EEG signal with the determination and integration of multiple characteristics of the EEG. For measuring the level of sedation, a strip with sensors is placed on the patient's forehead.

Few specific studies are available on the use of the different types of sedation scales in palliative care (Gonçalves et al. 2008; Arevalo et al. 2012), so their use seems to be linked to the preferences and experience of each team. A detailed description of each scale is beyond the scope of this chapter. The sedation scales are summarised in Boxes 4.3–4.7.

7.   Concerns regarding relatives and the care team

Even though the period of sedation could be considered to be short, with a reported mean duration of 2.5 days (Porta-Sales 2001), this is

---

Box 4.3 Ramsay scale adaptation (Institut Català d'Oncologia)

1 Anxious and/or agitated
2 Cooperative, oriented and tranquil
3a Agitated response to verbal stimulus
3b Calm response to verbal stimulus
4a Agitated response to light glabellar tap or mild pain stimulus
4b Calm response to light glabellar tap or mild pain stimulus
5 Patient exhibits a sluggish response to light glabellar tap or pain stimulus
6 Patient exhibits no response

Box 4.4 Consciousness Scale for Palliative Care (CSPC)

1 Awake
2 Awake when called by name and stays awake during conversation
3 Awake when called by name but falls asleep during conversation
4 Reacts with movement or brief eye opening, but without eye contact, when called by name
5 Reacts to trapezius muscle pinching
6 Does not react

---

enough time to generate relevant clinical, emotional and ethical issues that ought to be diligently identified and addressed by the care team, due to their potential deleterious impact on the relatives' bereavement. From a clinical point of view, the presence of death-rattle (Wildiers & Menten 2002), i.e. noisy or arrhythmic breathing, can be interpreted as patient suffocation, which in people's minds is always a horrible way of dying. Other frequent physical problems relate to the appearance of body movements, such as shiver, myoclonus or even seizures, which are usually interpreted as patient suffering.

Apart from concern with the patient's physical symptoms, other concerns quite frequently arise with the relatives. In some studies (Morita 2004a; Van Dooren et al. 2009), it was found that between 25% and 51% of relatives express some concerns about sedation. The main causes of concern related to the true aim of sedation (i.e. to relieve the

Box 4.5 Richmond Agitation Sedation Scale (RASS)

+4 Combative, violent, danger to staff
+3 Pulls or removes tube(s) or catheters; aggressive
+2 Frequent non-purposeful movement, fights ventilator
+1 Anxious, apprehensive, but not aggressive
0   Alert and calm
−1 Awakens to voice (eye opening/contact) >10 seconds
−2 Light sedation, briefly awakens to voice (eye opening/contact) <10 seconds
−3 Moderate sedation, movement or eye opening. No eye contact
−4 Deep sedation, no response to voice, but movement or eye opening to physical stimulation
−5 Unarousable, no response to voice or physical stimulation

Box 4.6 Glasgow Coma Scale

Eye opening response:

• Spontaneous – open with blinking at baseline: 4 points
• To verbal stimuli, command, speech: 3 points
• To pain only (not applied to face): 2 points
• No response: 1 point

Verbal response:

• Oriented: 5 points
• Confused conversation, but able to answer questions: 4 points
• Inappropriate words: 3 points
• Incomprehensible speech: 2 points
• No response: 1 point

Motor response:

• Obeys commands for movement: 6 points
• Purposeful movement to painful stimulus: 5 points
• Withdraws in response to pain: 4 points
• Flexion in response to pain (decorticate posturing): 3 points
• Extension response in response to pain (decerebrate posturing): 2 points
• No response: 1 point

Head injury classification:
Severe head injury – GCS score of 8 or less
Moderate head injury – GCS score of 9 to 12
Mild head injury – GCS score of 13 to 15

Box 4.7 Bispectral monitoring (BIS) index

BIS index	100	Awake, responds to normal voice
range	80	Responds to loud commands
		Or mild prodding/shaking
	60	General anaesthesia
		• Low probability of explicit recall
		• Unresponsive to verbal stimulus
	40	Deep hypnotic state
	20	Burst suppression
	0	Flat line EEG

patient's suffering *or* to hasten death) (27%), to possible patient suffering (29%) or to the relatives' own suffering (18%) (Van Dooren et al. 2009). The most commonly reported causes of relatives' suffering are remorse (e.g. for having given consent, or for the patient receiving no feeding or hydration), being unable to cope (e.g. with the patient's physical deterioration, or lost verbal communication), pressure to hasten death or cause euthanasia, and family disagreements. Van Dooren et al. (2009) found that the relatives' concerns increase as the length of palliative sedation increases (mean 46 h versus 19.5 h; P<0.05).

Other types of concern that can arise in the care team include personal emotional transference and projection. In view of all of these issues, the approach shown in Box 4.8 is advised.

The first and most important point is that everyone in the team involved in the care of the sedated patient as well as her family must be aware of the relevance and high likelihood of problems that can arise, and acknowledge the importance of preventing and treating them.

It is crucial to predict and prevent clinical symptoms, so the first step is to inform the relatives in advance of the possibility that such symptoms can occur and what they mean, which preventative measures can be taken and which remedies are available. In general, relatives are thankful for this information because it reduces some of their worries and allows them to continue to collaborate in the care of the patient. The

---

Box 4.8 Common situations accompanying palliative sedation and how to approach them

- Acknowledge their existence.

Clinicians

- Inform the relatives in advance.
- Assess regularly.
- Provide clear information (perhaps even in written form).

Relatives

- To be checked regularly for doubts or signs of exhaustion.
- To be offered understanding and practical help.
- Be available.

Team

- Be aware of the risk of personal transference.
- Change the carer at risk (if possible).
- Provide team support.

---

clinical team should regularly check (using open questions) for doubts, physical or emotional tiredness, and practical needs, and should always show an attitude of availability.

Health professionals must have a proactive attitude and regularly assess the level of sedation, general discomfort, and other potential issues such as death-rattle (Wildiers et al. 2009), noisy breathing, fever (checked by hand), full bladder or myoclonus. In the case of home care, it is advisable to give clear and written information about what to do and how, and from whom to obtain advice and help quickly (obviously in accordance with the local healthcare organisation). The team members should be aware of the risk of personal transference, for example in cases of a sedated patient of the same age, the patient's resemblance to a relative of a team member, or previous personal close involvement. If possible, the team member at risk should be advised to engage in other duties for the time being, and should always be offered the team's understanding and support.

8.   Conclusion

At the very least, the aim of palliative sedation is to protect patients with a far-advanced disease and a limited life expectancy against a certainty of suffering that is physical, emotional, or both, and which cannot be alleviated without reducing or even removing the patient's awareness. Palliative sedation is a dynamic anaesthetic technique and, like any other invasive medical procedure, it has its own technical and ethical requirements. Both must be complied with accurately and recorded in the patient's medical records. Consequently, palliative sedation procedures must be appropriately documented: which refractory symptom or symptoms indicate the palliative sedation; the whole decision-making procedure; drug selection, route and titration; assessment of sedation and sedation scale used; prevention of foreseen problems; and recording of the accompanying events and the actions taken. Due to the dynamic nature of palliative sedation, the care team should always be available and attend to potential problems and needs during the procedure.

In general, it can be said that some kind of informal consensus exists regarding the type of drugs to be used, but a standardised system of recording the procedure is lacking, as is a consensus on which type of items to check in order to guarantee the technical and ethical appropriateness of the procedure. The lack of an international agreement is one of the major barriers for large multicentre international studies and one of the reasons for the persistence of the confusion between palliative sedation and other procedures such as euthanasia, which is still a cause of concern among some professionals and members of the public.

In general, intermittent and transient sedation do not usually pose significant ethical dilemmas, but major concerns seem to arise with continuous palliative sedation until death. Daily clinical practice suggests that some personality traits or behavioural factors could be related to the need for prescribing continuous deep sedation. What these factors are, and the roles they play, is something to be explored in the future, mainly because identifying patients 'at risk' could allow for some proactive work regarding their decision-making in order to support the patient and lessen anxiety related to end-of-life care. Other insufficiently understood problems with the use of continuous deep sedation may be related to social, cultural or disease factors.

Even though it may be difficult to reach, an international agreement on a better operational framework for initiating and monitoring palliative sedation is still needed. In particular, what is lacking is an internationally agreed protocol and a common sedation scale, allowing the identification of factors prognostic of success or failure of the sedation.

After more than 20 years of taking part in professional discussions about what is, or is not, palliative sedation, and how to address the ethical dilemmas and technical issues relating to its use, the author still finds most lay people to be incapable of such a refined professional dialogue. The confusion between palliative sedation and euthanasia, which continues to cause mental suffering in patients and their families, still persists. Therefore, a key challenge for the future for palliative care professionals is to plan, promote and conduct educational programmes on palliative sedation, both for the public and for healthcare professionals, in order to make it clear that palliative sedation is a normal medical practice and an ethically sound procedure for treating avoidable suffering in patients at the end of life, and that it is entirely different from euthanasia.

5　Clinical aspects of palliative sedation

Nigel P. Sykes

1.　Introduction

The use of sedative drugs has always been a part of symptom management in palliative care. Although such use has come to arouse ethical concern in more recent years, the practice is not new. The start of the palliative care movement is generally traced back to the foundation by Dame Cicely Saunders of St Christopher's Hospice in London in 1967, but in her earlier writings that predated this event, Saunders was already discussing the place of sedative drugs in achieving comfort for distressed patients with advanced illness who were nearing the end of their life. In particular, she recognised that sedative use would sometimes be required for the relief of mental distress, but with emphasis that this was only as an adjunct to the giving of properly attentive time, not as a replacement for it (Saunders 1960). More specifically, there was a role for sedatives in the management of anxiety or agitated confusion (Saunders 1965).

2.　Difficulties of definition

The question arises as to what is meant by a sedative drug and – the matter that bedevils discussion of this subject currently – what is meant by 'sedation'? As early as 1958, Saunders was clear that, if a sedative were required, a drug with this specific property should be used, i.e. one whose primary mode of action is to reduce anxiety and induce a sense of relaxation. What concerned her at the time was the use of opioids (drugs related to morphine) as sedatives (Saunders 1958), as although this class of medication has the popular reputation of making users drowsy, their value in palliation is as powerful analgesics. In this role, if used appropriately, persistent drowsiness should not occur (Bruera et al. 1989) and it is an impediment to the acceptance of these enormously useful drugs by patients whose pain they could relieve if professionals characterise them as sedatives, a function that they perform only inefficiently.

Turning to the question of what is meant by 'sedation', Saunders wrote: 'It should hardly ever be necessary to use the very heavy sedation that completely smothers the patient's personality, although many who see these patients only occasionally do not believe that it is possible to avoid this' (Saunders 1967: 16–17). This statement goes to the heart of the current ethical debate about sedation in palliative care. For some, the word 'sedation' conjures up an image of an ill person rendered comatose by a heavy-handed cocktail of drugs, depriving her of any opportunity of communication with either her family or God and so destroying the possibility of any final resolution either social or spiritual. At the same time she is prevented from using her remaining psychic resources to wrestle her way through to a final acceptance of her impending death or to conjure meaning out of the life that now lies behind her. In fact sedation to unconsciousness is uncommon in palliative care, contrary to what many professionals who do not routinely care for dying people appear to believe.

However, the ethical concern goes beyond any issue of smothering the patient's personality to a perception that sedation is, intentionally or not, a practice that shortens life. As such it has been characterised as 'slow euthanasia' (Billings & Block 1996) or 'physician assisted death' (Rady & Verheijde 2010). An encouragement to this point of view has been the evidence that in recent years officially reported cases of euthanasia have declined in The Netherlands at the same time that the totals of end-of-life sedation have risen (Rietjens et al. 2008a). Is it easier just to sedate someone to death rather than use the life-terminating administration of a muscle relaxant, so avoiding the bureaucratic burden and potential reputational risk of reporting to the authorities an act of euthanasia? Possibly relevant is the finding that although only a small minority of Dutch doctors gave sedative medication with the explicit intention of hastening death, the proportion who did so was two to three times as great as that found in other European countries (van der Heide et al. 2003). The practice of sedation in end-of-life care therefore becomes tainted by association, a situation worsened if the association also includes withholding or withdrawal of artificial nutrition and hydration (which is actually an entirely separate issue).

In the use of the word 'sedation' by clinicians there is a confusion of purposes. Sedation can mean the giving of sedatives for specific symptom control, e.g. seizures, or the management of delirium in the absence of correctable factors. It can also be a treatment for insomnia. It may imply an attempt to make a patient unaware of an intractable symptom by reducing her consciousness level. Not surprisingly, perhaps, an expert survey achieved only 40 per cent agreement with a single definition of sedation (Chater et al. 1998). This is no doubt also why the literature contains such a confusing array of names for the practice of sedation.

Symptom intractability is a condition for initiating palliative sedation, according to existing guidelines. Yet it is not immediately apparent what it means, although it is said to imply something more than a symptom being merely 'difficult' (Claessens et al. 2008). Cherny and Portenoy helpfully proposed that an intractable symptom is one that does not respond to 'available' treatment or, importantly, a symptom for which the available treatment is unacceptable to the patient because of either insufficiently rapid action or excessive side-effects (Cherny & Portenoy 1994). This definition has important consequences because it makes intractability *contextual* rather than *universal*. A symptom that is intractable in one place, or when experienced by one person, may not be intractable if it occurs in another place or another individual. It has been reported that sedation is used more frequently by physicians who judged symptoms to be intractable without actually trying the potential treatments for them (Morita 2004b). It also appears that doctors with higher levels of professional burnout or less confidence with psychological modes of care are more likely to use sedation (Morita et al. 2002a). While subsequent widely published guidelines for sedation have advised consultation with a specialist in palliative care (de Graeff & Dean 2007; Dean et al. 2012) who in turn might need to consult more widely (Cherny & Radbruch 2009), this is not a feature of the Dutch national guidelines, where physicians are enjoined to seek specialist advice only if they doubt their own skills in this area: just 9 per cent of Dutch general practitioners involved in Rietjens' survey (Rietjens et al. 2008a) had sought such advice, raising the possibility that the potential treatments for symptoms were simply not known by the clinicians concerned.

3.   Indications for palliative sedation

Why, in fact, are sedative drugs used in palliative care? This seems to be a chief concern of health professionals, especially doctors, regarding end-of-life decision-making (Raijmakers et al. 2012). It often seems to be supposed that the prime need for sedation arises from the requirement to subdue the suffering caused by uncontrolled pain. In practice this is not the case. In an international multicentre study of sedation in 387 patients cared for by palliative care units, Fainsinger et al. (2000) found that only 1.8% of patients were given sedatives because of pain.

Breathlessness, at 6.5%, was over three times more common as an indication, but by far the commonest, applying to 15.2% of patients and accounting for 53.5% of instances of sedation, was the management of agitated delirium. This fits with evidence that delirium, with or without agitation, occurs in up to 85% of people as they approach the end of life (Massie et al. 1983).

4.   Approaches to sedative use

It is not only the reasons for sedative use that vary but also the manner in which these drugs are applied. As will emerge later, the approach to sedative use indicates the motivation for such use and has a bearing on how it might be judged ethically. In particular, a key distinction is whether a sedative is given in a relatively large dose from the outset or whether initial doses are low and are then built up according to the clinical response. The former approach is likely to produce a rapid diminution of consciousness, which Porta Sales (2001) has termed 'sudden sedation'. The latter approach initiates a process of relaxation that, if continued and deepened, will also lead to a significant reduction of consciousness level but which can be held steady or reversed at any point according to whether the clinical distress has been relieved. This point has been noticed elsewhere, for instance by Broeckaert and colleagues, who write that palliative sedation 'is *not* a matter of inducing deep, continuous and definitive sleep, but of reducing consciousness for as long and as deeply as necessary, intermittently or continuously, to relieve pain and/or suffering adequately as an ultimate palliative treatment for refractory symptoms' (Broeckaert et al. 2009: e12; emphasis in original). However, not everyone agrees with this (Rietjens et al. 2009b).

A helpful effort to judge the characteristics of any particular example of sedative use proposes the use of five subcategories or dimensions that are illustrated schematically in Figure 5.1 (Morita et al. 2001c). These are:

1. Depth of sedation, ranging from 'mild', in which communication is still possible, to 'deep', in which there is almost or complete unconsciousness.
2. The pattern of sedation described as either intermittent or continuous until death.
3. Whether sedation is the primary intention of the intervention and is achieved by the use of sedative drugs, or arises as an adverse effect of some other therapy, e.g. drowsiness resulting from unusually high doses of opioids given for pain.

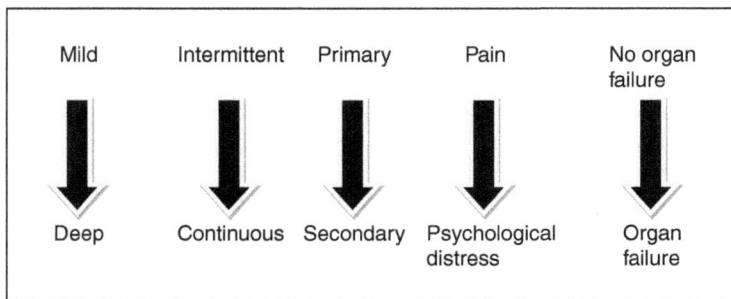

Figure 5.1 Classification of end-of-life care sedation (Morita et al. 2001c).

4. The indication for sedation, whether physical or mental.
5. The type of patient, defined according to their degree of organ failure and likely prognosis using a standard assessment tool.

It can be seen that the full spectrum of approaches to sedative use can be accommodated within this scheme. Hence, without prejudging what any individual practitioner might consider to be an appropriate approach to sedation, this classification could be used to compare and contrast different examples of sedative practice that have been described. It could also be used prospectively as an aid to team discussion and decision-making when the use of sedation is being proposed for a particular patient.

5.   The frequency of use of palliative sedation

The proportion of patients who require the use of sedatives in the closing days of life appears to vary alarmingly, all the way from 1% (Fainsinger 1998) to 88% (Turner et al. 1996). Concerningly, this situation does not appear to be improving as time goes on. For instance, a recent prospective study from Belgium of the use of all depths and lengths of sedation across eight palliative care units showed a rate of 7.5% (Claessens et al. 2011). Yet a retrospective study from a single palliative care unit in The Netherlands, by a group whose definition of sedation is that it be deep, continuous and until death, showed a rate of 43% (Rietjens et al. 2008b).

It might be supposed that a study that focused on just the use of the highest level of sedation – the implication of the term 'continuous deep sedation' – would have shown a *lower* prevalence than a survey of all types and degrees of sedative use. This was the proposed explanation of the difference between the Fainsinger and Turner studies: the former looked only at cases where the clear intention had been to induce deep sleep, whereas the latter included all instances of sedative use. Yet the Claessens et al. paper, which is apparently more inclusive than the investigation of Rietjens and co-workers – inclusive enough that the two groups have corresponded in print about the contrast in their definitions of sedation (Rietjens et al. 2009b; Broeckaert et al. 2009) – reports a frequency of sedation barely a fifth as great.

6.   Assessing the depth of palliative sedation

These reports and others similar to them expose the huge difficulty of discussing sedative use around the end of life: it is wholly unclear that different authors are actually talking about the same entity. Sedation in Rietjens' study was said to be 'deep' – implying a deeper level of sleep or unconsciousness – but it is not stated how such depth was assessed. A range of tools is available to rate the level of consciousness. Best known is the widely used Glasgow Coma Scale (Teasdale & Jennett 1974) but there are also scales that have been tested in a palliative care context, notably the Communication Capacity Scale (Morita et al. 2001b) and the Consciousness Scale for Palliative Care (Gonçalves et al. 2008).

A feature common to all these scales is that for the definition of the deepest level of unconsciousness (interpreted as the deepest level of sedation) they require the infliction of pain upon the patient. The form of painful stimulus varies: supra-orbital pressure for the Glasgow Coma Scale, an unspecified method of causing pain or else a change in patient position for the Communication Capacity Scale, and trapezius pinch for the Consciousness Scale for Palliative Care. For a specialty such as palliative care that exists specifically to improve the comfort of its patients, staff are likely to experience a cultural conflict if required to do the opposite and provoke pain in those for whom they are caring. This would perhaps be especially so if the purpose of causing pain was supposedly to monitor a therapeutic intervention whose avowed aim was to relieve distress. If the distress is relieved, why investigate any further? Hence it seems unsurprising that the most common measure of the depth of sedation is the physicians' unsubstantiated report.

Still without evidence that any objective assessment has been made, it has been suggested that the depth of sedation tends to increase as death approaches (Claessens et al. 2011). In this study, 45 per cent of patients originally given 'mild' sedation were said to be receiving 'deep continuous' sedation by two days before death. However, this is based

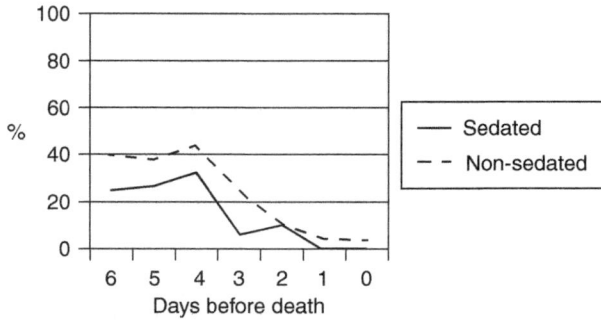

Figure 5.2 Comparison of percentage of patients spontaneously awake in sedated and non-sedated groups during the last week of life (n = 23) (derived from Fainsinger et al. 1998).

on only nine patients and it is not clear how the sedative doses changed in the interim. It is a common observation – as well as common sense – that people dying as a result of gradually progressive disease do not move from clear consciousness to the inertness of death in the twinkling of an eye. So when we are told that the level of sedation deepens as death approaches the possibility suggests itself that all or part of this process is actually the natural trajectory of dying. It has been reported, for instance, that even five days prior to death 50 per cent of palliative care patients not receiving sedatives are unable to manage complex communication (Morita et al. 2003b).

Two studies have explored this issue by assessing the proportions of palliative care patients who were spontaneously awake, or who were rousable, during the last week of life according to whether or not they were receiving sedative medication (Fainsinger et al. 1998; Kohara et al. 2005). The resulting curves (Figures 5.2, 5.3 and 5.4) show the sedated and non-sedated groups following parallel paths of reduction of consciousness level, with the two lines virtually overlapping for the last 48–72 hours of life. At the same time, even in the sedated group, no more than 20 per cent of patients are unrousable until they are entering the last two days prior to death. These results, from two widely differing cultures, indicate firstly that sedative use is not synonymous with unconsciousness and secondly that, regardless of whether sedatives are used, the level of consciousness spontaneously diminishes as death approaches. Sedation will therefore become 'deeper' in the last days of life, but this does not necessarily reflect either some tendency on the part of doctors to elevate sedative use as the patient becomes sicker or even an accumulation of existing sedative drugs as metabolism slows (even though such a thing can, of course, happen).

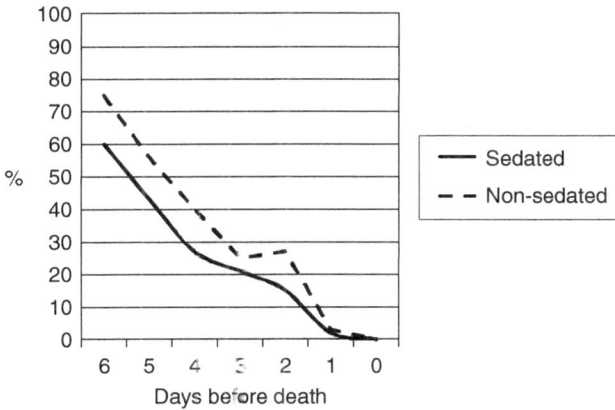

Figure 5.3 Comparison of percentage of patients spontaneously awake in sedated and non-sedated groups during the last week of life (n = 124) (derived from Kohara et al. 2005).

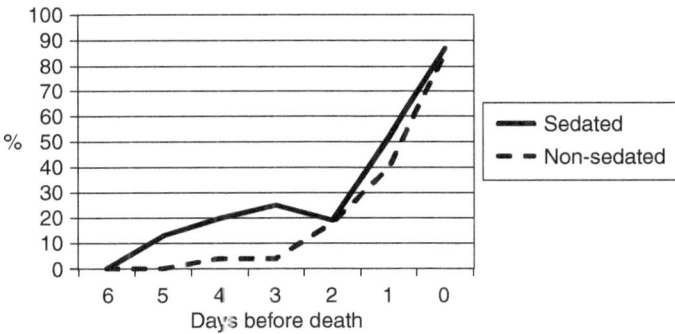

Figure 5.4 Comparison of percentage of unrousable patients in sedated and non-sedated groups during the last week of life (n = 23) (derived from Fainsinger et al. 1998).

Although the act of sedation is commonly assumed to involve the induction of drowsiness or even loss of consciousness, it is worth pointing out that the root of the word *sedation* is the Latin *sedatio* meaning 'soothing' or 'allaying'. The intent to precipitate sleep would be served by a soporific, not a sedative. The primary purpose of sedation is therefore the soothing or allaying of distress, by implication in a general way where the cause of the distress does not lend itself to specific treatment or where such treatment proves inadequate on its own. This is the palliative understanding of sedation, remembering that 'palliation' derives from the Latin *pallium* meaning 'cloak': palliation is therefore the cloaking of a symptom when a cure or specific treatment for its cause is unavailable. Properly understood, the clinical purpose of sedative drugs in palliation is the reduction of irritability or agitation, i.e. the relief of distress. Sleep is not the intention but may occur either if a high enough sedative dose is required to relieve the distress, or if a tired, ill patient is enabled to be comfortable and relaxed.

7.   Continuous and intermittent palliative sedation

A further aspect of sedative use that, alongside depth, is presented as an indication of the aggressiveness of the approach being taken, is that it is being given continuously. This may be by regular parenteral injections or, more often, by continuous infusion, usually subcutaneously. However, it is far from clear that the giving of a sedative continuously rather than intermittently actually marks any change in the intention with which the drug is being given. It has just been noted that sedation is a response to a symptom. Intermittent symptoms may be managed adequately by intermittently administered treatment, but continuous symptoms need continuous relief. A parallel is the regular use of morphine in persistent pain from cancer, where giving opioid analgesia 'by the clock' so that blood levels were maintained above the minimum effective concentration transformed cancer pain relief (World Health Organisation 1986).

Guidance accompanying the Liverpool Care of the Dying Pathway, which is widely used to manage the last 48 hours or so of a patient's life in UK hospitals and care homes, suggests use of a continuous subcutaneous infusion if three or more 'as required' doses of sedative have been given in 24 hours (MCPCIL 2010). Without implying that this guidance is unreasonable, given that the first priority is the patient's comfort, it would therefore not be surprising if a substantial proportion of end-of-life patients received continuous administration of medication. Practice in the author's own unit mirrors this approach, with 30 per cent of patients receiving sedatives doing so only on an 'as required' basis, receiving a median dose of 2.5 mg midazolam on a median of two occasions (Dunn et al. 2008). The remaining 70 per cent of patients have continuous subcutaneous infusions in order to provide smooth and constant symptom relief. So 'as required' rapidly becomes 'continuous', but continuous sedative administration is neither rare nor necessarily sinister.

8.   Proportionality

There is a growing consensus that the essence of an ethical approach to sedative use in palliative care is *proportionality* (Morita et al. 2002b; de Graeff & Dean 2007; Broeckaert 2009; Cherny & Radbruch 2009; Hasselaar et al. 2009b; Quill et al. 2009; Dean et al. 2012). In other words, the dose of sedative used is only that needed to provide adequate relief of the target symptom. This mode of use of sedatives is analogous to that of other symptom control measures, the use of opioids for pain, again, being a good example. A low initial dose is titrated higher against the response until distress is relieved, i.e. the dose used is proportional to severity of distress. Hence relief of distress is the endpoint, not a particular level of consciousness.

As symptoms differ in their intensity and individuals vary in their response to drugs, so the precise level of a 'proportionate' sedative dose will differ between patients. However, the levels of sedative dose used in palliative care practice have been investigated. Midazolam is the most commonly used sedative in palliative care (Sykes & Thorns 2003a) and so is the drug for which most data are available. Mean midazolam doses reported range from 22 to 70 mg/24 h, but may individually be as high as 240 mg/24 h (Mercadante et al. 2009). In our own study of 238 palliative care patients at the end of life, the overall mean midazolam dose was 25.7 mg/24 h (median 23.0 mg/24 h), which compares well with the mean dose of 32.7 mg/24 h (median 25.8 mg/24 h) reported by Fainsinger et al. across four study sites spread over four continents (Fainsinger et al. 2000). Meanwhile the equivalent figure for patients who had received midazolam continuously throughout the last week of life was 54.5 mg/24 h (Sykes & Thorns 2003b). As will be discussed below, our patients receiving sedatives survived as long, or longer, than those who had no sedation (Table 5.1). In addition, those who experienced the longest periods of sedation also received the highest doses of sedative. Both these findings suggest that the timing of patients' deaths resulted from their disease rather than the amount of sedative they had been given.

9.   The effect of palliative sedation on length of life

This question of whether sedation hastens a patient's death is, of course, the crucial ethical issue concerning this area of practice. There is no disputing that a level of sedative use high enough to cause respiratory depression can precipitate death. However, we have seen that a cornerstone of competent sedative use in palliative care is proportionality to

Table 5.1 *Effect of sedation on palliative care patients' survival*

Study	Without sedation	With sedation
Stone et al., 1997 (UK)	19.1 days	18.6 days
Ventafridda et al., 1990 (Italy)	23 days	25 days
Chiu et al., 2001 (Taiwan)	24.7 days	28.5 days
Sykes and Thorns, 2003a (UK)	14.2 days	38.6 days
Kohara et al., 2005 (Japan)	39.5 days	28.9 days

the symptom that it is intended to manage. So, does the practice of sedation within palliative care routinely shorten patients' lives? Table 5.1 lists the survival times recorded in the studies that have examined this issue. In only one of the five studies (Kohara et al. 2005) was survival noticeably shorter in the patients receiving sedatives than in those who did not receive sedatives. In three of the studies the sedative group lived longer on average than the non-sedative group, in one case (Sykes & Thorns 2003b) markedly so. The proposed explanation here was that the predominant indication for sedative use was agitated delirium and the onset of this symptom is known to be a situation that families caring for such a patient at home find hard to cope with. It is therefore suggested that patients in whom agitated delirium was a prominent feature of their final phase of life would be likely to be admitted to the inpatient unit where the study was performed at a somewhat earlier stage of their illness than those who did not show this symptom.

On average the actual duration of sedative use in palliative care is short. A review by Porta Sales (2001), updated by the present author and including a total of 1,900 patients from ten studies published in either English or Spanish, found the mean duration of sedation to be 2.5 days (range 1.3–3.9 days). In combination with the evidence of a lack of shortening of survival under a palliative care service through the use of sedatives, this suggests that sedation is indeed generally a response to symptoms associated with the onset of dying.

10.   Artificial nutrition and hydration in the context of palliative sedation

The concern to distinguish sedative use in palliative care from euthanasia or deliberate life-shortening has led to particular concerns about the use of artificial nutrition and hydration (ANH) when sedatives are being used, and about the appropriateness of giving sedatives to relieve existential distress, i.e. the patient's radical inability to tolerate the type of life that her condition is now obliging her to lead.

The two issues are linked in that existential distress does not necessarily correlate with physical deterioration and so, if the person's ability to eat and drink is compromised by sedation, this is more likely to hasten her death than if she had already physically deteriorated to the point where her oral intake was much diminished or absent. Within the last three weeks or so of life, the benefit of clinically assisted hydration appears doubtful. Its use has been observed to be associated with exacerbation of oedema, ascites and pleural effusions, while making no improvement in the level of confusion or the ability to communicate (Morita et al. 2005d). Correspondingly, it has been suggested that if fluids are given in this situation the volume be limited to no more than one litre per day (Dalal et al. 2009). Given that most sedative use occurs well within the last three weeks of a terminally ill patient's life, there seems to be no justification for suggesting that it should routinely be accompanied by assisted hydration, still less nutrition.

The decision about ANH is really quite separate from the decision to use a sedative. It is based on a perception as to whether the person's ability to eat and drink has been compromised by sedation and, if so, whether this is to a degree that in itself might possibly exacerbate discomfort or be for a duration that might influence the timing of death. If either of these situations might be present, the addition of ANH would be indicated and, if guidelines on sedation are to avoid giving the sense of sedation being euthanasia by stealth, they should not have a blanket prohibition on the use of ANH.

A patient ceasing to eat as a result of her level of sedation has been suggested to the author as a practical criterion of 'deep' sedation. How often does this happen in practice? By way of example, the author analysed all deaths occurring in the inpatient palliative care unit where he works during a random recent month. Fifty-five patients had died during this period, of whom 51 (93%) had had at least one dose of midazolam, the unit's sedative agent of choice. In 35 people (64% of those who had been given midazolam) the drug had been given by continuous subcutaneous infusion. Of the infusions, 14 (40%) had started within 48 hours of death and the same number between three and seven days before death. All of the patients concerned had either already stopped eating or continued to eat until three to five days before their death. The remaining seven infusions lasted between one week and one month. Of these patients, five also continued to eat until three to five days before death while the other two had gastrostomy feeding. Depending on one's view of what constitutes palliative sedation, these results could indicate a sedation rate of 93 per cent, as this was the proportion of patients who received a sedative drug, yet with zero cases of 'deep' sedation as none of them ceased to eat or drink as a result of the introduction of a sedative drug.

11.   Sedation for existential distress

In relation to existential distress, it has been argued that it is even harder than with a physical source of discomfort to tell whether such distress is really intractable (Cherny & Radbruch 2009). This is partly because the level of distress can be variable and idiosyncratic and partly because a wide variety of psychological approaches are available that take both skill and time. This means that the care team must have a wide multiprofessional base with access, for instance, to psychiatry, social work and chaplaincy (Dean et al. 2012). They should also be skilled in psychological care, know the patient and family, and have made repeated assessments. Not every team can easily satisfy these requirements, but as standard approaches to existential distress have low morbidity, the use of sedation to cover up a care team's therapeutic shortcomings is more ethically problematic than ever.

Of course, some sedative use in the sense of a modest dose of an anxiolytic may be regarded as an entirely orthodox component of the management of this type of situation. It may also be helpful to provide limited spells of deeper sedation to enable the patient to sleep as a period of 'time out', after which they may feel stronger to reappraise their situation or engage with approaches such as cognitive behaviour therapy. However, in a patient who is not at the end of life the induction of sleep for extended periods should surely be a truly exceptional occurrence.

12.   The place of the doctrine of double effect

The possibility that treatments may shorten a patient's life is often defended ethically by recourse to the doctrine of double effect, derived from Catholic moral theology (Boyle 2004). Briefly, this states that a harmful effect of treatment, even one resulting in death, is permissible providing that it was not intended, arose as a side-effect of a beneficial action *and* that the harmful effect was not the means of achieving the beneficial effect. In recent years this doctrine has been invoked most frequently in connection with pain control or the use of sedation in palliative care. Its use involves the judgement of intention and has been criticised on that account (Quill 1997). However, intention is something that is judged in the legal system every day and it does not seem insurmountable to find ways in which the professional's intention in using a sedative treatment could be assessed. Nambisan (2012) has provided a useful list of steps that practitioners should take in order to indicate that their intention in the use of a sedative is to relieve distress rather than to end or shorten life:

• Act within accepted practice guidelines, with a proportional approach.
• Document clearly and fully.
• Make sedation decisions as part of a multidisciplinary team.
• Where possible, involve patient and carers in sedation decisions.
• Show a clear indication for use of sedation, with consideration of alternatives.
• Demonstrate consideration of using ANH.
• Note evidence that patient is already near to dying.

Having said this, the evidence already cited that sedation in the context of palliative care is accomplished without curtailing patients' lives (we do not know if this is the case in other care settings) means that the doctrine of double effect is not needed in order to excuse the practice. Although valid, its continual mention tends to produce the impression that there is something that needs to be excused, which is unhelpful (Fohr 1998).

13.   Conclusion

Sedation continues to mean different things to different people. In specialist palliative care units the use of sedatives in the last days of life is not associated with shortened survival overall. Most use of sedatives is not for uncontrollable pain but for the management of restlessness and confusion occurring as part of the process of dying.

Impaired consciousness is common at the end of life with or without sedatives and the aim of sedative use is to relieve distress, not to induce sleep. Whatever the indication, the key to ethical use of sedatives is proportionality. If this is the case, the use of a sedative medication will be an act of mercy for our patients whose distress cannot be relieved by other means. It will be a myth that it shortens patients' lives and the term palliative sedation will not be a euphemism for euthanasia.

6 Understanding the role of nurses in the management of symptoms and distress in the last days of life

Eleanor Wilson and Jane Seymour

1. Introduction

The role and experiences of nurses in continuous sedation until death cannot properly be understood without situating that practice within the wider context of nurses' roles in and attitudes towards the management of the patient's last days of life. Nurses who care for dying people have a central role in assessing patients' needs for pain and symptom control and enabling their timely access to appropriate medications. In some contexts, nurses may have responsibility for deciding when to commence medications that have been medically prescribed or how to titrate medications already in situ to relieve a patient's distress. In assuming these roles and responsibilities, nurses are likely to encounter practical, emotional and ethical challenges and need high levels of knowledge and expertise (Bruce et al. 2006). However, nurses often perceive that the contribution they make to the management of patients' symptoms and distress in end-of-life care is poorly understood and undervalued; this means they are unlikely to feel that they have the support they need to effectively develop and implement this aspect of their role (Burt et al. 2008; King et al. 2009; Walshe & Luker 2010). As we will see below, the 'moral distress' that nurses frequently experience when they are involved in symptom control or non-treatment decisions can be exacerbated when they participate in continuous sedation until death.

The existing literature on symptom control in end-of-life care, including that relating to continuous sedation, places primary emphasis upon the experiences, practices and attitudes of physicians. This is in spite of evidence that good quality end-of-life care is dependent upon team-working between nurses and physicians (Xyrichis & Lowton 2008). There are a number of literature reviews relating to the nurse's role in palliative and end-of-life care and the problems they experience when caring for terminally ill people (Georges &

Grypdonck 2002; Bliss & While 2003; Lowey 2008; Frank 2009; Walshe & Luker 2010). These show that nurses' contribution to 'teamwork', and thus to decisions about patient care and treatment, is heavily influenced by the organisations and contexts in which they work. Factors like lack of continuity of care and enduring stereotypes about nurses' 'place' may mean that nurses feel that they lack the authority or ability to participate in the medical decision-making process (Georges & Grypdonck 2002; Frank 2009). This is a barrier to the process whereby shared goals of patient care can be established, with potentially significantly negative implications for the well-being of patients and their families (Bliss & While 2003; Xyrichis & Lowton 2008).

This chapter explores these issues by way of presenting a pragmatic synthesis of international research published in English relating to nurses' views, opinions and experiences regarding their role in decision-making in end-of-life care. In undertaking the literature review, we used a set of inclusion and exclusion criteria to focus our search for evidence relating to nurses' decision-making in the end-of-life care context,[1] and used a range of keywords to search a selection of databases. We searched for research published since 1990. Hand searching of reference lists in the papers retrieved was also undertaken.[2] Our initial search yielded a total of 140 papers that we reviewed by title, abstract and full text according to the inclusion and exclusion criteria. We included 26 papers reporting 26 studies as a result of this process. We applied a framework analysis approach (Ritchie & Spencer 1994) to the empirical findings reported in each paper in order to establish common themes across the whole body of research.[3]

---

[1] We included papers, published in English, that contained material on: (1) nurses' involvement in decisions relating to medications, drug dosages, and sedation for pain and symptom management for adults in palliative and end-of-life care contexts; and (2) nurses' involvement in non-treatment decisions (e.g. withdrawal or withholding of treatment, including artificial nutrition and hydration). We excluded papers that: focused on physician-assisted suicide or euthanasia; that reported research outside palliative or end-of-life care contexts; or were non-empirical.

[2] The search terms used included: nurs$4; nurse role; palliative care; end of life care; decision making; medication; prescribing; and sedation. The databases searched were: British Nursing Index; Embase; Medline; CINAHL; and Ovid full text.

[3] Framework analysis is particularly useful in the production of policy and practice based findings. Its purpose is to classify and summarise data while maintaining the individual responses. Familiarisation of the data was undertaken by reading and re-reading of papers and a thematic coding scheme was developed. These themes were then charted and condensed into sub-themes.

2.   Overview

Most of the research we reviewed had been published since 2008, although we found some isolated studies published between 2001 and 2007. The research was conducted in ten different countries, primarily the UK (n = 9). Eight papers were found to report studies conducted in northern Europe and Scandinavia, five reported research conducted in Japan and four papers reported on studies conducted in the USA and Canada. No papers were found reporting studies from Australia or New Zealand. Both quantitative and qualitative studies were identified, using a range of survey, interview, focus group and observational methods of data collection. The studies included in the review encompass nurses working in hospital, hospice and community settings, including nursing homes, with differences evident depending on the country in which the research was conducted. Most of the UK research was based in the community (King et al. 2003; Dunne et al. 2005; Cruickshank et al. 2010; Griggs 2010; Faull et al. 2013; Lawton et al. 2012), including in nursing homes (Enes & de Vries 2004; Watson et al. 2006), with only one study exploring the experiences of UK hospice nurses (Zinn & Moriarty 2012). Research reported in the Japanese studies included both hospital nurses (Doutrich et al. 2001; Morita et al. 2004c; Miyashita et al. 2008) and community based nurses (Hirano et al. 2011; Yamagishi et al. 2012). Research from North America focused on the views of hospital or hospice nurses, or both (Beel et al. 2006; Rietjens et al. 2007; Bach et al. 2009; Patel et al. 2012). The studies carried out in northern Europe and Scandinavia were predominantly nationwide surveys of nurses across all care settings (Hilden et al. 2004; de Veer et al. 2008; Venke Gran & Miller 2008; Inghelbrecht et al. 2009, 2011; Brinkkemper et al. 2011); although two smaller studies accessing the views of community nurses (Karlsson et al. 2010) and nursing home nurses (Hov et al. 2009) were also identified.

In the following sections, we provide a close examination of themes identified in the body of research. We begin by exploring in broad terms the key elements that nurses identify as being integral to their decision-making role in end-of-life care, including detecting a patient's needs, providing support to the patient's family and acting as a communication liaison with other professionals. Then we examine how the role of nurses is constituted in relation to the use of medications and the withdrawal or withholding of treatment at the end of life. Finally, we examine the research, reported in seven articles, that specifically addresses nurses' views and experiences about their role in continuous sedation.

3.   Decision-making in end-of-life care: the nurses' role

In this section, we comment on three particular themes that were identified: anticipating and preparing to meet patients' needs; providing support to patients' families, and providing information to and communicating with other healthcare professionals.

3.1.   *Anticipating and preparing to meet patients' needs*

Nurses identified that anticipating patients' needs and being 'prepared' were crucially important to their effectiveness as decision-makers in end-of-life care. This means continually monitoring a patient's condition and ensuring that the necessary additional support, medications and equipment are in place at the right time to meet their evolving needs effectively (Enes & de Vries 2004; Bach et al. 2009; Cruickshank et al. 2010; Griggs 2010; Patel et al. 2012). Thus, for example, English community nurses who took part in qualitative interviews designed to elicit their understandings of a 'good death' talked repeatedly about the importance of the proactive, rather than reactive, identification and management of patients' symptoms at the end of life (Griggs 2010). However, nurses in this study perceived that the extent to which they could effectively 'prepare' and then make the necessary decisions to meet needs was heavily dependent upon the existence of wider processes and structures (such as the availability of medications 'out of hours') that were beyond their control or influence. This finding is also echoed in another study of English community care nursing by Cruickshank et al. (2010).

In a very different context, nurses in a North American study based in an intensive care unit (Bach et al. 2009) similarly emphasised that crucial aspects of their daily work included the prediction of dying patients' needs and then interactive work to negotiate with physicians in reaching decisions about how best to meet these. This sometimes involved 'prompting' physicians to consider a change in focus from curative care. These findings are echoed in comparative research conducted in the USA and Japan among hospital nurses who reported seeking to educate and persuade physicians to move to a palliative approach, in which futile interventions could be withdrawn or withheld and the focus could be shifted to ways to comfort patients and relieve their suffering (Doutrich et al. 2001).

Shedding light on a different aspect of the same theme, a survey of nurses providing terminal care to older people in England shows that they placed emphasis on the importance of the practical aspects of preparing for death, such as finances, wills and funeral arrangements, as well as on the importance of helping patients to prepare for future loss of capacity by making decisions in advance. The latter was seen as essential to avoid the 'routine' application of life-sustaining treatments or transfer to hospital, which was perceived by nurses to adversely affect the quality of patients' deaths and the bereavement experience of their relatives (Enes & de Vries 2004).

3.2.   *Providing support to the family*

Providing support to patients' families, especially when providing care in the domestic home, emerged from several of the studies as a core aspect of the nurses' role in end-of-life care, albeit with interesting cultural differences. While the most obvious manifestation of this aspect of the nurses' role is the provision of hands-on care to relieve the potential burden on relatives, other important activities include: acting as a guide for family members to enable them to provide care to their relative; supporting and validating patients' and families' decisions; enabling channels of communication within families; providing information to patients and families, including interpretations of physicians' advice; and providing support, both practically and emotionally, including into bereavement. These activities, and how they overlap with the theme of 'anticipation and preparation' described above, are captured particularly clearly in a study of family assistance and caregiving by 31 Japanese nurses to the families of elderly patients, conducted in a context where home death rates are much lower (12 per cent) than in other parts of the world (Hirano et al. 2011). The paper presents a useful framework for further study of the nurses' decision-making role in end-of-life care, with community nurses being shown to undertake a continuous process of assessment to judge whether a family would be able to cope with caring for the patient at home. This process of assessment involved gathering information, and making predictions about whether the family had the ability to provide the care that a dying person needs. The nurses' attention then turned to visualising what was going to happen in the immediate future, what help was required by the family, and, finally, to making a decision about the place of death in collaboration with the family as the death approached. The promotion of consensus within the family and the provision of support to them as they said goodbye to their relative were critically important. Hirano et al. (2011) conclude that this aspect of nurses' work involves the dynamic balancing of multiple decision-making components.

Although in another cultural context and sharply differing care setting, an American study of critical care nurses posits a similar conceptual framework to that of Hirano et al. (2011) and enables a deeper understanding of the nurses' family-focused role in end-of-life care and how this relates to decision-making (Bach et al. 2009). The framework of this study spans four major themes: 'being there'; 'a voice to speak up'; 'enable coming to terms'; and 'helping to let go'. Of special note in this study is the work that nurses do in explaining and interpreting for patients and their families; this involves the difficult challenge of balancing truth with hope to enable the patient and family to make appropriately informed decisions. A study of community nurses in England (Dunne et al. 2005) similarly reveals the complexity that nurses face in relation to communication with patients and families as death approaches. Being asked 'difficult questions' and dealing with the range of patients' and families' emotions were seen as particularly challenging by nurses, especially where anger was expressed. The district nurses in this study reported experiences of being asked to collude with relatives in order to hide the truth from a patient, which created complex moral dilemmas for them (Dunne et al. 2005). The challenges associated with the disclosure of truth are examined in another English study of nurses caring for elderly terminally ill people, where nurses reported the difficulties they faced when working in situations where patients were unaware of the severity of their condition, but where their families knew they were likely to be terminally ill (Enes & de Vries 2004).

Further interesting light is shed on the moral dilemmas associated with the family support aspect of the nurse's role by a small Swedish study of community palliative care nurses (Karlsson et al. 2010). Here we see that although the nurses were autonomous practitioners and decision-makers, their autonomy was greatly constrained by the network of relations surrounding them. In this study, powerlessness and frustration were experienced by nurses both in relation to unrelenting demands from family members and in relation to unequal power differentials between themselves and physicians. These meant that physicians did not always observe nurses' requests (often at the behest of families) to provide pain relief or to reduce futile interventions. This issue recurs again in the next theme in relation to nurses' roles in providing information to others.

3.3.   Providing information and communicating with other professionals

Nurses play a key role in providing information to other staff to enable the wider process of care planning and decision-making surrounding patients, but will often encounter a range of structural and contextual features that disrupt the relationship between the provision of this information and patient care decisions (Doutrich et al. 2001; Venke Gran & Miller 2008; Bach et al. 2009; Patel et al. 2012; Zinn & Moriarty 2012). For example, in an English locality-based study of this issue (King et al. 2003), community nurses providing a 24-hour service reported in focus groups how challenging it was to liaise with specialist palliative care services that did not operate 'out of hours'. Community nurses reported that this resulted in delays in meeting patients' needs even when they provided information to specialists in a timely manner. Moreover, community nurses perceived that lack of understanding on the part of 'specialists' about the roles of 'generalist' services thwarted collaborative decision-making in patient care, even though this was an agreed aim (King et al. 2003). Similar difficulties are reported in a study evaluating the introduction of the Liverpool Care Pathway for the Dying Patient[4] in eight UK nursing homes (Watson et al. 2006). The use of such a pathway assumes that nurses, care assistants, family members and GPs will discuss and collaboratively decide, first, whether a patient is dying and, second, how to manage end-of-life care. However, in this study, such teamwork was profoundly lacking; most nurses felt uncomfortable about having any input into GPs' decision-making processes and reported 'going along' (Watson et al. 2006) with the GP's view, even where the resulting decision was perceived by the nurses to be to the detriment of a patient's best interests. A major contributor to this submissive stance was a lack of familiarity between GPs and nurses in the homes and a lack of confidence on the part of the nurses, even though they knew the patients in their care extremely well.

Experiences of challenging communication or conflicts between nurses and other health professionals (usually nurse–doctor relationships) that affected decision-making in patient care are frequently reported in the other studies we reviewed (Enes & de Vries 2004; Miyashita et al. 2008; Inghelbrecht et al. 2009; Griggs 2010; Karlsson et al. 2010; Brinkkemper et al. 2011). While most of the studies reviewed used qualitative methods to explore these issues, some insight into the prevalence of this problem is provided by data from a nationwide survey of 6,000 nurses in Flanders (Belgium) about their role in end-of-life

---

[4] The Liverpool Care Pathway for the Dying Patient is an integrated care pathway aimed at improving quality of care in the last days and hours of life. It is recommended by the Department of Health in England and Wales and can be used in any care setting to plan the most appropriate care, including a review of medications, for the individual at the end of life. www.liv.ac.uk/mcpcil/liverpool-care-pathway/ (last accessed 21 October 2012).

decisions (Inghelbrecht et al. 2009). This study found that, while 50 per cent of the nurses believed that physicians are usually prepared to listen to their opinions about the care of terminally ill patients, more than a third (35 per cent) felt that they were in a subordinate position to physicians, which made communication about patient care decisions challenging. Inghelbrecht et al. (2009) conclude that while nurses may wish to be involved in decision-making in end-of-life care, recognition is needed of the challenges they face in communicating with physicians and further training is required to empower nurses to represent their views assertively to the wider healthcare team.

4.   The nurse's role in symptom control and non-treatment decisions

We have already seen that nurses' decisions about patients' end-of-life care are inhibited in a variety of complex ways, from perceived emotional and moral constraints that operate in the everyday minutiae of patient and family care, to structural issues shaping the organisation of services, and by differentials of power and influence between nurses and other actors, especially medical practitioners. We now turn to examine how these operate in the specific context of the nurse's role in relation to symptom control and 'non-treatment' decisions.

A key theme which emerges from the body of research reviewed is that nurses frequently experience moral distress when involved in end-of-life care involving symptom control or non-treatment decisions. This has a number of antecedents, including a lack of perceived confidence or knowledge (Karlsson et al. 2010) and a lack of resources such as time and specialist advice (Cruickshank et al. 2010), which, as we have seen, also operate in the wider context of end-of-life care. However, much more fundamentally, when nurses are required to engage with care which involves questions of how best to control a patient's distress or when to limit or withdraw life-sustaining treatment, they experience at one and the same time a sense of burdensome responsibility and a lack of power or influence to meet those responsibilities. A qualitative Norwegian study of 14 nurses working in two nursing homes illustrates this most clearly, with nurses described as 'caught between too much responsibility and too little formal power' (Hov et al. 2009: 655). In this study, nurses were interviewed on two occasions to encourage them to talk about cases of patient care in which they had encountered a dilemma relating to non-treatment decisions. The nurses considered that they knew the patients' situations and their wishes for care well, because of the continuous and close contact they had had with them.

However, they experienced a series of challenges in reaching certainty about what was in the patients' best interests and in developing an unambiguous care plan that could be followed. Clear criteria were lacking for when curative treatment was inappropriate, and there were few opportunities to establish shared goals of care for any individual patient because of lack of physician availability or lack of interest among physicians in end-of-life care. When nurses tried to communicate their views, it would depend on the individual physician whether their perspective was considered; this meant that important information was sometimes neglected. On the other hand, some physicians (often because of lack of time) simply wished to 'rubber stamp' the nurse's view about what decision should be made. This led to high levels of anxiety and a sense of vulnerability among the nurses:

> If I told that physician, 'I don't think he needs parenteral hydration. Shouldn't we rather give palliative treatment?' Then the physician might say, 'OK'. You can say that we are mini-doctors who only need a boss to authorise it on paper, and that is challenging. (Hov et al. 2009: 655)

Hov et al. (2009) conclude that nurses are in a liminal position, in which they are often compelled to take the lead in, or implement, decisions that should be the remit of physicians while, at other times, having their knowledge and expertise marginalised: this paradoxicality damages the nurses' sense of professionalism and, at the same time, puts them at risk of exceeding their professional responsibility and remit, with all the potential legal and ethical consequences that this may give rise to.

The findings from Hov et al. (2009) are echoed throughout the other studies we reviewed. A nationwide panel survey of 489 nurses in The Netherlands (de Veer et al. 2008) shows that the majority (77%) preferred to be involved by physicians in non-treatment decisions, especially where these may hasten death,[5] and that the majority (68%) across all types of care settings are involved in talking to patients and their families about end-of-life care decisions. A slightly higher percentage wished to be involved in decisions about pain and symptom relief (79%). The background characteristics of the nurses, along with the type of care setting they work in, are associated with both the expressed desire to be included in decision-making at the end of life and whether they feel that they have been involved in the decision-making process by physicians. De Veer et al. (2008) show that nurses who work more hours and have a higher level of education and training are more likely

[5] A smaller proportion (49%) of nurses wished to be involved in decisions about euthanasia or physician-assisted suicide.

to prefer to be involved. As we have already seen, similar findings are reported on the basis of a much larger nationwide survey of 6,000 nurses from Belgium which led to the conclusion that: 'more attention should be paid to interdisciplinary consultation, because nurses have an important bridging function between patient and physician' (Inghelbrecht et al. 2009: 657). Similar conclusions are reached on the basis of a nationwide survey of 3,328 Japanese nurses, seeking their views on decisions about clinically assisted hydration for terminally ill cancer patients cared for in palliative care or oncology units (Miyashita et al. 2008). This survey shows that one-third of nurses felt that physicians did not respect their opinions. Echoing the detailed qualitative findings of Hov et al. (2009), Miyashita et al. (2008) report that nurses experience considerable distress, often because the physician-given orders they are expected to carry out conflict with their understandings of patients' and families' wishes.

Several studies that we reviewed reported that nurses are sometimes prepared to challenge physicians about treatment decisions, usually because of a desire to uphold or advocate for the wishes of the patient or family (Doutrich et al. 2001; Hilden et al. 2004; Bach et al. 2009). However, on the whole, nurses are shown to lack the confidence to challenge physicians' decisions and feel instead compelled to comply with, or justify to patients and families, decisions they have had no part in making. In studies based in community and care home settings, nurses are shown to experience frustration that critical decisions about pain and symptom management are reliant on GPs, whose knowledge may be out of date or who lack experience in the care of the dying (Enes & de Vries 2004; Griggs 2010; Karlsson et al. 2010). This can result in decision-making being delayed, meaning that some patients have very poor symptom management at the end of life.

In some contexts, particular historical features complicate issues of a more general nature. For example, research from the UK draws attention to the existence of heightened anxiety about the use of controlled drugs in the wake of the Shipman case of the early 2000s.[6] This has been perceived to intensify a generalised reluctance exhibited by GPs to take timely decisions about pain and symptom management (King et al. 2003; Griggs 2010) or to consult others about the use of drugs. Some commentators conclude that the Shipman affair has been so influential that it has been to the widespread detriment of patient care

---

[6] Harold Shipman was convicted in 2000 of murdering 15 of his elderly patients using a lethal dose of morphine. It is thought he may have killed at least 250 patients over his 23 years as a GP in England. In 2004, he died after hanging himself in prison.

(Faull et al. 2013). In the UK, a trend towards 'anticipatory prescribing' (involving GPs preparing 'just in case' prescriptions which nurses then implement at a time of their choosing) has been actively encouraged because of the widespread recognition of such problems. This in turn has been shown to give rise to a new set of challenges for nurses, most clearly reported by Faull et al. (2013) in a study of community health professionals involved in home-based palliative care in one locality. In this study, nurses reported encountering problems relating to gaining access to drugs once prescribed, as well as not always being able to successfully encourage GPs to prescribe in advance. This was often because of a lack of reliable links between professional teams or disciplines, which meant that trusting relationships had not been adequately established. Many GPs (especially when working 'out of hours') felt, on the one hand, that they had neither sufficient nor reliable information about the patients to whom they were expected to provide prescriptions. On the other hand, regardless of the quality of information they had about patients, GPs felt that they could not always rely on continuity of nursing care. This meant that they felt insecure about prescribing potentially dangerous controlled drugs and perceived that nurses often were reluctant to give the drugs prescribed. This led to poor symptom control for patients at a time when they most required it:

[W]hen you have a [different] nurse going in every night they were very, very reluctant to give the dose that [the patient] had been having and they would tend to go with the lowest dose on the range, which caused difficulties with pain control ... not knowing the patient, not knowing the family, not knowing me, not knowing the team, and being asked to give what seemed a lethal dose of morphine. (GP, reported in Faull et al. 2013: 4)

Such issues are even more sharply revealed in practice surrounding continuous sedation for patients with palliative care needs, to which the last section of our review now turns.

5.   Nurses' role in continuous sedation for patients with palliative care needs

As we have seen, nurses are involved in end-of-life care decisions, although often not as much as they would like, usually because of problematic relationships with physicians (Inghelbrecht et al. 2009). Moreover, nurses often assume a leading role in taking decisions about the use of medications to control symptoms (and in some cases in taking non-treatment decisions), but may be hampered by limited knowledge and experience with such medications, by organisational issues which heighten their sense of risk and by the paradoxicality of having too much responsibility without the necessary professional status or power. The concept of 'moral distress' captures nurses' perspectives in this area and is even more marked as a theme in the limited research available that has explored nurses' experiences with continuous sedation (Morita et al. 2004c; Beel et al. 2006; Rietjens et al. 2007; Venke Gran & Miller 2008; Brinkkemper et al. 2011; Inghelbrecht et al. 2011; Patel et al. 2012; Zinn & Moriarty 2012). Thus, for example, Morita et al. (2004c) refer to the 'serious emotional burden' experienced by some Japanese nurses involved in continuous sedation, while Beel et al. (2006) use the metaphor of a 'quagmire' to capture the difficult and complex issues Canadian nurses perceived to be associated with continuous sedation.

In Norway, Venke Gran and Miller (2008) report a survey of 73 nurses involved with continuous sedation, finding that their role involves administering and monitoring medications, assessing the effectiveness of the medications and providing compassionate care to patients and their families. Most of the nurses in this study perceived there to be ethical problems associated with continuous deep sedation, usually relating to the removal of the patients' ability to communicate with their families or to inform the nurse whether they remained in pain and distress. A survey of nurses from Belgium (n = 1,678) (Inghelbrecht et al. 2011) shows that many believe continuous sedation to be partly or explicitly intended to hasten death and feel that the quality of communication they have with physicians about this practice is inadequate, especially with regard to its goal and its likely effect. Brinkkemper et al. (2011) report on a much smaller survey of nurses (n = 201) employed in The Netherlands as 'medical technical assistants' to aid GPs in carrying out continuous sedation. Findings show that the nurses agreed with the indication by the physician for performing continuous sedation in 93% of the cases, but that in spite of this high level of agreement 21% of nurses had refused to carry out a GP's orders in the previous year. Reasons for refusal to carry out a GP's orders included unclear or incorrect prescriptions of drugs and nurses believing that continuous sedation was being started too soon. Specifically with regard to timing, 19% of nurses believed that the start of sedation was poorly timed, either too late or too early.

One exception to this general picture comes from an exploratory study (Zinn & Moriarty 2012), based in a Scottish hospice, in which a very small number of nurses (n = 5) involved in continuous sedation (by way of being responsible for titrating the prescribed doses) took part in qualitative interviews over a period of three months. Nurses reported that they felt empowered by support from physicians and that their judgement about the levels of sedation patients required was respected. Nurses took confidence from a collaborative teamwork approach and their own experience. Three (out of the total of five) were able to engage in informed discussion in their research interview about the ethical issues involved, such as primary intent, proportionality and the doctrine of double effect (Zinn & Moriarty 2012). Nurses' confidence was linked to having the courage to use sedative medications that had been prescribed, and to the sense that all decisions about patients' care at this time were taken collaboratively with medical colleagues. This meant that nurses were able to gain experience with sedation practice in a supportive environment. Clearly the very small sample size of this study means that we cannot draw any generalisable conclusions about nurses in hospices, but nonetheless the findings are interesting to compare with those of other studies which tend to portray a rather more mixed picture about nurses' experiences.

In reflecting on how to reduce the sense of emotional burden experienced by some Japanese nurses working in hospital and palliative care units with regard to continuous sedation, Morita et al. (2004c) suggest that the feeling of burden is exaggerated by these nurses' lack of skills and experience when dealing with people with refractory symptoms, by their limited knowledge of continuous sedation, by having insufficient time and by the patients' wishes not being clear. In their survey of almost 3,000 nurses 7 per cent reported a belief that sedation would hasten death, with most of these individuals being younger nurses with less clinical experience who reported a high emotional burden (Morita et al. 2004c). Closely mirroring those factors highlighted in the Scottish study (Zinn & Moriarty 2012) as being perceived by nurses to be helpful, Morita et al. recommend that a team approach is taken to resolve differences of opinion between professional staff, especially between nurses and physicians, and that the education and training of both nurses and physicians should focus on interpersonal and ethical skills (Morita et al. 2004c). In a different cultural context, Beel et al. also note that insufficient knowledge of continuous sedation was a cause of concern for Canadian nurses, reporting that nurses were often unfamiliar with the terminology surrounding the practice and unsure what the differences might be between continuous sedation and practices aimed primarily at shortening or ending life (Beel et al. 2006). In the latter study, a particular challenge perceived by nurses was that of establishing the indications for which continuous sedation might be appropriate, with confusion reported to be associated with whether existential suffering was a legitimate reason for continuous sedation. In another study from North America (Patel et al. 2012), nurses perceived that a definition of 'palliative sedation' should be agreed and clear indications for its use should be set out before a policy for the practice could be developed. The nurses in this study had a variety of opinions about whether continuous sedation was appropriate for the management of non-physical symptoms. Some felt that physical and non-physical suffering, while having different mechanisms, should each be treated in the same way; others felt that using sedation for non-physical suffering, especially when it was not clearly linked in some way to the patient's physical symptoms, was unethical. Some nurses also perceived that the distress of families about patients' suffering could be a compelling reason for considering the use of sedation. Patel et al. (2012) report that nurses in their study felt that this area of practice needed to operate within a wider context of interdisciplinary team-working. This echoes the conclusions of Venke Gran and Miller, reporting on the significance of the findings of a survey of Norwegian nurses, who recommend the 'development of interdisciplinary guidelines for determining the ethical use of palliative sedation and care of patients in local hospitals and palliative care units' (Venke Gran & Miller 2008: 537).

Perspectives from North American nurses can also be found in a study by Rietjens et al. (2007) comparing the experiences of 16 nurses from a palliative care unit and a medical intensive care unit, all of whom had a largely positive stance towards the value of continuous sedation in end-of-life care. However, the issue of whether or not non-physical suffering was a legitimate indication for the use of continuous sedation again emerged as a concern, mainly because this was something outside of the nurses' expertise and previous experience. Echoing the findings of Patel et al. (2012), some nurses thought that the distress of the family about the patient's suffering was a key consideration to take into account when deciding to start continuous sedation. In addition, they had a range of opinions about whether continuous sedation was associated with life being shortened, and some were unclear about the differences between the practice and euthanasia. Thus, for example, one respondent said the following:

I remember having questions about – because it was all new to me – what was an appropriate intervention? Was this euthanasia? Was this physician-assisted suicide? Was I being asked to actually kill a human being? And so I remember having to do a lot of reflection upon that to explore those notions. (Nurse, cited in Rietjens et al. 2007)

Participants generally subscribed to one of three views: first, that continuous sedation did not hasten death; second, that it could shorten the dying process but that this was acceptable as it was the only way to address refractory symptoms; and, third, that only a 'fine line' separated continuous sedation and the practice of euthanasia (Rietjens et al. 2007). Concerns were mainly expressed by those nurses who had little previous experience of the practice. This finding echoes the conclusions of Morita et al. (2004c), who recommend educational programmes concerning the minimal life-shortening risks of continuous sedation, and the ethical principles differentiating sedation from euthanasia.

6.   Conclusion

The review reported in this chapter has pooled small-scale qualitative research with larger quantitative studies to shed some light on nurses' experiences and views about an area of practice that has been studied comparatively rarely. We have shown the importance of nurses being able to engage in anticipatory planning to meet the needs of patients and their families, showing that across different cultural and care contexts this is perceived by nurses to lead to better quality care, especially in terms of appropriate pain and symptom control. It is clear that nurses feel that they play an important role in providing information to other staff to facilitate the wider process of care planning and decision-making surrounding patients. Yet they will often encounter a range of power relations and structural and contextual features that they perceive to be disruptive to the relationship between the provision of this information and patient care decisions.

When we focused on nurses' roles in and experiences of symptom control and non-treatment decisions in end-of-life care, including continuous sedation, we found that many nurses feel caught between having too much responsibility and not enough power, which leaves them in an ambiguous position. An overarching theme of moral distress emerges, which has a number of antecedents, including a lack of perceived confidence or knowledge, lack of resources including time and specialist advice, and differentials in professional power which lead to the marginalisation of nurses' views and positions. Specifically in relation to continuous sedation, we found that some nurses experience significant emotional burden and are profoundly concerned about the ethical and moral dimensions of the practice. Some feel that they have unclear communication with physicians about the aims and intended effects of continuous sedation and do not understand the relevant ethical principles or issues. The presence of a supportive interdisciplinary team and clear guidelines for practice are regarded as essential.

Similar issues emerged from all the studies included in the review, reflecting very little difference between the various countries from which the research originated. However, Japanese nurses were identified as especially lacking in confidence to challenge physicians, due to the status hierarchy between nurses and doctors in that country. In the UK, the legacy of the Shipman case appeared to have negatively influenced patient care, especially in the community. We found only a few studies from North America and none from Australia or New Zealand. Those that we found from North America did not extend to the study of community-based nurses and so it is not clear whether the findings about community nurses reported in this chapter are shared by their colleagues in other continents. It is also worth noting, however, that the definitions of a 'community nurse' and of the term 'hospice' may vary internationally, so comparisons are often complex.

The research that we found reports the views and opinions of nurses and does not provide a commentary about what happens in practice. For this reason, ongoing research[7] is using mixed methods approaches to gain insight into medical and nursing practice with end-of-life decision-making, with a special focus on continuous sedation (Seymour et al. 2011).

Our review highlights that nurses do want to be involved in end-of-life decisions and can provide essential insights into patients' preferences and health status. They also often have strong, close links with the patients and their families, creating a bond of trust and the right milieu for shared decision-making. These strengths should be embraced and built upon to improve communication, team-working and decision-making with the ongoing aim of improving end-of-life care for patients and families.

---

[7] A study funded by Marie Curie Cancer Care, and entitled 'Understanding the role of nurses in decisions to use anticipatory prescriptions to manage symptoms and distress in the last days of life: a prospective community based case study using mixed methods', is being carried out over 2011–13 by J. Seymour, S. Payne, C. Seale, N. Mathers and J. Brown.

7 Principle and practice for palliative sedation: gaps between the two

David Orentlicher

1. Introduction

End-of-life care has long suffered from gaps between principle and practice. For several aspects of care, many physicians do not observe guidelines that have been developed by professional associations or rules that have been established by lawmakers. For example, even though patients may refuse life-sustaining treatment regardless of their prognosis, some physicians will not honour requests to withhold or withdraw life-sustaining treatment from patients with good prognoses. And even though people have a right to determine their end-of-life care by leaving an advance directive with their wishes, some physicians fail to provide care in accordance with a patient's advance directive (Orentlicher et al. 2008: 251–2, 255–7, 295).

The gaps between principle and practice are troubling in a number of ways, but especially so for the treatment of pain and other suffering. Many physicians do not respond appropriately to suffering at the end of life, leaving their patients with insufficient palliation for their pain and other severe discomfort. Changes in professional guidelines and the law for end-of-life care have been spurred by a desire to ensure that patients do not suffer – practitioners, scholars and policymakers have recognised that good patient care requires attention not only to length of life but also to quality of life. Unfortunately, relief of suffering remains an elusive goal for many patients.

To some extent the gaps between principle and practice signal the need for reforms in principle. Physician-aid-in-dying,[1] for example, is

---

[1] Physician-aid-in-dying is often described as physician-assisted suicide. I prefer 'physician-aid-in-dying' because the term 'suicide' tends to connote conduct that should be prevented, as when a distraught college student dies after jumping from a bridge. However, when terminally ill individuals are suffering greatly from illness, the choice to ingest a lethal dose of medication is understandable and can be viewed as morally justified.

prohibited in most jurisdictions, leaving patients in most parts of the world without access to a potentially valuable option.

Gaps between principle and practice can also reflect deficiencies in practice. Physicians can be slow to reshape their delivery of care in response to reforms in professional standards and legal rules. As in other areas of medicine, a key barrier to quality care lies not in the governing guidelines but in physician behaviour.

As I discuss in this chapter, gaps between principle and practice are a problem for palliative sedation just as they are for other kinds of end-of-life care.[2] And, just as with other kinds of end-of-life care, there are problems with both principle and practice.

For an example of problems with principle, consider the fact that professional standards may give insufficient weight to the requirements of good patient care. Under Dutch and Norwegian guidelines, patients must have a life expectancy of no more than two weeks to be eligible for palliative sedation (Førde et al. 2008: 431; Hasselaar et al. 2009a: 431). However, many people will develop suffering that cannot be relieved by other treatments when their life expectancy is longer than two weeks, and it may be possible to respect the reasons for restricting access to palliative sedation with a cut-off measured in weeks or months rather than in days.

For an example of problems with practice, studies indicate that the use of palliative sedation can depend more on the personal or institutional philosophies of healthcare providers than on the needs or desires of patients. As with other end-of-life practices, studies of palliative sedation practices show wide variations in the frequency of use and the reasons for use from doctor to doctor and from hospital to hospital (Peruselli et al. 1999). Some patients may lack access to palliative sedation, even though they desire it and meet eligibility criteria for it, because their healthcare providers misunderstand or disagree with prevailing professional and legal standards (Cherny & Radbruch 2009: 582).[3]

The unwillingness of some healthcare providers to offer palliative sedation in appropriate circumstances may be driven in large part by a community ethic that disfavours the practice. After all, physician values

[2] Palliative sedation, as I use the term, refers to the practice of deeply sedating patients, even to unconsciousness, when they are suffering intolerable pain that cannot be relieved by other palliative therapies (Cherny & Radbruch 2009: 581).
[3] To be sure, while patients may be eligible for palliative sedation, their physicians are still entitled to practise according to their own moral beliefs. We do not expect obstetricians who oppose abortion to perform the procedure for their patients who desire an abortion. Still, when physicians are uncomfortable providing palliative sedation, their patients should have access to sedation from other healthcare providers.

are shaped by societal values, and palliative sedation will be viewed differently in different cultures. Accordingly, studies find important variations in patterns of practice. Physicians in some countries may be less likely to offer palliative sedation than physicians in other countries, and physicians in some communities of a country may be less likely to offer palliative sedation than physicians in other communities of the country.

For an example of differences across national boundaries, palliative sedation is provided more than twice as often in Belgium and The Netherlands as in Denmark or Sweden (Miccinesi et al. 2006: 124–5; Anquinet et al. 2012: 34). The United States provides a useful illustration of differences among communities within a single country. Physicians in the southern United States are more likely than physicians in the Northeast or West Coast to oppose the use of palliative sedation (Curlin et al. 2008: 116).

To some extent, differences in use of palliative sedation in different communities make sense. If local values favour a particular practice, one would expect it to be provided more frequently than in a place where local values disfavour the practice. Still, the influence of community values can result in frustration of the preferences of patients who do not share the values of their communities' majorities.

Since most of the data on actual practices are based on experiences in Europe and Japan, comparisons between the United States and other countries are difficult to make. Nevertheless, one important difference may exist between US practices and European practices. European physicians may be more willing to recognise 'existential' suffering as a justification for sedation. While professional guidelines in the United States reject existential suffering as a justification for palliative sedation (US Veterans Health Administration 2007: 487–8; American Medical Association 2008: 3–4, 6),[4] some professional guidelines in Europe leave room for existential suffering to serve as a justification for sedation. For example, according to the guidelines of the European Association for Palliative Care:

Occasionally, when patients approach the end of life, sedation may be considered for severe non-physical symptoms such as refractory depression, anxiety, demoralization or existential distress. (Cherny & Radbruch 2009: 584)[5]

---

[4] According to the Veterans Health Administration policy, palliative sedation for existential suffering is not justified 'in the absence of severe, refractory clinical symptoms'.

[5] The Dutch national guideline allows consideration of existential suffering but only because the guideline also requires that patients be within a week or two of death and therefore are at a stage of their illness at which they are very seriously ill and their bodies are breaking down. 'In other words, the issue here is never solely existential suffering.' Indeed, according to the guideline, for those patients who have no refractory symptoms but want palliative sedation to avoid 'consciously experiencing the end

2.   Palliative sedation principle and practice

I have mentioned some of the gaps between principle and practice for palliative sedation. What other gaps exist? I will start by identifying the key principles. Then, I will compare principle and practice.

When the US Supreme Court rejected a constitutional right to physician-aid-in-dying (which the court described as physician-assisted suicide), some of the justices relied on the premise that patient suffering can be relieved without resort to aid-in-dying. Justice Sandra Day O'Connor, for example, saw no need for a right to aid-in-dying because 'a patient who is suffering from a terminal illness and who is experiencing great pain has no legal barriers to obtaining medication, from qualified physicians, to alleviate that suffering, even to the point of causing unconsciousness and hastening death' (*Washington* v. *Glucksberg* 1997: 736–7). Similarly, Justice Stephen Breyer believed that a right to aid-in-dying could not be justified as long as the law allowed doctors to provide 'patients with drugs sufficient to control pain despite the risk that those drugs themselves will kill,' including those 'very few individuals for whom the ineffectiveness of pain control medicines can mean, not pain, but the need for sedation which can end in a coma' (*Washington* v. *Glucksberg* 1997: 791–2).

As the statements by Justices O'Connor and Breyer suggest, palliative sedation is supposed to be a rarely used treatment of last resort for terminally ill patients who are experiencing pain, shortness of breath, nausea or other physical suffering that is unbearable and that cannot be relieved without deep sedation. Professional guidelines take the same view – palliative sedation 'should be a "last resort" to be used only for dying patients with a very short life expectancy and refractory symptoms' (Raus et al. 2011: 34).[6]

In other words, the option of palliative sedation helps assure us that while everyone must die, no patient need suffer. Even in the uncommon situation in which standard palliative treatments are unable to provide relief, there should be no need to turn to physician-aid-in-dying for help. Palliative sedation responds to any kind and any level of suffering.[7]

---

of life', palliative sedation is not indicated (KNMG 2009b: 24–5). Guidelines issued by the Norwegian Medical Association do not allow for palliative sedation in cases of existential suffering (Førde et al. 2008: 431).

[6] For similar positions, see Cherny and Radbruch (2009: 584) and Rietjens et al. (2009a: 410).

[7] As discussed later, when palliative sedation is limited to patients with a very short life expectancy, it may not be available for all patients whose suffering cannot be relieved by other palliative therapies.

While some physicians practise in accordance with the standard characterisation of palliative sedation practice, others do not. For example, palliative sedation may be used when suffering is not persistent and unbearable. In a study of palliative sedation for patients dying at home in Belgium, researchers found that patients were not experiencing unbearable suffering in about one-third of cases (Anquinet et al. 2011: 10).

It also is not always the case that palliative sedation is rarely used (Raus et al. 2011). In studies that look at the practices of palliative care units or hospices, researchers report frequency rates for palliative sedation of anywhere from a few per cent to 25% or even 50% (Peruselli et al. 1999; Fainsinger et al. 2000; Cowan & Palmer 2002; Sykes & Thorns 2003a; Claessens et al. 2008).[8] When studies consider the prevalence of palliative sedation among all deaths, the range narrows, but in many countries palliative sedation is not a rarely provided treatment. Analyses of palliative sedation practices in Flanders (Belgium), The Netherlands and the UK found that deaths in 2007 (2010 for The Netherlands) were preceded by palliative sedation in 15%, 12% and 17% of cases, respectively (Anquinet et al. 2012: 37; Onwuteaka-Philipsen, et al. 2012: 909).[9] In Denmark, Switzerland and Sweden, on the other hand, rates for 2001–2 were lower, at 2.5%, 4.8% and 3%, respectively (Miccinesi et al. 2006: 124–5).[10]

Palliative sedation practice also deviates from principle because it often is provided for reasons other than the relief of severe physical suffering from terminal illness.[11] While early studies reported that palliative sedation was used primarily to relieve physical suffering unresponsive to other treatment, later studies have found an increased use

---

[8] Part of the variation in frequency rates reflects differences in how narrowly or broadly a study defines palliative sedation (Rietjens et al. 2004: 181–2; Claessens et al. 2008: 328).

[9] The UK rate may reflect an overestimate of the prevalence of palliative sedation (Seymour et al. 2011: 2).

[10] These palliative sedation rates may have changed in the intervening decade. The study found a palliative sedation rate of 5.7% in The Netherlands for 2001–2002 (Miccinesi et al. 2006: 125), while a more recent study found palliative sedation rates in The Netherlands of 8.2% in 2005 and 12.3% in 2010 (Onwuteaka-Philipsen et al. 2012: 909).

[11] As mentioned earlier, while professional guidelines generally reject palliative sedation for existential suffering, there is at least a minority view allowing sedation for existential suffering (Cherny & Radbruch 2009: 584). Among experts in medical ethics, the level of support may be even higher. In a European survey of mostly German ethicists, more than half thought palliative sedation permissible for incurable mental suffering, though support dropped a little if artificial nutrition would be withheld (Simon et al. 2007: 4).

of palliative sedation to relieve 'existential' or 'psycho-existential' suffering, which can include feelings of anxiety, despair, meaninglessness and other forms of mental anguish (Claessens et al. 2008: 325; Bruce & Boston 2011: 2733–4). In a study at a palliative care unit in Germany, for example, anxiety or psychological distress was the main reason for palliative sedation of 29% of patients between 1995 and 1999 and 47% of patients between 2000 and 2002 (Muller-Busch et al. 2003).

Other studies also find that palliative sedation is often provided for relief of existential suffering. Among Japanese oncologists and palliative care physicians, 38% reported the use of palliative sedation for psychological distress (Morita et al. 2002a: 750),[12] and an international survey of palliative care experts found that anguish, anxiety or emotional distress accounted for about one-third of palliative sedation cases (Chater et al. 1998: 259, 261).

While the use of palliative sedation has been extended to relieve existential suffering in some patients, we should worry that it may not be made available to protect other patients from needless physical suffering. For many years, studies have found that substantial numbers of patients die without relief of their pain, with shortness of breath or other discomforting symptoms. In the SUPPORT study of US patients hospitalised with a diagnosis of life-threatening disease, family members reported that among the patients who died, half did so without adequate treatment for their pain (Support Principal Investigators 1995). Similarly, a study of patients who died while hospitalised in Italy found that 48% of those who suffered from severe pain received no pain relievers at all (Toscani et al. 2005: 36). Other studies have shown similar failures to treat pain in dying patients (van den Beuken-van Everdingen et al. 2007: 1441; Escobar Pinzon et al. 2012).[13] For many of these patients, palliative therapies other than palliative sedation would probably be sufficient. Still, there are undoubtedly a number of patients who do not receive the palliative sedation they should be receiving.

There are other gaps between principle and practice. As with medical treatments generally, palliative sedation should be administered only with the informed consent of the patient or the patient's family or of another surrogate decision maker (Chambaere et al. 2010: 491). In some settings, that is almost always the case. According to a national Dutch study, consent was obtained from patient or family in 96% of

[12] The 38% figure represents use of continuous deep sedation. Forty-six per cent of the physicians administered intermittent-deep sedation and 64% administered mild sedation for psychological distress.
[13] However, some healthcare providers have made substantial strides in responding to patient pain (Walling et al. 2010).

cases (Rietjens et al. 2006: 750). However, a study of palliative sedation practices in Flanders (Belgium) found that consent was not obtained from patient or family in 20% of all cases and in 27% of hospitalised patients who died after palliative sedation (Chambaere et al. 2010: 491–2).[14] One-third of ICU nurses in a European study reported that patients and/or family were not routinely involved in decisions about whether to withhold or withdraw life-sustaining treatment (Latour et al. 2009: 115).

Access to palliative sedation should depend on the needs of patients, but use of palliative sedation appears to depend to a large extent on the preferences of the patients' physicians. In a study of 2 hospitals and 56 palliative care units in Italy, researchers did not find any correlation between the need for control of patient symptoms and the likelihood that patients would receive palliative sedation (Peruselli et al. 1999: 239). Moreover, other studies have found that patient access to palliative sedation may turn on the physician's field of practice or other personal attributes. In one study, for example, researchers found that the use of palliative sedation to relieve psychological distress varied by type of physician. That study reported on practices in The Netherlands, where 36% of medical specialists viewed anxiety as an indication for palliative sedation while 65% of nursing home physicians did so (Hasselaar et al. 2008: 538). In the UK, non-religious doctors are more likely to provide palliative sedation (Seale 2010: 48–9), and a US study found that a physician's ethnicity or religion could affect whether the doctor objected to the use of palliative sedation (Curlin et al. 2008: 116–17).[15]

A Japanese study also indicates how a physician's personal views may play a role in governing access to palliative sedation. In a survey of attitudes and practices for palliative sedation among oncologists and palliative care physicians, researchers found that doctors were more likely to favour palliative sedation for their patients when they expressed a greater preference for palliative sedation for their own end-of-life care (Morita et al. 2002a: 761).[16]

[14] In another Belgian study, failure to obtain consent occurred in about one-quarter of cases involving the 'alleviation of pain and symptoms with possible life-shortening effect' (De Gendt et al. 2009: 103). Palliative sedation cases were a subset of the alleviation cases, so may have had a higher or lower level of non-consent.
[15] In a study of Australia and six European countries, however, researchers found small differences across countries among different physicians based on their religion, although differences might be big within countries (Cohen et al. 2008: 251).
[16] In a study of US internists, researchers did not find any correlation between physicians' belief in the value of palliative care and the likelihood of physicians reporting that they had referred patients for palliative care (Ahluwalia & Fried 2009).

The intent of the physician in providing palliative sedation also may depart from what is permitted by principle. Many commentators prefer palliative sedation to physician-aid-in-dying because it is not supposed to hasten death. While aid-in-dying achieves its goal of symptom relief by ending the patient's life, palliative sedation can relieve suffering without shortening the patient's lifespan. To be sure, palliative sedation may sometimes hasten death, but principles of 'double effect' permit physicians to offer treatments that may cause death when the risk of death is an unintended side-effect rather than an intended outcome (Cowan & Palmer 2002: 244; Lo & Rubenfeld 2005: 1812). Professional guidelines require that palliative sedation not be used to intentionally cause a patient's death (American Medical Association 2008; Chambaere et al. 2010: 490).

However, a number of scholars have warned that palliative sedation can easily become a form of 'slow euthanasia', with physicians sedating the patient and then withdrawing all nutrition and hydration to ensure that the patient dies (Billings & Block 1996; Orentlicher 1997b). Studies generally find that in a substantial minority – and sometimes a majority – of palliative sedation patients, nutrition and hydration are withdrawn (Claessens et al. 2008: 326). Moreover, researchers have found that many decisions to provide palliative sedation may reflect an intent to hasten death. In the Belgian study of Chambaere et al. mentioned above, hastening death was intended by physicians in 17% of patients who received palliative sedation (Chambaere et al. 2010: 491–2). In a Dutch study, there was a partial intent to hasten death in 47% of cases and an explicit intent to hasten death in 17% of cases (Rietjens et al. 2004: 183, 2006: 751). In a UK study, palliative sedation was associated with a higher rate of requests by patients or families for a hastening of death; it also was associated with a higher rate of other end-of-life decisions that were driven in part by the physician's intent to hasten death (Seale 2010: 49).[17]

Although there is evidence that palliative sedation is sometimes administered with the intent to hasten death, it is not clear that it actually has such an effect. Most studies that have looked at the question do not find any shortening of life. To be sure, the data are not definitive. In one study that looked at palliative sedation accompanied by the withdrawal of artificial nutrition and hydration (ANH), physicians

[17] However, these associations may not reflect cause and effect. For many patients, intractable suffering may lead to a desire for palliative sedation and for a hastened death, but the palliative sedation may be a response to the intractable suffering independently of the intention for a hastened death (Seale 2010: 51).

believed that life was shortened by more than a week in 27% of patients (Rietjens et al. 2004). But other studies have not found a difference in survival between patients receiving sedation and comparable patients who were not sedated, even when some of the sedated patients did not receive ANH (Muller-Busch et al. 2003; Claessens et al. 2008; Maltoni et al. 2012b). In addition, while physicians deviate from some elements of palliative sedation guidelines, they appear to follow the requirement that they limit sedation to patients with a life expectancy of no more than two weeks. Studies either find that sedated patients always die within a week or two (Fainsinger et al. 2000; Muller-Busch et al. 2003; Kohara et al. 2005), or they find that only 2–3% of patients survive for more than two weeks once they are sedated (Rietjens et al. 2008a; Chambaere et al. 2010).[18]

3.   Why the gaps between principle and practice?

To some extent, the observed differences between principle and practice may be outdated, because practice has changed since the studies were done. More likely, though, the gap between principle and practice reflects a number of other factors.

For example, even though palliative sedation is permitted by law, its use is controversial for many people. Some physicians view palliative sedation as ethically problematic and therefore will hesitate to offer it to their patients even when permitted under professional standards of care. In addition, the controversial nature of palliative sedation may lead professional groups to set unduly narrow limits for its use. Many patients who could benefit from palliative sedation would then be deemed ineligible for that option.

Furthermore, it is difficult to practise medicine according to someone else's preferences. Even when physicians make every conscious effort to be guided by the desires of their patients, they ultimately can see only through their own eyes. Physicians' assessments are inevitably coloured by their own value systems. If a physician views the benefit from palliative sedation as substantial, the physician is more likely to offer it than is a physician who views the benefit as less significant.

Variations in practice are common throughout medicine, whether dealing with end-of-life care for dying patients or routine surgeries

---

[18] With a life expectancy of a few days or maybe a week or two, the discontinuation of ANH may not have an effect on survival (Raus et al. 2012: 333). According to the Dutch guideline, palliative sedation should be accompanied by the withdrawal or withholding of ANH (KNMG 2009b: 25–6).

for young patients facing a long and healthy lifespan. Physicians often develop their practice patterns for idiosyncratic reasons, and that reality will influence the use of palliative sedation.

In addition to the empirical studies discussed earlier, a number of other studies illustrate how palliative sedation practices can be influenced by considerations other than the patient's healthcare needs. For example, in the study comparing palliative sedation in Flanders (northern Belgium), The Netherlands and the UK, there were significant differences in the frequency of use across the three countries even though there were no meaningful differences in demographic or medical characteristics of the patients in the three countries (Anquinet et al. 2012). Similarly, in a study comparing the northern, Dutch-speaking and southern, French-speaking communities in Belgium, palliative sedation was almost twice as common in the south (15% compared to 8% of non-sudden deaths), even after controlling for differences among patients (Van den Block et al. 2009).

In the study comparing northern and southern Belgium, other end-of-life practices, such as euthanasia or withdrawal of life-sustaining treatment were more common in the northern part of the country. The authors surmised that the Dutch-speaking community may be more receptive to end-of-life practices that are intended to have a life-shortening effect, while the French-speaking community may prefer treatments such as palliative sedation that allow for a longer life or that have their life-shortening effect indirectly (Van den Block et al. 2009: 85).[19]

Cultural values may influence not only the likelihood that palliative sedation is provided but also the reasons why it is provided. In a study of sedation administration by palliative care programmes in Israel, South Africa and Spain, researchers found that existential suffering was much more likely to serve as a rationale in Spain than in Israel or South

---

[19] Because of methodological differences (including data collection periods) between the substudies in the northern and southern parts of Belgium, there is also a possibility that the study by Van den Block et al. underestimated the palliative sedation rate in northern Belgium and that palliative sedation rates really are similar in the two parts of Belgium. In the northern Belgium, Netherlands, UK study, researchers found a 15% rate of palliative sedation for northern Belgium (Anquinet et al. 2012). It may be important that the two studies relied on data from different time periods. The 15% study was based on 2007 data while the 8% study was based on 2005–6 data. In addition, the studies gathered their information from different sources. Both studies involved retrospective questionnaires for physicians whose patients had died, but the 15% study surveyed attending physicians, while the 8% study surveyed general practitioners who were asked whether they or another physician had provided palliative sedation. It may be that by surveying general practitioners, the 8% study underestimated palliative sedation in hospitalised patients (Van den Block et al. 2009: 83).

Africa. The researchers thought that their finding reflected Spanish social practices around death. As part of a 'conspiracy of silence' about dying, Spanish patients are less likely to be told of a cancer diagnosis than are patients in other countries, making conversations about end-of-life care difficult (Fainsinger et al. 2000: 264).

As mentioned earlier, we should not be surprised that palliative sedation rates vary with differences in cultural values. The preferences of patients will reflect the values of their communities. Nevertheless, when medical practice is driven by community sentiments, there will be many patients who do not share their communities' values and who therefore will not have their healthcare needs met.

To some extent, the gaps between principle and practice for palliative sedation may reflect a view by physicians that professional guidelines are too restrictive. Under the Dutch guideline, for example, one criterion for palliative sedation is a life expectancy of no more than two weeks (KNMG 2009b).[20] However, in a study of physician attitudes in The Netherlands, some doctors felt that other aspects of the patient's clinical situation could justify palliative sedation when life expectancy was three weeks or more (Rietjens et al. 2009a: 413). Similarly, even though the Dutch guideline restricts palliative sedation to patients with refractory physical symptoms, such as pain, shortness of breath or delirium, some physicians felt that the distinction between physical suffering and existential suffering was not necessarily a valid one and that they would therefore consider providing palliative sedation to patients whose suffering was predominantly existential (Verkerk et al. 2007: 667; Rietjens et al. 2009a: 410, 413–14).

Physician views about end-of-life care have caused gaps between principle and practice before, as in the case of decisions about life-sustaining treatment. For example, while under legal rules and prevailing ethical principle it is just as permissible to withdraw care as to withhold it, many physicians and laypersons believe it is more problematic to withdraw care than to withhold it, and physicians may be slower to withdraw care than to withhold it. The withdrawer of care seems more responsible for a patient's demise than a withholder of care. Yet in some ways it is more problematic to withhold than to withdraw. If treatment is withheld, the opportunity is lost to find out whether medical care can provide an unexpected benefit. On the other hand, treatment is withdrawn only after it fails to provide sufficient benefit (Orentlicher et al. 2008: 244).

---

[20] The guideline also contemplates palliative sedation for patients with a life expectancy longer than two weeks in 'highly exceptional situation[s]' (KNMG 2009b: 26–7).

As mentioned earlier, another gap between principle and practice exists with regard to the withholding of life-sustaining treatment from patients with an excellent prognosis. While a person's right to refuse treatment does not depend on the individual's medical condition or the nature of the treatment, some trial court judges will order a blood transfusion over the patient's objection for patients who are young and can be restored to excellent health (Orentlicher et al. 2008: 251).

These gaps between principle and practice for withdrawal of care reflect the same considerations that give rise to the gaps between principle and practice for palliative sedation. In particular, physicians bring their own moral perspective to their decision-making, and they may rely on their own views rather than on those of their patients.[21]

4.   How should we address the gaps between principle and practice?

If there are significant gaps between principle and practice, how should public policy address them? A full answer to that question is beyond the scope of this chapter. The principle–practice divide is common in the practice of medicine and needs to be addressed in its broader context.

Moreover, deciding whether a particular gap reflects a problem with principle or practice may require empirical data that are not available. For example, I observed that palliative sedation is used more often than would be expected for a therapy that is characterised as a rarely needed treatment of last resort. It may be the case that some physicians provide palliative sedation when other palliative treatments would be effective – a problem with practice – or it may be the case that policymakers have underestimated the need for palliative sedation – a problem with principle. In the absence of a systematic review of palliative sedation cases by palliative care experts, one cannot tell which explanation is more accurate.

Still, there are some observations that can be made about gaps between principle and practice for palliative sedation. As mentioned, some gaps reflect problems with principle, while others reflect problems with practice. Accordingly, different responses are needed for different gaps.

---

[21] Is it possible that differences in patient values rather than in physician values can explain some of the differences in access to palliative sedation and other end-of-life care? That may be part of the equation, but physicians generally exercise greater control than patients over decisions about end-of-life care (Orentlicher 1994b: 1280–8).

To the extent that physicians fail to observe appropriate principles, experience suggests that tighter monitoring of physician practices and the threat of legal enforcement can be effective. Professional associations may be able to fashion good guidelines, but they typically lack the ability or willingness to enforce them (Orentlicher 1994a: 591–605). If healthcare providers understand that the law will hold them to their professional responsibilities, they will be more scrupulous in adhering to them. Greater compliance with guidelines can also be achieved if physicians understand that compliance affords them protection from prosecution or other legal action. Thus, after the Royal Dutch Medical Association issued its 2005 guideline on palliative sedation, and the government informed physicians that they would not be prosecuted if they observed the guideline, physicians reported that they were more likely to obtain informed consent before administering palliative sedation. Doctors also reported that they were more likely to use appropriate drugs to sedate their patients (although that could reflect growing experience with palliative sedation rather than the guideline's impact, since Italy saw the same improvement) (Hasselaar et al. 2009a: 432, 435).[22] Although the Hasselaar et al. study did not have data on patient life expectancy before 2005, comparison of its post-2005 data with other pre-2005 data suggests that physicians also were more likely to adhere to the requirement that patients not have a life expectancy of greater than two weeks. After 2005, physicians reported that 7% of their palliative sedation patients had a life expectancy greater than two weeks (Hasselaar et al. 2009a: 433), while physicians in a pre-2005 study reported that 6% of palliative sedation patients had a life expectancy greater than one month, and 21% had a life expectancy of one to four weeks (Rietjens et al. 2004: 182).

In short, when physicians deviate from appropriate principles, greater enforcement by the legal system may be important. To make enforcement feasible, governments could require physicians to report their palliative sedation cases to public health authorities or review committees, as is required of physicians in Oregon and Washington for physician-aid-in-dying and of physicians in Belgium and The Netherlands for euthanasia and physician-aid-in-dying (Buiting et al. 2009).

---

[22] The impact of the Dutch guideline on reported physician practices may have been amplified by being perceived as having the force of law, a perception which appears to be held to a significant extent (Verkerk et al. 2007: 667; Hasselaar et al. 2009a: 432).

As indicated earlier, sometimes physician deviations from palliative sedation guidelines reflect problems with the guidelines. Physicians may find that they cannot meet their patients' needs by strict adherence to their professional standards. And we should expect a need for guidelines to evolve as they are implemented and studied. It would be surprising if palliative sedation guidelines worked perfectly.

As mentioned, physicians have expressed concern about the requirement that patients have a very short life expectancy in order to be eligible for palliative sedation. A patient may have a life expectancy of three or four weeks and yet need palliative sedation to relieve suffering. Under guidelines in The Netherlands, Norway, the United States and elsewhere, however, the patient would not be considered eligible for the sedation. While the exact terms vary from guideline to guideline, the different guidelines all require that the patient be very terminally ill: death should be expected 'within one or two weeks' (KNMG 2009b: 6), or the patient should be in the 'final stages of terminal illness' (American Medical Association 2008: 6), or the patient must have 'entered the final phase' of a terminal illness and be 'imminently dying' (US Veterans Health Administration 2007: 486) or patients should be in the 'very terminal stages of their illness with an expected prognosis of hours or days at most' (Cherny & Radbruch 2009: 584). When a principle does not allow for optimal practice, it usually should be modified to foster good practice.

That said, there may be good reasons to maintain some limits based on the life expectancy of patients. There are times when principles make sense even when they do not seem to permit optimal practices. If palliative sedation were available to any patient with unbearable suffering that cannot be relieved by other measures, then we would raise the risk of abuse. As mentioned earlier, some commentators worry that palliative sedation may be used as a form of slow euthanasia. Physicians could sedate patients with a life expectancy of a year or two, whose suffering is not truly refractory, and ensure the patients' demise by withholding nutrition and hydration. By restricting the use of palliative sedation based on life expectancy, the risks of abuse can be greatly reduced.

But even if the patient's life expectancy should be taken into account in setting guidelines, it is not clear that two weeks is the appropriate cut-off. We may draw a better balance between the need to relieve patient suffering and the need to protect patients from abuse by allowing palliative sedation for all terminally ill patients who satisfy the other criteria for the treatment (e.g. unbearable physical suffering that cannot be relieved by other palliative therapies), especially if we require that terminally ill patients with a life expectancy of more than two weeks possess decision-making capacity.[23] Such patients would be in a position to protect their own interests, and that would provide an important safeguard against abuse. Indeed, statutory proposals for legalised aid-in-dying in the United States include as one of their key requirements that the patients possess decision-making capacity.

I have observed that physicians often offer palliative sedation for the relief of existential suffering despite the fact that professional guidelines generally reject existential suffering as a justification for the treatment. Does this reflect a problem with principle or practice? As I have written before, if a patient is suffering severely and irreversibly, it should not matter whether the source of the suffering is physical, psychological or existential (Orentlicher 2001: 72). This suggests that the rejection of existential suffering needs rethinking.

On the other hand, just as the two-week life expectancy principle is designed to reduce the risk of abuse, so is the existential suffering principle. We need to ensure that when patients choose options for the relief of suffering that may shorten their lives, their choices reflect informed and considered decisions rather than thinking clouded by irrationality, misunderstanding or diminished mental capacity. While physicians can assess decision-making capacity directly, these assessments are imperfect (Orentlicher 2001: 62–3). To protect against the possibility that a patient will incorrectly be viewed as making an informed and considered decision for a palliative treatment that could shorten the patient's life, drafters of professional guidelines or legal rules commonly look for 'objective' measures of suffering. Objective measures provide reassurance that the patient is making a genuine choice for treatment – if we can be confident that the patient really is suffering, then we have identified a legitimate reason for the patient's choice. And symptoms of physical pain seem much more objective than the highly subjective symptom of existential suffering (Orentlicher 2001: 72–3). In this view, the existential suffering exclusion is regrettable for the undue suffering that it imposes on some patients, but is necessary to reduce the risk of premature death for other patients.

How one should come down on the balance between reducing the risk of premature deaths and preventing undue suffering is not always clear, but we can resolve the question in a way similar to the one I suggested for the two-week life expectancy principle. If other safeguards

---

[23] Patients would be terminally ill if they had a life expectancy of no more than six months.

are able to protect against the misuse of palliative sedation, the existential suffering safeguard may not be necessary. Indeed, this is essentially the view taken by the Dutch guidelines, which observe that when patients have reached the last week or two of life, they are 'very seriously ill … and their bodily functions are breaking down. In other words, the issue here is never solely existential suffering' (KNMG 2009b: 25). In short, as long as palliative sedation is limited to patients expected to die within two weeks, it seems unnecessary to reject existential suffering as a justification. Of course, this means that relaxation of the two-week requirement makes it more difficult to relax the existential suffering exclusion.

Finally, it is important to remember that any reforms of palliative sedation guidelines should be undertaken as part of a broader reform of palliative care. The troubling persistence of unrelieved suffering among patients with terminal illness may not reflect a substantial failure to use palliative sedation properly. Rather, it likely reflects a failure to use other palliative therapies aggressively enough. Physicians often are too reluctant to use pain-relieving medications at the high doses that dying patients may need.

5.   Conclusion

The gaps between principle and practice for palliative sedation are important, but not unique. Gaps between principle and practice are common with other end-of-life practices. Some of the gaps reflect troubling failures with physician practices, as with the failure to obtain informed consent. Other gaps reflect problems with palliative sedation guidelines, as with the requirement that patients have a life expectancy of no more than two weeks.

Because the gaps between principle and practice reflect a mix of problems with principle and problems with practice, responses to the gaps must include greater enforcement of some of the professional standards and reforms of other standards.

8   The legal permissibility of continuous deep sedation at the end of life: a comparison of laws and a proposal

Evelien Delbeke

1.   Introduction

Continuous deep sedation (CDS) at the end of life is a medical practice that is widely accepted and used. It is broadly agreed that if a patient is in intolerable pain that cannot be treated otherwise (i.e. has so-called refractory symptoms), then CDS should be started.

Probably because of this widespread acceptance and use, little has been written to date on the *legal* permissibility of CDS. Nonetheless, CDS does not come without problems: a life-shortening effect is often attributed to CDS. If a patient dies (earlier) because of this medical treatment, the caregiver who performed CDS might be found to be criminally liable. Therefore, it is important to examine the legal status of CDS and to explore the conditions under which CDS is legally justified.

2.   Legal status of continuous deep sedation

First of all, we need to examine whether CDS poses any legal problems at all. CDS is often combined with the decision to withhold artificial nutrition and hydration (ANH). This section, however, is limited to CDS *with* ANH. The effects of the withholding of ANH in patients who are continuously and deeply sedated are examined in section 4.

2.1.   Liability

It is often said that CDS shortens the patient's life. There are studies indicating that, although sedation at the end of life is generally a safe measure for many patients, a small risk of hastened death for individual patients exists, for example through respiratory depression, aspiration and haemodynamic compromise (Cherny & Radbruch 2009). If CDS

This chapter is a shortened and translated version of a chapter in Delbeke (2012).

does indeed shorten life, then this inevitably has legal consequences. As noted earlier, when CDS causes the (earlier) death of the patient, the caregiver providing CDS may be criminally liable. Depending on the exact intentions and circumstances, causing (earlier) death can be classified as murder, or as voluntary or involuntary manslaughter.

However, others are of the opinion that CDS has no life-shortening effect, or at least that no such effect has been proven (Sykes & Thorns 2003b; Maltoni et al. 2009). These authors refer to clinical studies showing no difference in the length of survival between sedated and non-sedated patients (Ventafridda et al. 1990; Morita et al. 2001a).

However, CDS does not have to be lethal for it to be a criminal offence. In Belgium, for example, when someone administers a drug that is potentially lethal, and when this causes an incurable disease or handicap to the victim, she is also criminally liable.[1] The fact that the consciousness of the patient is lowered or permanently removed as a result of the administration of sedatives in CDS might be sufficient for criminal prosecution.

This leads to the conclusion that, whether or not CDS *in itself* has a life-shortening effect, in any event it could be classified as a criminal act. It is self-evident that such a state of affairs is not desirable as it would severely interfere with good and adequate pain management. Accordingly, several countries have provided a legally valid justification for CDS in order to counteract this possibility of CDS being held to be a criminal act.

2.2.   Possible grounds of justification

Various grounds have been advanced in order to justify CDS as a legally acceptable act. I shall discuss the doctrine of double effect, the concept of necessity, the concept of normal medical practice and the approach of explicit permission by law.

2.2.1.   Doctrine of double effect

The ground of justification that is probably best known in the context of pain management is the doctrine of double effect. According to this doctrine, an act that has a foreseen harmful effect that cannot be separated from the intended good effect is justifiable if the physician only intended the good effect and not the harmful one (Latham 1997; Quill et al. 1997a; Williams 2001). In the case of CDS, this means that the caregiver foresees the patient's death as a consequence of CDS, but administers CDS with the intention only to relieve the patient's

---

[1] See Article 403 of the Belgian Penal Code.

suffering, and not to cause death. The doctrine of double effect thus relies on the *intent* of the caregiver.

This doctrine is predominantly relied on by the courts in the UK,[2] the USA[3] and Canada[4] to justify pain management techniques, such as CDS, which may have a life-shortening effect.

However, the doctrine of double effect cannot serve as an adequate justification for CDS, for several reasons. First, the doctrine is completely dependent on the *intention* of the agent, and it is very difficult to know what her exact intention was at the moment of her act. Moreover, while providing CDS a caregiver might act with multiple intentions, e.g. not only to relieve pain but also to hasten death (Williams 2001; Kuhse 2004). This was shown in a Flemish study on continuous sedation: in no less than 17 per cent of cases, there was found to be a (co) intention to hasten death (Chambaere et al. 2010). Finally, and most importantly, the doctrine is inconsistent with principles of criminal law. Even if one does not intend the consequences of one's act, but foresees them and nevertheless proceeds with the act, one is criminally liable (Price 1997; Otlowski 2000; Jackson 2006). The criminal punishment may be less severe because the agent did not intend the patient's death, but the agent will be held liable because she *knew* her act might lead to the patient's death.

2.2.2. Necessity
Some make an appeal to the legal concept of necessity. According to this concept, a criminal act can be justified if it was necessary to prevent greater harm.

The concept of necessity implies a conflict between two goods, one of which is considered more important and thus given priority. In

[2] See *R* v. *Adams* (1957) and *Airedale NHS Trust* v. *Bland* (1993). There is, however, doubt whether the doctrine of double effect can still be applied after the judgment of the House of Lords in *R* v. *Woollin* (1998). See also Pattinson (2006) and McLean (2007).
[3] See *Vacco* v. *Quill* (1997), pages 802 and 808, footnote 11: 'Just as a state may prohibit assisting suicide while permitting patients to refuse unwanted lifesaving treatment, it may permit palliative care related to that refusal, which may have the foreseen but unintended "double effect" of hastening the patient's death'.
[4] See *Rodriguez* v. *British Columbia* (1993), paragraph 57; Judge Sopinka ruled that: 'The administration of drugs designed for pain control in dosages which the physician knows will hasten death constitutes active contribution to death by any standard. However, the distinction drawn here is one based upon intention – in the case of palliative care the intention is to ease pain, which has the effect of hastening death, while in the case of assisted suicide, the intention is undeniably to cause death ... In my view, distinctions based upon intent are important, and in fact form the basis of our criminal law. While factually the distinction may, at times, be difficult to draw, legally it is clear.'

the context of palliative care, the conflict exists between maintaining the patient's life on the one hand, and alleviating the patient's severe suffering on the other hand. In the case of CDS, the alleviation of the patient's severe suffering is considered more important.

This ground of justification implies two conditions. First, one can only appeal to the concept of necessity when no less far-reaching means are available to achieve the alleviation of the suffering (subsidiarity). Second, the dose of sedatives administered to the patient should not be higher than that needed to alleviate the patient's suffering (proportionality).

This ground of justification was used by the Bundesgerichtshof (German Supreme Court) in the 'Dolantin' case in 1996. In this case, three physicians were prosecuted for administering 300 mg Dolantin (pethidine – an opioid) and two ampoules of Atosil (promethazine – an antihistamine) to an 88-year-old terminally ill patient. There was some disagreement between the experts as to whether the administered dose was lethal. Nevertheless, the court decided that being able to have a dignified and pain-free death is a higher good than being able to live a little longer but in severe pain. The court thus clearly applied the concept of necessity.

To my mind, applying the legal concept of necessity as the only ground of justification for pain management and CDS would not be satisfactory, for two reasons. First, this concept is meant for exceptional cases, to permit – under very strict conditions – an exception to the general rule. It can hardly be said that pain management is an exception to the rule – it is a well-accepted practice that takes place daily. Second, this concept would not provide caregivers with legal certainty. Necessity is subject to the judgment of the court when it comes to prosecution. It is the court that decides whether the conditions required for necessity are fulfilled. As a consequence, a caregiver would never be certain *in advance* about the legal consequences of her act.

2.2.3.   Normal medical care as set out in a professional guideline

A third approach to the legal justification of CDS is to consider it to be 'normal medical practice', i.e. not different from any other medical treatment, and to lay down specific rules in a guideline drawn up by a professional medical association or a multidisciplinary commission.

This approach can be seen in The Netherlands, where CDS is justified on the same legal ground as any other 'normal' medical treatment: the so-called 'medical exception' (Leenen et al. 2007; Griffiths et al. 2008). The Royal Dutch Medical Association has published an extensive guideline on palliative sedation, in which the conditions for CDS are laid out (KNMG 2009a).

A guideline has the advantage of being easily adaptable to changes in medicine and in moral values. Nonetheless, it has to be stressed that CDS is potentially a criminal matter. Guidelines do not have the same legal force as legislation (Hyman 1996). They do have legal relevance as they are often referred to when interpreting the law. They can enable a clearer specification of a legal requirement. Nonetheless, it is the task of the legislator (and not of a professional medical association or a multidisciplinary commission) to determine the basic framework, the conditions under which an act as far-reaching as CDS is permitted, especially since there is the underlying risk that it may be found to be a criminal act.

2.2.4. Statutory legislation

A final possible avenue for the legal justification of CDS is to permit it explicitly by law, and so provide it with a clear ground of justification in the law which neutralises the underlying risk of it being considered a criminal act.

As far as pain management is concerned, this approach can be found in Belgium. The Belgian Acts on Patients' Rights and on Palliative Care[5] stipulate that a patient has a right to adequate pain management and a right to palliative care, which is defined as the entirety of multi-disciplinary care, on a physical, psychological, social and moral level.

Even more explicit examples of this approach can be found in the laws of France and Luxembourg. Their legislation even takes into account the possible life-shortening effect of pain management and of CDS, and lays down the requirements that have to be met.

Thus, in France, Article L. 1110-5 of the Law on Public Health[6] provides that:

If the physician notices that he can only alleviate the suffering of a person, in an advanced or terminal stage of an incurable and severe disease, whatever the cause, by administering a treatment that might, as a secondary effect, shorten the patient's life, he must inform the patient of this.[7]

---

[5] Wet van 22 augustus 2002 betreffende de rechten van de patiënt and Wet van 14 juni 2002 betreffende de palliatieve zorg. For details, see References (Laws section).

[6] Code de la Santé Publique. For details, see References (Laws section).

[7] Author's translation from French. In the original, the Article states: 'Si le médecin constate qu'il ne peut soulager la souffrance d'une personne, en phase avancée ou terminale d'une affection grave et incurable, quelle qu'en soit la cause, qu'en lui appliquant un traitement qui peut avoir pour effet secondaire d'abréger sa vie, il doit en informer le malade.'

Luxembourg has a similar legal provision. Article 3 of Luxembourg's Act of 16 March 2009 regarding palliative care, advance directives and support at the end of life[8] provides that:

The physician has the obligation to adequately alleviate the physical and psychological suffering of the person at the end of life. If the physician notices that he can only adequately alleviate the suffering of a person, in an advanced or terminal stage of an incurable and severe disease, whatever the cause, by administering a treatment that might, as a secondary effect, hasten the patient's death, he must inform the patient of this and obtain his consent.[9]

In my opinion, the approach of enacting statutory legislation – in which the legislator explicitly takes into account the possible life-shortening effect of pain management – is the most preferable of the four approaches discussed here. First, it explicitly removes the possibility of CDS being found to be a criminal act by using a legal instrument that has the same legal force as the criminal law. Second, this approach provides caregivers with a clear framework in which the crucial requirements are defined. The latter, of course, can be further refined in a guideline.

3.   Conditions for the permissibility of CDS

There are four conditions determining the permissibility of CDS: (1) there has to be an indication for CDS; (2) CDS has to be proportional; (3) there has to be informed consent by or on behalf of the patient; and (4) certain procedural requirements have to be met.

I shall look into each of these, starting with a discussion of the indications for CDS. In this context, the main questions that arise are, first, what kinds of symptoms may qualify as 'refractory', and, second, does the patient have to be dying in order for CDS to be permissible?

3.1.   Indications for CDS

3.1.1.   Refractory symptoms
It is generally agreed that CDS can only be initiated in patients who are suffering severely due to *refractory* symptoms (Quill & Byock 2000;

---

[8] Loi du 16 mars relative aux soins palliatifs. For details, see References (Laws section).
[9] Author's translation from French. In the original, the Article provides that: 'Le médecin a l'obligation de soulager efficacement la souffrance physique et psychique de la personne en fin de vie. Si le médecin constate qu'il ne peut efficacement soulager la souffrance d'une personne en phase avancée ou terminale d'une affection grave et incurable, qu'elle qu'en soit la cause, qu'en lui appliquant un traitement qui peut avoir pour effet secondaire d'avancer sa fin de vie, il doit l'en informer et recueillir son consentement.'

Cherny & Radbruch 2009). A symptom is considered to be refractory when there is no other method than CDS that can be used for palliation within an acceptable time frame and/or without unacceptable adverse effects (Cherny & Radbruch 2009).

Refractory symptoms can be physical and/or psychological. Physical refractory symptoms include, amongst others, agitated delirium, dyspnoea, pain and convulsions (Cherny & Radbruch 2009). Psychological refractory symptoms include, for example, anxiety, existential distress and refractory depression (Cherny & Radbruch 2009).

It is commonly accepted that CDS can be indicated in cases of untreatable *physical* suffering. However, the question arises as to whether CDS could also be started in cases of *mere* psychological suffering (and thus without a physical component because, for example, the physical suffering is controlled through other pain medication). Different stances are taken on this issue.

Some are of the opinion that CDS is not the right answer to mere psychological refractory suffering, e.g. existential distress. They argue that this type of suffering should be treated in other ways, for example with social assistance, spiritual counselling or non-sedative drugs (Jansen & Sulmasy 2002; American Medical Association 2008). However, I would argue that this view underestimates psychological suffering, suffering which can be as severe as physical suffering. When psychological suffering does not respond to any other treatment, I consider that one cannot maintain that CDS is unjustified merely because there is no physical suffering.

Others contend that psychological suffering should be treated with *intermittent* sedation (Rousseau 2005a; Cherny & Radbruch 2009). They point to the fact that patients with existential suffering often become trapped in a downward spiral of fear, sleeplessness and tiredness. Sedating such patients for a short time might allow them to regain their strength. It is indeed important to try less drastic treatments first, before starting CDS, if it is thought they can alleviate the patient's suffering. However, this stance does not resolve the question as to whether CDS is justified when intermittent sedation does not alleviate the psychological suffering of the patient.

In a final approach, with which I agree, CDS is accepted for severe psychological suffering that cannot be treated otherwise (Morita 2004a; Schuman-Olivier et al. 2008; Cassell & Rich 2010). As already mentioned, psychological suffering can be as severe as physical suffering. There is no reason why patients with refractory psychological suffering should be excluded from a right to adequate pain management. Excluding mere psychological suffering from the range of application of

CDS would underestimate its severity. Indeed, empirical studies indicate that CDS is applied increasingly frequently in cases of psychological suffering (Muller-Busch et al. 2003; Hasselaar et al. 2008).

Obviously, it cannot be denied that, compared to physical suffering, it is more difficult to diagnose psychological suffering as refractory. Psychological suffering will inevitably need to be assessed more strictly than physical suffering. The refractory nature of the psychological suffering should at least be repeatedly assessed by a physician specialised in mental health care and with sufficient expertise (Cherny 1998; Hauser & Walsh 2009).

3.1.2.   Dying or non-dying patients

The majority of medical and legal commentators presuppose one crucial condition for the (legal) permissibility of CDS: the patient has to be terminally ill. Death has to be expected within hours, days or, at most, two weeks.

The reasons given in the literature for restricting CDS to dying patients are limited. According to some, CDS for non-dying patients does not satisfy the requirement of proportionality (Schuman-Olivier et al. 2008). CDS in patients expected to survive longer is regarded as disproportionate and ethically unacceptable: a sustained existence without any consciousness would be purposeless.

However, from a legal point of view, it seems strange to allow access to adequate pain management only to dying patients. I consider that the core determining factor for the permissibility of CDS should be the otherwise untreatable and intolerable suffering of the patient. Every patient has a right to adequate pain and symptom management and it should not be restricted to those with a limited life expectation.

In any event, the requirement for a limited life expectancy can be circumvented. The patient can herself decide to no longer take food and fluids. By doing this, she precipitates the dying process, since humans can only survive for a maximum of two weeks without fluids. It may be clear that requiring this decision of a patient who is suffering intractably in order for her to receive adequate pain management is neither desirable nor acceptable. It would affect the right to self-determination of the patient, since she would be forced to starve herself in order to receive adequate pain management. I therefore conclude that access to CDS should not be limited to dying patients. Non-dying patients who are suffering intractably also have a right to adequate pain management and to CDS.

There is, however, one important distinction between CDS for dying and for non-dying patients. Lo and Rubenfeld correctly point to the fact that, in a non-dying patient, it will be more difficult to conclude that the symptoms are intractable. The more extended time frame available with the non-dying patient allows a wider range of palliative options to be considered and tried (Lo & Rubenfeld 2005). In dying patients, on the other hand, their limited time frame will often lead to the diagnosis of suffering as otherwise untreatable.

In view of the difficulties of assessing the refractory nature of the suffering in non-dying patients, extra (procedural) conditions are justified for CDS to be correctly applied, such as an additional compulsory consultation (beyond the consultation required in all cases of CDS) and/or a certain waiting period before CDS can be started (to ensure that the patient's decision has been thought through carefully).

3.2.   Proportionality

A second crucial condition for CDS is its proportionality. The patient's consciousness should only be lowered to the degree necessary to alleviate the suffering (Lo & Rubenfeld 2005; Sanft et al. 2009). This implies that CDS should only be started when other (less far-reaching) types of sedation are not, or are not expected to be, effective (Morita et al. 2001c).

Proportionality also implies that an appropriate sedative is used. In medical guidelines, midazolam is suggested to be the most appropriate sedative because it has a rapid onset (Lo & Rubenfeld 2005; Cherny & Radbruch 2009). However, other sedatives are sometimes needed, for example when midazolam has adverse effects (Cherny & Radbruch 2009).

Finally, the dose of the sedative(s) has to be proportional and carefully titrated. The medical history and specific characteristics of the patient should be taken into account in this context (Claessens et al. 2008; Cherny & Radbruch 2009).

3.3.   Informed consent

The third requirement for CDS concerns the informed consent of the patient. CDS should only be started when the patient or her representative has consented. Although this seems to be a very obvious requirement, studies show that this condition is often not respected. For example, Chambaere et al. have found that, with one-fifth of all sedated patients in Flanders (Belgium) in 2007, neither patient nor family had given consent for sedation (Chambaere et al. 2010).

In order for consent to be valid, the patient or her representative has to be informed about the risks and the adverse effects of CDS (and thus of the possible life-shortening effect) and of possible alternatives for CDS. The patient's (or representative's) consent has to be explicit. Since CDS has a possible life-shortening effect and very severe consequences (complete absence of consciousness), implied consent is not sufficient. Usually, consent to a medical treatment does not have to be in writing. However, in CDS, the consciousness of the patient will be taken away. The patient will never regain consciousness, which is almost or even just as radical as death. From the onset of CDS, the patient will never again be able to take decisions. To my mind, these severe consequences justify a requirement for written consent.

When a patient is physically unable to give consent in writing (e.g. because she is paralysed), an adult representative could provide written consent for her in the presence of the physician. Only in an emergency should starting CDS be allowed without written consent.

3.4.   Procedural requirements

When applying CDS, certain procedural requirements have to be met. These procedural conditions primarily aim at guaranteeing transparency in the medical practice of CDS.

A first important procedural requirement is that a second opinion be obtained from another physician. CDS requires very specific knowledge, not only as to the refractoriness of a symptom but also as to the dose of sedatives and the depth and length of sedation. Therefore, I consider that the physician who considers starting CDS in a patient should seek a second opinion from an independent physician capable of assessing the refractoriness of the suffering of the patient. If only psychological suffering is concerned, I consider that the physician should consult *two* other physicians.

Second, the decision to sedate should be discussed within the care team that is treating the patient (e.g. nurses, psychologists). Communication with the family of the patient is also important, both because they are closely involved and to avoid potential reproaches afterwards (Alpers 1998).[10]

Finally, it is important to have good medical record keeping (Alpers 1998). The medical record should include notes on conversations with the patient, the reason for starting CDS, the (reasons for a specific) dose of sedatives, the side-effects, the patient's (or representative's) consent, the second opinion(s), etc.

---

[10] Alpers found that in cases of pain management which had come to a lawsuit, it was the family who had instituted legal proceedings.

4.   Permissibility of CDS without artificial nutrition and hydration

CDS is often combined with the decision to withhold artificial nutrition and hydration (ANH). A Flemish study has found that in 57 per cent of cases of CDS in Flanders in 2007, artificial nutrition and hydration was withheld (Chambaere et al. 2010). In this section, the requirements for CDS *without* ANH are set out. First, however, the possible life-shortening effect of CDS without ANH will be explored.

4.1.   *Life-shortening effect of CDS without ANH*

As with CDS with ANH, the question arises as to whether CDS without ANH has a life-shortening effect. Several commentators are of the opinion that it does not. It is noted that CDS is often only started in patients who have already stopped eating and drinking (Claessens et al. 2011) and that it would be unethical to force ANH upon them. Moreover, it is argued that CDS without ANH does not have a life-shortening effect because it would only be applied to dying patients who have less than two weeks to live. Within this limited time frame, lethal dehydration cannot occur (Hasselaar et al. 2009a; Claessens et al. 2011).

This stance immediately limits the scope of CDS without ANH to dying patients. What if a non-dying patient is suffering unbearably and her suffering cannot be treated otherwise? Is it possible to withhold ANH from this patient? And what if the physician misjudges the patient's life expectancy? The literature is not unanimous on the precise period required for lethal dehydration to occur. Some say hours to maximum of a few days (Cherny & Radbruch 2009), others one week (Verhagen et al. 2005), two weeks (Royal College of Physicians and British Society of Gastroenterology 2010), or even three weeks (Quill et al. 2000).

To assess the life-shortening effect of CDS without ANH, we should not limit ourselves to conditions under which CDS without ANH is thought to be permissible. Therefore, in our view, it is more correct to state that CDS without ANH has a life-shortening effect, except when the life expectancy of the patient is clearly shorter than the time frame in which lethal dehydration occurs.

4.2.   *Legal classification*

Since CDS without ANH can have a life-shortening effect because of the withholding of ANH, the question arises as to how CDS without ANH should be legally classified. Some are of the opinion that CDS

and the withholding of ANH should not be considered to be two separate decisions. After all, they say, the state of unconsciousness is not
a natural consequence of the disease but is artificially created by the
physician. It is this state of unconsciousness that prevents the patient
from eating and drinking. Because of that, CDS without ANH should
be considered as an entirety as it can hardly be said that it is a procedure
in which we simply allow nature to take its course (Orentlicher 1997a;
Kuhse 2004; Cellarius 2011)

Nonetheless, it should be noted that the need to start CDS is prompted
by the patient's underlying disease and because the patient has refractory symptoms. The decision to start CDS is justified because there is
a *clear indication* for CDS. CDS is not started just to keep the patient
unconscious, but to control otherwise untreatable pain.

It is intrinsic to this type of treatment that a decision also has to be
made whether or not ANH will be given. The decision to start CDS
does not necessarily imply that ANH has to be withheld. The decision
to withhold ANH requires its own justification and should be considered separately from the decision to start CDS.

4.3.   A justified decision to withhold ANH in CDS

If the withholding of ANH in a continuously and deeply sedated patient
necessitates its own justification, the question arises as to when the
withholding of ANH can be justified. In order to answer this question,
a distinction needs to be made between dying and non-dying patients.

4.3.1.   Dying patients

Certain authors argue that it cannot be justified to withhold ANH in a
patient who is continuously and deeply sedated, because it is not necessary to alleviate the patient's suffering (Orentlicher 1997a; Williams
2001; Cantor 2006). According to them, withholding ANH would only
aim at hastening the patient's death.

However, this approach loses sight of the fact that a patient *with decisional capacity* has the right to refuse treatment, even if it concerns a
life-prolonging treatment. Consequently, when ANH is withheld in
a dying patient with decisional capacity in whom CDS is started, it
is her right to refuse treatment that justifies the withholding of ANH
(Orentlicher 1997a; Williams 2001; Cantor 2006). Whether or not
ANH will be administered during CDS is a decision that can only be
taken by the patient, if she has decisional capacity.

As far as withholding ANH in a dying patient *without* decisional
capacity is concerned, the principles of representation come into play.
An incompetent patient has to be represented. It is the representative

who has to make the decision whether or not ANH should be started, thereby respecting certain standards.

4.3.1.1. Actual or probable wishes of the patient   First, the representative should follow the actual wishes of the patient. This means that if the patient has stated something in the past about ANH in the context of CDS, those explicit wishes should be followed. This is the so-called subjective standard.

Often, however, the patient will not have expressed explicit wishes. Sometimes it is possible – by reflecting on the patient's moral values and view of life – to determine what the patient would have decided herself if she still had decisional capacity. This is known as the standard of the probable wishes of the patient. If it is indeed possible to determine what the patient herself would have decided if she were still capable, then the representative has to respect those probable wishes.

4.3.1.2. Best interests of the patient   If it is impossible to determine what the actual or probable wishes of the patient are, a decision has to be made in accordance with her best interests. According to this standard, the representative has to take the decision that best represents the interests of the patient. The standard of the best interests of the patient is rather an objective one in which the advantages of the medical treatment are balanced against its disadvantages.

The crucial question is what this standard in fact entails for the decision as to whether or not ANH should be given to a deeply sedated dying patient. There is general agreement in many quarters that giving ANH to a dying patient is not in her best interests. With a dying patient who does not eat or drink any more, it is clear that death is imminent (Claessens et al. 2008). It would be completely futile to give ANH to such a patient as it would not benefit her survival or her well-being.

Even when the dying patient still has oral or artificial intake of food and fluids, providing ANH is not in her best interests, for two reasons. First, ANH in dying patients is contraindicated because it can cause adverse effects, such as oedema, ascites, bronchial secretion, etc. (Gezondheidsraad 2004). Second, it is futile to provide ANH to patients who are inevitably dying and who are completely unconscious.

4.3.2.   Non-dying patients

In section 3 above, on the conditions for CDS, it has already been mentioned that the majority of commentators limit the permissibility of CDS to dying patients. This is even more the case for CDS without ANH. It is stated that CDS without ANH can only be started in patients who are dying and who have a life expectancy of less than two weeks. Only in those circumstances would CDS without ANH have no life-shortening effect. Only then would it be proportional (den Hartogh 2006a).

Only a few commentators think there are no grounds to require the imminent death of the patient for CDS without ANH. According to Cellarius, no such grounds can be found in the traditional principles for CDS, namely the right to self-determination, proportionality and the doctrine of double effect (Cellarius 2008). Cantor too is of the opinion that the approaching death of the patient is not a necessary condition to start CDS without ANH (Cantor 2006).

Here, again, a distinction needs to be made between patients *with* and patients *without* decisional capacity. As noted earlier with respect to the dying patient with decisional capacity, the justification for the decision on whether or not to withhold ANH in a non-dying patient is the patient's right to consent to or refuse a treatment. A non-dying patient also has the right to refuse treatment, even if it is life-prolonging or life-saving. In treatment decisions, the right to self-determination outweighs the principle of proportionality. The caregiver has to respect the patient's decision.

I therefore conclude that CDS without ANH is permissible in a non-dying patient, as long as the decision has been made by a properly informed patient who has decisional capacity.

A non-dying incompetent patient also has the right to adequate pain management and to alleviation of pain. Nonetheless, the refractory suffering of a non-dying incompetent patient will generally be assessed more strictly, first of all because of her incompetency. The caregiver can only rely on observations (facial expressions, moaning, muscle tension, etc.) to assess the suffering. Second, the patient is not dying, which allows a longer time frame to seek alternatives to treat the patient's suffering.

The non-dying patient without decisional capacity, in whom CDS is started, has to be represented. If the patient ever expressed any wishes concerning ANH during CDS, those wishes have to be respected (this is the subjective standard discussed above).

However, it is rather unlikely that a patient, while still competent, has expressed wishes concerning ANH during CDS. Accordingly, it is likely that the representative will have to consider what the patient would have decided if she were still competent (the standard of the probable wishes). Thus, for example, it is possible that, at an earlier stage of life, the patient declared that she would not want any life-prolonging treatment were she ever to be in a state of permanent unconsciousness, e.g. coma or permanent vegetative state. Such statements can serve as a starting point for withholding ANH in the patient who will be continuously and deeply sedated.

If it is impossible to determine what the patient herself has or would have decided, a decision has to be made in her best interests. How are best interests to be understood in the case of CDS without ANH in an incompetent non-dying patient? In my view, it is appropriate to compare such patients to patients in an irreversible comatose or vegetative state, since they too lack any consciousness and since the state could continue for years.

It seems to be generally agreed that it is not in the best interests of a permanently unconscious patient to provide her with life-sustaining treatment, such as ANH (Dresser 1986; Shepherd 2006). In the famous British case of Tony Bland, the question arose as to whether ANH should be continued in a 17-year-old who was in a permanent vegetative state. One of the judges in the House of Lords explicitly stated that: 'it is not in the interests of an insentient patient to continue life-sustaining care and treatment' (*Airedale NHS Trust v. Bland* 1993).

Specifically in the context of CDS, Gevers takes the view that: 'it is possible that even if the death of an unconscious patient is not imminent, continuation of feeding and providing fluids is no longer indicated, and becomes disproportional or even pointless taking into account the overall situation of the terminal patient. In particular, it may only lengthen a life which is only bearable due to continuous deep sedation' (Gevers 2004: 365).

Nevertheless, the question as to whether life has enough intrinsic value in cases of irreversible unconsciousness has no objective or legal answer. It is fully dependent upon a person's view of life and the extent to which one values quality of life higher than life itself. Both choices imply a value judgement. Since the decision to start or withhold ANH is not a strictly medical one, I believe it should be made by the patient's representative. Considering the consensus on the permissibility of withholding ANH in an irreversibly unconscious patient, I consider that the representative is allowed to decide that ANH be withheld for the continuously and deeply sedated patient.

5.   CDS versus euthanasia

In the final section of this chapter, CDS is compared with euthanasia, as it has often been described as merely being a slow form of euthanasia (Billings & Block 1996; Orentlicher 1997a). This dispute finds its origin either in the fact that euthanasia is prohibited and CDS is not, or in the fact that, for example as in Belgium, euthanasia is permitted but is subject to very strict conditions while there are no such conditions for CDS.

Some argue that CDS has the same result as euthanasia (i.e. the (social) death of the patient), that CDS is applied with the same intention (to let the patient die), and that the only difference lies in the length of the dying process (Billings & Block 1996). In Belgium, according to some commentators, CDS is often applied to circumvent the severe conditions of the Act of 2002 on euthanasia.[11] Others contest this. They argue that CDS has no life-shortening effect and that it is not applied with the intention to shorten or end the life of the patient (Materstvedt et al. 2003; Claessens et al. 2011). However, this position is hard to defend when CDS is combined with the withholding of ANH in patients with a life expectancy longer than two weeks. Some also find a difference in the fact that CDS could be reversible (Legemaate 2006). However, this line of argument cannot be accepted, as it would not be *continuous* deep sedation if one planned to interrupt the sedation.

However, the conditions for the permissibility of CDS without ANH set out in this chapter are closely comparable to the conditions stipulated in the laws governing euthanasia in The Netherlands, Belgium and Luxembourg. The patient has to be suffering unbearably (this can be physical or psychological suffering), the suffering has to be untreatable, the patient must make a written request, the physician must consult another independent physician and a second physician if the patient is not terminally ill, etc.

Where euthanasia is legally permitted, the determinative factor in deciding between CDS and euthanasia should be the choice of the patient. It is the patient's choice whether she wants a quick death through euthanasia or a slower (more 'natural') death through CDS. The only other limiting factor is of course the willingness of the physician. A physician is not obliged to practise euthanasia.

6. Conclusion

This chapter started by examining the legal status of CDS. I have shown that CDS has an underlying criminal quality, not merely because of its possible life-shortening effect, but particularly because the patient will be unconscious until death.

---

[11] The Belgian newspaper *De Morgen* carried an article on 25 March 2009, quoting palliative care expert and euthanasia advocate Professor Wim Distelmans as saying that there is something hypocritical about palliative sedation.

Several possible grounds of justification were explored, such as the doctrine of double effect and the legal concept of necessity. However, these were found to be legally unsatisfactory and I concluded that statutory legislation, in which the lowering of consciousness and the possible life-shortening effect of CDS are explicitly taken into account, is necessary to neutralise the underlying risk that administering CDS could be found to be a criminal act and thus to provide caregivers with legal certainty.

In the second part of this chapter, the conditions for continuous deep sedation were discussed. Overall, four conditions were identified: (1) the patient has to suffer intractably; (2) CDS has to be proportional; (3) there has to be an informed consent, from the patient or her representative; and (4) certain procedural requirements have to be met.

However, the majority of the medical and legal authors on this subject add another condition – that the patient has to be terminally ill and that her death has to be expected within two weeks. The most frequently invoked reason for this further requirement is that CDS has no life-shortening effect under those circumstances. CDS is often combined with the decision not to start artificial nutrition and hydration. Since one can survive without fluids for approximately two weeks, it would be impossible for a deeply sedated patient to die of dehydration within her final two weeks. Furthermore, it is often stated that CDS is only permitted in cases of physical suffering, and that mere psychological suffering should be treated, among other means, by psychological and spiritual counselling.

This chapter has questioned and ultimately rejected the presupposition that the patient has to be terminally ill and/or that her suffering has to be physical. The core determining factor for the permissibility of CDS should be the otherwise untreatable and intolerable suffering of the patient. Every patient has a right to adequate pain and symptom management and this should neither be subject to a limited life expectancy nor to a certain type of suffering.

As far as the withholding of artificial nutrition and hydration (ANH) is concerned, I have emphasised that every patient has the right to refuse life-prolonging treatment. If the patient is incompetent, her representative has, in principle, the authority to decide whether or not ANH will be given.

Finally, the relation of CDS to euthanasia has been clarified. According to some, CDS is a slow form of euthanasia. I have argued that the conditions under which CDS (without ANH) is permitted are virtually identical to those for euthanasia. In those countries where euthanasia is legal, euthanasia or CDS should be the patient's choice, in consultation with the treating physician.

9 The Dutch national guideline on palliative sedation

Johan Legemaate

1. Introduction

Since 2003 a lot of discussion has taken place in The Netherlands about 'terminal sedation', also known as palliative sedation. The discussion revolved around the criteria and the conditions which must be met for such sedation to be initiated, and also about the relationship between the practice of sedation and euthanasia. In 2003, the former Attorney-General Joan De Wijkerslooth suggested that palliative sedation should perhaps be covered by the Dutch Euthanasia Act (Legemaate 2004). The government responded by informing Parliament that palliative sedation should be regarded as normal medical practice (Sheldon 2003). In the third national study of medical decisions in end-of-life care, published in 2003,[1] data on palliative sedation appeared for the first time (Rietjens et al. 2004). In its response to this study, the Dutch government stressed that it was important for the medical profession itself to develop a national guideline regarding terminal sedation.

In September 2004, at the request of the Ministry of Health, Welfare and Sports, the Royal Dutch Medical Association appointed a committee which was given the task of drawing up this guideline (hereafter: the committee). The committee consisted of a medical ethicist, two medical oncologists, two general practitioners, two nursing home physicians, one anaesthesiologist, two nurses and two representatives (a lawyer and a doctor) of the Royal Dutch Medical Association. In December 2005, the national guideline on palliative sedation (hereafter: the guideline) was finalised and offered to the Secretary of State for Health, Welfare and Sports (KNMG 2005). In 2009, the guideline was updated (KNMG 2009b) in order to clarify a number of misunderstandings and to add the most recent information on the medicines to

The author gratefully acknowledges the comments of Marian Verkerk, Eric van Wijlick and Alexander de Graeff.

[1] Previous national studies were published in 1991 and 1997.

be used for continuous sedation. The guideline aims to clarify questions and misunderstandings regarding palliative sedation, both at a conceptual level and in medical practice (Legemaate et al. 2007; Verkerk et al. 2007). It has proven to be of great value for medical practitioners. In this chapter, the structure and contents of the guideline will be described, as well as the ongoing discussion in The Netherlands with regard to its underlying assumptions.

2.   Definition and aim of palliative sedation

The terms palliative sedation, sedation in the final phase of life, terminal sedation and deep sedation may have different meanings, but are often used synonymously. The guideline prefers the term 'palliative sedation', as it makes quite clear that this sedation takes place in the framework of palliative care. In the guideline, palliative sedation is defined as 'the deliberate lowering of a patient's level of consciousness in the last stages of life' (KNMG 2009b). The objective of palliative sedation is to relieve suffering, and lowering consciousness is the means to achieve this. It is very important that palliative sedation is given for the right indication, proportionally and adequately. According to the guideline, it is the degree of symptom control, not the level to which consciousness is lowered, that determines the dose and combinations of the sedatives used and the duration of treatment. The assessment and decision-making processes must focus on adequate relief of the patient's suffering, so that a peaceful and acceptable situation is created. Palliative sedation may be given in the last phase of life, in the case of an imminently dying patient.

According to the guideline, palliative sedation may be used in two ways: (1) continuous sedation until death; or (2) short-term or intermittent sedation. The practice that has given rise to the ethical, legal, social and political debate is the former (Legemaate et al. 2007). This is the practice the guideline focuses on.

3.   Indication and conditions

In the guideline, the indication for palliative sedation is formulated as follows: the presence of one or more refractory symptoms which lead to unbearable suffering for the patient. A symptom is or becomes refractory if none of the conventional treatments are effective (within a reasonable time frame) and/or these treatments are accompanied by unacceptable side-effects. Pain, dyspnoea and delirium are the most common refractory symptoms which in clinical practice lead to the use of palliative sedation, although existential suffering could also constitute a refractory symptom. Another requirement for initiating deep and continuous sedation is that the patient must have a life expectancy of no more than one to two weeks. The physician may then decide to initiate deep sedation which, in principle, continues until death. The guideline is based on the assumption that if deep and continuous sedation is administered, no artificial hydration will be given (Quill & Byock 2000). If life expectancy is less than two weeks, it is assumed that withdrawing artificial hydration will not hasten death. If the patient is expected to live longer, the situation is different, because in that case the patient would die sooner than would otherwise be the case, due to dehydration, and hence the crucial distinction between sedation and the active termination of life could be blurred.

4.   The distinction between palliative sedation and euthanasia

The process of drafting the guideline was preceded by a debate amongst lawyers, ethicists and medical professionals about the relationship between palliative sedation (in particular continuous sedation until death) and actions intended to terminate life (in particular euthanasia). The committee has taken the view that palliative sedation is a normal medical procedure and must be clearly distinguished from termination of life, because there is no evidence that palliative sedation – if administered carefully – hastens death.

Towards the end of the patient's life, a variety of medical and other procedures and decisions may become necessary (Gevers 2004; Legemaate 2004). They may include decisions to withdraw particular kinds of treatment, not to resuscitate, to intensify symptom control measures, to abstain from artificially administering fluids, to provide palliative sedation and even to terminate life (via euthanasia, physician-assisted suicide or termination of life without request). It should be stressed that, although these procedures and decisions may be closely interconnected, they each have their own particular characteristics and specific criteria (Gevers 2004). It is not uncommon for a number of different procedures to be employed or decisions to be taken, either simultaneously or sequentially, during the last stages of a patient's life.

Both at the policy level and in practice, there is some confusion about the distinction between palliative sedation and euthanasia. Palliative sedation, as described in the guideline, is a way of ensuring that patients are unaware of their symptoms and therefore relieved of suffering in the period immediately prior to death. Palliative sedation, the guideline maintains, is different from euthanasia in that it does not result in shortening the patient's life. Indeed, no current evidence supports the claim that palliative sedation, if carried out in accordance with good medical practice, shortens life. Consequently, a clear distinction should be drawn between the two. Palliative sedation is the treatment of choice if the patient no longer wishes to suffer but does not wish to take the assisted suicide or euthanasia route. If the patient feels that her suffering is so unbearable that she no longer wishes to remain alive, euthanasia is the more obvious choice in countries where it is legal. The patient may have good reasons for preferring euthanasia to palliative sedation, for example she may wish to remain lucid enough to continue communicating with her loved ones in her final days.

Another important difference is that palliative sedation can be initiated at a time when the patient is (temporarily or permanently) incapable of giving consent, if the physician feels that this is the best course.

It follows from the position taken by the guideline that a patient with a life-threatening condition but without refractory symptoms cannot 'opt' for palliative sedation. Palliative sedation is only an option in the presence of an indication of the kind described in section 3 above. This means that, properly practised, palliative sedation cannot be used to 'get around' the requirements and procedures for euthanasia and achieve the same aim (i.e. of shortening life) in a more gradual and surreptitious way. Palliative sedation is therefore not a form of 'slow euthanasia'. The main differences between palliative sedation and euthanasia can be summed up as follows:

1. Palliative sedation relieves suffering by lowering consciousness; euthanasia does so by terminating life.
2. Palliative sedation does not in itself shorten life, euthanasia certainly does. Indeed, palliative sedation may even prolong life to some extent (because it prevents exhaustion as a result of suffering).
3. Palliative sedation is in principle reversible; termination of life is not.

If practised properly, palliative sedation must be considered to be a normal medical procedure. This means that the indications for it and its use in medical practice are determined by current standards within the medical profession, and that it is a patient's right to receive palliative sedation (like other normal medical procedures), provided the accepted indications and preconditions are present, and that it cannot therefore be refused by the physician. Euthanasia, and termination of life generally, is not regarded as a normal medical procedure; there is therefore no such thing as a 'right' to euthanasia even in countries where it is legal (Legemaate 2004). Since palliative sedation is seen as normal medical practice specific legal arrangements, such as those mentioned in the Euthanasia Act, are not required.

It should be noted, however, that there is an overlap between the indications for palliative sedation and those for euthanasia; thus, in some situations, palliative sedation and euthanasia may both be possible options. However, this is not always the case.

5.   Decision-making procedures

5.1.   The initial proposal

The issue of palliative sedation may be raised in various ways. The patient and/or her representative may request it, either explicitly or indirectly in the form of a request to relieve suffering. Equally, staff caring for the patient may raise the possibility of administering continuous sedation, if they believe that the patient's situation is developing in such a way as to require it, now or in the near future.

5.2.   Determination of the indications for palliative sedation

Once the question of initiating palliative sedation has been raised, the patient's situation must be assessed thoroughly in the light of the indications for palliative sedation set out above. This assessment should include information provided by the patient's physicians and other carers as well as by the patient herself and her loved ones because such information could be important. Through their regular close contact with the patient and her loved ones, other carers are often in a better position than the attending physician to assess the patient's overall situation. On the basis of their observations, monitoring and recording of symptoms, they can generally provide background information in support of the expressed desire or need for sedation. From this information, a picture can be built up of the patient's overall situation, in terms of case history, diagnosis and prognosis. The guideline emphasises that the continuity of cooperation, coordination, exchange of information and communication among the various carers is crucial. Poor cooperation and coordination can produce discrepancies in the information received by the various parties involved and these can cause anxiety for the patient, loved ones and indeed staff. To avoid this, clear agreements are needed between all concerned, especially when the patient is being cared for at home, where contact between the parties will generally be less regular.

The assessment must culminate in a decision on palliative sedation by the attending physician. This decision should specify the aim of sedation (relieving suffering caused by a particular refractory symptom), its nature (temporary, intermittent or continuous), its level (superficial or deep), the choice of drugs and the dose to be administered. The decision itself and its underlying considerations must be recorded in the patient's file. The file should also contain a record of consultations with the patient and/or with her loved ones, within the team of professional carers, and with any outside specialists.

As with other forms of medical intervention, sufficient expertise is essential in making a responsible decision when palliative sedation is at issue. If the attending physician possesses insufficient expertise concerning the treatment of refractory symptoms and/or is in doubt about key issues such as medical indications and life expectancy, an appropriate expert should be consulted – preferably a palliative care specialist. Given the nature and content of palliative sedation and the medical indications set forth in the guideline, the committee saw no need to insist that an expert physician should be consulted at all times before deciding to initiate palliative sedation.

Acute situations can arise in which the attending physician is unable to take the steps listed above before deciding to administer palliative sedation. In that case, the physician has the discretionary power to make the decision on the basis of the patient's condition. In such cases, the steps listed above must be completed as soon as possible afterwards: that is, all relevant information must be recorded in the patient's file, and consultations should be held with the other carers and/or a specialist consultant where applicable.

5.3.   *Discussion with the patient and/or her representative*

The general rules set out in the Dutch patients' rights legislation (Medical Treatment Contracts Act) (Sluijters & Biesaart 2005) also apply to palliative sedation. The main principle is that of a patient's informed consent. If the patient is no longer competent to take an informed decision, the physician must consult her representative (Gevers 2006). In both cases, it is crucial that the information on which consent is to be based should be provided in a form that is comprehensible to the patient and/or her representative. There are three possible situations: (1) discussion with the patient; (2) discussion with the representative of the incompetent patient; and (3) acute situations in which neither the patient nor her representative can be consulted. These three situations are discussed below.

5.3.1.   Discussion with the patient

Wherever possible, palliative sedation should not be initiated without the consent of the patient. Staff should be proactive in ensuring that consent is sought at a time when the patient is still competent to make decisions. This means that the possibility should be discussed with the patient, if at all possible, well before the stage when palliative sedation is the only remaining option. Staff caring for the patient should therefore take the initiative and explain to the patient why it is important to discuss the possibility of palliative sedation at that relatively early stage.

The guideline also contains a list of specific issues that, in principle, need to be discussed with the patient or her representative. These issues are grouped in three categories: palliative sedation as such, specific wishes and views of the patient, and other aspects. They need not all be addressed on the same occasion and, indeed, may not all be relevant in the particular case. As noted earlier, the process of information giving/seeking and discussion may well be spread over a number of different conversations.

5.3.2.   Discussion with the representative of an
incompetent patient

If the patient is no longer competent to give consent, the decision must be discussed with her representative. The Medical Treatment Contracts Act lists the people eligible to take on this role (Sluijters & Biesaart 2005). In order of eligibility: the patient's legal representative (a guardian or mentor appointed by the court), if there is one; any authorised representative; her spouse, partner or companion; or otherwise a parent, child, brother or sister (Article 7:465 of the Dutch Civil Code). The patient's right of informed consent is then transferred to her representative. However, decisional competence is not a black-or-white matter. Patients may be only partially incompetent, and even if completely incompetent, they may still have relevant feelings on the matter and ways of making them clear. In such cases, the patient should be involved in the decision-making process as far as possible.

The Medical Treatment Contracts Act requires that the patient's representative should take the decision on the patient's behalf. However, this does not preclude the possibility that the representative (usually a relative) may elect to leave the decision to the physician(s) involved in the case, either because she feels they have greater expertise or because she is unwilling to assume the responsibility of taking such a momentous decision. Another possibility – at least in theory – is that the representative refuses to give consent for palliative sedation. In that case, however, the physician has discretion – in the interests of the patient – to ignore the feelings of the representative and decide to initiate palliative sedation without consent. In such a situation, the physician can always consult a specialist if this is considered appropriate or desirable. As a rule, however, it is extremely important that a consensus should be reached between medical staff and the patient's loved ones about the aim of the treatment (to relieve suffering and not to shorten life), the procedure that is appropriate to achieve this and the consequences that it is likely to have. Such agreement is in the interests of both the patient and her loved ones.

5.3.3.   An exceptional situation: acute sedation
As explained in the previous sections, the general rule is that palliative sedation should not be initiated without the consent either of the patient herself or, if she is incompetent, her representative. In acute situations, however, there may not be time to seek such consent if the patient is experiencing unbearable suffering and is likely to die in the very near future (in a few minutes or hours). Such situations can arise, for example, in the case of an arterial haemorrhage associated with a head or neck tumour, or respiratory distress caused by a pulmonary haemorrhage due to bronchial carcinoma. For complications of this kind, no treatment is available and care must be directed at making the patient unaware of her unbearable suffering. Generally speaking, the patient herself will be incapable of giving properly informed consent at that stage and action will have to be taken too quickly for it to be possible to consult the representative. In these circumstances, responsibility for the decision lies with the attending physician(s). The patient's representative must, however, be informed as quickly as possible of the decision and its consequences.

In cases where the patient is incompetent but has no representative, the attending physician, likewise, has discretion to decide to initiate palliative sedation on the basis of the indications listed in these guidelines and any other relevant information (e.g. views expressed by the patient in the past, signs of suffering, etc.).

6.   Consultation and other aspects

As with all other forms of medical treatment, there must always be sufficient expertise on which to base the decision to initiate palliative sedation. A doctor who is responsible but has insufficient knowledge of the treatment of refractory symptoms, is uncertain about the correctness of the indication and/or has insufficient knowledge as to how to administer sedatives should consult an expert, preferably a palliative care specialist.

The initiation of palliative sedation is an emotionally charged moment, especially if it leads to a rapid loss of consciousness so that communication with the patient is lost. The doctor should be present when continuous sedation is initiated, because sometimes intervention is necessary. In the subsequent phase, the administration of sedation can be left largely to nurses and or other health professionals if necessary.

Good documentation is essential. The relevant data about the patient's situation must be recorded in the file: why the decision was made to initiate palliative sedation; how sedation was administered; an assessment of its effect; and what criteria must be met to adjust the dosage. The treating physician should visit the patient at least once a day. Optimal palliative care also includes giving attention, support and counselling to the patient's family and close friends. During the course of events leading up to palliative sedation and during its administration, they play an important role: they function as carers, observers, information providers and representatives of the patient, in addition to their role as partner, family member, close friend or acquaintance. They go through their own process of uncertainty, feelings of guilt, fear, sorrow and mourning. Giving information and explanations to the family, working with them and assessing the situation with them are all essential to a satisfactory procedure and a good farewell.

There should also be care for the carers. Throughout the whole process, care and support should be available for the various care providers who are involved in the patient's situation. This requires good communication, reflection and support for care providers. Attention to and reflection on the whole situation after the death of the patient requires careful observation and a high quality of care.

7.   Discussion

The Dutch national guideline, which was published in 2005 and updated in 2009, interprets palliative sedation as: 'the deliberate lowering of a patient's level of consciousness in the last stages of life'. A distinction is made between two forms of palliative sedation: short-term/intermittent sedation and continuous sedation until the moment of death. The latter (continuous sedation until death) involves the withholding of food and drink (administered artificially). For this reason, the guideline sees continuous sedation until death as acceptable only if, as well as complying with various other conditions, the patient has a life expectancy of less than two weeks. The information on which the guideline is based shows that, in these circumstances, withholding food and drink will not, in itself, have any effect on the patient's life expectancy. If continuous sedation until death were to start earlier, there could (possibly) be such an effect, and this would blur the distinction between palliative sedation and actively terminating life (whether on request or otherwise).

This example shows how the possible implications of classification and definition in terms of medical ethics and/or legal acceptability can have an impact on the definition or formulation of the conditions and requirements to be observed. Under the guideline, palliative sedation in the case of a patient with a life expectancy of less than two weeks is seen as a 'normal medical intervention'. In other cases, there may be reasons for viewing palliative sedation as a form of actively ending life. Just like the definition of euthanasia established in the 1980s, this is typical of the way in which these issues are dealt with in The Netherlands, where solutions reached generally enjoy broad support, both within the medical profession and in the wider society. This does not mean that these choices and developments are not subject to critical discussion in the country, but these discussions focus primarily on exceptions and individual cases rather than on basic principles and general frameworks (Legemaate 2012).

Initially, palliative sedation was associated with the termination of life. In recent years it has been stressed more and more often that palliative sedation is normal medical practice. However, it remains important to define explicit criteria and conditions for the use of palliative sedation in order to contribute to sound medical practice in this area. It is in this light that the contents of the guideline should be seen. The guideline has stripped the debate about palliative sedation of spurious elements and has made physicians and other care providers aware of the standards and starting-points for sound practice. The guideline tries to deal as carefully as possible with the various aspects involved (clinical, ethical, legal). There is good reason to do so, since there are fundamental values at stake (Gevers 2004).

The guideline reflects the consensus within the Dutch medical profession. Nevertheless, several aspects of the guideline have been and continue to be criticised. With regard to the requirement that death is to be expected in one or two weeks, it has been argued that such a moment is very difficult to determine. A second point of criticism focuses on the guideline's failure to create an obligation to consult an independent expert in all cases of palliative sedation (den Hartogh 2006a; Janssens et al. 2012). Furthermore, critics have taken the position that the borderline between palliative sedation and euthanasia, both conceptually and in practice, is so thin that a physician who decides to sedate a patient should always consult an independent colleague, or at least should do so in cases in which death is not imminent (den Hartogh

2012; Janssens et al. 2012). The guideline is also criticised for the way it deals with situations in which the patient refuses food and water, and thereby may influence the indication for palliative sedation and – as a result – the time of her death. It has been argued that the guideline does not preclude these situations, thereby creating doubt about its conclusion that palliative sedation is normal medical practice rather than termination of life (den Hartogh 2006a, 2006b). The inclusion of existential suffering as a possible refractory symptom has also been criticised (Daverschot 2010)

Recently, Janssens et al. voiced a strong opinion with regard to the guideline. They argue that:

[I]n the guideline, palliative sedation is portrayed as normal medical treatment in order to contrast it with euthanasia. Palliative sedation is normalised, and inherent morally problematic aspects are given insufficient attention ... Since the consequences of palliative sedation are severe, meticulous assessment of the refractoriness of symptoms is indicative of good care. The guideline's argumentation in favour of optional consultation may be in need of revision. Considering consultation optional only because mandatory consultation makes palliative sedation look like euthanasia seems an unpersuasive argument. (Janssens et al. 2012: 667)

They conclude that key elements of the guideline that serve to depict palliative sedation as normal medical treatment lack convincing power. In their view a revision is indicated, 'making palliative sedation a little less normal' (Janssens et al. 2012: 667). The views expressed by these authors show that, although there is a consensus amongst Dutch health professionals with regard to the main features of the guideline, some of its aspects continue to be discussed. At the same time, there is increasing evidence that the guideline is successful in influencing medical practice since a study, performed in 2008, shows that palliative sedation practice in The Netherlands largely reflects the recommendations made in the national guideline. According to this study, issues needing further attention include the pressure felt by physicians to start palliative sedation, as well as the possible life-shortening effect of palliative sedation as perceived by some physicians (Swart et al. 2011).

10 Continuous deep sedation at the end of life: balancing benefits and harms in England, Germany and France

Richard Huxtable and Ruth Horn

1. Introduction

Although various terms and definitions are used to describe continuous deep sedation (CDS) at the end of life (Morita et al. 2002a; Aubry et al. 2010), there is broad agreement that this involves the use of medication to induce and maintain unconsciousness until the patient dies, in order to relieve refractory symptoms. CDS generates significant controversies, regarding its arguable life-shortening effect (e.g. Sykes & Thorns 2003a; Maltoni et al. 2009; Rady & Verheijde 2010), the sustained privation of consciousness, the (frequently) associated discontinuation or withholding of food and fluids (Rady & Verheijde 2012) and the possibility that the practice can be used as a camouflage for euthanasia (Tännsjö 2004a; Jansen 2010). CDS accordingly prompts substantial questions about what it means to 'benefit' – and, indeed, to 'harm' – the terminally ill patient whose symptoms appear intractable.

In this chapter we consider how these questions are dealt with legally, practically and ethically in three countries: England, Germany and France. Common to these countries is the prohibition of euthanasia and a long-established (if beleaguered) principle that would appear to support the use of CDS: the doctrine of double effect (DDE), according to which purportedly 'bad' effects (like death or the removal of consciousness) might be justified, provided they are not directly sought but are merely pursuant to the achievement of some greater good (like the removal of otherwise intractable symptoms). Yet, there are, of course, also important differences between the three jurisdictions, not least in terms of the legal frameworks that govern palliative (and related terminal) care.

In order to illustrate the areas of similarity and difference, a common case study can be instructive. The case we describe below is based on a real case, albeit suitably anonymised (Horn 2009):

Mrs Martin, a 54-year-old cancer patient in the terminal stage who is considerably confused, has become extremely agitated, prompting the oncology team to request input from specialist palliative care services. The palliative care doctors associate Mrs Martin's confusion with the progression of her cancer and her imminent death. In her confusion, Mrs Martin behaves aggressively towards the care team, her body thrashing, such that items cannot safely be stored in her immediate vicinity. Neither antidepressants nor weaker sedative drugs can calm her.

Communication with Mrs Martin is currently impossible. Communication was difficult before, since she refused to discuss her cancer with the team or her family. According to her husband, Mrs Martin always avoided discussing her problems and fears, following a family trauma during her childhood. Neither he nor their children ever speak with the patient about her illness.

The palliative care team believes total sedation[1] offers the only possibility for calming Mrs Martin. Two days later the sedation is discontinued but, soon after waking, Mrs Martin becomes extremely agitated again, without becoming responsive to her environment.

The palliative care team conclude that sedation should continue until Mrs Martin's death. They decide that the delivery of food and fluids by clinically assisted means (such as through a nasogastric tube) would be inappropriate considering her terminal stage. Long discussions are held with the family and the rest of the care team. Although the palliative care team are keen to control Mrs Martin's symptoms so that she might have a peaceful death, they also recognise the need to protect her family and the staff. A broad consensus is reached that this will be the most appropriate course. Two days after Mrs Martin is sedated, she dies.

Is the decision taken in Mrs Martin's case acceptable – professionally, legally and ethically? Crucially, what counts as 'beneficial' and what counts as 'harmful' when dealing with an adult patient in such a situation? In the following section we first focus on the professional and legal dimensions of these questions, as they pertain to England, Germany and France.

---

[1] 'Mild' sedation involves decreased consciousness; 'deep' or 'total' sedation removes consciousness (Cherny & Radbruch 2009).

2.   Legal and professional perspectives in England, Germany and France

2.1.   England

English healthcare law (generally that pertaining to England and Wales) has developed from numerous roots – including the civil law of tort, the family law and public law – to become its own body of law. Yet, the legal approach to end-of-life care is particularly indebted to the criminal law, particularly on homicide. In this jurisdiction, the harshest available penalty (mandatory life imprisonment) is reserved for murder, which essentially involves the intentional causation of death. Prompted by developments in medical science, the courts (and, to some extent, Parliament) have sought to clarify when and how healthcare professionals might avoid committing this crime when caring for terminally ill patients. Two distinctions have emerged as fundamental: one, between intending and (merely) foreseeing a result; another, between (positively) acting and (negatively) omitting to act.

The first difference originated in the 1957 trial of Dr John Bodkin Adams (Palmer 1957). Adams, a GP, was charged with murdering an 81-year-old patient, after an autopsy revealed high levels of barbiturates and opioids. The doctor argued he had intended only to kill pain, not his patient. Directing the jury, the trial judge, Devlin J, noted:

If the first purpose of medicine, the restoration of health, can no longer be achieved there is still much for a doctor to do, and he is entitled to do all that is proper and necessary to relieve pain and suffering, even if the measures he takes may incidentally shorten life. (Davies 1998: 347)

The jury acquitted. Devlin J's principle thereafter became an 'established rule', gaining acceptance in the highest court (*Airedale NHS Trust* v. *Bland* 1993: 370D) and subsequently being applied in other trials involving opioids like diamorphine (Huxtable 2007: 84–114).

The second distinction, between acts and omissions, is also well established. An omission can be culpable – provided, that is, that the person who omitted to provide the necessities for life had been under a duty to do so. Various rulings have clarified when the duty might (not) be present. The leading ruling concerns Anthony Bland, who was in a persistent vegetative state (PVS) (*Airedale NHS Trust* v. *Bland* 1993). In line with the wishes of his family and doctors, the House of

Lords confirmed that it would be lawful to remove artificial nutrition and hydration[2] (ANH), with the inevitable (and, according to the Law Lords, intentional) shortening of Anthony's life, since the doctors were no longer under a duty to provide this, in view of medical opinion that there was no benefit in continued treatment of this sort. Comparable decisions have been reached for incapacitated adults afflicted with other conditions, like the minimally conscious state (MCS) (e.g. *W* v. *M and S and A NHS Primary Care Trust* 2011).

According to the relevant legislation (Mental Capacity Act 2005), the existence and scope of the duty turns on the 'best interests' of the patient (Huxtable 2012). The Act also emphasises the obligation to respect the autonomy of the incompetent patient, who – whilst competent – may have appointed a healthcare proxy (by conferring a 'lasting power of attorney') or made her wishes known in advance (such as via an 'advance decision to refuse treatment'). Similarly, the adult patient who retains the capacity to make the relevant decision can discharge the doctors from their duty to sustain life by issuing a contemporaneous refusal of (even life-saving) treatment (e.g. *Re B (Adult: Refusal of Medical Treatment)* 2002).

Legally, the duty to maintain life therefore finds its limits when death is (only) foreseen or attributable to a permissible omission. These limits are reflected and to some extent clarified in professional guidance (e.g. General Medical Council 2010). Of course, if these limits have not been reached, then the duty persists – especially the obligation to refrain from active, intentional killing. Exceptions to this obligation are not unprecedented, but they have been narrowly drawn (e.g. *Re A (Children) (Conjoined Twins: Surgical Separation)* 2000). Although the law tends to be lenient in operation (Huxtable 2007; Director of Public Prosecutions 2010), the formal resistance to legalised assisted dying continues to withstand legal challenge (e.g. *Case of Pretty* v. *the United Kingdom (Application No. 2346/02)* 2002; *R (on the application of Purdy)* v. *Director of Public Prosecutions* 2009; *R (on the application of Tony Nicklinson)* v. *Ministry of Justice* 2012) and calls for reform (e.g. Commission on Assisted Dying 2011). Such resistance might be unsurprising, as research 'suggests a culture of medical decision making informed by a palliative care philosophy' (Seale 2006: 8).

---

[2] Artificial nutrition and hydration is generally referred to as clinically assisted nutrition and hydration (CANH) in the UK. For consistency with the other chapters of this book, the term ANH is used in this chapter.

2.2.   France

In France, a law of 22 April 2005 (Law n° 2005-370) clarified patients' rights and the boundaries of legal and illegal practices in end-of-life care. Although the law condemns any (positive) act that 'provokes death', it establishes the physician's right to 'let die' a terminally ill patient. As now stated in the Public Health Code (Code de la Santé Publique, CSP), a terminally ill patient has the right to refuse 'every' treatment, including ANH (Article L.1111-4, CSP). Yet, in the same article (L.1111-4), it is stated that the doctor is not required to accept such a request and may 'do all that is possible in order to convince the patient' to continue treatment when the refusal thereof endangers the patient's life.

The legal focus on the physician's, rather than the patient's, judgement (Thouvenin 2008: 404–5) becomes even more apparent in Article L.1110-5 CSP. This article specifies that therapeutic acts which 'seem futile or disproportionate or have no other effect than only artificial maintenance of life ... *can* be suspended or not be undertaken' (our italics). The physician therefore enjoys the power to decide: she can withhold or withdraw futile or disproportionate treatments, but is not obliged to do so. The physician is, however, advised to 'preserve the dignity of the dying person and assure quality of life by dispensing [palliative care]' (Article L.1110-5 CSP). At this point the law introduces the idea that it might be acceptable for life to be shortened, provided that this is only foreseen and not intended; in such a situation, 'if the doctor finds that he can ease the suffering of a person in an advanced or a terminal stage of a serious and incurable disease ... only by administering a treatment that may have a life-shortening side effect, he has to inform the sick person ... the surrogate, the family or a close person. The procedure must be recorded in the medical notes' (Article L.1110-5 CSP).

A revised version of Article 37 of the French Code of Medical Ethics (Code de Déontologie Médicale, CDM) – which is part of the CSP and thus legally binding – further confirms the obligation to dispense palliative care. The patient's right to receive such care (Article L.1110-9 CSP) would seem to imply that there is a right to receive sedation as a last-resort option for treating refractory suffering. In its comments on Article 37 CDM, the French Board of Physicians (Ordre National des Médecins) has emphasised the principle of proportionality when employing analgesics and sedatives, i.e. doses should be administered proportionately and progressively. This principle seeks to guard against abuse, in the form of intentional killing using sedative drugs (Baumann et al. 2011).

The new version of Article 37 CDM also included a specific note requiring the use of sedation (and/or analgesics) when life-sustaining treatment is being withdrawn from patients in a vegetative state. This revision arose in 2010, following the removal (without sedation) of a gastric tube from a patient in a vegetative state, Hervé Pierra. After having endured seizures, Mr Pierra died six days after the tube was removed (Mission d'évaluation de la loi n° 2005-370 du 22 avril 2005 relative aux droits des malades et à la fin de vie 2008: 204–16). Mr Pierra's parents thereafter began a media campaign for the legal right to euthanasia, although this remains contrary to French law. In 2011, Michel Salmon, a patient with locked-in syndrome, refused ANH and he died three weeks later, while receiving CDS (Gorget 2012).

In addition to the law, there is pertinent professional guidance. In 2002, the French Society for Accompaniment and Palliative Care (Société Française d'Accompagnement et de Soins Palliatifs, SFAP) first published recommendations for the use of sedation for patients with uncontrollable distress. These guidelines were revised in 2004 following the parliamentary report (Mission d'information sur l'accompagnement de la fin de vie 2004) that preceded the 2005 law. Following Mr Pierra's case and the report evaluating the implementation of the law of 2005 (Mission d'évaluation de la loi n° 2005-370 du 22 avril 2005 relative aux droits des malades et à la fin de vie 2008), the SFAP reviewed their recommendations again in 2008. In addition to the principle of proportionality, the SFAP, in line with the CDM, emphasises the importance of using sedation in consultation with specialists in pain management, and, where possible, after consultation with the patient or the family.

Despite such guidance, evidence suggests ongoing confusion about the distinctions between sedation and euthanasia. Some doctors appear to resist the use of sedative drugs for fear of hastening death (as one might detect in the case of Mr Pierra), while others use such measures with this precise aim (Horn 2013). Significantly, the latter group appear more resistant to engaging with palliative care specialists. Indeed, collaboration between French hospital services and palliative care advisory teams is not always harmonious (Mino & Lert 2003; Horn 2013), which raises questions about the willingness of doctors from 'curative' services to consult with palliative care specialists before employing sedative medication.

2.3.   Germany

Like English and French law, German criminal law (*Strafgesetzbuch*, StGB) prohibits the intentional causation of death (Section 216 StGB).

The atrocities committed by Nazi doctors have cast a long shadow here, under which people prefer not to talk of 'euthanasia', preferring to replace this term with 'active/direct assistance in dying'. Legally, this remains a crime, in its positive and direct form; however, again as elsewhere, what some term 'passive' assistance in dying (i.e. withdrawing life-sustaining treatment) and 'indirect' assistance in dying (i.e. administering analgesics with the aim of relieving pain, albeit at the purported risk of shortening life) are both lawful practices.

In the wake of the Nuremberg Trials, medical decision-making today is dominated by concerns for the patient's right to autonomy and physical integrity, which is enshrined in Article 2 II 1 of the German constitution (the so-called Fundamental Law or *Grundgesetz*, GG). Regarding indirect assistance in dying, the Higher Regional Court of Frankfurt stated in 1998:

> ... a medical intervention that implies the risk of causing death is something different than a medical act that aims to cause death, because such an act does not serve the health of the concerned person. (20 W 224/98 1998)

This position was reconfirmed by the Federal Supreme Court in 2010 in a case in which the daughter of an 80-year-old comatose patient removed her mother's feeding tube, in accordance with her mother's previously expressed wish and on the advice of her lawyer. Underlining the consistency of the act with the patient's previously expressed wish, the judges stipulated that indirect assistance in dying, where the primary aim is not to cause death, is not unlawful (2 StR 454/09 2010).

Likewise, the German Medical Association (Bundesärztekammer, BÄK) has, since the 1990s, emphasised the difference between 'indirect' or 'passive' (lawful) and the 'direct' or 'active' (unlawful) assistance in dying. In its 2011 statement on end-of-life care, the BÄK repeats that:

> [P]alliation of the suffering of a dying person can be of such importance that an eventual inevitable shortening of life may be acceptable. (Bundesärztekammer 2011)

Research into the attitudes of German healthcare professionals seems to echo the BÄK view: Simon et al.'s (2007) study revealed that 98 per cent of medical and nursing professionals regarded the use of sedation in dying patients with refractory physical symptoms as acceptable. However, only 61 per cent considered acceptable the use of sedation in dying patients with incurable mental suffering. Schildmann et al.'s (2010) survey of members of the German Association for Palliative Care (Deutsche Gesellschaft für Palliativmedizin, DGP) later found that 78.1 per cent of physicians estimated that the treatments they employed to alleviate suffering in terminally ill patients had a possible life-shortening effect. For such physicians, it seems foreseeing – but not intending – death may be permissible, and adherence to this distinction enables them to distinguish their practices (permissible) from euthanasia (impermissible).

2.4.   Sedating Mrs Martin?

Although the jurisdictions do differ in their respective normative commitments (see Horn 2013), the legal and professional frameworks governing the use of CDS in England, France and Germany share some common features. First, to recap, if she were in England, Mrs Martin's care would be likely to be informed by a palliative care philosophy. Her confusion, and prior resistance to discussing her situation, make it difficult to discern her autonomous wishes (if any); at the time of the crisis, she would almost certainly be classed as incompetent under the Mental Capacity Act 2005, according to which capacity hinges (*inter alia*) on comprehension and communication. Any decision would therefore have to accord with Mrs Martin's best interests. Even in the absence of a formally conferred lasting power of attorney, her family could help the doctors to determine where these interests lie. And the doctors, in turn, might take comfort from Devlin J's principle: they may therefore direct their efforts towards relieving Mrs Martin's distress, even if such measures 'may *incidentally* shorten life'. On the same basis they might also refrain from providing Mrs Martin with food and fluids through tubes. Indeed, all of this can occur without the need for judicial oversight, since Mrs Martin is not afflicted with one of the disorders of consciousness for which judicial input is required (PVS and MCS) – although, of course, the courts are available to decide if a decision is needed.

Had Mrs Martin been a patient in France, then, again, the legislation and guidelines indicate that sedation could have been provided. Of course, she would need a willing doctor, and the successful relief of her symptoms would seem also to hinge on that doctor consulting appropriately with palliative care services. Furthermore, the SFAP (Aubry et al. 2010) cautions against the use of CDS in order to relieve the distress of the patient's family or healthcare providers. In France, then, Mrs Martin's benefit seems to be the central issue – but how benefit for (and to) her is interpreted and achieved seems, crucially, to rely on the physicians charged with her care. Considering the fact that only 12 per cent of physicians in a survey conducted in 2007 and 2008 knew that they have to take into account the patient's wish when making decisions

(Mission d'évaluation de la loi n° 2005-370 du 22 avril 2005 relative aux droits des malades et à la fin de vie 2008: 15), the benefit might be considered from a purely medical point of view. And even then, there is evidence that only a few doctors know the DDE (Mission d'évaluation de la loi n° 2005-370 du 22 avril 2005 relative aux droits des malades et à la fin de vie 2008: 15) or collaborate with palliative care specialists during the last days of life (Lalande & Veber, 2009: 4, 63).

Physicians in Germany, meanwhile, might hesitate to sedate, given the lack of consent from Mrs Martin (Horn 2013). However, they might well find comfort in the GMA's insistence that activities which only 'indirectly' shorten life can be justified. This idea that there is a distinction to be drawn between the foreseen (or indirect) and the intentional shortening of life has recurred throughout our survey of legal and professional norms in England, France and Germany. The implication – apparently supported by some empirical research into professionals' attitudes – would appear to be that CDS involves limiting the patient's life, albeit justifiably. But is this implication clinically accurate? And is this an ethically appropriate way of framing this issue?

3.   Balancing benefits and harms (clinically, ethically and legally)?

3.1.   In the clinic

In order ethically to evaluate CDS we need first to understand the practice: good ethics relies upon good facts. Here questions of benefit and harm come to the fore. The benefit would appear to be the relief of otherwise intractable symptoms, but the implied harm seems to be that life will be shortened or consciousness removed (Rady & Verheijde 2010). Yet, the proven and potential properties of CDS are not beyond dispute: many studies confirm that CDS has no life-shortening effect (Chiu et al. 2001; Morita et al. 2001a; Sykes & Thorns 2003a; Claessens et al. 2008; Radha Krishna et al. 2012); some find that it can even have a life-prolonging effect (Bakker et al. 2008; Maltoni et al. 2009; Mazer et al. 2011); but others detect a small risk (1.8–3.9 per cent) of respiratory and/or circulatory suppression, at least for some terminally ill patients during the last days or couple of weeks of life (Sykes & Thorns 2003a; Morita et al. 2005c). These findings require further consideration.

The risks appear clearest when an excessive dose is administered, since here the life-shortening effect will be most obviously detectable (Irwin 2001). Indeed, studies from The Netherlands (in which voluntary euthanasia is lawful) have suggested that some physicians there have used sedative medication with the primary intention of hastening death (Rietjens et al. 2004; Sheldon 2007). Yet, where relief of symptoms is the primary aim, the European Association of Palliative Care (EAPC) recommends that the doses be increased gradually, in proportionate response to the patient's symptoms (Cherny & Radbruch 2009). As Morita et al. (2002a) suggest, the use of rapid, heavy doses in order to avoid confronting the psychological distress of patients can otherwise blur the line between euthanasia and sedation. Swart et al. (2012c) have similarly found that physicians who start with mild sedation appear inclined towards maintaining the patient's ability to interact with others, whereas those who have an earlier preference for deep sedation tend to fear facing up to their patients' suffering, favouring the maintenance of sedation until death.

Of course, the approach favoured by the EAPC requires physicians to be capable of determining the proportionate dose for the particular patient. This will not always be straightforward: Swart et al. (2012a) point to the difficulty of predicting end-of-life disease trajectories in non-cancer patients, for whom there might be unexpected deterioration and then death, and thus for whom appropriate doses can be difficult to assess. They add that this unpredictability also leads physicians to overestimate the life-shortening effect of sedative medication. Indeed, Sykes and Thorns (2003a) believe that the risk is entirely absent, at least when the patient is in the last hours (<48 h) of life. The risk will nevertheless be present for other patients: for example, Rady and Verheijde note that responding to breakthrough restlessness and agitation by escalating doses can lead to 'fatal respiratory or circulatory depression and life-shortening effect in dehydrated and hypoxic' terminally ill patients (Rady & Verheijde 2010: 209). It appears that the risk is run where the patient is not yet in her last hours of life, which would explain why the EAPC stipulates that 'continuous deep sedation should be only considered if the patient is in the very terminal stages of their illness with an expected prognosis of hours or days at most' (Cherny & Radbruch 2009: 584).

It seems, then, that we need to distinguish between the use of CDS in the last hours of life and its use elsewhere, such as in the treatment of patients who might have weeks or months left to live. There is a potential problem here, of course, concerning the accuracy of diagnoses and prognoses and thus the appropriate classification of a patient who is in the last hours of life. But, assuming that an agreeable criterion for differentiation can be found and applied, a distinction does appear to be warranted between the two groups of patients. The first group contains patients in their last hours of life who seem likely to benefit from the relief of associated symptoms and unlikely to have their lives correspondingly shortened (provided, that is, that their clinicians refrain from administering large single doses or substantially escalating the levels). The benefit to a patient like Mrs Martin, who seems to occupy this group, would appear to reside in the relief of symptoms, both psychological and physical (Breitbart & Alici 2008). In such cases, even withholding ANH cannot be responsible for limiting the patient's lifespan; indeed, the introduction of tubes might be considered a cruel imposition on a dying patient, who is likely already to have forgone the delivery of food and fluids by more 'natural' means. For patients like Mrs Martin, the harm 'inflicted' by CDS (even with the associated denial of ANH) seems unlikely to be death. Instead, the harm appears to be the deprivation of consciousness.[3] There is, however, something of a paradox here, since this 'harmful' deprivation simultaneously provides the means by which the patient will benefit, since it is this deprivation that enables her to avoid her distressing symptoms.

The second group of patients encompasses those in their last weeks or months, who are experiencing unbearable suffering. Here – for at least a small number of such patients – the perceived threat appears not merely to concern consciousness, but also life. But, given cases like that of Hervé Pierra (who suffered for six days from seizures without having received sedation), there would appear to be patients who might benefit from total sedation. Yet, cases like that of Michel Salmon also suggest that CDS is unlikely to shorten life even if the patient has months left to live: this deeply sedated locked-in patient died three weeks after ANH was withdrawn, which seems to correspond with the estimated lifespan of a person lacking hydration (Jansen & Sulmasy 2002; Ganzini et al. 2003). Given these facts, how should the benefits and burdens of CDS be balanced for the occupants of either group of patients?

3.2.   *In ethics*

The principle of balancing benefits and burdens that was articulated by Devlin J in the English courts, and is detectable also in Germany and France, is commonly known as the doctrine of double effect (DDE). Associated with Catholic theology and first formulated by the medieval theologian Thomas Aquinas (*Summa theologiae* II-II, q. 64, a. 7), the doctrine distinguishes between intended and foreseen 'bad' outcomes,

---

[3] Clive Seale made this point during a workshop held at Queen Mary, University of London (19 February 2010).

allowing the latter to be brought about only when four conditions have been satisfied (Marker 2011: 101):

1. The act is good in itself or at least ethically neutral.
2. The good effect is not obtained by means of the bad effect.
3. The bad effect, although foreseen, is not intended for itself, but only permitted.
4. There is a proportionately grave reason for permitting the bad effect.

In 1957, the year in which Devlin J effectively endorsed the principle in the trial of Dr Adams, Pope Pius XII also explicitly confirmed that the principle could apply to the suppression of pain and consciousness, a position affirmed in the 1980 'Declaration on Euthanasia' (Congregation for the Doctrine of the Faith 1980). For its supporters, the doctrine captures a crucial moral distinction, which they sometimes seek to illustrate through the use of thought experiments:

Imagine a pot-holer stuck with two people behind him and the water rising to drown them. And suppose two cases: in one he can be blown up; in the other a rock can be moved to open an escape route but it will crush him to death ... There might be people ... who, seeing the consequence, would move the rock, though they would not blow up the man because that would be choosing his death as the means of escape. This is a far from meaningless stance, for they thus show themselves as people who will absolutely reject any policy making the death of innocent people a means or end. (Linacre Centre 1982: 49)

Many critics complain that such applications are 'contrived' (Singer 1993: 210) and lacking in 'intuitive plausibility' (Glover 1977: 91) and that the purported success of the distinction 'depends on how the action is described, and crucially on how to set limits to the redescription of any action' (Harris 1985: 44). Condemning the principle, Rachels refers to Pascal's satirical criticism: 'where we cannot prevent the action at least we purify the intention' (Rachels 1986: 92). Supporters nevertheless insist that the DDE captures genuine differences – not only conceptual and moral (in the differentiation between intended and foreseen outcomes), but also experiential (as the act of killing is said to feel significantly distinct from that of relieving symptoms) (Gillon 1999).

The defenders seem particularly inclined towards a narrow account of intention, which counts as intentional that outcome which is primarily or directly aimed at, as opposed to that which is merely secondary, indirect or only foreseen. Critics also reject this interpretation of intention and its ensuing account of moral responsibility. For one thing, they say, intentions may be multilayered (Quill 1993). Moreover, they claim that we might rightly be held accountable for more than the ends that we directly aim to achieve. Beauchamp and Childress have thus suggested that intentional action must encompass both ends and means: the means chosen must at least be tolerated, which for them signals that foreseen consequences must count as intended (Beauchamp & Childress 1994: 208–11). John Harris, meanwhile, has argued that persons should be held to account for the 'worlds' they voluntarily bring about, i.e. for the consequences of their free choices (Harris 1997: 36–40).

Harris's reference to the consequences of one's free actions hints at a major difference between many of the supporters and critics of the DDE. Proponents appear to take a deontological line, in which duties, rights and intentions dominate, rather than consequences as such, while many opponents tend to adopt a consequentialist perspective, in which right and wrong are judged in terms of outcomes. According to consequentialist critics like Peter Singer, the DDE smuggles in 'a disguised quality of life judgment', since it implicitly signals that the allegedly prohibited result – death – need not be a bad thing for suffering patients (Singer 1993: 210). Singer would therefore prefer this evaluation to be made out in the open, ousting the usual presumption in favour of prolonging life. Many defenders of the doctrine, however, remain committed to the preservation of life; indeed, for its Catholic proponents, the sanctity of human life is a core commitment. But this too troubles opponents. For the doctrine to succeed at all, it requires prior moral work, specifically defining what will count as 'good' and 'bad' consequences. If such work appeals to an authority like God, then atheists and those with alternative faith-based commitments will have little reason to accept such sovereignty and might therefore have good reason to reject the doctrine (Glover 1977: 86–91).

Still the proponents insist that one need not be a (particular type of) theist to recognise the intrinsic value of human life (Keown 2002) and that intention remains fundamental. According to Sulmasy (2000), intention can be relatively easily tested, by asking the agent: how would you feel if the foreseen prohibited result did not ensue – would you feel that you had failed in what you set out to achieve? If the agent did not feel they had failed, then this result seems not to have been intended.

For such proponents, running the risk of a 'bad' outcome is preferable to embracing the undoubtedly bad outcome that would ensue if the DDE were to be abandoned. Without such a principle, they say, there is a risk that many clinicians would abandon the use of opioids and sedatives, so as to avoid the taint of euthanasia, and many patients would accordingly die in pain and distress (Sulmasy & Pellegrino 1999). This is a risk worth taking seriously, particularly in light of empirical research from the UK, which has found that 'the belief that opioids hasten death is widely held' amongst patients, which in turn 'has a significant impact on pain management, as patients felt that an offer of opioids signified imminent death' (Reid et al. 2008). Notably, the authors found that 'opioids were more acceptable if healthcare providers had confidence in opioids and side-effects were well managed' (Reid et al. 2008). Of course, these findings could also promote the dissemination of better information regarding the effects and the appropriate use of opioids in pain management.

3.3.   In the law

Unfortunately (but perhaps unsurprisingly), confusion and a lack of confidence have spilled over into the legal realm. The law as stated and as applied in England vividly illustrates the problems (Huxtable 2007: 84–114). The most pertinent examples from the case law in this jurisdiction concern the use of opioids, rather than sedatives (Huxtable 2008), and the cases reveal that the law can be unclear, unfair and even dangerous.

First, the judges are not always consistent in the ways that they conceptualise and apply Devlin J's principle. Some judges seem to see the principle as straightforwardly expressing the doctrine of double effect and, thus, primarily concerned with protecting intentions to achieve permissible outcomes from the full force of the criminal law. Devlin J himself appeared inclined towards this interpretation, when he described the doctor as 'entitled to do all that is proper and necessary to relieve pain and suffering, even if the measures he takes may *incidentally* shorten life' (our italics). But Devlin J also – or perhaps alternatively – thought his principle was concerned with causation: 'the proper medical treatment that is administered and that has an incidental effect on determining the exact moment of death is not the cause of death in any sensible use of the term' (Devlin 1985: 171–2). At least one of Devlin J's successors appears to have added a third reading of the principle, according to which the doctor who pleads double effect is guilty of a crime, but he or she can claim a substantive defence for their actions, constructed along the lines of accepted professional practice (Arlidge 2000). This idea – that the doctor is a murderer, albeit a justified one – is remarkable and is unlikely to sit well with practitioners of palliative care.

The legal uncertainty seems to reflect some of the underlying philosophical and clinical confusion. But perhaps the precise category in which the relevant principle is stated should only trouble the criminal lawyers; maybe the rest of us need only concern ourselves with whether the law is being fairly and consistently applied. However, here too there is cause for concern, since double effect reasoning does not appear available to everybody. Case law in England reveals that a member of the public who foresees (but does not intend) the adverse outcome of their actions might be held criminally culpable, including for murder (*R* v. *Woollin* 1998). Doctors, meanwhile, can continue to rely on the principle.

Whether the principle applies to the right doctors, in the right circumstances, nevertheless remains open to question. There appear to be three types of doctors who appeal to the doctrine: those who *use* it, those who *confuse* it and those who *abuse* it (Forbes & Huxtable 2006: 395). The *first group* seems likely to comprise experts in palliative care, who will be well versed in the stories told by the data we surveyed earlier. Even for these experts there may still be a 'grey zone of ambiguous intentions' (Douglas et al. 2008: 394) but, generally, they seem most likely to know which doses will involve risk to that patient's life, and when they will therefore need the DDE close to hand.

The *second group* are likely to lack this expertise and they may err in various ways, such as over-reporting death as a consequence of palliation, under-treating pain and distress, or even over-dosing their patients, sometimes with fatal consequences. Such errors can range from relatively harmless mistakes, all the way up to grossly negligent or reckless practice, which could result in conviction for manslaughter (Huxtable 2007: 106–7).

More problematic is the *third group*, who discuss double effect, but who, really, directly intend to end life, whether for beneficent reasons (as in euthanasia) or from more nefarious motives. Even Dr Adams was not all that he appeared. Adams had inherited under the deceased patient's will; too 'paltry' a reward, observed the trial judge, for a respected GP to risk the death penalty (the then mandatory sentence for murder). However, the reward may not have been so meagre, as Adams inherited under 132 wills over the course of a career caring for many elderly patients. Apparently the prosecution case was poorly handled; if Adams had been prosecuted for the alleged killing of a different patient, then a conviction might have resulted (Huxtable 2007: 98). There therefore appear to be sound clinical, ethical and legal reasons why double effect needs careful consideration, both in principle and in practice.

4.   Conclusion: striking the balance?

Even excluding extreme cases, these diverse clinical, ethical and legal considerations provide conflicting accounts of how CDS might benefit and/or harm patients like Mrs Martin. Yet, it seems consensus – or at least compromise – can be constructed from the competing accounts of what it means to value human life that seem to underlie these considerations.

Three accounts of the value of life appear to be in play, which respectively emphasise its intrinsic, instrumental and self-determined nature (Huxtable 2007, 2012). Proponents of the *intrinsic* value of life (like those who espouse the sanctity of life) argue that life itself matters, such that it should not intentionally be brought to a premature end. Yet, such proponents acknowledge that there are limits, which the DDE helps to clarify. Advocates of the *instrumental* value of life object to the DDE and argue that life is only a vehicle for achieving other goods: where the vehicle is sufficiently damaged – say, where there is extensive suffering and inability – then it might be permissible to bring such a life to an early end. Adherents to the *self-determined* value of life, meanwhile, emphasise notions like autonomy and thus leave the determination to the liver of the life – she may decide what makes life valuable for her, and whether or not to continue with that life.

Each of the perspectives commands support in the laws of England, Germany and France, albeit to different extents (Huxtable 2007; Horn 2012, 2013). This might signal inconsistency, but we might do well to prevent the dominance of any one: the intrinsic value of life may be too closely associated with (particular) religious doctrine, while preoccupation with perceived suffering might raise the spectre of eugenics, as Peter Singer discovered when lecturing in Germany (Singer 1993: 337–59). Even the ever-popular autonomy might do insufficient work in the context of CDS, if someone like Mrs Martin has not indicated her wishes in advance or nominated a proxy. But, equally, we should not necessarily abandon any of these perspectives. Their prevalence and tenacity in end-of-life debates must tell us something.

Yet, even retaining something of each moral tradition, there remains the problem that the accounts can point in different directions. However, there may still be room for consensus: it seems unlikely that anyone would wish to see patients dying in pain, or distressed and suffering. Even supporters of assisted dying might be unlikely to want this practised unnecessarily, i.e. when patients' needs can be tackled without ending life, although some might still prefer assisted dying to CDS. Proponents of each position might still support the use of CDS. Those in favour of the intrinsic value of life might insist that this is a matter of intending to achieve a permissible outcome (relief of symptoms). Those who favour life's instrumental value might argue that the DDE is hypocritical and they would prefer to go further, with euthanasia also being permitted. But, in the absence of such a development, even these critics would probably prefer that CDS still be allowed. Those who prefer self-determination might add the caveat that CDS should occur, at least wherever possible, at the (current or previous) behest of the suffering patient.

Of course, each proponent might still have cause to complain: of boundaries being wrongly extended; of boundaries not being sufficiently extended; and of clinicians' interests dominating over patients' wishes. Even if consensus is not entirely likely or defensible, a case can still be made for compromise, where CDS can continue. Compromise on moral matters looks appropriate when there is great uncertainty and complexity, not every competing value can be respected simultaneously, a decision is needed and the disagreeing parties must continue to coexist as peacefully as possible (Huxtable 2012: 132–5). These conditions are amply satisfied here, with uncertainty and complexity particularly rife: diagnosing and prognosticating about terminal illness is seldom straightforward; the effects and side-effects of drugs are unpredictable; and judgements about the value of life (and, indeed, consciousness) remain contentious.

The idea of compromise in end-of-life ethics is gaining currency (Huxtable 2007, 2012; Mullock 2012). How might a compromise on CDS appear? Like the consensus position, compromise might simply be what we have, i.e. CDS may be practised, according to the DDE and thus within specified boundaries. Of course, to count as a compromise, which splits the difference between disputants, the boundaries need to be carefully drawn and policed. This should at least involve ensuring that the true properties and potentials of the relevant drugs are known (by clinicians, lawyers and the public alike), so that distinctions can be made between those who use the drugs within the boundaries, those who abuse them and those who are confused. To recap, the DDE seems most applicable where the patient is suffering but not near the end of life; elsewhere, no one needs to be unduly fearful of the assumed life-shortening effect of CDS.

Drawing up the boundaries necessitates further debate, to which this volume makes a useful contribution. Disputants should advance their claims in a reflective, reliable and respectful manner, so that the most suitable compromise is found (Huxtable 2012: 135–40). Where the lines will finally be drawn remains to be seen; for now, we hope to have defended the middle ground, which strikes an appropriate balance between the different benefits and harms at stake in these debates.

11 Can the doctrine of double effect justify continuous deep sedation at the end of life?

Kasper Raus, Sigrid Sterckx and Freddy Mortier

1. Introduction

The doctrine of double effect (DDE) plays a very influential role in medical ethics as well as in clinical practice (Beauchamp & Childress 1994) and it is very frequently invoked as a justification for several practices and decisions at the end of life. For example, both non-treatment decisions and decisions to administer pain-relieving drugs with a possible life-shortening effect are considered by many to be justified by DDE. Moreover, DDE also sharply distinguishes these practices from practices such as physician-assisted suicide and euthanasia, which, according to DDE, are unjustified and therefore impermissible.

For the purposes of this chapter, we will focus on another end-of-life decision, namely continuous deep sedation at the end of life (CDS), the practice whereby a doctor significantly reduces or takes away a patient's consciousness until death follows. Several commentators consider CDS to be more like non-treatment decisions or the alleviation of pain and symptoms than like euthanasia or physician-assisted suicide, and thus to be justified according to DDE (Boyle 2004; Cavanaugh 2006). Arguably, the doctrine of double effect even serves as one of the main legal justifications of CDS in some jurisdictions, as can for example be seen by a statement from the US Supreme Court in the case of *Vacco* v. *Quill*, one of the most influential US Supreme Court rulings on end-of-life decisions, where the court stated that: '[a]lthough proponents of physician-assisted suicide and euthanasia contend that terminal sedation is covert physician-assisted suicide or euthanasia, the concept of sedating pharmacotherapy is based on informed consent and the principle of double effect' (*Vacco* v. *Quill* 1997: 807).

The authors would like to express their deepest gratitude to David Albert Jones and Paul Schotsmans for their highly useful comments on an earlier draft of this chapter.

In this chapter, we will investigate whether DDE can in fact be unproblematically invoked to justify continuous deep sedation. Since we will discuss the application of DDE, its history is not particularly relevant to the purposes of this chapter. Nonetheless, its many uses in the past (as a mere casuistic principle, an intuitively valid moral guideline, a paradigm of a full ethical theory, etc.) do indicate that there is considerable difference of opinion over the implications of DDE for moral conduct.

2.   Different interpretations of DDE

2.1.   Introduction

As mentioned above, no single agreed upon interpretation of DDE exists, and thus there are relevant differences among those who accept the doctrine. What is agreed upon is the function of DDE. The doctrine was originally introduced as a solution to an action problem, where an agent wishes to do good (follow a right rule), but cannot do so without causing some harm.[1] DDE solves this problem by stating that an agent may cause harm as a side-effect, provided that this harm is unintentional and that the intention is to do good. Thus, applying DDE to complex and concrete ethical cases (such as end-of-life decisions) serves its proper function. As, for example, Joseph Mangan argues: '[The doctrine of double effect] is not an inflexible rule or mathematical formula, but rather an efficient guide to prudent moral judgment in solving the more difficult cases' (Mangan 1949: 41).

The subject of debate is the question as to what theoretical moral framework DDE belongs to, or, as Joseph Boyle puts it: 'who is entitled to double effect?' (Boyle 1991: 475). According to some commentators, DDE is essentially a *theoretical construction* that is closely tied to an absolutist deontological framework and functions to make that framework coherent (Duff 1976). Oderberg, for example, argues that DDE forms 'one of the indispensable planks of any moral system worthy of serious consideration' (Oderberg 2004: 211). Others consider it to be a *practical tool* or way of reasoning that allows practical problems to be dealt with (Boyle 2004; Cavanaugh 2006), and as such not dependent on any specific moral theory. Joseph Boyle, for example, notes that: '[t]he logic of double effect (...) has application in medical

---

[1] DDE was, historically, invoked by Thomas Aquinas as a justification for some forms of self-defence, where an agent wants to protect her own life but cannot do so without causing harm to her assailant.

ethics and the law, quite independently of the particular moral framework in which it was developed and has a natural function in moral reasoning' (Boyle 2004: 59).

It is possible to roughly distinguish three groups among those who use and defend DDE. The first group, the largest one, includes those thinkers who adhere to the classical interpretation of DDE and situate themselves within the natural law tradition.[2] Thinkers in this group include Mangan, Anscombe, Boyle and Sulmasy, all of whom are discussed below. More often than not, when DDE is invoked to justify CDS, an interpretation belonging to the natural law family of interpretations of DDE is used.

The second group includes thinkers who are sympathetic to DDE, but situate themselves outside the natural law tradition (e.g. Philippa Foot and Warren Quinn). Quinn's interpretation is highly influential, but he describes DDE in such a way that it is inapplicable to end-of-life issues (Quinn 1993). For Quinn, DDE distinguishes between two types of agency – *direct* agency and *indirect* agency. In *direct* agency an agent deliberately infringes on a victim's rights to further her own plans, while in *indirect* agency an agent infringes a victim's rights, but this infringement is in no way essential to the aim the agent wishes to achieve. Thus, according to Quinn: 'we need, ceteris paribus, a stronger case to justify harmful direct agency than to justify equally harmful indirect agency' (Quinn 1993: 184–5).

In Quinn's interpretation, DDE applies only to cases where one (or more) person(s) is being harmed and one (or more) different person(s) is being benefited. Since the person being benefited cannot be the same as the one being harmed, Quinn's interpretation of DDE excludes *intra*personal dilemmas and applies only to *inter*personal dilemmas (e.g. abortion or self-defence). This interpretation then does not apply to continuous deep sedation since, in this case, the patient receiving sedation is the same person being both harmed and benefited.

Finally there are also thinkers who are, arguably, revisionist in their interpretation of DDE, namely the proportionalists (discussed below). Distinguishing between these three groups is important, for in this chapter we will mainly discuss the application of the classical (i.e. natural law) interpretation of DDE to CDS, so our comments need not necessarily apply to *all* interpretations and revisions of DDE.

---

[2] This is not surprising since DDE originated within the Roman Catholic moral tradition.

2.2.   The classical formulation

As a theoretical concept, DDE has known many different formulations. One of the classical formulations has been set out as follows by Joseph Mangan:

[A] person may licitly perform an action that he foresees will produce a good and a bad effect provided that four conditions are verified at one and the same time:

(1) That the action in itself from its very object be good or at least indifferent
(2) That the good effect and not the evil effect be intended
(3) That the good effect be not produced by means of the evil effect; and
(4) That there be a proportionally grave reason for permitting the evil effect.
     (Mangan 1949: 43)

In view of the first condition, this formulation of DDE assumes that some actions are absolutely good (i.e. good in themselves), and that others are absolutely bad (i.e. bad in themselves). Which acts are absolutely right, which are absolutely wrong and which are merely relatively right or wrong cannot be determined by DDE itself but depends upon other principles or reasons. This is why many commentators claim that DDE requires a deontological framework in order to function properly and only makes sense as one of a number of principles.

DDE deals with relative wrongs, i.e. its application is limited to actions that are not clearly and absolutely wrong. If such an action has both a good and a bad effect and satisfies the four conditions mentioned above, then, according to this formulation of DDE, it is *permitted*. It should be noted that DDE only permits certain actions, but in no way confers an obligation to act; one may always choose not to perform an action that is permitted by DDE (Spielthenner 2008). Actions that do not satisfy these four conditions are considered unjustified and thus *impermissible.*[3]

A good example of a debate in which DDE has played a very influential role, is that concerning abortion (Connery 1977). If one considers an embryo or fetus to be a person (or at least a potential person) it would seem that all types of abortion are forbidden on the ground that it is always wrong to kill a person. Applying DDE, however, allows one to maintain the general rule against killing, while still allowing some forms of *therapeutic* abortion (i.e. abortion to remove a serious health threat to the mother).

---

[3] Thus one could say that DDE has more strength as a *prohibitive* principle than as a *permissive* principle.

A case to which the classical formulation of DDE applies is the so-called Hysterectomy Case: suppose that a woman in the early months of pregnancy is discovered to have cancer of the uterus and a hysterectomy is required to save her life. When applying Mangan's formulation, this action is allowed if and only if:

1. When a woman suffers from a cancerous uterus, a hysterectomy *in itself* is good or at least neutral.[4] Since a hysterectomy is neutral in this case, condition (1) is fulfilled.
2. The good effect is the saving of the mother's life, while the bad effect is the death of the early fetus (the 'unborn child'). If the physician does not intend to kill the fetus, but rather intends only to save the mother's life, condition (2) is fulfilled.
3. In this case the mother's life is saved by the removal of the uterus and not by the death of the unborn child. Hence condition (3) is also fulfilled.
4. Arguably, saving the mother's life is a proportionally grave reason for allowing the death of the unborn child, so condition (4) is also fulfilled.

Since all the conditions seem to be fulfilled, then, according to DDE, the hysterectomy may legitimately be performed.

This case is often contrasted with the so-called Craniotomy Case, which involves a controversial procedure that was first discussed by Catholic moralist thinkers in the nineteenth century (Connery 1977), and has been discussed extensively, for example by H.L.A. Hart (1986). In this case, described as follows by Marquis: '[T]he head of an unborn child is lodged in its mother's birth canal. Suppose that the head cannot be dislodged without crushing the baby's skull. Suppose that if the child is not dislodged, the mother will die' (Marquis 1991: 518).

At first sight, the Craniotomy Case is similar to the Hysterectomy Case in that there is both a good and a bad effect. When applying the four conditions, however, the differences become apparent. First, it is clear that crushing the unborn child's skull is not in itself good or neutral (condition (1) is not met). Furthermore, since one cannot crush the

[4] It is clear that, without qualification, a hysterectomy is not in itself neutral since it involves exposing a body to significant risks. What justifies hysterectomy in the case of a woman with a cancerous uterus is the principle of totality, which states that one part of the body may be harmed for the sake of the health of the whole body. As noted earlier, classical DDE functions only in combination with other principles. These principles are here taken to justify the hysterectomy before DDE is applied. DDE is then 'brought in' to morally assess the additional complication that the woman needing the hysterectomy is carrying a fetus in her womb.

unborn child's skull without killing her, the good effect of saving the mother is obtained through the evil effect, thereby clearly violating condition (3). In this case it is impossible to produce the good effect without the bad effect, so one has to *intend* the bad effect, thereby violating condition (2). What about condition (4)? Arguably, saving the mother's life is a proportionally serious reason to allow the unborn child to die. Setting aside the problem that 'killing' may have a different impact on proportionality than 'allowing to die' (the former making the death of the unborn child worse than the latter), it might be conjectured that the proportionality requirement is satisfied. Overall then, the Craniotomy Case fails to fulfil three out of four of the conditions and thus, according to the classical formulation of DDE, is unjustified.

The classical formulation of DDE, which is referred to in many articles and textbooks, has been criticised for having certain problems. As a result, several other formulations of DDE have been proposed. Before looking into these, we will first discuss the 'redescription problem' since this will become relevant later on in this chapter.

2.3.   The redescription problem

As shown above, classical DDE relies strongly on what one's intentions are, versus what one brings about as a 'side-effect'. One of the most important commentators in this respect is Elisabeth Anscombe, who attempted to find a good criterion for intention and closeness in her book *Intention*. She acknowledges that a major problem in determining one's intention is that 'a single action can have many different descriptions' (Anscombe 1958: 11). One of the examples she uses is of a person sawing a plank, an action that could be described as 'sawing a plank', or 'sawing oak', or 'sawing one of Smith's planks'. These are all descriptions of the same action but are not all necessarily performed intentionally by the person sawing the plank. The person might, for example, not realise that the plank is of oak or that it is one of Smith's planks and cannot therefore be said to intentionally saw oak or one of Smith's planks.

However, *knowledge of* what one is doing does not suffice for establishing intentionality according to Anscombe. The person sawing the plank might, for example, saw planks for a living and thus only have the intention to do her job. What you intend to do must in some way also provide the *motivation* or *reason* for you to act the way you do. One's intention in acting then is the answer one would give to the question: 'Why are you doing what you are doing?' The answer might, for example, be: 'to do my job', or 'to help Smith by sawing one of the planks', thereby establishing the intention. Also, because Anscombe believes that intention is not something that is purely inside the agent's head, one's actions must be in accordance with the answer one gives to the 'Why?' question, thereby making intention a bit more objective. As an example, Anscombe asks us to '[c]onsider the question "Why are you going upstairs?" answered by, "To get my camera"' (Anscombe 1958: 35). Now if one were to answer 'But your camera is right here' and the other person were to respond: 'I know but I'm still going upstairs to get it', one might question this person's self-claimed intention in going upstairs.

When related back to the Craniotomy Case, this would mean that we could ask the physician 'Why did you crush the baby's skull?', to which the physician might respond: 'To be able to remove the baby from the birth canal and thereby save the mother's life'. In this case, although 'killing the baby' would be a correct description of the physician's action, it is not, as such, intended because it does not provide the reason for the physician's action.[5] The downside, however, is that this makes the intention of an action depend strongly on what the agent says her reason for acting was.

The problem of redescribing intentions in classical DDE was also acknowledged by Philippa Foot, who has discussed DDE from outside the natural law tradition. She pointed out that there is a problem with condition (1), namely that the action must in itself be good or at least neutral (Foot 1978). The problem is that DDE makes a distinction between a good or neutral action and the effects it brings about, thereby allowing that every action can be redescribed to fit this action structure. In the Craniotomy Case, for example, one might say that the physician merely intends to reduce the size of the unborn child's skull with the bad side-effect that the unborn child dies and the good side-effect that the mother survives. The death of the unborn child can then be said to be unintentional in the sense that the death of the unborn child was not the reason for performing the craniotomy (cf. Anscombe's interpretation of intention). When redescribed like this, the Craniotomy Case fits DDE. However, this redescription can be applied in almost any case, making almost every case fit DDE, thereby making it a catch-all principle. The only way to solve this, would be to formulate some sort of 'criterion of closeness', linking intended actions to their closely related side-effects so that they are inseparable from

---

[5] Even though the physician might be aware of the fact that her action necessarily causes the baby's death.

each other. Foot, however, concluded that no proposal would actually solve the redescription problem.

Joseph Boyle, in an influential contribution to the debate, acknowledged that the classical formulation of DDE falls victim to the redescription problem, and made an attempt to solve this problem *within* the classical (natural law) interpretation of DDE. He accepted the impossibility of formulating a 'closeness criterion' and proposed to focus on the intentional structure of actions:

> On this conception, one intends one's ends, the state of affairs one aims to achieve in action, and one also intends one's means, that is the precise steps one takes to achieve one's ends. Features of one's voluntary actions which are not one's ends or means are side effects. Side effects are consequences or other aspects of one's actions which are neither the goal one seeks in acting nor the precise state of affairs one is committed to realizing for the sake of these goals. (Boyle 1991: 479)

So instead of focusing on actions and the effects they bring about, Boyle focuses DDE on the state of affairs one is committed to bring about. The replacement of 'actions' by a language emphasising intended versus foreseen states of affairs results in a two-condition formulation of DDE:

> The double effect doctrine states that such harms [i.e. of the kind involved in DDE cases] may be brought about if two conditions are met:
>
> (1) the harms are not intended but brought about as side effects; and
> (2) there are sufficiently serious moral reasons for doing what brings about such harms. (Boyle 1991: 476)

This alternative formulation led Boyle to treat certain cases differently as compared with Mangan's 'classical' formulation. The Craniotomy Case, for instance, is a genuine case of valid DDE reasoning for Boyle, because the physician is only committed to realising a state of affairs in which the mother is saved. The death of the unborn child is in no way essential to the state of affairs the physician is committed to. This shows how theoretical disagreements about the proper formulation of DDE can result in a different evaluation of particular ethical dilemmas.

2.4.   Proportionalism

As mentioned earlier, a revised form of DDE reasoning is advocated by an increasing number of thinkers. One of these revised interpretations is known as 'proportionalism'. This interpretation of DDE is controversial, as shown by the fact that a former Pope, John Paul II, compared proportionalism to consequentialism and condemned both in his Encyclical Letter *Veritatis Splendor* (Pope John Paul II 1993).[6]

Proponents of this reading of double effect ('proportionalists') consider the classical interpretation of DDE to be problematic in view of its reliance on an erroneous view of causality and intention (Kaczor 1998; Kalbian 2002). For Peter Knauer, arguably the first proportionalist, intention cannot be seen as being detached from proportionality. In a self-defence case, for example, I can only claim to intend to defend myself if the violence I use is proportional to the goal of defending myself. Thus, if I use a disproportional level of violence, I cannot claim that my intention was merely to defend myself. Knauer argued that:

The purely physical series of events is irrelevant to the moral qualification of good or bad ... If there is a commensurate reason for the permitting or causing of the evil, the means is effectively willed only in its good aspect. (Knauer 1967: 149)

Proportionalism thus distinguishes between a *psychological* intention and a *moral* intention; even when a person *psychologically* intends (i.e.

---

[6] The Pope noted that, with regard to the problem of the 'sources of morality' (what does the moral assessment of man's free acts depend on?), 'there have emerged in the last few decades new or newly-revived theological and cultural trends which call for careful discernment on the part of the Church's Magisterium'. (Pope John Paul II 1993: 74)

  With regard to consequentialism, he stated that this theory 'claims to draw the criteria of the rightness of a given way of acting solely from a calculation of foreseeable consequences deriving from a given choice'. Proportionalism, according to him, 'by weighing the various values and goods being sought, focuses rather on the proportion acknowledged between the good and bad effects of that choice, with a view to the "greater good" or "lesser evil" actually possible in a particular situation' (Pope John Paul II 1993: 75)

  He stated: 'Such theories however are not faithful to the Church's teaching, when they believe they can justify, as morally good, deliberate choices of kinds of behavior contrary to the commandments of the divine and natural law. These theories cannot claim to be grounded in the Catholic moral tradition. Although the latter did witness the development of a casuistry which tried to assess the best ways to achieve the good in certain concrete situations, it is nonetheless true that this casuistry concerned only cases in which the law was uncertain, and thus the absolute validity of negative moral precepts, which oblige without exception, was not called into question' (Pope John Paul II 1993: 76).

  The reason for the fundamental incompatibility of these theories with the Catholic moral tradition is of course that, according to that tradition, certain kinds of behaviour are intrinsically evil. As explained by the former Pope: '[T]he consideration of ... consequences, and also of intentions, is not sufficient for judging the moral quality of a concrete choice. The weighing of the goods and evils foreseeable as the consequence of an action is not an adequate method for determining whether the choice of that concrete kind of behaviour is "according to its species", or "in itself", morally good or bad, licit or illicit. The foreseeable consequences are part of those circumstances of the act, which, while capable of lessening the gravity of an evil act, nonetheless cannot alter its moral species' (Pope John Paul II 1993: 77).

wilfully brings about) a certain action, when there is a grave reason for performing that action she does not necessarily *morally* intend that action. Thus, according to proportionalists, any action that has both good and bad effects may rightfully be performed if the good effect is proportional to the bad effect. This allows proportionalism to escape the criticism of redescription, but quite possibly at the cost of allowing too much, since according to proportionalism every evil can be rightfully caused or allowed to happen, as long as there is a proportionate reason for doing so.

Proportionalism will not be discussed further in this chapter, since the proportionalist interpretation of DDE is often so different from the classical interpretation that addressing the distinction between the two would merit a chapter of its own. Indeed, many proportionalist thinkers are very critical of the classical formulation of DDE. A good example is Joseph Selling, who argues that DDE has been overextended and that its application has become so common, that it has trumped moral thinking. He argues that amending DDE so as to fit any moral question regarding what is permitted is unnecessary and instead advocates a revision of the methodology of ethics so that the essentially limited scope of DDE (and of other principles) may be replaced by a comprehensive system of moral principles[7] (Selling 1980).

Let us now turn to the application of DDE to end-of-life practices, and to CDS in particular.

3.   DDE and end-of-life practices

3.1.   *The Standard Vatican Case*

The classical example of applying DDE to end-of-life practices concerns the administration of drugs to a terminally ill patient with the intention of preventing, lessening or taking away the patient's suffering, with the foreseen but unintended side-effect of life-shortening. Let us call this the *Standard Vatican Case*, as the applicability of DDE to it is clearly formulated in the Declaration on Euthanasia (1980) issued by the Vatican's Congregation for the Doctrine of the Faith:

At this point it is fitting to recall a declaration by Pius XII, which retains its full force; in answer to a group of doctors who had put the question: 'Is the suppression of pain and consciousness by the use of narcotics ... permitted

---

[7] In his opinion, DDE '*may*' (his emphasis) function at the level of concrete moral decision-making, but it has 'absolutely nothing' to do with an overall 'objective' level of making moral statements (Selling 1980: 56–7).

by religion and morality to the doctor and the patient (even at the approach of death and if one foresees that the use of narcotics will shorten life)?' the Pope said: 'If no other means exist, and if, in the given circumstances, this does not prevent the carrying out of other religious and moral duties: Yes.' In this case, of course, death is in no way intended or sought, even if the risk of it is reasonably taken; the intention is simply to relieve pain effectively, using for this purpose painkillers available to medicine. (Congregation for the Doctrine of the Faith 1980, Section III)

This case clearly falls under the classical formulation of DDE where the action of administering pain-relieving drugs has the good intended effect of relieving suffering and the bad side-effect of hastening death.

3.2.   Questions concerning the application of DDE to end-of-life cases

Although it is clear that DDE is invoked to justify certain end-of-life practices, for example in the Standard Vatican Case, some concerns about the applicability of the doctrine to end-of-life scenarios have been expressed.

First, as was discussed above, not all interpretations of DDE apply to end-of-life cases. This was the case with the interpretation by Warren Quinn. Second, some issues regarding the applicability of condition (4) arise. The reason for allowing the patient to die should be proportional to the suffering that is prevented. In the self-defence case discussed by Thomas Aquinas, for example, DDE allows one to kill in self-defence. Here, condition (4) is satisfied because one life is saved (your own) and one is taken (the assailant's), creating a perfect balance. But how can the evil of causing death be weighed against the prevention of suffering, if non-accidentally causing the death of an innocent person is considered to be an absolute evil? The solution to this problem for DDE is, again, redescription. In order to make the Standard Vatican Case work, one has to redescribe death as a certain state of affairs. By viewing not death itself, but the span of time by which life is shortened, as what should be balanced against the reduction of suffering in an imminently dying person, a favourable equilibrium or an imbalance in the direction of the good might be achieved. If we assume that the difference between a 'natural' point of dying and the precipitated point of dying can be expressed as the description of some state of affairs (a counterfactual one), the proportionality can be assessed.

Thus the application of DDE to end-of-life decisions is not uncontroversial. Nevertheless, since many commentators do believe that the doctrine applies to these cases, this chapter will not focus on these difficulties but specifically discuss DDE's application to end-of-life cases and CDS. However, we do acknowledge that end-of-life cases might in some important respects be different from classical DDE cases. Our criticisms of the application of DDE to CDS need not therefore apply automatically to the application of DDE to other cases.

4.   DDE and continuous deep sedation at the end of life

In the previous section, we have attempted to show how DDE is used as a justificatory principle in what we have called the Standard Vatican Case. When it comes to CDS, some commentators believe that the Standard Vatican Case is sufficient to justify this practice, while others have modified the Standard Vatican Case to make it apply to CDS. In this section, we shall investigate whether any of these formulations can adequately justify CDS.

4.1.   *Applying the Standard Vatican Case*

The first application of DDE to CDS that we will discuss comes from Joseph Boyle, who considers the Standard Vatican Case to be sufficient to justify CDS (see also Cavanaugh 2006). According to Boyle:

The use of terminal sedation to control the intense discomfort of dying patients appears to be an established procedure within palliative care. But sometimes the amount of sedative needed to control suffering has the effect of shortening the patient's life ... Invoking double effect addresses these worries [that terminal sedation might be a form of euthanasia]: the intent of the physician prescribing the life-shortening analgesics is to control the suffering, not to shorten life. (Boyle 2004: 51)

In order to illustrate the application of DDE to CDS more clearly, we can represent it schematically, after having introduced the following conventions. They are compatible, as far as we can see, with Boyle's interpretation of DDE, and start from the current standard account of intentions (following Anscombe (1958) and Bennett (1995)). According to this account, as mentioned earlier, one's intentions in acting are defined by which of one's beliefs explain one's acting that way. When acting, people have beliefs about what states of affairs they are bringing about and some of these beliefs explain why we do what we do: they are the reasons why we act. These beliefs are the *intentions* behind the act. So:

let Φ stand for a proposed act (e.g. administering sedatives);
let E stand for a state of affairs that is an effect of doing Φ (e.g. reducing the patient's suffering);

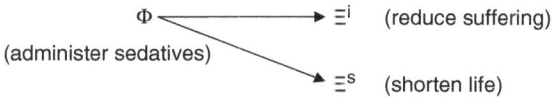

Figure 11.1 Boyle's application of the Standard Vatican Case.

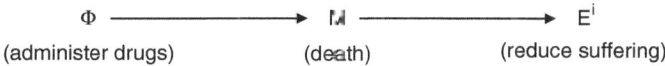

Figure 11.2 Euthanasia Case.

let i and s be indexes on E, denoting respectively 'intentional' and 'non-intentional' (side-effect);

let M stand for an E that is intended as a 'means' (it is thus by definition an E^i); and

let A $\rightarrow$ B stand for 'A contributes to B' (with 'contributes' signifying either causal relations, or relations that are made true under some description of what is happening, or some other kind of contribution,[8] with A and B ranging over M, E and Φ).

Boyle's statement above may then be represented as in Figure 11.1.

This is simply the Standard Vatican Case. Its counterpart may be called the Euthanasia Case (Figure 11.2).

According to this view, from the perspective of DDE there is no relevant difference between sedation and the alleviation of pain and symptoms with a possible life-shortening effect.

However, this application of DDE to CDS gives rise to some problems. First, some commentators do not agree that, in CDS, life-shortening is a side-effect. This is obviously a discussion about 'closeness',[9] where the answer to the question whether DDE can be applied to CDS depends on how close one perceives the connection to be between administering sedatives and shortening of life.

A second problem with the formulation suggested by Boyle is that it does not consider loss of consciousness as either a means or a side-effect of CDS, even though CDS is a practice that *necessarily* includes loss

---

[8] For example, by allocating scarce medical resources to one group, another group may not get what it needs. Yet giving the resources to one group is not the *cause* of the other not getting what it needs. Similarly, omissions are not necessarily the *causes* of what happens, although they may *condition* that chains of events continue working as they are.

[9] See our discussion of the redescription problem in section 2.3 above.

of consciousness. Furthermore, reducing consciousness is not only *by definition* part of CDS, it could also be argued that permanently reducing consciousness can be considered an absolute wrong. Some commentators reject the latter claim and point to the fact that we have no obligation to always maintain consciousness. Indeed, we frequently reduce our consciousness (or allow it to be reduced) intentionally (e.g. undergoing general anaesthesia for painful surgery) or as a side-effect (e.g. consuming alcohol). There is, however, a relevant difference between these cases of lowering consciousness and continuous deep sedation, in that CDS *permanently* takes away consciousness. Taking away consciousness completely and permanently can constitute either a *direct* harm or an *indirect* harm. Paraphrasing Quinn, a direct harm is one that comes to its victim from the agent's intentionally involving her in something, so that the aim of the agent is furthered precisely by that involvement. An indirect harm is one that comes about even though it is either not intended in this purposive way for the victim, or what is purposively intended does not contribute to the harm (Quinn 1993: 184–5). Frances Kamm argues that CDS is a direct harm:

In terminal sedation, we intend (not merely foresee), on an occasion, the cessation of rational agency, though this will not be conducive to future rational agency. We even intend to prevent future rational agency, all done as a means of stopping pain. (Kamm 1999: 602)

On this view, taking away consciousness is bad, since it takes away all rational agency as a means of stopping pain. Moreover, unlike taking alcohol and undergoing general anaesthesia, which do not undermine *future* rational agency, CDS *does*, since the patient will not regain consciousness.

One could also argue that taking away consciousness permanently until death represents an *indirect* harm since it deprives the patient of the possibility to perform certain essential duties or even of the possibility to experience future pleasures. On this view, bringing a patient intentionally into a state of unconsciousness does not necessarily constitute a harm in itself, but it does harm the patient in a non-intended way. The Vatican seems to hold this view, as can for example be seen in an opinion of the Congregation for the Doctrine of the Faith (1980), according to which:

[P]ainkillers that cause unconsciousness need special consideration. For a person not only has to be able to satisfy his or her moral duties and family obligations; he or she also has to prepare himself or herself with full consciousness for meeting Christ. Thus Pius XII warns: 'It is not right to deprive the dying person of consciousness without a serious reason.' (Congregation for the Doctrine of the Faith 1980, Section III)

But what constitutes a 'serious reason'? In his original speech, quoted from in the Declaration on Euthanasia, Pius XII seems to suggest that a serious reason for decreasing consciousness could be when continued pain or suffering gives 'opportunity for new sins' (Pope Pius XII 1957, para. 41; authors' translation from Spanish), although what this means is somewhat vague. The more recent Declaration on Euthanasia lists three conditions for the rightful use of painkillers, including when they 'suppress' consciousness.[10] The first condition, known as the principle of last resort, is that no other means exist to relieve the patient's suffering. The second condition is that the suppression of consciousness should not prevent the patient from carrying out other religious and/or moral duties. In order words, the indirect harm inflicted by continuous sedation should be diminished as much as possible. The final condition is that death should in no way be intended or sought and that the intention must be confined to effective pain relief.

Some commentators assume that the 'serious reason' for causing unconsciousness is circumscribed by these three conditions for the rightful use of 'decreased' consciousness.[11] However, the passage that calls for a serious reason is clearly limited to 'painkillers that cause unconsciousness', i.e. to what we call continuous deep sedation.[12]

Accordingly, the text does not offer a full justification for permanently taking away consciousness. Again, undergoing general anaesthesia and consuming alcohol do not permanently impede one's capacity to fulfil certain (religious or other) duties, but taking away consciousness completely until death *does*. This seems to be precisely why Pius XII, in his speech, made a strong distinction between, on the one hand, sedation that leaves the patient with some moments of competence and clarity (maintaining the possibility to fulfil religious duties), and, on the other hand, sedation that deprives the patient of all mental capacities and thus of all ability to do what should be done (e.g. to reconcile herself to God).

---

[10] The encyclical letter *Evangelium Vitae*, rephrasing the passage from the Declaration on Euthanasia, uses the expression '*decreased* consciousness' (Pope John Paul II 1995: 65; our italics).

[11] M. Davis, for example, summarises the two passages as follows: 'The [Congregation for the Doctrine of the Faith] reiterated Pope Pius XII's teaching on the use of terminal sedation. Painkillers that may cause unconsciousness may be used if no other treatment can relieve pain, and if the person has been given the opportunity to make his/her spiritual duties. The CDF emphasised that the intention in using these painkillers was to relieve pain and not to cause death' (Davis 2008: 1).

[12] The encyclical letter *Evangelium Vitae* reproduces the duality between 'mild' and 'deep' sedation. In the latter case, it uses the expression '*deprive* the dying person of consciousness' (Pope John Paul II 1995: 65; our italics).

The latter kind of sedation, which is the topic of this chapter, was therefore clearly condemned by Pius XII when he said: 'Anaesthesia used at the approach of death, with the only goal of avoiding a conscious end of life for the patient, will not be a significant victory of modern therapeutics, but rather a truly deplorable practice' (Pope Pius XII 1957, para. 42; authors' translation from Spanish). Apparently, the Congregation for the Doctrine of the Faith does believe that a proportionally sufficiently serious reason for permanently taking away consciousness might sometimes exist (but it does not clearly identify that reason).

Our main point, however, is that, whatever that reason may be, it is difficult to see how DDE could be applied to it in a plausible way. If one were to accept that taking away (momentary) consciousness as a means (and thus intending it) is not a wrong in itself, it would still be necessary to show how it is possible to perform CDS without *also* intending to take away consciousness permanently (the so-called indirect harm). Consider the case of someone who would claim: 'Well, I intended to perform CDS, but only by taking away the patient's consciousness, albeit not permanently'. That amounts to a performative paradox.

4.2.   *The Non-Standard Vatican Case*

Some commentators, for example Jansen and Sulmasy, have included 'permanent loss of consciousness' in their application of DDE to CDS:

> The rule of double effect, when applied to the issue of terminal sedation, maintains that it is not immoral to render a patient unconscious as a side effect of treating specific symptoms if 1) one does not aim at unconsciousness directly, 2) unconsciousness is not the means by which one intends to relieve symptoms, and 3) one has a 'proportionate reason' for taking such action. (Jansen & Sulmasy 2002: 847)

To make their view clearer, Jansen and Sulmasy introduce two contrasting cases. First, Joe's Case: Joe is terminally ill from cancer and his suffering is worsening. Because no other therapies help, his physician prescribes increasing doses of benzodiazepines until the pain caused by the cancer is controlled. The dose required to achieve this control precipitates a coma. Joe dies two days later.[13]

---

[13] This is a simplified case description. In fact Jansen and Sulmasy also add the requirement of patient consent to their description, a condition that is altogether irrelevant to the validity of DDE.

The doctrine of double effect

193

Φ ⟶ E^i (reduce suffering)
(administer sedatives)
                      E^s (permanent loss of consciousness)

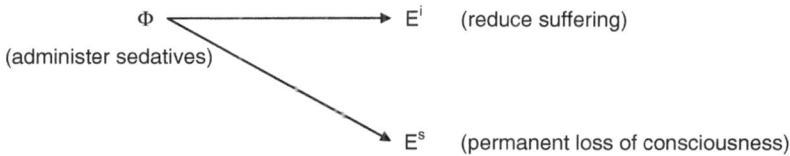

Figure 11.3 Non-Standard Vatican Case.

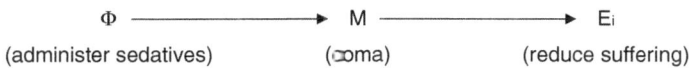

Φ ⟶ M ⟶ E_i
(administer sedatives) (coma) (reduce suffering)

Figure 11.4 Terminal Sedation Case.

This case is contrasted with Janet's Case: The facts are as in Joe's Case, but Janet's suffering is blocked by sedating her deeply.[14]

Thus, in Joe's Case, Jansen and Sulmasy start from the structure of the Standard Vatican Case, but modify it to include the permanent loss of consciousness as the relevant side-effect rather than the hastening of death. This is presented schematically in Figure 11.3.

As mentioned above, some commentators note that loss of consciousness has the *additional* side-effect of preventing future experiences. For the sake of completeness, one could therefore include this as an additional effect to the permanent loss of consciousness. However, as this is not central to the application of DDE and would only complicate the scheme (as it would be a side-effect of a side-effect), we shall ignore this here.

This scheme can then be called the *Non-Standard Vatican Case*. It can be contrasted with Janet's Case, which Jansen and Sulmasy consider to be unjustified and to be more like the Euthanasia Case, where an undesirable means is used to produce a good effect. One could call Janet's Case the *Terminal Sedation Case* and schematically this would be as in Figure 11.4.[15]

The Non-Standard Vatican Case seems to be a more accurate application of DDE to CDS than the Standard Vatican Case, since it explicitly includes permanent loss of consciousness as an unintended side-effect.

[14] Again, Jansen and Sulmasy's case is different, as they let Jane ask to be put in a coma. Again, they confuse an application of DDE from the point of view of what a *physician* is allowed to do with the application of DDE to a *patient's* request to have consciousness taken away.
[15] Note that the Congregation for the Doctrine of the Faith believes that such a scheme can be justified, as shown in section 4.1 above.

In the Non-Standard Vatican Case, 'preserving consciousness' properly takes the place that 'preserving life' has in the Standard Vatican Case: consciousness is, like life, a fundamental good that should not be intentionally and permanently diminished or taken away for the sake of preventing or diminishing suffering. That consciousness is a positive good is often missed in discussions about the ethical acceptability of CDS: taking consciousness away, or diminishing it, is often implicitly seen as a neutral thing compared to the evil of shortening life. In fact, the claim that sedation does not intentionally shorten life is sometimes mentioned as its main virtue compared to *both* the Standard Vatican Case and the Euthanasia Case (Cavanaugh 2006).[16] Yet, consciousness, as the condition of any kind of *meaningful* life, is obviously a positive value. Heyse-Moore, for instance, points out that some patients, even in pain, seem to value it: 'We try to avoid sedating patients where possible. Patients don't usually like it, nor do their relatives. Preservation of consciousness is rightly seen as an important priority' (Heyse-Moore 2003: 469).

Nevertheless, some questions can be raised concerning the Non-Standard Vatican Case. First, although this application of DDE introduces preserving consciousness as a positive value in the debate, it does so *by leaving out possible life-shortening*. However, since CDS is often accompanied by a withdrawal of artificial hydration and nutrition, the possibility of life-shortening cannot be excluded, and (if present) should be considered relevant for the application of DDE.

Second, and more importantly, DDE, in this version, does not serve as a justification for CDS, but rather as an answer to the question as to how to protect the value of consciousness when the pharmacologically induced and permanent diminishment of consciousness appears to be the only way (besides death) of reducing pain. According to this application of DDE, the *deliberate* use of sedatives to cloud consciousness constitutes a direct harm (as in Janet's Case) and is the equivalent of euthanasia. This is problematic for two reasons.

First, most of the definitions of CDS (or of 'palliative' or 'terminal' sedation) include the intentional lowering of consciousness. Gevers (2004), for example, uses the term 'terminal sedation' and defines it as: 'the administration of sedative drugs with the aim to reduce the consciousness of a terminal patient in order to relieve distress' (Gevers 2004:

---

[16] According to Cavanaugh, the advantage of CDS is that in doing CDS, the doctor does not intend the life-shortening, unlike with euthanasia where the doctor intends the patient's death. Thus Cavanaugh ignores the role of 'permanent loss of consciousness' and the question as to whether one may use a coma as an intended means for pain or symptom relief.

360). However, when CDS is defined in this way, it describes a practice that is unjustified and impermissible according to the Non-Standard Vatican application of DDE.

Second, since CDS includes the administration of sedatives (i.e. consciousness-lowering drugs), the question arises as to how a physician could administer these drugs while at the same time *not* intending to take away consciousness as a means to reduce suffering. Of course, different types of drugs are administered to patients at the end of life, and for some of these drugs, their administration need not necessarily be accompanied by an intention to lower consciousness. Certain analgesics and anxiolytics, for example, are administered with the aim of relieving pain and anxiety respectively, but have a sedative effect. In these cases, the reduction of consciousness could be claimed to be a side-effect.[17] However, the drugs most commonly used and recommended for sedation at the end of life, such as midazolam, levomepromazine and propofol, have the lowering of consciousness as their primary function. In small dosages, the reduction is minimal (but still present), while in high dosages these drugs induce a deep coma. It is clear that the effect of these drugs is a reduction of consciousness, and that, when administering them, one cannot claim reduction or loss of consciousness to be a side-effect. This is true even if one is aiming at the lowest possible reduction of consciousness.

One could attempt a redescription and construe the case so that loss of consciousness or coma is interpreted as a side-effect of the cutting off of neuro-physiological processes. ('I only had the intention to interrupt normal neurological processes, not to induce a coma!'). CDS would then fall under the Non-Standard Vatican Case and thus be justified according to DDE. The problem with this 'DDE-saving' reply is that consciousness is – depending on one's preferred theory of consciousness – either identical to brain processes or supervenient on them (i.e. determined by brain processes). Both alternatives imply that the closeness between the physical processes and the experiential processes is infinite (their distance is zero). It is inconceivable (unless one adopts a dualist theory of the mind–body relationship) that conscious experience could survive the undercutting of its physical basis.

One might, however, still question whether using a *coma* as a means of relieving suffering is not in some relevant ways different from using *death* as a means to relieve suffering. For commentators such as Jonathan Glover it is clear: what is of value is not the 'biological life',

---

[17] Although these drugs can in fact also be used with the explicit aim of reducing consciousness.

but the consciousness that comes with it, and thus a 'life of permanent coma [is] in no way preferable to death' (Glover 1977: 45). This would imply that no ethically relevant difference exists between killing someone and permanently taking away her consciousness. Other commentators, however, see permanent coma as different from death for two reasons. First, they value life as such and claim that a patient in a coma can still be said to be alive (although permanently unconscious) and be allowed to die a natural death. Second, they note that CDS is – theoretically speaking – reversible. On these grounds, these commentators could claim that it is not incoherent to say that one may sometimes use permanent unconsciousness as a means to relieve suffering but never death.

To this we would answer that, even if it is true that putting someone in a permanent coma is a lesser evil than killing that person, this does not make it a good. As we have argued earlier, there are good reasons to consider the permanent removal of consciousness as a wrong. Since we are dealing with *continuous* deep sedation, it is clear that the intention with which it is performed is to sedate the patient permanently until her death. Therefore, we would submit that inducing a coma for pain relief cannot become 'DDE-allowed' by claiming that inducing a permanent coma is a lesser evil than killing.

4.3.   The Non-Standard Vatican Case and life-shortening

As noted in the previous section, the Non-Standard Vatican Case does not include the possible life-shortening of CDS. If we include the possible life-shortening, we would obtain the scheme shown in Figure 11.5. Or something like the scheme shown in Figure 11.6.

Both schemes have the advantage of including both the permanent loss of consciousness and the shortening of life as relevant means or side-effects, but both involve problems. In the first scheme, two bad side-effects (shortening of life and permanent loss of consciousness) have to be balanced against the good intended effect of reducing suffering. This might create a problem with the proportionality condition (although one might also argue that, since death is itself (permanent) unconsciousness, adding unconsciousness to unconsciousness makes no difference).

The problem with the second scheme is that, although death is considered here to be an unintended side-effect, it still remains the case that taking away consciousness is deliberately intended in order to reduce suffering. Thus, as in the Non-Standard Vatican Case, only those types

Φ ━━━━━━━━━━━━━━━━━━▶ E^i
(administer sedatives)   (reduce suffering)

                                                   E^{s1}
                                                   (permanent loss of consciousness)

                                                   E^{s2}
                                                   (patient dies)

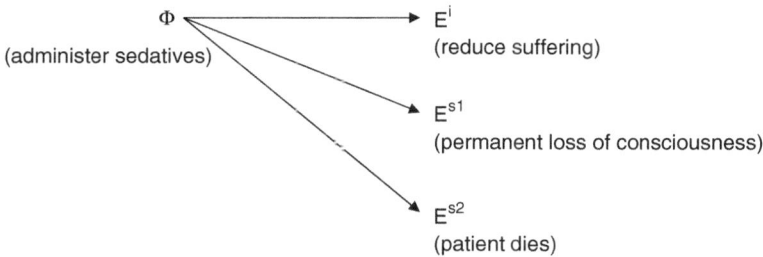

Figure 11.5 Non-Standard Vatican Case and life-shortening scheme 1.

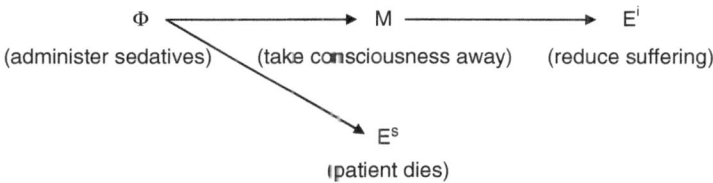

Φ ━━━━━━━━━━▶ M ━━━━━━━━━━▶ E^i
(administer sedatives)   (take consciousness away)   (reduce suffering)

                         E^s
                         (patient dies)

Figure 11.6 Non-Standard Vatican Case and life-shortening scheme 2.

of sedation where permanent loss of consciousness is a side-effect will be permitted and, as noted earlier, such a claim is unconvincing in cases of CDS.

It might, however, be possible to apply the 'proportionalist' version of DDE (see section 2.4 above) here, since this version allows an agent to use an evil as a means, provided that the good effect represents a good reason for doing so. In this case it could be claimed that – in some last resort cases – preventing suffering is a proportionate reason for using permanent loss of consciousness as a way of relieving that suffering. This interpretation of DDE, however, is controversial and can be said to have more in common with moral theories that allow a lesser evil to be committed to stop or prevent a greater evil, than it has with classical DDE.

4.4. Combining CDS with the withdrawal of artificial nutrition and hydration

The practice of CDS is often combined with the withholding or withdrawing of artificial nutrition and hydration (ANH). In Belgium, for example, the decision to use CDS has been reported to be combined with a decision to withhold or withdraw food and fluids in 57 per cent

$$\Phi + \Delta \longrightarrow M \longrightarrow E^{i1} + E^{i2}$$

(administering sedatives + no ANH)   (taking consciousness away)   (reducing suffering + avoiding futility)

$$E^s$$

(patient dying)

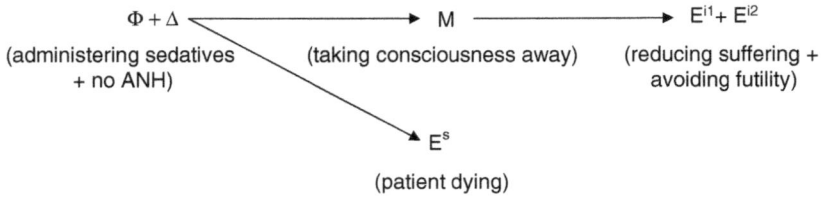

Figure 11.7 DDE applied to CDS without ANH.

of all sedation cases (Chambaere et al. 2010). It is therefore interesting to investigate whether and how DDE might apply to these cases, on the assumption that the life-shortening effect of withdrawing or withholding ANH may be real.[18] Schematically one could construe such cases as shown in Figure 11.7.

This application combines all the elements of CDS that are commonly thought to be relevant. Yet this application of DDE actually *combines two practices*, so in order to analyse this application one needs to look at the individual decisions.

Does DDE apply to the withholding of ANH? It is commonly claimed that DDE does in fact justify this, but only if, additionally, a distinction is maintained between *ordinary/proportionate* and *extraordinary/ disproportionate* means.[19] In withholding *extraordinary/disproportionate* means (such as a ventilator), the patient is spared excessive pain from

[18] For example, Gillian Craig, a specialist in geriatrics, has noted that: 'If death is imminent few people would feel it essential to put up a drip but ethical problems arise if sedation is continued for more than one or two days, without hydration, as the patient will become dehydrated. Dehydration can result in circulatory collapse, renal failure, anuria and death' (Craig 1994: 140). See also the discussion of this topic in the Introduction to this volume (Chapter 1).

[19] As Donald Henke explains in an interesting overview of the history of the development within the Catholic tradition of the distinction between 'ordinary' and 'extraordinary' means, confusion arose from the way in which the healthcare community used those terms, in contrast to their traditional theological meaning (Henke 2007: 66–7). Quoting Bryan Jennett (Jennett 2002: 105), Henke notes that, initially, 'ordinary was taken to mean generally available and widely used, whilst extraordinary would include advanced technological methods that were scarce and expensive'. With its Declaration on Euthanasia (1980), according to Henke, the Congregation for the Doctrine of the Faith attempted 'to clarify the distinction between what the medical community understood as the definitional characteristics of the terms ordinary and extraordinary ... and the theological understanding, which was significantly more nuanced than simple ease or difficulty in application ... The declaration proposed that the terms used by moral theologians and medical personnel should shift away from the ordinary-extraordinary distinction ... to a different set of terms that would be more specific' (Henke 2007: 67). Indeed, in the Declaration on Euthanasia, the question is raised as to whether it is necessary in all circumstances to have recourse to all possible remedies. According to the Congregation for the Doctrine of the Faith:

a treatment that offers no reasonable hope of benefit, even if withholding the treatment may shorten the patient's life. In these cases, all the conditions for classical DDE are fulfilled. However, when *ordinary/proportionate* means are withheld, DDE's proportionality condition is not met. Marquis, for example, argues that: 'A decision *not* to use *ordinary* means of sustaining life ... is not justified by a *proportionate* reason to bring about the bad consequence. Hence, a physician who deliberately refrains from *ordinary* means of sustaining life *must be intending* the death of her patient' (Marquis 1991: 521; our italics).

The classical example of such ordinary/proportionate means is ANH. Thus DDE may justify certain non-treatment decisions, but *not* the withholding of food and fluids. Especially not in permanently unconscious patients, since these patients – being unconscious – can suffer no harm from the treatments they are receiving and so withdrawing food and fluids cannot be proportional to the suffering that is spared. The application of DDE to CDS combined with withdrawal or withholding of ANH therefore is problematic.[20]

Furthermore, even if one believes that withdrawing or withholding ANH is permitted by DDE, the use of sedatives to intentionally

'In the past, moralists replied that one is never obliged to use "extraordinary" means. This reply, which as a principle still holds good, is perhaps less clear today, by reason of the imprecision of the term and the rapid progress made in the treatment of sickness. Thus some people prefer to speak of "proportionate" and "disproportionate" means. In any case, it will be possible to make a correct judgment as to the means by studying the type of treatment to be used, its degree of complexity or risk, its cost and the possibilities of using it, and comparing these elements with the result that can be expected, taking into account the state of the sick person and his or her physical and moral resources' (Congregation for the Doctrine of the Faith 1980, Section IV). Thus, as Henke rightly concludes, the key message from the Declaration in this regard is that whether a means is proportionate or disproportionate cannot be decided by merely considering the means in themselves. Rather, contextual factors (including patient-specific factors) must also be taken into account.

In other Vatican documents, the terms 'ordinary' and 'proportionate' appear to be used together. See, for example, the Congregation for the Doctrine of the Faith's *Responses to certain questions of the United States Conference of Catholic Bishops concerning artificial nutrition and hydration* (2007), approved by Pope Benedict XVI: 'The administration of food and water even by artificial means is, in principle, *an ordinary and proportionate means* of preserving life. It is therefore obligatory to the extent to which, and for as long as, it is shown to accomplish its proper finality, which is the hydration and nourishment of the patient. In this way suffering and death by starvation and dehydration are prevented' (Congregation for the Doctrine of the Faith 2007, response to the first question; our italics).

[20] According to proponents of the proportionalist interpretation of DDE, what constitutes *disproportionate* means depends on the particular circumstances and values at stake. In this interpretation, withdrawing ANH can sometimes be considered *proportionate* (e.g. if hydration and nutrition have side-effects that threaten a patient's dignity), making DDE potentially applicable. The proportionalist interpretation, however, is not the interpretation of DDE we are concerned with in this chapter.

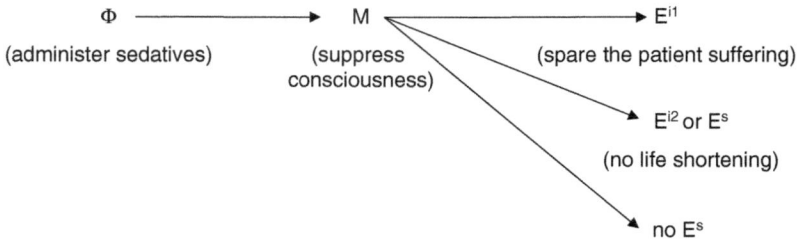

Figure 11.8 Non-Construable Case.

lower consciousness is not permitted by DDE, as we argued earlier. Accordingly, when combining these practices, one is at best adding a right to a wrong, thereby making a wrong.

4.5.   *The Non-Construable Case*

Another possible case exists which we will call the Non-Construable Case (Figure 11.8). This is the most frequently encountered version in clinical and ethical discussions of CDS.

In this case, consciousness is taken away in order to spare the patient suffering. There is no negative side-effect, but a second (either intended or unintended) positive effect, namely: not shortening life.

This case is not positively construable by means of DDE: Mangan's conditions (2) and (3) do not obtain because there is no bad effect. There are only two positive effects. One could, as noted earlier, claim that there is a negative side-effect since suppressing consciousness prevents further opportunities for positive acts or experiences. This point, however, is very rarely made in the literature on CDS and DDE. Moreover, this would still not make this case a case of DDE reasoning, since the line linking Φ to M and M to E^{i1} either simply represents a prohibition – if one believes that suppressing consciousness is not allowed in order to bring suffering under control – or describes intending a lesser evil in order to avoid having to intend a greater one.

We would submit that the morality that is at work in clinical practice regarding CDS is actually *not* DDE (in spite of all the lip service paid to this doctrine), but rather the morality of choosing the (seemingly) lesser evil over the greater one, i.e. consequentialism. This means that *directly intending* 'evils' (whether coma or death) should be allowed if one wants one's medical ethic to correspond to ongoing clinical practice. But whatever one may think about this, DDE does not apply to the kind of scheme mentioned above.

5.   Concluding remarks

Although the doctrine of double effect is a very frequently invoked justification for CDS, its application to this end-of-life practice turns out to be problematic. Classical DDE does *not* allow an intentional and permanent reduction of consciousness in order to diminish a patient's suffering. Only the construction under which the permanent loss of consciousness is a *side-effect* of administering sedatives, rather than its end, is a candidate for a green light from classical DDE. In cases of CDS, such a claim is unconvincing.

We have also attempted to show that the most frequently encountered case in clinical ethical discussions is in fact not construable under DDE reasoning. The reason is that there is often claimed to be no bad side-effect for CDS, since the practice does not shorten life. So what happens in these justifications of CDS only *looks* like applying DDE. But what justifies CDS in this case is most clearly *not* DDE, but a different type of reasoning that weighs the evil of taking away consciousness against the good of reducing suffering. This is an ethical justification which Magnusson (2006) has called 'the devil's choice', in which an agent finds herself in a situation where every choice available to her involves an evil, and she chooses the lesser one.

This ethic seems to be the reason why the existing guidelines concerning CDS recommend the use of this practice only as a 'last resort'. The last resort case is of course the paradigm case where there is no good choice for the physician to make. In these cases, taking away consciousness is the only available way to reduce otherwise terrible suffering.

12   Palliative sedation, consciousness and personhood

Timothy Holahan, Thomas Carroll, Claudia Gonzalez and Timothy E. Quill

1.   Introduction

Palliative care and hospice medicine are envisioned as essential elements of the standard of care for patients who are experiencing suffering in the setting of serious or life-threatening illness. However, despite the advances in perception, accessibility, delivery and performance of palliative care, a subset of patients still experience severe suffering refractory to standard palliative treatments. Palliative sedation is one option that can be employed, usually as a last resort, to ameliorate suffering in these situations. There are several types of palliative sedation, each of which may be appropriate in different settings. When a clinician is considering palliative sedation to relieve suffering, one important consideration is the relationship between consciousness and personhood. Our purpose for this chapter is to define the various types of palliative sedation, and to consider how these interventions may affect an individual's consciousness and personhood. We will also discuss the ethical reasoning behind the different types of palliative sedation, and how these considerations might affect a clinician's practice.

2.   Types of sedation

There are three types of sedation that we will define for the purposes of this chapter: ordinary sedation, proportionate palliative sedation and palliative sedation to unconsciousness.[1] The first, *ordinary sedation*, is the result of attempts to relieve a symptom without necessarily impairing consciousness. This type of sedation is used in everyday clinical

---

[1] So, for the purposes of this chapter, we will divide palliative sedation into two categories: proportionate palliative sedation and palliative sedation to unconsciousness (Quill et al. 1997b). Although the ultimate goal of each of these interventions is the relief of otherwise intractable suffering, the means are sufficiently different to justify this distinction.

practice. Pain, anxiety, depression and insomnia are among the symptoms whose treatment may result in mild sedation during the course of treatment. Temporary decreases in alertness may be the desired effect of some of these pharmacological interventions, but no lasting impairment in consciousness would be intended. Over-sedation would be an unintended side-effect which would warrant dose titration downward or rotation of the therapeutic agent if necessary to reduce the degree of sedation. Examples from everyday practice would include the treatment of anxiety with low dose benzodiazepines or using low dose hypnotics to improve sleep. The goal of such treatment is the specific relief of suffering due to these symptoms, and the risk of permanently impairing consciousness or unintentionally hastening death would be negligible.

The second type of sedation, proportionate palliative sedation (PPS), is one of the 'last-resort' options that can be employed to relieve symptoms in cases of refractory suffering (Quill et al. 2009). Its purpose is to relieve physical, psychosocial and, in some cases, existential suffering that is not responsive to less aggressive measures. PPS usually involves the administration of sedating medications in gradually increasing doses until a level of decreased awareness is reached that is sufficient to relieve the patient's intractable suffering. Achieving this end using the minimal amount of sedation needed is the goal, although, when necessary, sedation may gradually progress to complete unconsciousness. The risk of hastening death when low levels of PPS are sufficient to relieve suffering is relatively small, but the risk increases in proportion to the depth of sedation. PPS is usually used alongside other symptom-relieving measures to help achieve a patient's comfort, including antipsychotics and analgesics. If sedation to full unconsciousness is required to relieve the suffering, such a depth of sedation is viewed as an anticipated but unintended side-effect.

There is general acceptance of PPS when used to relieve otherwise intractable physical suffering at the end of life. In addition to the relief of 'strictly' physical symptoms, clinicians may also find themselves considering PPS to relieve coexisting psychosocial and/or existential suffering, including severe refractory depression, post-traumatic stress disorder or relentless anxiety. This indication is, however, much more controversial for patients whose suffering is *primarily* psychosocial and/ or existential rather than physical. We will come back to this distinction later in this chapter.

In summary, PPS employs the minimum amount of sedation needed to achieve adequate relief of suffering. While this intervention could conceivably hasten death in some cases, the doctrine of double effect applies when the intention of PPS is to relieve severe otherwise intractable suffering, and the potential obliteration of consciousness or hastening of death is a foreseen, but unintended, consequence.

The third type of sedation, palliative sedation to unconsciousness (PSU), is another distinct 'last resort' option where, as with PPS, the ultimate goal is also to relieve intense, refractory symptoms in dying patients (Quill et al. 2009). However, PSU is more controversial than PPS because unconsciousness is an intended endpoint rather than a potentially foreseeable but unintended outcome. The use of PSU can be justified in cases where the symptoms are so extreme that nothing short of unconsciousness can provide relief. When undertaking PSU, sedating medications are rapidly titrated over a period of minutes to hours until the patient is totally sedated. Other coexisting palliative medications are continued as the sedated patient will no longer be able to report pain or other uncomfortable symptoms. Because the fully sedated patient will no longer be able to report potential physical discomfort, clinicians generally err on the side of aggressive concomitant symptom management in these cases, but this is admittedly an inexact process.

PSU is more ethically controversial than PPS. This is especially the case if a patient's suffering is predominantly psychosocial or existential, or if a patient is requesting PSU in the context of a desire for a hastened death. Such requests will be considered later in this chapter.

When considering PSU, the doctrine of double effect may or may not be invoked to justify the practice. If the bad effect includes altering consciousness, then it cannot be invoked since consciousness is intentionally altered as part of the practice. If the bad effect involves the risk of hastening death, then the doctrine might be invoked if neither the patient nor the clinician explicitly intends to hasten death. The consenting patient is sedated to unconsciousness to relieve otherwise untreatable symptoms, and will ultimately die from the underlying disease or insufficient intake of nutrition and hydration. The primary goal of both patient and clinician is to relieve suffering, but there may be some ambiguity as to whether hastening death is intended by either party (Quill 1993). This is different from PPS which, as mentioned earlier, uses the least amount of sedation needed to relieve the symptom. With PSU, unconsciousness is the intended endpoint, which makes it more extreme and potentially controversial. PSU is generally considered in cases of symptoms that are so severe that nothing short of complete lack of awareness can reasonably be predicted to provide relief. It should be relatively rare in comparison to PPS, which is a preferred approach to lesser degrees of suffering.

In this regard, consider the following case:

> DD was a 60-year-old African American man with locally
> metastatic oropharyngeal cancer that had invaded and encased
> his carotid artery. The lesion had been extensively treated in the
> past with radiation and surgery, and there was now an open ulcer
> filled with tumour leaving his carotid visible and oozing. Surgery
> and radiation therapies had been administered repeatedly, and
> had given him some extra time. Now all consulting teams agreed
> that the artery was likely to rupture very soon, and there were no
> effective treatments remaining to prevent this. He was terrified
> about bleeding out, but also wanted to maintain alertness as
> much as possible so he could fully enjoy his family for the time
> that remained. He wanted sedation to be minimised for as long
> as possible so he could interact fully with his family, but he also
> wanted reassurance that the clinical team would be ready to provide
> palliative sedation to unconsciousness should he begin to actively
> bleed. After extensive discussions with the patient, his family,
> the palliative care team and the ethics team, plans were made to
> rapidly provide PSU should rapid bleeding occur. After several
> weeks on the palliative care unit where he was fully alert, one
> morning his vessel began to rupture, and he was rapidly sedated
> until he was unconscious to escape the terror he anticipated would
> accompany bleeding out. The patient was unarousable for his final
> hours as the medical team tried their best to support the family and
> manage the severe bleeding. The family was very grateful for the
> weeks he had spent fully alert in the palliative care unit, but also
> were appreciative and understanding of the need for PSU in this
> circumstance to address his terminal symptoms.

In 2008, the House of Delegates of the American Medical Association
(AMA) adopted a report by its Council on Ethical and Judicial
Affairs (CEJA) entitled *Sedation to Unconsciousness in End-of-Life Care*
(American Medical Association 2008). This report lays out parame-
ters for providing palliative sedation to the point of unconsciousness
for dying patients whose symptoms are refractory to standard palliative
care. The report suggests a consensus about the permissibility of PSU
to respond to severe and otherwise intractable *physical* suffering, but it
also states that severe *psychological* suffering may warrant using PSU
after all other treatments have been exhausted. However, it also states
that PSU is not indicated in the case of purely existential suffering (fear
of death, isolation, etc.) (Cassell & Rich 2010).

Providing PSU in the absence of severe physical suffering remains very controversial, and there is little consensus in the literature about its permissibility, which leaves practising clinicians in a difficult position when faced with patients whose severe suffering is more psychosocial or existential than physical. In the absence of very clear, intractable physical suffering, clinicians must use their own clinical and ethical judgement, with involvement of experts in this area (palliative care, ethics, psychiatry), to help sort through these difficult cases. It is incumbent upon any clinician who cares for patients with advanced diseases to be familiar with the different types of palliative sedation and the associated ethical principles. PPS and PSU potentially allow for ethically and legally accepted responses to extremes of suffering when less extreme interventions are ineffective.

3.   Consciousness and personhood

One of the more challenging aspects of palliative sedation is how the inevitable reduction in the patient's consciousness associated with the practice affects her personhood. There is certainly no universally accepted view regarding the relationship between consciousness and personhood. At one end of the spectrum, consciousness awareness may be viewed by some patients as a necessary condition for experiencing personhood, and such patients may therefore want to minimise any sedating medications even under the most dire of circumstances (Singer 1995). In the middle ground there may be a spectrum of views that place varying weight on the degree of self-awareness that is able to be preserved as well as the presence of any level of consciousness at all (e.g. being able to perceive the presence of loved ones without necessarily being able to verbally respond). At the other end of the spectrum, a person who is fearful about losing control of her self-awareness may desire total sedation at the end of life as soon as cognition becomes even minimally impaired at all to preserve what remains of her personhood which she feels is being destroyed by the ravages of disease.

Cassell characterises the essence of suffering as the disintegration of the person (Cassell 1982), but the relationship between physical suffering and loss of perceived personhood is extremely variable and individual. Some patients may tolerate extremes of physical symptoms without suffering severely, whereas others may find significantly less severe symptoms threatening to their integration as a person. Other patients may experience being in control of their minds and bodies as at the core of personhood, and when this control is failing it may be experienced as unacceptable suffering. When a person is suffering so severely that her personhood is experienced as disintegrating, then PPS or PSU may be the only legally permissible avenue available to help her find relief. In that sense, PPS or PSU can help preserve what remains of personhood when it is being assaulted by the ravages of advanced disease.

What might PPS or PSU mean to patients in relation to the relief of suffering? If consciousness is viewed by an individual as a necessary component of personhood, then PSU should be reserved for the most extreme and irreversible cases. The goal of PPS is to preserve consciousness as much as possible, and therefore in such circumstances it may be more likely to preserve personhood. However, the linkage of personhood to consciousness is likely to differ from one person to the next, and, importantly, the strength of the relationship between the two may change over time and in the face of extremes of suffering towards the very end of life. Other people believe that the essence of the person is maintained until death no matter whether the person is conscious or unconscious. This would make the lack of consciousness potentially associated with either PPS or PSU easier to accept. However, as noted earlier, there are cases where the physical or existential suffering is so severe that the loss of consciousness becomes necessary to relieve the distress, arguably preserving what remains of personhood.

In this regard, consider the following case:

> *AA was an 87-year-old Jewish immigrant who had survived the death camps during the Holocaust in World War II. He suffered from end-stage congestive heart failure, and had been intubated twice in the previous two months. He was a man who valued being in charge of his life and making his own decisions. While intubated in the intensive care unit, he would experience flashbacks about his experiences during the war. He would become extremely agitated, requiring that he be restrained and totally sedated. He talked about the terror he experienced during these flashbacks and memories of his concentration camp experience upon being extubated. Despite his poor prognosis and the reactivation of these devastating memories during his hospitalisations, he continued to opt for full resuscitation including a trial of intubation and cardiopulmonary resuscitation if and when he experienced another exacerbation unless there was no meaningful prospect of recovery. In an attempt to avoid these distressing symptoms, his attending physician discussed with AA the option of immediately sedating him to unconsciousness if and when he had another heart failure exacerbation requiring intubation. Although the patient still hoped to recover from any new exacerbation, he also agreed in advance*

with a plan to withdraw potentially life-prolonging treatments if he did not respond within a few days to our interventions. Shortly thereafter he had another exacerbation necessitating intubation. He was sedated to unconsciousness while attempts were made to treat this acute heart failure exacerbation. Unfortunately, he did not respond to aggressive heart failure management, and several days later life-sustaining treatments were withdrawn when the medical team agreed that there was no reasonable prospect of his being successfully extubated. He was kept sedated to unconsciousness until he died.

4.   Ethical consequences of reducing consciousness when employing PPS or PSU

There is no guarantee that an individual's abstract view of the relationship between consciousness and personhood is immutable, and so the experiences of significant suffering may affect that individual's view of this relationship. Although there are no data specifically addressing this evolution, analogous data suggest that people's views regarding their own advance directives tend to change over time with the experience of illness and debility (Fried et al. 2007). Therefore it seems reasonable to ask whether a similar temporal instability exists for a person's perception of the relationship between consciousness and personhood.

Although no empirical data specifically address this topic, an individual's previously expressed, or inferred opinions about the relationship between consciousness and personhood can at least provide a starting point for discussion. More challenging are the cases in which the patient lacks the ability to effectively take part in such a challenging discussion. In this situation, substituted judgement on the part of surrogates is appropriate, as with any other medical decision for incapacitated patients. In the absence of sufficient knowledge of a patient's preferences, the team and any surrogate decision-makers would be left with only the 'best interests' standard to guide decision-making.

It is widely agreed within palliative care that consciousness should be preserved to the greatest degree possible while providing a level of relief from suffering that is acceptable to the patient. The surrogate decision-maker would represent the patient using substituted judgement if the patient is not capable of making decisions. For patients experiencing a level of refractory suffering sufficient for consideration of palliative sedation, an ethical and practical tension will inevitably emerge between preservation of consciousness, the risk of hastening death and relief of suffering. The most straightforward situation is when the patient has decisional capacity, or can at least express her subjective experience of suffering and willingness to accept decreased or complete lack of consciousness to escape that suffering. However, more ethically complicated situations arise when the patient is incapacitated or otherwise unable to speak for herself. In these scenarios, the determination of how to balance relief of suffering, the risk of hastening death, and the preservation of consciousness falls to surrogate decision-makers and the healthcare team. In such circumstances, the determination of suffering is inevitably from the outside-looking-in. Unfortunately, under such circumstances we can never be completely sure that we are correct in our determination of the patient's intensity of suffering.

This question of who is best to judge suffering for an incapacitated patient does not yield a universal answer. We suggest that a team approach be employed that includes family members or friends who know the patient well, nurses who are at the bedside and hopefully are experienced in using non-verbal pain rating scales, and healthcare providers who are skilled in the practice of palliative medicine. Any given situation may call for a specific combination of individuals, with each member providing input into decisions about apparent intensity of suffering at various levels of consciousness. It is also important to assess for factors that may influence an individual clinician's judgement with regard to the patient's intensity of suffering, including, for example, over-identification with a patient who reminds a clinician of his own parents and/or feelings of guilt on the part of family members who can no longer care for a patient at home.

5.   Decision-making regarding PPS and PSU

Palliative sedation is a medical procedure and, as such, the usual approach to determination of decision-making authority should apply. Patients, or their surrogate decision-makers, should be engaged in a balanced discussion of the possible risks and benefits of the treatment. As with all risk/benefit discussions, we strongly encourage the medical team to not only communicate their best objective estimates of the patient's clinical condition, but also to provide patients and their loved ones with a reasoned and thoughtful recommendation that includes what is known about the patient's previously stated wishes and values in the current clinical context (Quill & Brody 1996). Consideration of palliative sedation is often undertaken at times of great stress and sadness. This stressful environment makes providing compassionate recommendations on the part of the medical team all the more important.

Alleviation of patients' suffering and maximisation of their quality of life are among healthcare teams' most important responsibilities. These goals of medical care were articulated in antiquity and apply with equal importance today. In accepting an individual as a patient, physicians enter into a trust relationship that imparts certain rights and responsibilities onto both parties. Neither these rights nor responsibilities are unlimited, however, and as such cannot in principle obligate a physician to violate personal beliefs.

While individual physicians may have strongly held views and values about what kind of sedation they might offer and under what circumstances, these limits should take into consideration conventional medical ethics as well as personal beliefs. Principled limits to what care a physician will offer a patient must be applied uniformly and discussed openly. This conversation should be initiated as early as possible in the course of the patient–physician relationship. When a physician feels obligated to turn down an otherwise indicated last resort treatment such as PPS or PSU because it violates her own personal moral values or beliefs, she must then initiate the transfer of care to another physician who is willing to consider the intervention in question. On the other hand, turning down a request for PSU based on suffering that is primarily existential (a practice that is much more controversial especially under these clinical circumstances) would warrant continued searching along with other members of the healthcare team for other ways to better address the patient's intractable suffering (see the next case example).

We strongly urge anyone who cares for sick and dying patients, especially in a hospital, palliative care or hospice setting, to thoughtfully consider their own position on the use of PPS and PSU as last resort options before such a situation presents itself. Insight into how one's own beliefs interface with the ethical issues raised by palliative sedation is essential to minimise conflict and potential delays in care that may result from unanticipated tension between indicated treatment and a physician's personal moral code.

6.   Existential suffering

There has been much debate in the literature regarding what clinical scenarios warrant consideration of palliative sedation. There seems to be general agreement that 'physical' symptoms (e.g., pain, dyspnoea, nausea) that are refractory to aggressive, competent management should be sufficient for consideration of palliative sedation. We certainly agree that refractory physical symptoms that are causing unacceptable suffering create an appropriate environment for consideration of palliative sedation, especially towards the end of life. Again, in this setting, although it might ultimately result in sedation to unconsciousness if lesser degrees of sedation were inadequate, PPS would be much less controversial than PSU in that with the former the least amount of sedation to adequately relieve the suffering will be provided.

More controversial has been whether refractory existential or emotional suffering should be an indication for either type of palliative sedation, especially for patients who are not otherwise near the end of life and when the practice includes withholding or withdrawing artificial hydration and nutrition. There are guidelines/recommendations in the literature that accept intractable existential suffering as an indication for palliative sedation in the setting of advanced stages of terminal illness after the failure of all other interventions (Rousseau 2001; Fine 2005). In general, we take the position that the distinction between physical and psychosocial/existential suffering is an artificial one, and that the intensity of an individual's 'total pain' is independent of its source, as elaborated by Cassell three decades ago (Cassell 1982). However, we urge caution when considering sedation where an individual's suffering is predominantly existential or psychological and seems to the clinician and the multidisciplinary team to be out of proportion to their underlying physical illness. Although the mind–body dichotomy is artificial, most medical professionals are more skilled at assessing and managing physical sources of suffering as compared to those of an existential or emotional aetiology. This is of particular concern when the existential or emotional suffering is primary, being unrelated to an identifiable physical ailment.

Suffering due to primary non-physical sources, while serious and deserving of careful assessment and intensive management, generally does not rise to the level of a terminal condition. While there may be exceptions, this lack of a terminal nature of the underlying primary illness also makes the argument for using palliative sedation much more difficult to accept in principle.

In this regard, consider the following case:

> *A 45-year-old nurse with a history of life-long depression had been tried on multiple antidepressant medications individually and in combination, as well as several courses of electroconvulsive therapy. He had been in intensive psychotherapy for many years. He saw his condition as irreversible and overwhelming. Indeed by many*

objective measures his suffering was extreme and distressing, and it appeared to be unresponsive to multiple standard and non-standard therapies which he had diligently tried. Having read about legally available palliative options of last resort, he asked whether palliative sedation to unconsciousness might be available to him. After multiple discussions about his suffering and other ways to approach it including several additional psychiatric consultations, his request for PSU was ultimately turned down because of the absence of a terminal illness and because the desire for death was likely in large measure a symptom of his underlying depressive disorder. This discussion continued for several years while the clinician tried to help him find some other approaches to this seemingly intractable suffering.

Some patients who have a combination of severe physical and existential distress may ask a healthcare provider to help hasten death in an attempt to relieve their suffering. These situations are not uncommon and can present a challenging situation for the clinician. Such requests may stem from multiple sources of existential or physical suffering, such as overwhelming physical pain, hopelessness, fear of burdening others, loss of control, severe depression and unbearable spiritual suffering. There is also a possibility that the request for hastening death stems from profound ambivalence about continuing to live with unbearable distress. These situations can be intimidating to the clinician and may initiate some self-examination regarding the clinician's own beliefs. It is important to understand the different options available to patients with intractable suffering, other than hastening death, in order to have a firm grasp of how to respond to such a patient. We would recommend the following approach:

The first step is to thoroughly evaluate the source of the patient's suffering, and to ensure that its multiple dimensions are understood and that good faith efforts have been made to address them (Quill & Arnold 2008). Usually one begins by evaluating and potentially treating the physical dimensions of suffering (pain, dyspnoea, other symptoms), but subsequently other dimensions (psychosocial, psychiatric, spiritual, existential) must also be addressed. Frequently the need for escape through sedation can dissipate when total suffering is understood and treated. If the unacceptable suffering is more psychosocial and/or existential than physical, involvement in the evaluation of experts from psychiatry, chaplaincy and social work should be strongly considered. Every effort should be made to find other avenues to address and alleviate a given patient's total suffering. However, there will be a relatively small number of cases of intractable, irreversible suffering despite comprehensive assessment and treatment, and it is in those cases where last resort options might be explored in earnest.

Indeed, in these refractory cases, clinicians begin to consider the different possibilities that a patient has available as a last resort to hasten death (Quill et al. 2010). PPS and PSU are among these options, and in comparison to other possibilities they are relatively flexible and enable clinicians to respond to a wide range of suffering. Other methods, including aggressive symptom management, withholding or withdrawing life-sustaining therapies, voluntarily stopping eating and drinking, physician-assisted suicide and voluntary active euthanasia, will not be explored here.

7.   Requests for hastened death

The manner by which to respond to a request for an escape from suffering that potentially includes hastening death in the setting of intractable suffering may also be a challenge for physicians and other healthcare providers. This conversation can often be uncomfortable as well as intimidating. However, developing a systematic approach can help the patient and family to thoughtfully work through this process. Ideally, any discussion about interventions that might hasten death requires the patient to have full capacity. If the patient lacks capacity and is suffering severely, decisions may need to be made by surrogate decision-makers using substituted judgement with guidance from a knowledgeable clinician. However, these 'once-removed' discussions are significantly more complicated because one has to infer the patient's wishes rather than hear them directly. Here we suggest a stepwise approach when faced with a patient who is inquiring about options for hastened death, and in particular PPS or PSU, as the mechanism by which this goal might be accomplished (Quill et al. 2010; Quill & Arnold 2009). Discussions with family members of incapacitated patients using substituted judgement should follow a similar sequence.

First, clinicians need to clarify what exactly is being asked of them. Is the patient asking about options in the future in the case of potential intractable suffering, or is she seeking to end her life at this moment based on the current situation? There may also be an underlying fear of death (or of the suffering associated with it) that needs to be addressed. *Second*, the patient and the family need to be assured that the clinician will continue to help them through this difficult process, no matter what unfolds. *Third*, the clinician should ensure that the patient fully understands the medical situation. The patient's level of suffering needs to be explored, to make certain that it is proportionate to her request.

A psychologist or psychiatrist may be of help, especially if psychosocial or existential suffering is a large part of the puzzle. *Fourth*, other potential dimensions of the patient's suffering should be explored. Are there underlying feelings of guilt, being a burden, or depression? *Fifth*, a response needs to be provided to the emotions associated with the request. Clinicians should try to imagine being in the patient's situation, re-examine their own feelings about the request, and discuss their reactions with a trusted colleague. If there are parts of the patient's request that the clinician is uncomfortable providing, the question arises in what other ways the clinician can help the patient. *Sixth*, any physical, emotional or spiritual suffering must be intensively treated. This may involve medical interventions as well as the counselling help of a psychologist, social worker or chaplain. Many patients will reconsider their request for hastened death once their symptoms are comprehensively managed. *Seventh*, the clinician should respond in an attentive way to the patient's request. It is critical to understand exactly what the patient is asking for after her symptoms have been managed. Oftentimes the patient may be seeking a way out in the future if her suffering becomes unbearable, an escape route she may or may not turn out to need.

Despite intensive evaluation and management, requests for hastened death may sometimes continue or resurface regularly in the course of a terminal illness. In these cases, clinicians should continue to have open communication with the patient as well as with the patient's family and loved ones. The clinician should make an effort to fully understand the request. It can also be helpful to discuss the situation with other members of the healthcare team, including chaplains, social workers and nurses. It is imperative to understand the legal, ethical and medical implications of the particular request. In these situations, a palliative care or ethics consultant can be helpful to further assist the primary medical team.

In this regard, consider the following case:

> *Mr X was a 66-year-old man with a history of a malignant brain tumour diagnosed and treated with radiation and surgery approximately 20 years previously. He now presented to the palliative care clinic with progressive weakness and decline in function. These symptoms had been worsening over a five-year period. The aetiology of this rapid decline was unclear, but it was thought to be secondary to an amyotrophic lateral sclerosis-like process probably triggered by his initial treatment with whole brain radiation. At the time of presentation, Mr X was suffering both physically and existentially. He was becoming severely weak and*

debilitated, and he was having difficulty with depression secondary
to his loss of function and resulting inability to do the things in
life he enjoyed. Over a two-year period his depression was treated
with medication and regular counselling. He also had multiple
discussions with the palliative care team regarding options for
hastening his death. He was very clear that, if his symptoms were
to become severe enough, he wanted options to relieve his suffering
by ending his life. Although he was suffering from physical,
psychological and existential distress, the healthcare team decided
that his physical suffering was not severe enough at the time to
warrant PPS or PSU. In fact, the patient would really have
preferred physician-assisted suicide (PAS), but this request could
not be honoured as he was not terminally ill and PAS is illegal in
the state of New York. The patient had seen multiple members of
the palliative care team and had many conversations with them
regarding his wishes. Since honouring his specific request was
not possible, the team ultimately decided that a discussion should
be undertaken with the patient regarding voluntary cessation of
hydration and nutrition.

Because the patient was not actively dying and because his
suffering was complex and difficult to understand fully, the
healthcare team took the time to go through a lengthy evaluation
process. The physicians reflected carefully on his request and
supported him emotionally during the evaluation process. The
discussion eventually included what last resort options the patient
could potentially access, including the possibility of voluntary
cessation of oral intake. He was also reassured that if his symptoms
worsened at any time, PPS could be considered. The patient
was very appreciative of the information about potential options
to escape his suffering if it became unbearable, and he actually
did relatively well over the next year. However, he subsequently
declined further functionally such that he became completely
bedbound and dependent for all of his activities of daily living.
At this time he made the decision to stop eating and drinking. He
was re-evaluated by the palliative care team, and they agreed to
support this action given his high level of irreversible suffering (both
physical and existential). His pain and other physical symptoms
were being well managed, and he was not found to be clinically
depressed when assessed by a palliative care physician as well as by
a psychiatrist and ethicist. He was then admitted to an inpatient
hospice setting where he stopped eating and drinking, and was
supported through the process and monitored closely for worsening

symptoms. Towards the very end of his life he developed severe delirium requiring PPS, which was provided given his request for relief of suffering if symptoms worsened. The patient died soon thereafter.

This case illustrates the dynamic process that should be employed in cases of severe suffering both anticipated and actual. There needs to be continuous communication with the healthcare team to help treat the patient, according to her wishes and to the dynamics of the clinical situation. Although here the team members were unable to honour the patient's initial request for medications to end his life, they continued to communicate with him to provide alternatives that were legally appropriate and ethically acceptable for the patient as well as the physician. Sometimes a patient's request for a hastened death may actually be a manifestation of frustration with an apparent lack of effective management options, as was evident in this case. Regardless of a patient's decision, providing intensive symptom relief is always imperative during the evaluation as well as during any intervention. In this case, when voluntarily stopping eating and drinking was eventually accepted and activated by the patient, PPS was still needed towards the very end of the patient's life, providing comfort during his last days.

This case also brings to light the issue of discussing potential future interventions with patients. This patient had a fear of intractable suffering at the very end of his life. If he experienced increased suffering in the future, he wanted reassurance that additional options would be available to relieve his suffering, even if they might result in hastening his death. It is important in these situations to discuss the fears of both the patient and the healthcare providers, and to have an open discussion with the patient about what options might be possible and beneficial. Part of this conversation should include the patient's views and priorities regarding the preservation of consciousness.

8.   Conclusion

There is often a role for palliative sedation in cases of intractable suffering towards the end of life. Palliative sedation is generally accepted in circumstances of extreme intractable physical suffering in the terminally ill, but it is more controversial in cases of suffering that is more psychosocial and existential rather than physical, when the patient is directly seeking a hastened death and/or when the patient is not otherwise near death. The responsibility of the clinician is to provide continuous assistance and support to the patient and her loved ones through this difficult time. When a patient is making a decision regarding palliative sedation, one must consider the patient's view of the relationship between consciousness and personhood. Many patients may want to preserve consciousness to the largest degree possible while achieving relief of suffering, in which case PPS would be most appropriate. Others may experience conscious awareness of suffering to be at the core of their distress, in which case PSU might be preferable. The relationship between consciousness, personhood and suffering is complex and very personal. Understanding it requires an open discussion with patients as well as their families and loved ones. An interdisciplinary approach is often necessary to fully explore this relationship, help resolve conflicts and alleviate the burdens being carried by everyone involved. Palliative sedation is a powerful intervention that allows relief from a wide range of suffering, but it also has a direct impact on consciousness and personhood. Although the implications of palliative sedation can sometimes seem overwhelming, our hope is that the concepts reviewed in this chapter will provide a method by which those involved in such decisions can find solace and comfort while ensuring that patients experiencing terrible suffering might find relief.

13 The ethical evaluation of continuous sedation at the end of life

Johannes J.M. van Delden

1. Introduction

In almost half of cases in which a patient dies, physicians have influenced the circumstances and/or the timing of the patient's death by means of an end of life decision (Onwuteaka-Philipsen et al. 2012). The figures quoted by Onwuteaka-Philipsen and colleagues on the prevalence of particular medical end-of-life decisions concern deaths occurring in 2010 in The Netherlands. However, European studies show that the opening statement of this chapter holds for other countries as well (van der Heide et al. 2003). There are many ways in which physicians can exercise this influence. Some of these are accepted as 'normal medical practice', for instance when a disproportional treatment is forgone. Others are considered tolerable only under strict conditions or even strictly intolerable, such as non-voluntary active euthanasia.

A relatively new phenomenon in the ethical discussion on end-of-life decisions is continuous sedation. Continuous sedation is used in terminally ill patients for whom normal medical treatments cannot relieve severe symptoms such as pain and agitation, and no option is left but to take away the patient's perception of these symptoms. Often, the decision to start continuous sedation is accompanied by the decision to forgo the provision of artificial nutrition and hydration (ANH) to these patients. The combination of these two decisions has made the ethical status of continuous sedation the subject of fierce ethical debate (Raus et al. 2011). Is it 'slow euthanasia' or is it a good palliative intervention that can take away the need for euthanasia completely?

A first observation to be made is that many seemingly descriptive definitions of continuous sedation contain normative claims (van Delden 2007). Examples of these are definitions of continuous sedation in which only certain intentions are recognised (usually the intention only to relieve suffering), only certain indications are held to be sufficient (usually refractory symptoms) or only certain patients are accepted (usually those whose life expectancy is less than one week).

These definitions are problematic because they obfuscate normative discussions and because they raise the question of what to call cases in which the same acts were performed but other intentions, indications or patients were involved. Generally speaking, one should adopt descriptive definitions of an intervention, allowing for a separate discussion about the conditions under which the intervention would be ethically acceptable. Applied to continuous sedation, this would lead to the following definition: continuous sedation is sedation until death follows (Chabot et al. 2005). It should be noted that this definition does not specify: a life expectancy for the patient; an indication for the intervention; or a specific intention. The condition that sedation is continued till death is a necessary condition in order to discriminate this intervention from the ordinary forms of sedation that are routine in medical practice, e.g. anaesthesia for a surgical operation.

Obviously, the consequence of this definition is that continuous sedation is reduced to a technique. The question as to the circumstances under which the use of this technique would be ethically acceptable still needs to be answered. To do so is the aim of this chapter.

2.   What determines the ethical status of continuous sedation?

A first issue to be addressed in determining the justifiability of continuous sedation is its seemingly problematic categorisation. This follows from the fact that, as noted earlier, *two* modes of conduct are often combined: an *act* (sedation); and an *omission* (forgoing the provision of ANH). In combining these two, continuous sedation ruins the peace of mind of those who equate the boundary between normal medical practice and intolerable medical conduct (such as euthanasia) with the distinction between omissions and acts. Obviously, those who reject the ethical relevance of this distinction will have fewer problems.

A second point to be made in this respect is that, whenever continuous sedation is combined with the forgoing of ANH, one should evaluate this as a single decision and not as two separate decisions. The line of reasoning that continuous sedation is a form of normal medical practice because 'only' palliative measures are used, and that, given the sedation, ANH should be considered as futile medical treatment (KNMG 2009a), is a salami-slicing technique. What happens in that case is that the physician argues for the first step only (sedation because of unrelievable symptoms) and then takes the situation that is created (we intentionally use an active verb here) as a new starting point from which to argue for the next step. This is clearly fallacious because, for a sound ethical evaluation, one has to take all steps into account in as far as these steps are planned or foreseeable. Not doing so means one does not properly take responsibility for the steps taken.

However, even when continuous sedation is evaluated as a single decision, one gets the impression that the most important issue in determining its ethical status is whether or not the physician, by applying continuous sedation, brings about death.

In The Netherlands, the Royal Dutch Medical Association (RDMA) has published a guideline for palliative sedation (KNMG 2009a). One of the guideline's main premises is the idea that continuous sedation, as opposed to euthanasia, is 'normal medical treatment'. The guideline draws a sharp ethical distinction between euthanasia and continuous sedation. Under continuous sedation, patients are said to die a natural death which does not result from the sedatives or the forgoing of the provision of ANH (if applicable), but from the underlying disease. The guideline recommends that the sedatives be titrated according to the needs of the patient with, supposedly, little or no life-shortening effect. The aim of the physician is to put an end to the experience of unbearable and hopeless suffering, rather than to the patient's life. Moreover, whereas euthanasia is irreversible, patients under sedation can be woken up again, for instance to say goodbye to a relative. Therefore, the guideline concludes, continuous sedation is not at all like euthanasia.

The construction of continuous sedation as common medical practice is founded on the stipulation of the following conditions: (1) the patient's life expectancy should be less than two weeks; and (2) the intention of the physician should be to relieve suffering and not to shorten the patient's life (Janssens et al. 2012).

The purpose of this chapter is twofold: to show that the argumentation strategy that is used to stress that continuous sedation is normal medical treatment is problematic; and to show that this strategy comes with a price, since other ethically relevant features of continuous sedation are obfuscated. The first we will deal with in the next section. The second we will return to in sections 4 and 5.

3.   Continuous sedation as common medical practice

In order to make continuous sedation an example of normal medical practice, the RDMA guideline seeks to exclude the possibility that life is shortened. Therefore, continuous sedation is only regarded as justifiable if the patient's life expectancy is considered to be less than two weeks. Implicitly, continuous sedation in patients with a longer life expectancy is deemed exceptional medical practice. This is problematic for several reasons.

First, estimating life expectancy is often difficult, if not impossible, certainly in cases in which death is not expected within hours. Physicians can predict an imminent death by looking at signs of a failing circulation, but these will occur only hours before death. To suggest that physicians can differentiate between someone who will die within one week, two weeks and three weeks is simply incorrect. A number of prognostic scores or indices have been developed in palliative care that permit an estimate of life expectancy by placing patients into broad groups that differ significantly in survival (Maltoni et al. 2005). The best known are the Palliative Prognostic (PaP) Score and the Palliative Prognostic Index (PPI). But even these do not allow one to make subtle differences between one, two and three weeks of life expectancy. Perhaps physicians can estimate what the life expectancy will be given a certain diagnosis and certain accompanying problems, but these will only be general predictions with large 'confidence intervals' (error margins), based on prognostic knowledge about the general course of illness. In cancer patients, this may work out reasonably well, but in many other diseases, courses of illness are much less predictable. It is relevant to note that a considerable percentage of the patients receiving continuous sedation suffer from other diseases or conditions than cancer (Rietjens et al. 2004, 2008a).

Second, even if physicians were able to differentiate between one, two or three weeks of remaining life expectancy, it is not at all clear whether there is enough justification to support the upper limit of two weeks. To put it bluntly, in the RDMA guideline, the function of the two-week limit is to give confidence that the patient will die from her disease before she dies from the dehydration involved in continuous sedation without ANH. The implicit assumption is that it takes about two weeks to die from dehydration. That may be correct in cases where one starts from a normal hydration status, but since most of the patients for whom continuous sedation is considered will have been seriously ill before, one can safely assume that their hydration status will not be optimal at the moment of starting continuous sedation. In such cases, it is unlikely that withholding ANH would lead to death only after two weeks. In other words, accepting a two-week limit actually means accepting that the moment of death of at least *some* patients will be determined by the dehydration that comes with continuous sedation (without ANH) and not by the underlying disease. The two-week limit is therefore not only an impossible criterion to use in real life, but it does not even do what it is supposed to do: to differentiate between cases in which the patient dies because of the disease and cases in which the patient dies because of dehydration.

Should this worry us? Is a time limit necessary in distinguishing ethically acceptable cases of continuous sedation from unacceptable cases? The limitation of continuous sedation to patients with a life expectancy of less than two weeks is not common internationally (Janssens et al. 2012). In many countries where euthanasia is prohibited, palliation is permitted in cases of unbearable and hopeless suffering by an informal common norm governing medical practice, even if it hastens death. Usually some form of the doctrine of double effect, in which foreseen but unintended side-effects are accepted, is quoted to justify this position. Some guidelines prohibit this practice, but certainly not all (Berger 2010).

Cellarius has argued that 'the traditional justifications of terminal sedation are unhelpful to supporting the imminence condition' (Cellarius 2008: 71). By the 'imminence condition', he refers to the condition that the use of continuous sedation must be limited to 'the dying phase' or 'the last stages'. Indeed, principles of subsidiarity (sedation being the lesser evil), proportionality (sedation being the proportionate answer to the magnitude of the problem) and double effect can be applied to early continuous sedation. But these arguments do not provide a justification for restricting continuous sedation to the dying phase. If the benefit of palliation outweighs the harm of an earlier death, if there are no other reasonable alternatives and if dosages are titrated according to the patient's need, the imminence condition still remains unaccounted for. Refractory symptoms are conditional for continuous sedation, not the moment when these occur. Cellarius concludes: 'if no robust justification for the imminence condition is forthcoming, we should reject the imminence condition and accept that cases of early terminal sedation will occur and will foreseeably and considerably hasten death' (Cellarius 2008: 72).

The Dutch guideline convincingly argues that refractory symptoms are conditional for continuous sedation. With regard to life expectancy, however, the main argument is the patient's possible premature death as a result of dehydration. The implicit assumption seems to be that, in such cases, continuous sedation should be regarded as 'euthanasia by other means'. However, palliation of refractory symptoms with an unintended but foreseen life-shortening side-effect is considered acceptable by the medical profession in most developed countries, including The Netherlands. If rendering the patient unconscious is the only possible way to relieve suffering, then even if the patient is not yet in the last stages of life, continuous sedation may be seen as the lesser evil, and unintended life-shortening effects may be accounted for. The decision to withhold ANH in these cases is a decision not to prolong life, and perfectly consistent with palliative care principles (Janssens et al. 2012).

So how far have we come with respect to the elements of an ethical evaluation of decisions to use continuous sedation? We need to know precisely what the physician did, what the effects of her acts were (in terms of shortening life and effect on consciousness) and in what condition the patient was. This information will enable us to judge the proportionality and the subsidiarity of the intervention. It should be noted that we certainly need to know more than what the physician intended. Intentions, to a large extent, are reconstructions of what one felt at the time of decision-making and they are hard to verify (Quill 1993). If what the physician did was the right palliative measure, and if it was therefore perfectly understandable that she hoped for the end to come, why hold it against her that she acted accordingly? We may assume that she did not intend to hasten the end of life, but even if we were wrong, we would evaluate her behaviour in the same way because her actions fulfilled the criteria of proportionality and subsidiarity: the bad consequence of the act was the lesser evil which could not have been avoided by acting in a different way. Using these criteria, some cases will be judged as ethically permissible; those cases will be called 'normal medical practice'. Other cases, for instance when continuous sedation is used only as a technique to bring about death on request, will turn out to be the ethical equivalent of active voluntary euthanasia.

4.   The other issue

In order to demarcate continuous sedation from euthanasia, the RDMA guideline excludes early continuous sedation because of its presumed life-shortening effect. We have seen that there are many reasons to question this strategy, but here we would like to point to another issue. By focusing on the possible life-shortening effect of continuous sedation, one may get the impression that this is the most ethically relevant aspect. However, we would submit that there is another issue, the loss of consciousness, that also merits attention when undertaking an ethical evaluation of continuous sedation. It is to this issue that we now turn.

The key aim of hospice care has always been to 'let the patients live until they die' (Saunders 1965). Continuous sedation frustrates this aim of hospice care (Janssens et al. 2012). Under deep continuous sedation, meaningful experiences, such as coming to terms with the approaching end of life, and communication with loved ones, become impossible. The patient is in a state of social death, deprived of any social interaction. Although the patient remains alive, her personality is gone. The moment of goodbye is separated from the moment of death. To the patient, deep continuous sedation, just like euthanasia, means the end of (conscious) life. For patients and loved ones, the distinction between euthanasia and deep continuous sedation may be less evident than it is for physicians (den Hartogh 2006b). Although the patient in deep sleep is still alive we cannot argue that she still leads 'a life'. Family members observe their loved one in deep sleep realising that she will not wake up any more (Steinhauser et al. 2000). As death approaches, communication with the dying patient becomes even more important to them, while at the same time the sedatives rule out the possibility of communication (Brajtman 2003).

These problematic aspects which are inherently associated with continuous sedation are barely touched upon in the RDMA guideline. The guideline labels continuous sedation as 'normal medical treatment', and any distinctions over conventional medical treatments are only hinted at. The guideline attempts to demarcate continuous sedation as clearly as possible from euthanasia. A demarcation from conventional medical treatment would only blur the guideline's key message. But since deep continuous sedation puts an end to conscious, i.e. biographical, life, the distinction between continuous sedation and conventional medical treatment *does* require careful attention. If this means that continuous sedation becomes less 'normal' and more problematic than it is now portrayed in the guideline, then so be it.

This obviously has implications for medical practice. Patients and family members should be prepared for the loss of meaningful contact. This, at least, should imply that they are made aware of the fact that they have to say goodbye *now*. In qualitative studies, we have often heard that the 'planned character' of continuous sedation has an alienating effect on family members (van Delden et al. 2011). In some way it is unreal, incomprehensible and impossible to grasp that in an hour's time you will have lost contact with your loved one. To be aware of this effect and to address it, even if they do not have the solution, may be the best that healthcare providers can do.

Thus, we would submit that continuous sedation should be treated as an option of last resort (Quill et al. 1997b), in view of, *inter alia*, the concomitant loss of consciousness.

5.   From decision to process

At this stage in our discussion, we need to broaden the scope from simply making a decision to engaging in a process. When undertaking an ethical evaluation of continuous sedation, we should do more than simply consider its effects in terms of life-shortening, relief of suffering and loss of consciousness. Such an approach runs the risk of conceptualising continuous sedation as a decision at a certain moment *in* time as opposed to a process *over* time. To evaluate a decision to use continuous sedation, we also need to look at the process of interaction between the healthcare providers who are involved and the patient.

In order to develop this argument, we will once again use the RDMA guideline as a stepping-stone. In the guideline, continuous sedation is depicted as the medical answer to a medical emergency (KNMG 2009a). Apart from the imminence condition, the requirement is made that the patient has to suffer from refractory symptoms. A first observation to make in this regard is that the reported incidences of continuous sedation make it hard to believe that this really applies to all cases. In 2010, continuous sedation was applied in 12 per cent of all deaths in The Netherlands (Onwuteaka-Philipsen et al. 2012). Such incidences are no exception in the international literature (Miccinesi et al. 2006; Seale 2009; Chambaere et al. 2010). To conclude that 12 per cent of patients die in intractable agony seems problematic. Modern palliative care is not omnipotent, but it can do better than that.

A second observation is that the idea of an 'emergency' suggests that the situation warrants extraordinary measures, but that brings us back to our earlier discussion about the permissibility of life-shortening effects. The real point to be made is thus that constructing continuous sedation as a response to a medical emergency obfuscates the fact that whether a symptom is refractory is *not* a medical fact beyond our influence. Qualitative research has shown that whether a symptom is seen as refractory or not has to do with various things that can be influenced (Swart et al. 2012d). *Location* matters: some interventions are available in hospitals or other healthcare institutions that are not available at home. Consequently, symptoms may be refractory sooner at home than they are in other settings. *Family* matters: pressure from family to 'just do something' may reduce the possibilities of trying alternative interventions (Raus et al. 2011). The *patient* matters: patient preferences contribute to a refractory state. Sometimes, patients do not want to go through any more suffering or are reluctant to try additional treatment options (Swart et al. 2012d).

This means that the necessity of continuous sedation is not a given, fully determined by the unalterable medical circumstances of the case, but, on the contrary, is something that is influenced by circumstances, patients and their healthcare providers. This insight reaffirms the importance of the process of interaction between patient, family and healthcare providers during the palliative phase. The *palliative phase* is understood here usually to be a longer period that precedes the *terminal phase*. The palliative phase is the one in which attention to the patient can help her to come to terms with her imminent death, which in turn reduces the experience of 'only suffering pointlessly'. If we are serious about continuous sedation being an option of last resort, both because of its potential for life-shortening and because of its effect on consciousness, then the palliative phase is the phase to be active in. This is the phase to think about continuous sedation, talk about continuous sedation and, if possible, prevent continuous sedation from being necessary. Continuous sedation should be one element of a process of advance care planning through shared decision-making between healthcare providers and patient. The interests of terminally ill patients are better served by providing attentive guidance during the palliative phase than by making 'ethically justifiable' decisions in the terminal phase, when no other options are left.

To call for attentiveness to the patient is not new, of course, certainly not in palliative care. But one gets the impression that the widespread attention on autonomy as a *right* has blurred the necessity of fostering autonomy as an *ideal*. Autonomy as a right is about sovereignty. It is about the right not to be interfered with if an autonomous person does not want to be interfered with. Hence the importance of living wills, the right to refuse treatment and the need to obtain informed consent before a treatment can start. All of this is indeed important, but it should not be seen as the whole story about good care. For that, more is needed. To properly care for someone as a healthcare professional means to acknowledge that illness, and certainly a terminal illness comes with a threat to the capacities to shape one's life and to live according to one's own standards, in accordance with the ideal of autonomy. One of the main tasks of healthcare providers in this respect is to act as a skilled companion, rather than to be a trouble-shooter (Kars 2012). Dialogue belongs in the realm of the first role, decision-making in the realm of the second.

None of the above purports to say that continuous sedation can or should be prevented in all situations, let alone that this could be achieved through a dialogue with the patient. That would be ridiculous. Rather, what we wish to emphasise is that, for an ethical evaluation of continuous sedation, we should not construct the use of continuous sedation as a decision, the acceptability of which is determined only by the circumstances of the moment of that decision. Continuous sedation should instead be conceptualised as a process in which there are many options to mitigate circumstances.

6.   Conclusion

We set out in this chapter to evaluate the features of an ethically justifiable use of continuous sedation as a technique to take away the
experience of otherwise untreatable symptoms that come with severe
suffering. We have argued that continuous sedation should be regarded
as an option of last resort, both because of its potential life-shortening
effects and because it leads to an end of the biographical life of the
patient. In order to evaluate such an intervention, we need to know precisely what the physician did, what she intended, what the effects of her
acts were (also in terms of shortening life) and what the condition of the
patient was. This information will enable us to judge the proportionality
and the subsidiarity of the intervention. We have also stressed, however,
that the moral pain of continuous sedation lies not only in its potential for life-shortening. Rendering a patient unconscious deprives her
of the possibility to live her life in the biographical sense. This has led
us to make some observations regarding the importance of adequately
accompanying a terminally ill patient during the last phases of her life.
Good palliative care not only takes the wishes of patients seriously but
also helps patients to shape their own lives and to remain moral agents.
By doing so, the number of cases of continuous sedation is likely to
diminish. Only thus can continuous sedation become what it should
truly be: an option of *last* resort.

14   Terminal sedation and euthanasia: the virtue in calling a spade what it is

Søren Holm

1.   Introduction

Among the many practices, and proposed practices discussed in the end-of-life area, terminal sedation (TS) (sometimes called palliative sedation, a terminology that seems to be preferred by physicians involved in palliative care (Broeckaert & Olarte 2002; Lynch 2003)) has until recently been one of the least discussed, being hidden behind seemingly more contentious practices like voluntary active euthanasia[1] and physician-assisted suicide.

It has, however, now become clear that terminal sedation is widely practised, even in countries where euthanasia and/or physician-assisted suicide is legalised (de Graeff & Dean 2007; Claessens et al. 2008, 2011; Bilsen et al. 2009; Chambaere et al. 2010). The popularity of terminal sedation seems to be linked to two factors: (1) it is not conceived of as euthanasia or assisted suicide by doctors and patients; and (2) it is not regulated, legally or professionally, as strictly as euthanasia and therefore leaves more 'wiggle room' for decision-making, for instance in cases where the competence of the patient is questionable. This chapter will argue that some forms of TS are close to euthanasia in their ethical implications and that those forms of TS therefore ought to be regulated in a similar way as euthanasia.

Although most discussions of these issues are relatively recent, one of the very early UK bioethics debates, between Zachary and Lorber about the treatment of newborns with severe spina bifida, was, at least partially, about non-voluntary terminal sedation, since Lorber proposed not only non-treatment, but also the use of sedatives and painkillers in doses that would render the infants completely lethargic. Combined with a 'feeding only on demand' policy, this clearly amounted to slow

---

[1] In the following, 'euthanasia' will, unless explicitly stated otherwise, mean 'voluntary active euthanasia'.

active euthanasia as pointed out by John Harris among many others (Harris 1981).

There is no complete agreement about the use of the term 'terminal sedation' at present (Morita et al. 2002b), but in the following I will use the definition proposed by Hallenbeck in one of the early papers concerning TS:

Terminal sedation is the induction and maintenance of a sedated state with the intent of relieving otherwise intractable distress, both physical and mental in a patient close to death. (Hallenbeck 1999: 222)

By way of contrast, Morita et al. have defined terminal sedation as 'the use of sedative medications to relieve intolerable and refractory distress by the reduction in patient consciousness' (Morita et al. 2002b: 447), while for Broeckaert et al. it is 'the intentional administration of analgesics and/or other drugs in dosages and combinations required to adequately relieve pain and/or other symptoms' (Broeckaert & Olarte 2002: 169).

The intractable distress can be caused by pain, dyspnoea, nausea, restlessness, insomnia, bleeding, or other symptoms and disease manifestations occurring in the terminal phase, and the distress is relieved by making the patient effectively unconscious. The reduction of the patient's level of consciousness does not necessarily have to be complete if the distress can be removed by a lesser reduction of consciousness. TS, however, will almost always diminish the patient's decisional competence and desire for food and water, since even moderate sedation has these effects.

2.   Types of terminal sedation

There are four main types of TS:

1. Continuous TS

   a. With continued hydration and nutrition
   b. Without continued hydration and nutrition

2. Intermittent TS

   a. With continued hydration and nutrition
   b. Without continued hydration and nutrition

In continuous TS, the sedated state is induced with the intention to maintain it until the patient dies and TS *is* maintained (except if a medical error occurs), whereas in intermittent TS the patient is brought back to consciousness at regular intervals to assess whether the distressing symptoms still persist, necessitating further sedation, or whether they have disappeared and the patient can be left in the conscious state. The argument in this paper will be that continuous TS, without continued hydration and nutrition, is very close to euthanasia, and should be regulated as such, whereas other forms of TS are less close to euthanasia.

The distinctions drawn above are relative clear, but one may doubt whether their importance is always understood by palliative care physicians. Broeckaert and Olarte, for instance, write:

> Are we suggesting here that one always has to start artificial hydration and nutrition as one starts palliative sedation? Not at all. It would rightly be considered pointless, futile and not in line with palliative care philosophy [*sic!*] to begin (once sedation is started) artificial hydration, still less artificial nutrition, in patients who had not been eating and drinking and were not artificially hydrated during the days before sedative drugs were administered. We are not discussing and certainly not advocating the artificial lengthening of the life of sedated patients. (Broeckaert & Olarte 2002: 171)

Here palliative care philosophy seems to dominate over clear thinking. The only way that one can plausibly claim that the provision of hydration in this situation is futile is if it does not matter whether the patient dies sooner or later, in which case active euthanasia seems eminently preferable to TS.

There is in theory no reason why TS could not be maintained for a very long time, but in practice it is almost only used in situations where death from the underlying disease process is expected within days or at the most a few weeks. This paper is restricted to a consideration of TS at the very end of life.

As with other end-of-life interventions, we can also in this case distinguish between voluntary, non-voluntary and involuntary forms of terminal sedation, but I will concentrate exclusively on an analysis of voluntary terminal sedation.[2] Accordingly, when I write 'terminal sedation' or 'TS' without specification it should be read as 'voluntary terminal sedation'. *Involuntary* terminal sedation is clearly ethically unacceptable for many of the same reasons that involuntary euthanasia is ethically unacceptable. No one should be terminally sedated against their will. In *non-voluntary* TS we have to distinguish between

---

[2] By involuntary TS I mean TS instituted against the known wishes of the patient, whereas non-voluntary TS is TS that is instituted for an incompetent patient where there is no knowledge of whether the patient wants TS or not. This usage parallels the standard usage in relation to active euthanasia.

continuous and intermittent TS in our analysis. Non-voluntary continuous TS is very similar to non-voluntary euthanasia, but in certain cases of non-voluntary intermittent TS it can be argued that the aim is to temporarily remove the suffering that leaves the patient decisionally incompetent in the hope that when she is awakened the distressing disease manifestations will have abated somewhat and the patient will be able to decide herself whether or not to continue TS. That non-voluntary TS does occur is clear from the other chapters in this book and from the reference by Morita et al. to the use of TS with patients with agitated delirium – it is difficult to see how a patient in a state of agitated delirium can give valid consent (Morita et al. 2000). However, while non-voluntary terminal sedation raises a few specific issues, they take us too far away from the topic of this chapter.

2.1.   TS without hydration and nutrition and double effect

If continuous TS is instituted without continued hydration and nutrition, it looks very much like a slow form of euthanasia. The patient is put into a state where she is unable to take water and food, hydration and nutrition is not provided, and she will eventually die from dehydration, if the underlying disease does not kill her first. This means that in patients with very short *and certain* life expectancy, even continuous TS without continued hydration and nutrition may not count as euthanasia, because it is known that the patient will die from her underlying disease. It is, however, rare that we can predict life expectancy with certainty, and there will therefore almost always be the possibility that this kind of TS will turn out to be equivalent to euthanasia. Broeckaert and Olarte (2002: 176) review a number of studies and find that the *mean* survival of patients after starting TS is between 2.4 and 3.2 days. They unfortunately give no information about the *range* of survival and we are therefore unable to say with any accuracy whether dehydration is a problem in continuous TS without hydration.

Is this analysis correct? If double effect reasoning is applied, it can, presumably, be argued that as long as the intention is only relief of distress, continuous TS without hydration and nutrition is not actually a case of euthanasia at all (de Graeff & Dean 2007; Lo & Rubenfeld 2005). However, this is an even more problematic argument than in the standard case of double effect reasoning where the provision of effective pain relief has a reduction in life expectancy as a side-effect. The reason it is even more problematic in the case of continuous TS without hydration and nutrition is that there is a perfectly straightforward intervention (continued hydration and nutrition, or at least continued hydration) that will allow one to achieve the desired outcome (relief of distress), without reduction in duration of life or a change in the cause of death.[3] What relieves the distress (i.e. has the desired effect) is the sedation, what causes the death (i.e. has the undesired effect) is not the sedation but the withholding or withdrawing of hydration and nutrition.[4] It is clearly possible to administer sedative drugs in such high doses that they have a life-shortening effect, but that is not part of standard TS, since complete sedation can be achieved with lower doses.

If an effective pain relief is possible which does not involve a risk of reducing life expectancy, then double effect thinking enjoins us to use that kind of pain relief and not a more risky form, and the same applies to TS. If adequate sedation is possible without a risk of reducing life expectancy, then that is the form of TS that should be used. Here it is important to emphasise that whether or not patients die earlier if TS without hydration or nutrition is instituted is largely irrelevant for the double effect analysis. What matters is what causes their death: is it the disease or is it the lack of hydration or nutrition? If a man is about to be executed by hanging and I shoot him while he is dropping, but before his neck has broken, I have still killed him even if I have only shortened his life by milliseconds. And if I give you a drug that cures your current terminal illness, but means that you will die from a side-effect in two years' time, it is still the case that I have killed you, even though you will live longer than you would otherwise have done.

An alternative analysis, of *voluntary* TS without hydration and nutrition, is to divide it into two components: (1) the withdrawal at the patient's request of hydration and nutrition; and (2) sedation to suppress symptoms, including symptoms caused by the withdrawal of hydration and nutrition. Even though a patient's decision to refuse hydration and nutrition might not be seen to be morally correct (e.g. because it constitutes suicide and suicide is seen as morally problematic), there is little doubt that a patient has the right to refuse hydration and nutrition. The only remaining question on this line of analysis is therefore whether sedation is justified in this situation. If there are already other symptoms of the underlying disease that in themselves justify sedation, it is

---

[3] Where the patient's life expectancy is very short, maintaining nutrition might not be necessary as long as hydration is maintained, since it takes a very long time to die of malnutrition, but not very long to die of dehydration.

[4] We should also note that many who see a distinction between TS and euthanasia also hold that hydration and nutrition are not properly classed as treatments that can be legitimately withheld or withdrawn. In their view, hydration and nutrition are basic essentials that should always be provided (Papal allocution 2004).

difficult to see how the addition of hunger and dehydration symptoms can invalidate that justification. The difficult case is thus the one where the only symptoms are those caused by the patient's refusal of hydration and nutrition. If these reach the threshold where TS would otherwise be contemplated, for instance in a patient with obstructed oesophagus and 'bad veins', then, on this line of analysis, it is again difficult to see why TS should not be instituted if the patient wants it.

This second line of argument does, however, crucially rely on a competent patient making the decision to request withdrawal of hydration and nutrition (or to cease taking food and fluids and to refuse artificial hydration and nutrition). If the patient is not competent, then withdrawal of hydration and nutrition can only unproblematically take place if continuation is futile. And if withdrawal gives rise to symptoms, then continuation is clearly not futile, because it would prevent the symptoms from occurring.

2.2.   TS with continued hydration and nutrition

TS with continued hydration and nutrition should not normally lead to a reduction in the remaining duration of life, and may in certain circumstances increase life expectancy, because it reduces the level of physiological stress on the patient's body.[5]

There may be cases where the hydration and nutrition provided are not sufficient to sustain life in the long run. If this is deliberate, intended or foreseen, these cases should not count as TS with hydration and nutrition, but should be classed as TS without hydration and nutrition. The distinguishing criterion is not whether some hydration and nutrition are provided, but whether enough is provided to sustain life.

3.   Are all kinds of terminal sedation akin to euthanasia?

It is sometimes claimed that terminal sedation is morally equivalent to euthanasia, and that it mainly functions as a hypocritical option for those who want to perform active euthanasia without admitting that they are doing just that (Gauthier 2001; Quill et al. 1997b).[6]

---

[5] This only holds if we are discussing *terminal* sedation, i.e. sedation 'in a patient close to death'. Sedation of a patient in chronic but non-terminal distress is a different matter and not the topic of this chapter.
[6] This seems actually to entail that TS is morally slightly worse than euthanasia in those cases where it involves hypocrisy, since if A is morally equivalent to B, but A entails a further element of hypocrisy not present in B, then A must, all things considered, be worse than B.

We have dealt with TS *without* continued hydration and nutrition in the previous section and have seen that this kind of TS is close to euthanasia, but what about TS *with* continued hydration and nutrition? The equivalence claim can be made in two ways, either by claiming that the *intention* of terminal sedation is equivalent to the intention of active euthanasia, or by claiming that terminal sedation is *functionally equivalent* to active euthanasia (i.e. it aims at and achieves the same goals or has the same consequences). Let us now look more closely at these two equivalence claims.

3.1.   Intention

Is the intention in active euthanasia and TS the same? In active euthanasia the intention of the person performing euthanasia is to kill the person who is having euthanasia, in order to fulfil that person's autonomous request for euthanasia and, in the large majority of cases, to relieve the suffering of the person in question (since there are a few cases where there is no current suffering, but where the intention is to prevent future suffering). As we have seen above, the same intention seems to be at play in many cases of TS without hydration and nutrition.

In TS with hydration and nutrition, the intention is to induce a state of unconscious sedation, in order to fulfil the person's autonomous request for TS and relieve her suffering. Are these two intentions the same?

In the case of *intermittent* TS they are clearly not the same, since intermittent TS involves an open-ended series of discrete choice-making nodes stretching into the future. Choosing intermittent TS is not a final decision in the same sense as choosing euthanasia or *continuous* TS.

But what about continuous TS *with* hydration and nutrition? If active euthanasia and TS are functionally equivalent, then they are also intentionally equivalent, unless some kind of double effect principle can be brought into play, which, as we have seen above, is doubtful. I discuss below whether there is functional equivalence, so here I will concentrate on the case where we assume no direct functional equivalence.

Remember that the kind of TS we are discussing here is TS *with* hydration and nutrition, and that there is therefore no element of shortening of life and *eo ipse* no element of intended,[7] foreseen or even foreseeable shortening of life. We can therefore assert that the shortening of life is not a foreseeable consequence of TS with hydration and nutrition,

---

[7] Except in cases where the healthcare professional and/or the patient mistakenly believe that TS with hydration and nutrition shortens life.

and so cannot be imputed as part of the intention. It can therefore not be argued convincingly that the physician claims that she intended not to shorten life (her subjective intention), but that she did so anyway in a foreseeable way, and that life-shortening is therefore part of her objective intention.

The shortening of life element is thus different in TS with hydration and nutrition and euthanasia (absent in one, but present in the other), but the elements of fulfilling an autonomous desire and relieving suffering are present in both. This, however, is a characteristic that TS with hydration and nutrition and euthanasia share with a widely disparate range of medical and non-medical interventions including giving someone an aspirin for headache, putting a plaster on a bruised knee, or buying an ice cream for a child after a visit to the dentist. We can therefore conclude that, *unless active euthanasia and TS with hydration and nutrition can be shown to be functionally equivalent, they are not intentionally equivalent.*

3.2.   *Functional equivalence and the definition of death*

Could it be convincingly argued that TS is morally equivalent to euthanasia because both bring about the immediate death of the patient (i.e. because they are functionally equivalent)? In the previous section, we have rejected this argument in its straightforward form in the case of TS with hydration and nutrition, because this does not shorten the life of the patient. However, perhaps this conclusion was too hasty because the argument relied implicitly on a traditional account of death. Since the introduction of brain death criteria for death, there has been a vociferous debate about the definition of death, and many now believe that death should not be defined according to traditional heart, brainstem or whole brain standards but according to a standard derivable from, or at least congruent with, the personhood view of moral status (Singer 1995; several of the essays in Rachels 1997). What matters, according to this view, is not the biological life of the organism, but the biographical life of the person. On this view, a person is dead when there is irreversible cessation of consciousness, even if the body and (large parts of) the brain live on.

One of the purposes of TS is to reduce or remove consciousness, since this is *ex hypothesi* the only way to remove the suffering caused by the distressing disease manifestations. Could we not say that a person dies when continuous deep TS is instituted? If at a given time *t* we have the option of instituting either continuous deep TS or euthanasia, could we claim that the person dies at time *t* in both cases, since that was when she lost consciousness for the last time?

Phenomenologically (from the first person perspective), this seems to make sense. The last time I am conscious is the last time I will experience myself as alive. This analysis raises a number of questions, and begs one as well. The question it begs is, not surprisingly, the question of the proper analysis of death. Those who explicitly argue that continuous deep TS is not euthanasia, and that continuous deep TS is morally acceptable in a way that euthanasia is not, typically reject a personhood account of moral status and hold a traditional view of death leading to traditional criteria for death (either heart, brainstem or whole brain). However, the argument we are discussing here relies on a quite different definition of death that explicit proponents of continuous deep TS would reject, or, if they accepted it, they would (have to) revise their moral assessment of TS.

Yet many proponents of continuous deep TS are not explicit proponents of only TS; they accept both continuous deep TS and euthanasia as morally acceptable, and may hold a personhood account of moral status, without having considered its implications for the definition of death.

The more 'neutral' questions our analysis raises are: (1) in what sense cessation of consciousness in TS is irreversible; and, following on from this, (2) whether the contingent nature of the level of consciousness during continuous deep TS should make us wary of pronouncing someone dead when they can very easily be 'resurrected', either intentionally or unintentionally. Even in continuous deep TS, the removal of consciousness is not irreversible in a strict sense of the term. The loss is intended to be permanent, not necessarily to be irreversible.[8]

In reality, loss of consciousness in TS is rather contingent; it depends on actively maintaining sedation, and this means that it can be reversed either deliberately or as a result of mistakes. With continuous deep TS we are therefore in a situation that if we declare someone dead when continuous deep TS is first instituted, she might, through medical error in not maintaining sedation, suddenly spring back to consciousness and life. In intermittent TS, we will, even more problematically, never be able to say whether the patient is alive or dead in the periods when TS is in place, until the patient 'dies' according to one of the traditional criteria. This should clearly make us wary of pronouncing someone dead when continuous deep TS is instituted. So, prospectively, there does seem to be a difference between continuous deep TS and euthanasia.

---

[8] In intermittent TS, there is no intention to induce a permanent loss of consciousness, and even less an intention to induce irreversible loss of consciousness. If consciousness is irreversibly lost as a result of intermittent TS procedures, this will be seen as a problem and not as a good thing.

This difference can also be brought out by considering a slightly different hypothetical form of continuous deep TS that we can call irreversible TS. Irreversible TS is the form of TS that is induced by an intervention that irreversibly removes consciousness, for instance by killing off a significant number of brain cells, or by destroying the brain's activating systems. A patient who has had irreversible TS would therefore be permanently, and irreversibly, unconscious. It should be obvious that irreversible TS is closer to euthanasia than continuous deep TS, and that by contraposition continuous deep TS is further away from euthanasia.

However, for those who hold a biographical account of death, linked to personhood considerations, it will still, retrospectively, be the case that the person died at the time that consciousness was lost for the last time. We don't often think about it (except when discussing organ donation from non-heart-beating donors), but according to the standard criterion for heart death we fix the time of death at the last heart beat, not at the time when heart function was irreversibly lost, which is often several minutes later. There is thus, in this case, a short time period where the person is dead, but not irreversibly so. And it is only retrospectively that we can ascertain the time of death with certainty.

4.   Terminal sedation and the idea of a good death

Many people express a desire to die peacefully in their sleep.[9] Terminal sedation could seem to be a simple way to fulfil this desire in difficult circumstances. I do, however, think that the issue is considerably more complicated.

There are at least two and possibly three different underlying distinctions at play here, explaining our desire for a peaceful death in our sleep. One is the distinction between a death with great suffering and one without great suffering, the second is the distinction between death after a long life and death after a relatively short life, and the third is the idea of dying after having sorted your life, put your house in order (as in the Old Testament story of the royal counsellor Ahithophel: 'When Ahithophel saw that his advice had not been followed, he saddled his donkey and set out for his house in his hometown. He put his house in order and then hanged himself. So he died and was buried in his father's tomb' (2 Samuel 17:23)).

It is reasonably clear that, for the person who is dying, death without suffering is generally a good thing (except in cases where the person for

---

[9] As put very memorably in the joke 'I want to die peacefully in my sleep like my father, not screaming in abject fear as the passengers on his bus!'

some reason craves final expiation through suffering),[10] that it is a good thing to die old rather than young, and that it is a good thing to die after having put your house in order and said farewell to your family rather than in a state of unpreparedness.

It is important to note, though, that the two last good things have no intrinsic connection to dying peacefully in your sleep. The connection is contingent: it just happens that more old people die peacefully in their sleep, and that more old people have put their house in order (because they expect to die in the not too distant future). If we, for instance, imagine a teenager dying suddenly in her sleep, we would not find that much less tragic than if she had died in an accident, even if the accident had caused her some suffering.

TS removes the suffering caused by the death process, but it does not make it possible to die after a long life instead of after a short one, and it does remove (in the case of continuous deep TS) or significantly reduce (in the case of intermittent TS) the opportunity to put your house in order or prepare yourself for death in any other way. TS thus only facilitates one element of a good death, and it is thus only the preferable strategy for a person who does not want euthanasia in three situations: (1) if the person in question has no interest in putting her house in order and saying farewell to her family; (2) if the disease manifestations are so distressing that they in themselves make communication with family, etc. impossible; or (3) if the suffering outweighs any positive benefits that could be obtained by further conscious existence. This means that the attractiveness of TS depends very much on a person's beliefs about what a good dying process would be like, since these beliefs are essential in situations 1 and 3 outlined above.

If we, as a society, are moving from an *ars moriendi* focusing on a gradual and orderly withdrawal from life, to a *managed death process* focusing on absence of suffering, then TS will be seen as more and more attractive, especially for those who think that euthanasia and physician-assisted suicide are morally problematic.

5.   Conclusion

In this chapter I have argued for two conclusions. The first is that terminal sedation with *maintenance* of hydration and nutrition is *sui generis*, it is not a form of active or passive euthanasia, and does not rely on any use of potentially problematic double effect reasoning. This follows

---

[10] See, for example, *The ills and evils Frate Jacopone called down upon himself in an excess of charity* (da Todi 1982: 164–5).

even if we accept the controversial view that death is the irreversible cessation of consciousness, since terminal sedation never involves the *irreversible* cessation of consciousness.

The second conclusion is that terminal sedation with *withdrawal* of hydration and nutrition has many ethically relevant similarities with euthanasia, and very few dissimilarities. If we are right in believing that euthanasia should be (strictly) regulated, because there are risks of misuse that need to be guarded against, then we should also think about regulating TS with withdrawal of hydration and nutrition. If we are, for instance, worried about non-voluntary or involuntary euthanasia, then we should also be worried about non-voluntary or involuntary TS, and if we are worried about the authenticity of requests for euthanasia, we should be similarly worried in the context of TS.

It is true that 'Everything is what it is and not something else', but equally true that there is intellectual and practical virtue in calling a spade what it is.

15   Terminal sedation: recasting a metaphor as the *ars moriendi* changes

Margaret P. Battin

1.   Introduction

Sometimes, one wonders, in applied ethics fields like end-of-life issues that have such a large component of empirical prediction, whether what one foresaw, or what one was alert to at some stage, still holds water in light of further developments. More recent thinking about death and dying offers the chance to reinspect what one wrote, a short half-decade ago, to see how the way an issue has been framed looks in light of changes in the medical and social scenery.

Some years ago, I looked at the issue of terminal sedation in a sceptical way. Does this account still make sense?

Back in 2008, I asked whether the turn to terminal sedation is 'pulling the sheet over our eyes' (Battin 2008). I observed that terminal sedation had become a new favourite in end-of-life care, an apparent compromise in the debate over physician-assisted dying, which offered something to each side of the dispute. Yet I noted that it was a compromise that sold out on most of the things that could be important – to both sides.

2.   Terminal sedation: a way out of the dispute over physician-assisted dying?

I argued that assisted dying can be justified on the basis of autonomy and mercy. According to the principle of autonomy, people are entitled to be the architects, as much as possible, of how they die. The principle of mercy requires that pain and suffering be relieved to the extent possible. Consequently, physician assistance in bringing about death is to be provided only when the person voluntarily seeks it *and* only when such assistance serves to avoid pain and suffering or the prospect of them.

Sections 2 and 3 of this chapter borrow heavily from Battin (2008).

I also explained that opponents of physician-assisted dying usually invoke, first, the principle of the sanctity of human life, a religious or secular respect for human life that is absolute (i.e. does not allow for any exceptions) and that is said to entail the wrongness of killing, suicide and murder. The second objection that is frequently raised by opponents of physician-assisted dying is that it might lead to abuse, either by threatening the integrity of the medical profession or by making people victims of assisted dying they did not want, as a result of institutional or social pressures.

Back in 2008, I observed that terminal sedation is often proposed as an alternative last-resort measure that can overcome the practical and ideological disputes surrounding physician-assisted dying. For example, in its 1997 rulings in the cases *Washington* v. *Glucksberg* and *Vacco* v. *Quill*, the US Supreme Court recognised the legality of providing pain relief in palliative care even if doing so might shorten the patient's life, provided that the intention was to relieve pain. However, as I scrutinised terminal sedation, I concluded that it was not much of a compromise after all, since it failed to meet the concerns that underlie the dispute regarding physician-assisted dying (autonomy, mercy, sanctity of life, abuse).

As to *autonomy*, one of the key concerns of proponents of physician-assisted dying, I noted that the central requirement of consent is not always met in decisions to use terminal sedation, for various reasons. First, terminal sedation is often used for patients who suffer from severe pain and for whom pain management has failed. However, if pain is severe enough, reflective, unimpaired consent may become impossible, necessitating surrogate decision-making.

Second and more importantly, even when consent is given in advance of the onset of intense pain, the focus of the consent is obscured. Terminal sedation may end pain, but it also ends life, in two ways: it immediately ends sentient life and the possibility for social interaction, and, when artificial nutrition and hydration (ANH) are withheld, a frequent practice, it also ends biological life. However, because the official assumption is that sedation is used only to end pain, without any intention of ending life, the patient cannot be asked for consent to end her life, but only to relieve her pain. Admittedly, some mention of the possibility that relieving pain might inadvertently shorten life could be included in the consent process, but if the acknowledgement that life will be ended were stronger than that, the question of what is actually intended would arise.

The popularity of what I called 'the new euphemism' in 2008, 'palliative sedation' – which meanwhile has become increasingly used instead of the more distressing label 'terminal sedation' – only reinforces the problem that the focus of consent is obscured. I argued that, by avoiding the word 'terminal' and hence any suggestion that death may be close, the most important feature of the practice is concealed and terminal sedation is confused with 'palliative care'. Consequently, the requirement of valid consent, and hence the principle of respect for autonomy, are undercut, even in cases where the patient's decision-making capacity is not impaired by severe suffering.

As to the other principle invoked by proponents of physician-assisted dying, the principle of *mercy*, terminal sedation is typically used only when the patient's suffering has become extreme (e.g. agitation, delirium, dyspnoea, seizures, urinary and faecal retention, nausea and protracted vomiting) and other palliative measures are not effective. As Lo and Rubenfeld have said: 'We turn to [sedation] when everything else hasn't worked' (Lo & Rubenfeld 2005: 1810).

Terminal sedation to unconsciousness may certainly provide relief from such suffering. However, some patients wish to avoid a long downhill course – especially its last stages. The use of terminal sedation 'to relieve suffering' presupposes that the patient is already experiencing suffering. It provides no rationale for sedating a patient who is not currently suffering, even if suffering is clearly in the offing.

A question that arose in my analysis was whether terminal sedation respects the principle of the *sanctity of life* (or principle of the wrongness of killing, in the sense of ending a person's life before it would 'naturally' end), a key concern of the opponents of physician-assisted dying. I found that terminal sedation does not respect this principle. Rather, it unarguably causes death, *and* does so in a way that is not 'natural'.

As to causing death, it is important to clearly understand that the practice of terminal sedation commonly involves two components: (1) inducing sedation; and (2) withholding ANH. The first is not intrinsically lethal, but the second is, if pursued long enough. Patients who are sedated to the extent involved in terminal sedation cannot eat or drink, and without ANH they will necessarily die, often if not always before they would have died otherwise.[1]

Death following terminal sedation is not 'natural' either (see Raus et al. 2011). The notion of 'natural' death usually refers to death that results from an underlying disease. Yet in terminal sedation death may result from, or be accelerated by, dehydration. This is not 'natural'

---

[1] Patients are sometimes sedated to unconsciousness with ANH continued, but this is not usual.

dehydration – it is induced by a physician.[2] If respect for the principle of the sanctity of life implies that a patient's life should not be caused to end, but rather that death must occur only as the result of the underlying disease process, then terminal sedation does not honour this principle.

With regard to the other main concern of opponents of physician-assisted dying, the risk of *abuse*, I noted back in 2008 that there is nothing in the practice of terminal sedation that offers greater protection against the possibility of abuse than is the case for physician-assisted dying. As to the risk that the practice may be applied to patients who have not requested or consented to it, and where it is not in their best interests, for example because, as is sometimes argued by opponents of physician-assisted dying, physicians are overworked, biased against patients of certain backgrounds, beholden to cost pressures, etc., I argued that there is no reason to assume that terminal sedation would be less subject to these abuses than direct aid-in-dying.

Indeed, direct aid-in-dying, at least as it is legally practised in, for example, Oregon, requires a series of safeguards – confirmation of a terminal diagnosis, oral and written requests, a waiting period and other criteria. The practice of terminal sedation, on the other hand, is not subject to legally binding safeguards.

3.   Managing perceptions

Nevertheless, a case may be made for terminal sedation. It offers a definitive response to uncontrollable suffering. The gradual induction of death over several days may appeal to some patients and their families, especially if this slow process is perceived as gentler and easier for the patient, and as permitting the family more time to absorb the reality of their loss. Terminal sedation may also be perceived as less final than physician-assisted death. However, as I already noted in 2008, the argument in favour of terminal sedation is one of perceptions:

[I]t may *feel* natural (even if it is not), it may *feel* safer (even if it offers less protection from abuse), it may *feel* like something the patient can openly choose (even if the choice is constructed in a way that obscures its real nature), and it may *feel* to the physician as if it is more in keeping with medical codes that prohibit killing (even if it still brings about death). We live in a society that tolerates many obfuscations and hypocrisies, and this may be another one we ought to embrace. (Battin 2008: 29)

---

[2] As noted, for example by Craig: 'If a dying patient [receives prolonged sedation, i.e. more than one or two days, without hydration] there may be reasonable grounds for doubt as to whether the patient died of the treatment or the disease' (Craig 1994: 141).

Yet we should embrace this practice with caution, and we should remain sceptical about efforts to promote it. In 2008, the American Medical Association Council on Ethical and Judicial Affairs issued a report entitled *Sedation to Unconsciousness in End-of-Life Care* (American Medical Association 2008). This report made an earnest effort to preclude many of the practical and ethical difficulties with terminal sedation by, for example, acknowledging the importance of patient or surrogate consent and emphasising the importance of interdisciplinary consultation and careful monitoring. The AMA also distinguishes between physical and existential suffering, thereby insisting that sedation may be appropriate in cases of uncontrollable physical suffering, but that for patients with severe existential suffering social support is recommended.

However, in its attempt to distinguish 'palliative sedation' (it avoids the expression 'terminal sedation') from euthanasia, the report undercuts its own courage in addressing these difficult issues by trying to argue that palliative sedation (the permissible strategy) has nothing in common with euthanasia (the impermissible strategy). Unfortunately, the report does not distinguish between *voluntary* euthanasia (legal in The Netherlands, Belgium and Luxembourg), *non-voluntary* euthanasia (of a patient no longer capable of expressing her wishes or of giving legally valid consent), and *involuntary* euthanasia (against the patient's wishes). It thus fails to notice that the Dutch/Belgian/Luxembourg and the Nazi senses of 'euthanasia' are entirely different, and that one could welcome the former while reviling the latter.

The AMA report distinguishes sedation from euthanasia (or physician-assisted suicide or aid-in-dying) on the basis of intention – thus applying the doctrine of double effect – and then attempts to infer intent from the pattern of practice: 'one large dose' or 'rapidly accelerating doses' of morphine may signify an intention to cause death, whereas 'repeated doses or continuous infusions' are benign. However, this view is extremely naive. What could equally well be inferred from repeated doses and continuous infusions is a clever attempt to cover one's tracks.

Nor is it clear what counts as 'large doses' in the AMA's framework. For example, as I asked in 2008:

Is a fentanyl patch in a fentanyl-naive patient 'rapidly accelerating' or 'continuously infusing' when opioid tolerance may be in question? If a hydromorphone infusion for a patient with myoclonus is increased overnight from forty milligrams per hour to one hundred, does the increase count as 'rapidly accelerating'? Are one hundred milligram boluses of hydromorphone given every fifteen to thirty minutes on top of a one hundred milligram/hour infusion considered to be 'large doses', or are they merely 'repeated' doses? (Battin 2008: 29)

Distinguishing between different sorts of intentions on the basis of observed practice is not only impossible but also morally indefensible. Such distinctions can only worsen the ethical unease and legal dread in physicians who try to ease their patients' dying. My point here is not that terminal sedation is wrong, but rather that it can be practised in a hypocritical way. The AMA report seems to provide the tools needed for such hypocrisy.

Because there is so much anxiety that terminal sedation might be confused with euthanasia, the characteristics that it shares with euthanasia are obscured or sanitised. This is where 'the sheet is pulled over our eyes', as I suggested in 2008. The implausible effort to draw a bright line between these end-of-life practices makes the practice of terminal sedation more dishonest than it should be. It makes what can be a decent and humane practice morally problematic.

Some of those who present terminal sedation as a 'compromise' seem to suggest that terminal sedation is the one and only way to deal with difficult deaths. However, many other last resort options are possible, including patient-elected cessation of eating and drinking and direct physician-assisted dying. If terminal sedation displaces these alternatives, it cannot be an acceptable 'compromise'. Knowing that pain is likely in some diseases and that, even with the best palliative care, not all pain can be relieved, some patients will prefer an earlier, gentler way out. Others will want to hang on as long as possible, in spite of extreme suffering. There is no reason why terminal sedation should not be recognised as an option for some patients at the end of life, but, as I concluded in my analysis in 2008, this practice should not be seen as the only option – or even the best option – for easing a bad death.

4.   Is the sheet pulled over our eyes?

The question is whether the sheet is pulled over our eyes, that is, whether there is something we should be seeing that the practice of terminal sedation veils. It may be an awkward metaphor, but I think it is revealing, in that the question it asks could be treated in many different ways. For instance, it could be treated as an *epidemiological* question – have rates of terminal sedation, perhaps in comparison to practices like euthanasia, gone up? (the answer is that they have, at least in The Netherlands and Belgium). It could be seen as a *conceptual* question, one that might be answered by examining the various different names for the practice: 'terminal sedation', 'palliative sedation', 'continuous deep sedation', and so on. Such an examination might give us some way of inferring how the practice is conducted and whether the character of consent and how consent is obtained vary from one label to another. Or it could be seen, as it often is, simply as a pragmatic *clinical* question: is terminal sedation as effective in reducing pain as some other symptom-management strategies? (The answer is yes, if you consider just the patient's immediate symptoms, since experience of them is completely obliterated in terminal sedation, but no if you think about the whole downhill course of a terminal illness, where terminal sedation is not typically introduced until the very end: the patient suffers, indeed intractably, until terminal sedation begins.)

Then, too, various ways of framing the question emphasise different ways of understanding *agency* in the question being asked. Is the sheet over our eyes? If so, how did it get there? Has the sheet been actively pulled over our eyes, and if so, by whom or what? In what party's interests would it be to do so? Could we have been or be pulling that sheet over our eyes ourselves? Is a sheet – imagine a bedsheet in a hospital setting – the appropriate metaphor, and, if so, are screening-off, veiling or cloaking the kinds of effect-descriptors that are appropriate?

Unlike pulling a sheet over some disturbing item, whether a spilled salad or a human corpse, in terminal sedation not everything is hidden: some parts of the practice are being foregrounded while other features of it are being obscured. Even if 'pulling the sheet over our eyes' is a clumsy metaphor to begin with, the various ways in which we can phrase it suggest how complex the issue of causation and responsibility in terminal sedation is.

However, all these ways of framing and reframing the question appear to operate against a societal background that is not challenged. In this volume, Søren Holm makes an enigmatic remark about changes in our contemporary *ars moriendi*, and even though his remark is, by his own account, 'just something that has been rumbling in the back of my mind',[3] I think it holds a key to something more of what is ethically unsettling about terminal sedation. Holm writes:

> If we, as a society, are moving from an *ars moriendi* focusing on a gradual and orderly withdrawal from life, to a managed death process focusing on absence of suffering then TS [terminal sedation] will be seen as more and more attractive, especially for those who think that euthanasia or physician-assisted suicide are morally problematic. (Holm, Chapter 14, this volume)

Surely many patients do see avoidance of pain as a primary goal. The development of hospice care, of better methods of pain and symptom

[3] Personal communication, 22 October 2012.

management, of better training of nurses and doctors in treating pain, and of better pain-control medications over the last several decades, responds to this goal. So does the development of terminal sedation, as a last resort when other methods of pain management fail. It is now considered a violation of medical ethics to 'let a patient suffer'.

But what Holm's brief remark hints at is the issue of the relationship between background context and the *ars moriendi* of a culture or subculture, i.e. the way people think of and go about dying. Such cultural conceptions change and evolve. Cultural assumptions can drive technological development, but technological developments can also reshape cultural assumptions.

In the developed world, the ubiquitous *ars moriendi* of the 1950s and 1960s was understood by both physicians and patients alike as to keep on fighting as long as possible: after all, the then-recent development of antibiotics made extended survival at the end of life possible, in part by making it possible to treat pneumonia, formerly the bedridden 'old man's friend'. Then, aided in part by the Catholic Church's recognition that life-prolongation was not morally required, there was some retrenchment in favour of (limited) patient autonomy. Respect for a patient's choice was the new watchword, and the dance between the physician and the patient, in which the physician tries to help the patient negotiate the sometimes treacherous shoals of dying, began to become the new *ars moriendi*. DNR orders, refusal of some life-prolonging treatment, even the refusal of ANH, became possible.

To be sure, physician-assisted suicide and euthanasia were sometimes also discreetly practised, as, it is assumed, has always been the case, though they were not part of the officially acknowledged *ars moriendi*. But these earlier assertions of patients' rights to avoid excessive attempts at life-prolongation were not necessarily targeted at the avoidance of *pain*, but kept open the possibility of a person's choosing, in concert with the physician, ways of negotiating dying so as to bring one's life to a meaningful close. That could mean choosing only therapies that would not interfere with cognitive function, or only therapies that were in accord with a person's other values. It need not have been that the end-of-life strategies that a physician and patient might choose were entirely focused on pain.

Terminal sedation, in contrast, is intended to obviate intractable pain and suffering at the end of life. It often arrives too late, as I have noted earlier (Battin 2008), and its strategies – reduction in conscious experience so that pain is no longer felt – make central quite a different value. This is part of Holm's point, but what Holm also hints at is a large medical/cultural reframing: a change away from autonomy as the central value (which it had never fully achieved) to something that could be far more potentially paternalistic, or unthinkingly over-interested.

Of course, patients want to avoid pain. But they may also want to avoid the obtundation that comes with some forms of pain management, something not possible if terminal sedation is employed. An *ars moriendi* based on avoidance of suffering might seem patient-centred, but it invites outside assessment that masquerades as objective (starting with the simplistic 'rate your pain on a 1–10 scale') and may undercut opportunities for autonomous choice. Patients in pain are offered medication, urged to take medication, or simply have it administered to them if the clinical perception is that they are in severe distress, and while this may often be the right thing to do, it is not automatically so.

5.   Conclusion

What is the bottom line, if we take seriously Holm's suggestion that pain-suppression is becoming the new *ars moriendi?* It has been tempting to think of terminal sedation as the, or rather a, solution to a problem that has been growing as lives have been extended by the achievements of modern medicine: longer lives, later dying, but also the risk of more pain. Terminal sedation is a good solution in some cases (viz., where it is in accord with the values of the patient and the family), whereas in other cases it is an inadequate, indeed deceptive pseudo-solution compared to other ways that life, and with it pain, might come to an end.

That is what I had argued half a decade ago, and I still believe it is the case. But it is only part of the story. That part of the story sees terminal sedation as a solution to a problem, whether a good solution or, as I had argued, often not a good one. But what Søren Holm lets us see is that the very practice of terminal sedation may itself be a symptom of a much more general issue: not just how do we relieve pain, but what should we say about a medical and social culture that is coming to value the relief of pain above any other value, including the value of life (after all, the court-recognised doctrine of double effect permits the use of pain-relieving drugs even when they will foreseeably, though not intentionally, shorten life), and, most importantly, the autonomy of the patient. Indeed, while suffering is a quintessentially subjective phenomenon, it is often assessed 'objectively' with a 1–10 scale. There is little uniformity, as has often been noted, in pain assessments. But the patient who answers 5 or above is treated. As noted earlier, it is now considered a violation of medical ethics to 'let a patient suffer', even though this may undercut discussion of the trade-offs in reducing alertness or preserving other values. This is, I think, yet another way in which the sheet is pulled over our eyes.

This is the real risk of terminal sedation as a response to intractable suffering at the end of life. Terminal sedation involves the administration of pain medication in the hands of others, and, once the process has begun, the patient no longer has a way of controlling the course of events on the way to death: what had been a gain in patient autonomy is erased. Even periods of 'lightening up' in the sedation level, intended to see if the patient is still in pain, cannot be controlled by the patient. But we have not yet come to question what role these assumptions play in the ways we think about death – nor, for that matter, whether the very development of terminal sedation (in the minds of some) as a legally and morally acceptable alternative to assisted dying *has altered our background assumption about how we should die, our societal ars moriendi,* to make it seem the appropriate, ideal solution for difficult clinical problems.

The argument I presented in 2008 I still think holds, but what Søren Holm should make us all see is that an argument like this does not take full account of the *larger social context* within which terminal sedation takes place, or the ways in which the larger social context might itself be influenced by the development and championing of terminal sedation as a solution to the problems of hard dying. It is something, I believe, that we should not tolerate as the normal, routine compromise solution to these problems, the default strategy for physicians and families, even though it should indeed be available to those patients who would welcome it.

References

Ahluwalia, S.C. and Fried, T.R. (2009) 'Physician factors associated with out-patient palliative care referral'. *Palliat Med* 23(7):608–15.

Alkire, M.T., Hudetz, A.G. and Tononi, G. (2008) 'Consciousness and anesthesia'. *Science* 322(5903):876–80.

Alonso-Babarro, A., Varela-Cerdeira, M., Torres, I., Rodriguez-Barrientos, R. and Bruera, E. (2010) 'At-home palliative sedation for end-of-life cancer patients'. *Palliat Med* 24(5):486–92.

Alpers, A. (1998) 'Criminal act or palliative care? Prosecutions involving the care of the dying'. *J Law Med Ethics* 26(4):308–31.

American Medical Association (Council on Ethical and Judicial Affairs) (2008) *Sedation to Unconsciousness in End-of-Life Care.* CEJA Report 5-A-08, American Medical Association. Available at www.ama-assn.org/resources/doc/code-medical-ethics/2201a.pdf (last accessed 24 April 2013).

Anquinet, L., Rietjens, J.A., van den Block, L., Bossuyt, N. and Deliens, L. (2011) 'General practitioners' report of continuous deep sedation until death for patients dying at home: a descriptive study from Belgium'. *Eur J Gen Pract* 17(1):5–13.

Anquinet, L., Rietjens, J.A., Seale, C., Seymour, J., Deliens, L. and van der Heide, A. (2012) 'The practice of continuous deep sedation until death in Flanders (Belgium), the Netherlands, and the U.K.: a comparative study'. *J Pain Symptom Manage* 44(1):33–43.

Anscombe, E. (1958) *Intention.* Oxford: Basil Blackwell.

Arevalo, J.J., Brinkkemper, T., van der Heide, A., Rietjens, J.A., Ribbe, M., Deliens, L., Loer, S.A., Zuurmond, W.W. and Perez, R.S. (2012) 'Palliative sedation: reliability and validity of sedation scales'. *J Pain Symptom Manage* 44(5):704–14.

Arevalo, J.J., Rietjens, J.A., Swart, S., Perez, R.S.G.M. and van der Heide, A. (2013) 'Day-to-day care in palliative sedation: survey of nurses' experiences with decision-making and performance'. *Int J Nurs Stud.* 50(5): 613–21.

Arlidge, A. (2000) 'The trial of Dr David Moor'. *Crim L R* 31–40.

Aubry, R., Blanchet, V. and Viallard, M.-L. (2010) 'La sédation pour détresse chez l'adulte dans des situations spécifiques et complexes'. *Médecine Palliative* 9(2):71–9.

AVVV, NVVA and STING (2006) *Begrippen en Zorgvuldigheidseisen met betrekking tot besluitvorming rond het levenseinde in de verpleeghuiszorg.* Utrecht: AVVV, NVVA, Sting.

Bach, V., Ploeg, J. and Black, M. (2009) 'Nursing roles in end-of-life decision making in critical care settings'. *West J Nurs Res* 31(4):496–512.

Baines, M., Oliver, D.J. and Carter, R.L. (1985) 'Medical management of intestinal obstruction in patients with advanced malignant disease. A clinical and pathological study'. *Lancet* 2(8462):990–3.

Bakker, J., Jansen, T.C., Lima, A. and Kompanje, E.J. (2008) 'Why opioids and sedatives may prolong life rather than hasten death after ventilator withdrawal in critically ill patients'. *Am J Hosp Palliat Care* 25(2):152–4.

Barbato, M. (2001) 'Bispectral index monitoring in unconscious palliative care patients'. *J Palliat Care* 17(2):102–8.

Battaglia, J. (2005) 'Pharmacological management of acute agitation'. *Drugs* 65(9):1207–22.

Battin, M. (2008) 'Terminal sedation: pulling the sheet over our eyes'. *Hastings Cent Rep* 38(5):27–30.

Baumann, A., Claudot, F., Audibert, G., Mertes, P.M. and Puybasset, L. (2011) 'The ethical and legal aspects of palliative sedation in severely brain-injured patients: a French perspective'. *Philos Ethics Humanit Med* 6:4.

Beauchamp, T.L. and Childress, J.F. (1994) *Principles of Biomedical Ethics*, 4th edn. Oxford University Press.

Becker, D.E. (2010) 'Nausea, vomiting, and hiccups: a review of mechanisms and treatment'. *Anesth Prog* 57(4):150–6.

Becker, D.E. (2012) 'Pharmacodynamic considerations for moderate and deep sedation'. *Anesth Prog* 59(1):28–42.

Beel, A.C., Hawranik, P.G., McClement, S. and Daeninck, P. (2006) 'Palliative sedation: nurses' perceptions'. *Int J Palliat Nurs* 12(11):510–18.

Belgrave, K. and Requena, P. (2012) 'A primer on palliative sedation'. *National Catholic Bioethics Quarterly* 12(2):263–81.

Benitez-Rosario, M.A., Castillo-Padrós, M., Garrido-Bernet, B. and Ascanio-León, B. (2012) 'Quality of care in palliative sedation: audit and compliance monitoring of a clinical protocol'. *J Pain Symptom Manage* 44(4):532–41.

Bennett, J. (1995) *The Act Itself*. Oxford: Clarendon Press.

Berger, J.T. (2010) 'Rethinking guidelines for the use of palliative sedation'. *Hastings Cent Rep* 40(3):32–8.

Bernat, J.L., Gert, B. and Mogielnicki, R.P. (1993) 'Patient refusal of hydration and nutrition: an alternative to physician-assisted suicide or voluntary active euthanasia'. *Arch Intern Med* 153(24):2723–31.

Billings, J.A. and Block, S.D. (1996) 'Slow euthanasia'. *J Palliat Care* 12(4):21–30.

Bilsen, J., Vander Stichele, R., Broeckaert, B., Mortier, F. and Deliens, L. (2007) 'Changes in medical end-of-life practices during the legalization process of euthanasia in Belgium'. *Soc Sci Med* 65(4):803–8.

Bilsen, J., Cohen, J., Chambaere, K., Pousset, G., Onwuteaka-Philipsen, B.D., Mortier, F. and Deliens, L. (2009) 'Medical end-of-life practices under the euthanasia law in Belgium'. *N Engl J Med* 361(11):1119–21.

Bliss, J. and While, A. (2003) 'Decision-making in palliative and continuing care in the community: an analysis of the published literature with reference to the context of UK care provision'. *Int J Nurs Stud* 40(8):881–8.

Blondeau, D., Roy, L., Dumont, S., Godin, G. and Martineau, I. (2005) 'Physicians' and pharmacists' attitudes toward the use of sedation at the end of life: influence of prognosis and type of suffering'. *J Palliat Care* 21(4):238–45.

Boorsma, M., Wanrooij, B. and Koelewijn, M. (2005) 'Sedatie in de palliatieve fase: naar een kalm einde'. *Huisarts & Wetenschap* 48(9):470–4.

Boyle, J. (1991) 'Who is entitled to double effect?'. *J Med Philos* 16(5):475–94.

Boyle, J. (2004) 'Medical ethics and double effect: the case of terminal sedation'. *Theor Med Bioeth* 25(1):51–60.

Brajtman, S. (2003) 'The impact on the family of terminal restlessness and its management'. *Palliat Med* 17(5):454–60.

Brandt, H.E., Ooms, M.E., Deliens, L., van der Wal, G. and Ribbe M.W. (2006a) 'The last two days of life of nursing home patients – a nationwide study on causes of death and burdensome symptoms in the Netherlands'. *Palliat Med* 20(5):533–40.

Brandt, H.E., Ooms, M.E., Ribbe, M.W., van der Wal, G. and Deliens, L. (2006b) 'Predicted survival vs. actual survival in terminally ill noncancer patients in Dutch nursing homes'. *J Pain Symptom Manage* 32(6):560–6.

Breitbart, W. and Alici, Y. (2008) 'Agitation and delirium at the end of life: "We couldn't manage him"'. *JAMA* 300(24):2898–910, E1.

Breitbart, W., Marotta, R., Platt, M.M., Weisman, H., Derevenco, M., Grau, C., Corbera, K., Raymond, S., Lund, S. and Jacobson, P. (1996) 'A double-blind trial of haloperidol, chlorpromazine, and lorazepam in the treatment of delirium in hospitalized AIDS patients'. *Am J Psychiatry* 153(2):231–17.

Brinkkemper, T., Klinkenberg, M., Deliens, L., Eliel, M., Rietjens, J.A., Zuurmond, W.W. and Perez, R.S. (2011) 'Palliative sedation at home in the Netherlands: a nationwide survey among nurses'. *J Adv Nurs* 67(8):1719–28.

Broeckaert, B. (2009) 'Advanced symptom control, not slow euthanasia: myths and issues regarding palliative sedation', in Bhatnagar, S. (ed.), *Freedom from Pain: Sixteenth International Conference of Indian Association of Palliative Care*. New Delhi: IK International Publishing, pp. 160–7.

Broeckaert, B. and Olarte, J.M.N. (2002) 'Sedation in palliative care: facts and concepts', in Ten Have, H. and Clark, D. (eds.), *The Ethics of Palliative Care – European Perspectives*. Buckingham: Open University Press, pp. 166–80.

Broeckaert, B., Claessens, P., Menten, J. and Schotsmans, P. (2009) 'Authors' reply: a descriptive definition of palliative sedation'. *J Pain Symptom Manage* 37(3):e11–12.

Broeckaert, B., Mullie, A., Gielen, J., Desmet, M. and Vanden Berghe, P. (2010) *Guideline Palliative Sedation*. Ethics Steering Committee of the Federation for Palliative Care Flanders [Sedation]. Available at www.pallialine.be/template.asp?f=rl_palliatieve_sedatie.htm (last accessed 24 April 2013).

Bruce, A. and Boston, P. (2011) 'Relieving existential suffering through palliative sedation: discussion of an uneasy practice'. *J Adv Nurs* 67(12):2732–40.

Bruce, S., Hendrix, C. and Gentry, J. (2006) 'Palliative sedation in end-of-life care'. *J Hospice Palliat Nurs* 8(6):320–7.

Bruera, E., Macmillan, K., Hanson, J. and MacDonald, R.N. (1989) 'The cognitive effects of the administration of narcotic analgesics in patients with cancer pain'. *Pain* 39(1):13–16.

Bruinsma, S.M., Rietjens, J.A., Seymour, J.E., Anquinet, L. and van der Heide, A. (2012) 'The experiences of relatives with the practice of palliative sedation: a systematic review'. *J Pain Symptom Manage* 44(3):431–45.

Buiting, H., van Delden, J., Onwuteaka-Philpsen, B., Rietjens, J., Rurup, M., van Tol, D., Gevers, J., van der Maas, P. and van der Heide, A. (2009) 'Reporting of euthanasia and physician-assisted suicide in the Netherlands: descriptive study'. *BMC Med Ethics* 10:18.

Bundesärztekammer (2011) 'Grundsätze zur ärztlichen Sterbebegleitung'. *Deutsches Ärzteblatt* 108(7):A346–8.

Burt, J., Shipman, C., Addington-Hall, J. and White, P. (2008) 'Nursing the dying within a generalist caseload: a focus group study of district nurses'. *Int J Nurs Stud* 45(10):1470–8.

Callahan, D. (2004) 'Terminal sedation and the artefactual fallacy', in Tännsjö, T. (ed.), *Terminal Sedation: Euthanasia in Disguise?* Dordrecht: Kluwer Academic Publishers.

Cameron, D., Bridge, D. and Blitz-Lindeque, J. (2004) 'Use of sedation to relieve refractory symptoms in dying patients'. *S Afr Med J* 94(6):445–9.

Cañas, F. (2007) 'Management of agitation in the acute psychotic patient – efficacy without excessive sedation'. *Eur Neuropsychopharmacol* 17(Suppl 2):S108–14.

Cantor, N.L. (2006) 'On hastening death without violating legal and moral prohibitions'. *Loyola University Chicago Law Journal* 37:101–25.

Caraceni, A., Zecca, E., Martini, C., Gorni, G., Campa, T., Brunelli, C. and De Conno, F. (2012) 'Palliative sedation at the end of life at a tertiary cancer center'. *Support Care Cancer* 20(6):1299–307.

Carrasco, G. (2000) 'Instruments for monitoring intensive care unit sedation'. *Crit Care* 4(4):217–25.

Carter, M.J., Gibbins, J. and Senior- Smith, G. (2008) 'Ketamine: does it have a role in palliative sedation?'. *J Pain Symptom Manage* 36(4):e1–3.

Cassell, E.J. (1982) 'The nature of suffering and the goals of medicine'. *N Engl J Med* 306(11):639–45.

Cassell, E.J. and Rich, B.A. (2010) 'Intractable end-of-life suffering and the ethics of palliative sedation'. *Pain Med* 11(3):435–8.

Cavanaugh, T.A. (2006) *Double-effect Reasoning: Doing Good and Avoiding Evil*. Oxford: Clarendon Press.

CBCEW (Catholic Bishops' Conference of England & Wales Dept. for Christian Responsibility & Citizenship) (2010) *A Practical Guide to The Spiritual Care of the Dying Person*. London: CTS.

Cellarius, V. (2008) 'Terminal sedation and the "imminence condition"'. *J Med Ethics* 34(2):69–72.

Cellarius, V. (2011) '"Early terminal sedation" is a distinct entity'. *Bioethics* 25(1):46–54.

Cellarius, V. and Henry, B. (2010) 'Justifying different levels of palliative sedation'. *Ann Intern Med* 152(5):332.

Chabot, B., den Hartogh, G. and van Delden, J.J.M. (2005) 'Een eng begrip. Pleidooi voor een sobere definitie van palliatieve of terminale sedatie'. *Med Contact* 60:1464–6.

Chambaere, K., Bilsen, J., Cohen, J., Rietjens, J.A., Onwuteaka-Philipsen, B.D., Mortier, F. and Deliens, L. (2010) 'Continuous deep sedation until death in Belgium: a nationwide survey'. *Arch Intern Med* 170(5):490–3.

Chater, S., Viola, R., Paterson, J. and Jarvis, V. (1998) 'Sedation for intractable distress in the dying – a survey of experts'. *Palliat Med* 12(4):255–69.

Cherny, N.I. (1998) 'Sedation in response to refractory existential distress: walking the fine line'. *J Pain Symptom Manage* 16(6):404–6.

Cherny, N.I. and Portenoy, R.K. (1994) 'Sedation in the management of refractory symptoms: guidelines for evaluation and treatment'. *J Palliat Care* 10(2):31–38.

Cherny, N.I. and Radbruch, L. (Board of the European Association for Palliative Care) (2009) 'European Association for Palliative Care (EAPC) recommended framework for the use of sedation in palliative care'. *Palliat Med* 23(7):581–93.

Chiu, T.Y., Hu, W.Y., Lue, B.H., Cheng, S.Y. and Chen, C.Y. (2001) 'Sedation for refractory symptoms of terminal cancer patients in Taiwan'. *J Pain Symptom Manage* 21(6):467–72.

Claessens, P., Menten, J., Schotsmans, P. and Broeckaert, B. (2008) 'Palliative sedation: a review of the research literature'. *J Pain Symptom Manage* 36(3):310–33.

Claessens, P., Menten, J., Schotsmans, P. and Broeckaert, B. (2011) 'Palliative sedation, not slow euthanasia: a prospective, longitudinal study of sedation in Flemish palliative care units'. *J Pain Symptom Manage* 41(1):14–24.

Claessens, P., Menten, J., Schotsmans, P. and Broeckaert, B. (2012) 'Level of consciousness in dying patients. The role of palliative sedation: a longitudinal prospective study'. *Am J Hosp Palliat Care* 29(3):195–200.

Cohen, J., van Delden, J., Mortier, F., Löfmark, R., Norup, M., Cartwright, C., Faisst, K., Canova, C., Onwuteaka-Philipsen, B. and Bilsen, J. (EURELD Consortium) (2008) 'Influence of physicians' life stances on attitudes to end-of-life decisions and actual end-of-life decisionmaking in six countries'. *J Med Ethics* 34:247–53.

Cohen, L.B., Dubovsky, A.N., Aisenberg, J. and Miller, K.M. (2003) 'Propofol for endoscopic sedation: a protocol for safe and effective administration by the gastroenterologist'. *Gastrointest Endosc* 58(5):725–32.

Commission on Assisted Dying (2011) *The Current Legal Status of Assisted Dying Is Inadequate and Incoherent...* London: Demos.

Congregation for the Doctrine of the Faith (1980) 'Declaration on Euthanasia – *Iura et bona*'. *AAS* 72,1:542–52, Documenta 38, 5 May 1980. Available at www.vatican.va/roman_curia/congregations/cfaith/documents/rc_con_cfaith_doc_19800505_euthanasia_en.html (last accessed 24 April 2013).

Congregation for the Doctrine of the Faith (2007) *Responses to certain questions of the United States Conference of Catholic Bishops concerning artificial nutrition and hydration*. August 2007. Available at www. vatican.va/roman_curia/congregations/cfaith/documents/rc_con_ cfaith_doc_20070801_risposte-usa_en.html (last accessed 24 April 2013).

Connery, J.S.J. (1977) *Abortion: The Development of the Roman Catholic Perspective*. Chicago: Loyola University Press.

Cowan, J.D. and Palmer, T.W.P. (2002). 'Practical guide to palliative sedation'. *Curr Oncol Rep* 4(3):242–9.

Cowan, J.D. and Walsh, D. (2001) 'Terminal sedation in palliative medicine – definition and review of the literature'. *Support Care Cancer* 9(6):403–7.

Craig, G. (1994) 'On withholding nutrition and hydration in the terminally ill: has palliative medicine gone too far?'. *J Med Ethics* 20:139–43.

Critchley, P., Plach, N., Grantham, M., Marshall, D., Taniguchi, A., Latimer, E. and Jadad, A.R. (2001) 'Efficacy of haloperidol in the treatment of nausea and vomiting in the palliative patient: a systematic review'. *J Pain Symptom Manage* 22(2):631–4.

Cronin, D. (1958) *The Moral Law in Regard to the Ordinary and Extraordinary Means of Conserving Life*. Rome: Pontifical Gregorian University.

Cruickshank, S., Adamson, E., Logan, L. and Brackenridge, K. (2010) 'Using syringe drivers in palliative care within a rural, community setting: capturing the whole experience'. *Int J Palliat Nurs* 16(3):126–32.

Curlin, F.A., Nwodim, C., Vance, J.L., Chin, M.H. and Lantos, J.D. (2008) 'To die, to sleep: US physicians' religious and other objections to physician-assisted suicide, terminal sedation, and withdrawal of life support'. *Am J Hosp Palliat Care* 25(2):112–20.

Czapiński, P., Blaszczyk, B. and Czuczwar, S.J. (2005) 'Mechanisms of action of antiepileptic drugs'. *Curr Top Med Chem* 5(1):3–14.

Dalal, S., Del Fabbro, E. and Bruera, E. (2009) 'Is there a role for hydration at the end of life?'. *Curr Opin Support Palliat Care* 3(1):72–8.

da Todi, J. (1982) *Jacopone da Todi – The Lauds* (translated by Hughes, S. and Hughes, E). London: SPCK.

Daverschot, M. (2010) 'Palliatieve zorg: juridische kanttekeningen bij de KNMG-Richtlijn palliatieve sedatie (versie 2009)'. *Pro Vita Humana* 17(2):54–60.

Davies, M. (1998) *Textbook on Medical Law*, 2nd edn. London: Blackstone.

Davis, M. (2008) 'Understanding terminal sedation'. *Bioethics Matters* 6(3):1–4.

Dean, M.M., Cellarius, V., Henry, B., Oneschuk, D. and Librach, S.L. (2012) 'Framework for continuous palliative sedation therapy in Canada'. *J Palliat Med* 15(8):870–9.

De Gendt, C., Bilsen, J., Mortier, F., Vander Stichele, R. and Deliens, L. (2009) 'End-of-life decision-making and terminal sedation among very old patients'. *Gerontology* 55(1):99–105.

de Graeff, A. (2008) 'De rol van consultatie bij palliatieve sedatie in de regio Midden-Nederland'. *Ned Tijdschr Geneeskd* 152:2346–50.

de Graeff, A. and Dean, M. (2007) 'Palliative sedation therapy in the last weeks of life: a literature review and recommendations for standards'. *J Palliat Med* 10(1):67–85.

Delbeke, E. (2012) *Juridische aspecten van zorgverlening aan het levenseinde*. Antwerp: Intersentia.

den Hartogh, G.A. (2006a) 'Palliatieve sedatie en euthanasia – commentaar op een richtlijn'. *Tijdschrift voor Gezondheidsrecht* 30(2):109–19.

den Hartogh, G.A. (2006b) 'Het recht op inslapen – Richtlijn houdt onvoldoende rekening met opvatting "goed sterven"'. *Medisch Contact* 61:1463–5.

den Hartogh, G.A. (2012) 'The regulation of euthanasia: how successful is the Dutch system?', in Youngner, S.J. and Kimsma, G.K. (eds.), *Physician-assisted Death in Perspective – Assessing the Dutch Experience*. Cambridge University Press, pp. 351–91.

Dev, R., Dalal, S. and Bruera, E. (2012) 'Is there a role for parenteral nutrition or hydration at the end of life?'. *Curr Opin Support Palliat Care* 6(3):365–70.

de Veer, A., Francke, A. and Poortvliet, E. (2008) 'Nurses' involvement in end-of-life decisions'. *Cancer Nursing* 31(3):222–8.

Devlin, P. (1985) *Easing the Passing: The Trial of Dr Bodkin Adams*. London: Bodley Head.

Director of Public Prosecutions (2010) *Policy for Prosecutors in Respect of Cases of Encouraging or Assisting Suicide*. London: Crown Prosecution Service.

Douglas, C., Kerridge, I.A.N. and Ankeny, R. (2008) 'Managing intentions: the end-of-life administration of analgesics and sedatives, and the possibility of slow euthanasia'. *Bioethics* 22(7):388–96.

Doutrich, D., Wros, P. and Izumi, S. (2001) 'Relief of suffering and regard for personhood: nurses' ethical concerns in Japan and the USA'. *Nurs Ethics* 8(5):448–58.

Drazen, J.M. (2003) 'Decisions at the end of life'. *N Engl J Med* 349(12):1109–10.

Dresser, R. (1986) 'Life, death and incompetent patients: conceptual infirmities and hidden values in the law'. *Ariz L Rev* 28(3):373–405.

Duff, R.A. (1976) 'Absolute principles and double effect'. *Analysis* 36(2):68–80.

Dumonceau, J.M., Riphaus, A., Aparicio, J.R., Beilenhoff, U., Knape, J.T., Ortmann, M., Paspatis, G., Ponsioen, C.Y., Racz, I., Schreiber, F., Vilmann, P., Wehrmann, T., Wientjes, C. and Walder, B. (NAAP Task Force Members) (2010) 'European Society of Gastrointestinal Endoscopy, European Society of Gastroenterology and Endoscopy Nurses and Associates, and the European Society of Anaesthesiology Guideline: Non-anesthesiologist administration of propofol for GI'. *Endoscopy* 42(11):960–74.

Dunn, J., Hall, E., McManus, J. and Young, H. (2008) 'How effective is the control of and communication about agitation and distress in the last 48 hours of life?'. *Palliat Med* 22(4):404.

Dunne, K., Sullivan, K. and Kernohan, G. (2005) 'Palliative care for patients with cancer: district nurses' experiences'. *J Adv Nurs* 50(4):372–80.

Dyer, C. (2007) 'Dying woman seeks backing for dose of morphine to hasten death'. *BMJ* 334(7589):329.

Easthope, G., Tranter, B. and Gill, G. (2000) 'Normal medical practice of referring patients for complementary therapies among Australian general practitioners'. *Complement Ther Med* 8(4):226–33.

Elsayem, A., Curry III, E., Boohene, J., Munsell, M.F., Calderon, B., Hung, F. and Bruera, E. (2009) 'Use of palliative sedation for intractable symptoms in the palliative care unit of a comprehensive cancer center'. *Support Care Cancer* 17(1):53–9.

Enck, R.E. (1991) 'Drug induced terminal sedation for symptom control'. *Am J Hosp Palliat Care* 8(5) 3–5.

Enes, S. and de Vries, K. (2004) 'A survey of ethical issues experienced by nurses caring for terminally ill elderly people'. *Nurs Ethics* 11(2):150–64.

Escobar Pinzon, L.C., Claus, M., Zepf, K.I., Fischbeck, S. and Weber, M. (2012) 'Symptom prevalence in the last days of life in Germany: the role of place of death'. *Am J Hosp Palliat Med* 29(6):431–7.

Fainsinger, R.L. (1998) 'Use of sedation by a hospital palliative care support team'. *J Palliat Care* 14(1):51–4.

Fainsinger, R., Miller, M.J., Bruera, E., Hanson, J. and Maceachern, T. (1991) 'Symptom control during the last week of life on a palliative care unit'. *J Palliat Care* 7(1):5–11.

Fainsinger, R.L., Landman, W., Hoskings, M. and Bruera, E. (1998) 'Sedation for uncontrolled symptoms in a South African hospice'. *J Pain Symptom Manage* 16(3):145–52.

Fainsinger, R.L., Waller, A., Bercovici, M., Bengston, K., Landman, W., Hoskings, M., Nunez-Olarte, J.M. and deMoissac, D. (2000) 'A multicentre international study of sedation for uncontrolled symptoms in terminally ill patients'. *Palliat Med* 14(4):257–65.

Faull, C., Windridge, K., Ockleford, E. and Hudson, M. (2013) 'Anticipatory prescribing in terminal care at home: what challenges do community health professionals encounter?'. *BMJ Support Palliat Care*, 3:91–7

Fine, P. (2005) 'The evolving and important role of anesthesiology in palliative care'. *Anesth Analg* 100(1):183–8.

Finnis, J., Grisez, G. and Boyle, J. (2001) '"Direct and "indirect": a reply to critics of our action theory'. *The Thomist* 65(1):1–44.

Fohr, S.A. (1998) 'The double effect of pain medication: separating myth from reality'. *J Palliat Med* 1(4):315–28.

Foot, P. (1978) 'The problem of abortion and the doctrine of double effect', in Foot, P. *Virtues and Vices: And Other Essays in Moral Philosophy*. Berkeley: University of California Press, pp. 19–32.

Forbes, K. and Huxtable, R. (2006) 'Clarifying the data on double effect'. *Palliat Med* 20(4):395–6.

Førde, R., Materstvedt, L.J. and Syse, A. (2008) 'Scandinavia', in Griffiths, T., Weyers, H. and Adams, M. (eds.), *Euthanasia and Law in Europe*. Portland: Hart Publishing, pp. 425–41.

Frank, R. (2009) 'Shared decision making and its role in end of life care'. *Br J Nurs* 18(10):612–18.

Fried, T.R., O'Leary, J., Van Ness, P. and Fraenkel, L. (2007) 'Inconsistency over time in the preferences of older persons with advanced illness for life-sustaining treatment'. *J Am Geriatr Soc* 55(7):1007–14.

Furst, C.J. and Hagenfeldt, K. (2002) 'Sedering i livets slutskede – definition och kliniska riktlinjer behovs'. *Lakartidningen* 99(39):3830–5.

Gambrell, M. (2005) 'Using the BIS monitor in palliative care: a case study'. *J Neurosci Nurs* 37(3):140–3.

Ganzini, L., Goy, E.R., Miller, L.L., Harvath, T.A., Jackson, A. and Delorit, M.A. (2003) 'Nurses' experiences with hospice patients who refuse food and fluids to hasten death'. *N Engl J Med* 349(4):359–65.

Gauthier, C.C. (2001) 'Active voluntary euthanasia, terminal sedation, and assisted suicide'. *J Clin Ethics* 12(1):43–50.

General Medical Council. (2010) *Treatment and Care Towards the End of Life: Good Practice in Decision Making*. London: General Medical Council.

Georges, J. and Grypdonck, M. (2002) 'Moral problems experienced by nurses when caring for terminally ill people: a literature review'. *Nurs Ethics* 9(2):155–78.

Gevers, J.K.M. (2006) 'Terminal sedation: between pain relief, withholding treatment and euthanasia'. *Med Law* 25(4):747–51.

Gevers, S. (2004) 'Terminal sedation: a legal approach'. *Eur J Health Law* 10(4):359–67.

Gezondheidsraad (2004) *Patiënten in een vegetatieve toestand*. The Hague: Gezondheidsraad.

Gillick, M.R. (2004) 'Terminal sedation: an acceptable exit strategy?'. *Ann Intern Med* 141(3):236–7.

Gillon, R. (1999) 'When doctors might kill their patients: foreseeing is not necessarily the same as intending'. *BMJ* 318(7196):1431–2.

Glare, P., Virik, K., Jones, M., Hudson, M., Eychmuller, S., Simes, J. and Christakis, N. (2003) 'A systematic review of physicians' survival predictions in terminally ill cancer patients'. *BMJ* 327(7408):195–8.

Glover, J. (1977) *Causing Death and Saving Lives*. London: Penguin Books.

Gonçalves, F., Bento, M.J., Alvarenga, M., Costa, I. and Costa, L. (2008) 'Validation of a consciousness level scale for palliative care'. *Palliat Med* 22(6):724–9.

Gorget, A. (2012) *A la Vie, A la Mort*. Documentary film broadcast by France 2, 11:40pm, 7 February 2012.

Gormally, L. (2004) 'Terminal sedation and sanctity-of-life in medicine', in Tännsjö, T. (ed.) *Terminal Sedation: Euthanasia in Disguise?* Dordrecht: Kluwer Academic Publishers.

Greenblatt, D.J. (1992) 'Pharmacology of benzodiazepine hypnotics'. *J Clin Psychiatry* 53(Suppl):7–13.

Greene, W.R. and Davis, W.H. (1991) 'Titrated intravenous barbiturates in the control of symptoms in patients with terminal cancer'. *South Med J* 84(3):332–7.

Greenhalgh, D.L. and Kumar, C.M. (2008) 'Sedation during ophthalmic surgery'. *Eur J Anaesthesiol* 25(9):701–7.

Griffiths, J., Weyers, H. and Adams, M. (eds.) (2008) *Euthanasia and Law in Europe*. Portland: Hart Publishing.

Griggs, C. (2010) 'Community nurses' perceptions of a good death: a qualitative exploratory study'. *Int J Palliat Nurs* 16(3):140–9.

Haduch, A., Wójcikowski, J. and Daniel, W.A. (2011) 'Effect of neuroleptics on cytochrome P450 2C11 (CYP2C11) in rat liver'. *Pharmacol Rep* 63(6):1491–9.

Hallenbeck, J. (1999) 'Terminal sedation for intractable distress'. *West J Med* 171(4):222–3.

Hallenbeck, J.L. (2000) 'Terminal sedation: ethical implications in different situations'. *J Palliat Med* 3(3):313–20.

Harris, J. (1981) 'Ethical problems in the management of some severely handicapped children'. *J Med Ethics* 7(3):193–201.

Harris, J. (1985) *The Value of Life: An Introduction to Medical Ethics.* London: Routledge and Kegan Paul.

Harris, J. (1997) 'The philosophical case against the philosophical case against euthanasia', in Keown, J. (ed.), *Euthanasia Examined: Ethical, Clinical and Legal Perspectives.* Cambridge University Press, pp. 36–45.

Hart, H.L.A. (1986) 'Intention and punishment', in Hart, H.L.A., *Punishment and Responsibility.* Oxford: Clarendon Press, pp. 113–35.

Hasselaar, J.G.J., Reuzel, R.P.B., van den Muijsenbergh, M.E.T.C., Koopmans, R.T.C.M., Leget, C.J.W., Crul, B.J.P. and Vissers, K.C.P. (2008) 'Dealing with delicate issues in continuous deep sedation. Varying practices among Dutch medical specialists, general practitioners, and nursing home physicians'. *Arch Intern Med* 168(5):537–43.

Hasselaar, J.G.J., Verhagen, S.C., Wolff, A.P., Engels, Y., Crul B.J.P. and Vissers, K.C.P. (2009a) 'Changed patterns in Dutch palliative sedation practices after the introduction of a national guideline'. *Arch Intern Med* 169(5):430–7.

Hasselaar, J.G., Verhagen, S.C. and Vissers, K.C. (2009b) 'When cancer symptoms cannot be controlled: the role of palliative sedation'. *Curr Opin Support Palliat Care* 3(1):14–23.

Hauser, K. and Walsh, D. (2009) 'Palliative sedation: welcome guidance on a controversial issue'. *Palliat Med* 23(7):577–9.

Hawryluck, L. and Harvey, W. (2000) 'Analgesia, virtue, and the principle of double effect'. *J Palliat Care* 16(Suppl, October):S24–30.

Henke, D.E. (2007) 'A history of ordinary and extraordinary means', in Hamel, R.P. and Walter, J.J. (eds.), *Artificial Nutrition and Hydration and the Permanently Unconscious Patient: The Catholic Debate.* Washington: Georgetown University Press, pp. 53–77.

Heyse-Moore, L. (2003) 'Terminal restlessness and sedation: a note of caution'. *Palliat Med* 17(5):469.

Hilden, H., Louhiala, P., Honkasalo, M. and Palo, J. (2004) 'Finnish nurses' views on end of life discussions and a comparison with physicians' views'. *Nurs Ethics* 11(2):165–78.

Hirano, Y., Yamamoto-Mitani, N., Ueno, M., Takemori, S., Kashiwagi, M., Sato, I., Miyata, N., Kimata, M., Fukahori, H. and Yamada, M. (2011) 'Home care nurses' provision of support to families of the elderly at the end of life'. *Qual Health Res* 21(2):199–213.

Hooten, W.M. and Rasmussen, K.G. Jr (2008) 'Effects of general anesthetic agents in adults receiving electroconvulsive therapy: a systematic review'. *J ECT* 24(3):208–23.

Horn, R. (2009) *Le debat sur l'euthanasie et les pratiques en fin de vie en France et en Allemagne. Une étude comparative.* Unpublished doctoral dissertation. Paris: Ecole des Hautes Etudes en Sciences Sociales.

Horn, R. (2013) 'Euthanasia and end-of-life practices in France and Germany. A comparative study'. *Med Health Care Philos* 16(2):197–209.

Horn, R. (2012) 'Advance directives in England and France: different concepts, different values, different societies'. *Health Care Annal,* published online 4 May 2012, doi: 10.1007/s10728-012-0210-7.

Hov, R., Athlin, E. and Hedelin, B. (2009) 'Being a nurse in nursing home for patients on the edge of life'. *Scand J Caring Sci* 23(4):651–9.

Huxtable, R. (2007) *Euthanasia, Ethics and the Law: From Conflict to Compromise.* London: Routledge-Cavendish.

Huxtable, R. (2008) 'Whatever you want? Beyond the patient in medical law'. *Health Care Annal* 16(3):288–301.

Huxtable, R. (2012) *Law, Ethics and Compromise at the Limits of Life: To Treat or Not to Treat?* London: Routledge-Cavendish.

Hyman, C. (1996) 'Pain management and disciplinary action: how medical boards can remove barriers to effective treatment'. *J Law Med Ethics* 24(4):338–43.

Inghelbrecht, E., Bilsen, J., Mortier, F. and Deliens, L. (2009) 'Nurses' attitudes towards end-of-life decisions in medical practice: a nationwide study in Flanders, Belgium'. *Palliat Med* 23(7):649–58.

Inghelbrecht, E., Bilsen, J., Mortier, F. and Deliens, L. (2011) 'Continuous deep sedation until death in Belgium: a survey among nurses'. *J Pain Symptom Manage* 41(5):870–9.

Irwin, M.H. (2001) 'Euthanasia. Figures for "slow euthanasia" should be included in data on physician assisted suicide'. *BMJ* 323(7316):809.

Jackson, E. (2006) *Medical Law. Text, Cases and Materials.* Oxford University Press.

Jackson, K.C. 3rd, Wohlt, P. and Fine, P.G. (2006) 'Dexmedetomidine: a novel analgesic with palliative medicine potential'. *J Pain Palliat Care Pharmacother* 20(2):23–7.

Jansen, L.A. (2010) 'Disambiguating clinical intentions: the ethics of palliative sedation'. *J Med Philos* 35(1):19–31.

Jansen, L.A. and Sulmasy, D.P. (2002) 'Sedation, alimentation, hydration, and equivocation: careful conversation about care at the end of life'. *Ann Intern Med* 136(11):845–9.

Janssens, R., van Delden, J.J.M. and Widdershoven, G.A.M. (2012) 'Palliative sedation: not just normal medical practice. Ethical reflections on the Royal Dutch Medical Association's guideline on palliative sedation'. *J Med Ethics* 38(11):664–8.

Jennet, B. (2002) *The Vegetative State: Medical Facts, Ethical and Legal Dilemmas.* West Nyack, NY: Cambridge University Press.

Jones, S.F. and Pisani, M.A. (2012) 'ICU delirium: an update'. *Curr Opin Crit Care* 18(2):146–51.

Kaczor, C. (1998) 'Double-effect reasoning from Jean Pierre Gury to Peter Knauer'. *Theoretical Studies* 59:297–316.

Kalbian, A.H. (2002) 'Where have all the proportionalists gone?' *Journal of Religious Ethics* 30(1):3–22.

Kamm, F. (1999) 'Physician-assisted suicide: the doctrine of double effect, and the ground of value'. *Ethics* 109(3):602.

Karlsson, M., Roxberg, A. and Berggren, I. (2010) 'Community nurses' experiences of ethical dilemmas in palliative care: a Swedish study'. *Int J Palliat Nurs* 16(5):224–31.

Kars, M.C. (2012) *Parenting and palliative care in paediatric oncology*. Dissertation. Utrecht University.

Kennett, A., Hardy, J., Shah, S. and A'Hern, R. (2005) 'An open study of methotrimeprazine in the management of nausea and vomiting in patients with advanced cancer'. *Support Care Cancer* 13(9):715–21.

Keown, J. (2002) *Euthanasia, Ethics and Public Policy: An Argument Against Legalisation*. Cambridge University Press.

King, N., Thomas, K. and Bell, D. (2003) 'An out-of-hours protocol for community palliative care: practitioners' perspectives'. *Int J Palliat Nurs* 9(7):277–82.

King, N., Melvin, J., Ashby, J. and Firth, J. (2009) 'Community palliative care: role perception'. *Br J Community Nurs* 15(2):91–8.

Klinkenberg, M., Willems, D.L., van der Wal, G. and Deeg, D.J. (2004) 'Symptom burden in the last week of life'. *J Pain Symptom Manage* 27(1):5–13.

Knauer, P. (1967) 'The hermeneutic function of the principle of double effect'. *Am J Juris* 12(1):132–62.

KNMG (Koninklijke Nederlandse Maatschappij ter bevordering van de Geneeskunde) (2005) *KNMG-richtlijn palliatieve sedatie*. Utrecht: KNMG.

KNMG (Koninklijke Nederlandse Maatschappij ter bevordering van de Geneeskunde) (2009a) *KNMG-richtlijn palliatieve sedatie*. Utrecht: KNMG.

KNMG (Koninklijke Nederlandse Maatschappij ter bevordering van de Geneeskunde) (2009b) *KNMG-Guideline for palliative sedation (2009)*. Available at http://knmg.artsennet.nl/Publicaties/KNMGpublicatie/Guideline-for-palliative-sedation-2009.htm (last accessed 24 April 2013).

Kohara, H., Ueoka, H., Takeyama, H., Murakami, T. and Morita, T. (2005) 'Sedation for terminally ill patients with cancer with uncontrollable physical distress'. *J Palliat Med* 8(1):20–5.

Krakauer, E.L., Penson, R.T., Truog, R.D., King, L.A., Chabner, B.A. and Lynch, T.J. (2000) 'Sedation for intractable distress of a dying patient: acute palliative care and the principle of double effect'. *Oncologist* 5(1):53–62.

Kuhse, H. (2004) 'Why terminal sedation is no solution to the voluntary euthanasia debate', in Tännsjö, T. (ed.), *Terminal Sedation: Euthanasia in Disguise?* Dordrecht: Kluwer Academic Publishers, pp. 57–70.

Lalande, F. and Veber, O. (2009) *La mort à l'hôpital*. Paris: Inspection générale des affaires sociales.

Latham, S. (1997) 'Aquinas and morphine: notes on double effect at the end of life', *DePaul J Health Care Law* 1(3):625–44.

Latour, J.M., Fulbrook, P. and Albarran, J.W. (2009) 'EfCCNa survey: European intensive care nurses' attitudes and beliefs towards end-of-life care'. *Nurs Crit Care* 14(3):110–21.

Lawton, S., Denholm, M., Macaulay, L., Grant, E. and Davie, A. (2012) 'Timely symptom management at end of life using "just in case" boxes'. *Br J Community Nurs* 17(4):182–3.

Lee, P.E., Gill, S.S., Freedman, M., Bronskill, S.E., Hilmer, M.P. and Rochon, P.A. (2004) 'Atypical antipsychotic drugs in the treatment of behavioural and psychological symptoms of dementia: systematic review'. *BMJ* 329(7457):75.

Leenen, H., Gevers, J. and Legemaate, J. (2007) *Handboek gezondheidsrecht. Deel 1: Rechten van mensen in de gezondheidszorg.* Houten: Bohn Stafleu van Loghum.

Legemaate, J. (2004) 'The Dutch Euthanasia Act and related issues'. *J Law Med* 11(3):312–23.

Legemaate, J. (2006) *Medisch handelen rond het levenseinde.* Houten: Bohn Stafleu van Loghum.

Legemaate, J. (2012) 'Classifications and definitions: Dutch developments', in Youngner, S.J. and Kimsma, G.K. (eds.), *Physician-assisted Death in Perspective – Assessing the Dutch Experience.* Cambridge University Press, pp. 21–33.

Legemaate, J., Verkerk, M., van Wijlick, E. and de Graeff, A. (2007) 'Palliative sedation in the Netherlands: starting-points and contents of a national guideline'. *Eur J Health Law* 14(1):61–73.

Lemiengre, J., Dierckx de Casterlé, B., Verbeke, G., Guisson, C., Schotsmans, P. and Gastmans, C. (2007) 'Ethics policies on euthanasia in hospitals – a survey in Flanders (Belgium)'. *Health Policy* 84(2–3):170–80.

Levy, M.H. and Cohen, S.D. (2005) 'Sedation for the relief of refractory symptoms in the imminently dying: a fine intentional line'. *Semin Oncol* 32(2):237–46.

Linacre Centre (The Linacre Centre for Health Care Ethics) (1982). 'Euthanasia and clinical practice: trends, principles and alternatives. A Working Party report', in Gormally, L. (ed.), *Euthanasia, Clinical Practice and the Law.* London: The Linacre Centre for Health Care Ethics, pp. 1–107.

Liu, J., Singh, H. and White, P.F. (1996) 'Electroencephalogram bispectral analysis predicts the depth of midazolam-induced sedation'. *Anesthesiology* 84(1):64.

Lo, B. and Rubenfeld, G. (2005) 'Palliative sedation in dying patients'. *JAMA* 294(14):1810–16.

Lowey, S.E. (2008) 'Communication between the nurse and family caregiver in end-of-life care: a review of the literature'. *J Hospice Palliat Nurs* 10(1):35–48.

Lundström, S., Zachrisson, U. and Fürst, C.J. (2005) 'When nothing helps: propofol as sedative and antiemetic in palliative cancer care'. *J Pain Symptom Manage* 30(6):570–7.

Lundström, S., Twycross, R., Mihalyo, M. and Wilcock, A. (2010) 'Propofol'. *J Pain Symptom Manage* 40(3):466–70.

Lynch, M. (2003) 'Palliative sedation'. *Clin J Oncol Nurs* 7(6):653–7.

Magnusson, R.R. (2006) 'The devil's choice: re-thinking law, ethics, and symptom relief in palliative care'. *J Law Med Ethics* 34(3):559–69.

Maltoni, M., Caraceni, A., Brunelli, C., Broeckaert, B., Christiakis, N., Eychmueller, S., Glare, P., Nabal, N., Viganò, A., Larkin, P., De Conno, F., Hanks, G. and Kaasa, S. (The Steering Committee of the European Association for Palliative Care) (2005) 'Prognostic factors in advanced cancer patients: evidence-based clinical recommendations – a study by the Steering Committee of the European Association for Palliative Care'. *J Clin Oncol* 23(25):6240–8.

Maltoni, M., Pittureri, C., Scarpi, E., Piccinini, L., Martini, F., Turci, P., Montanari, L., Nanni, O. and Amadori, D. (2009) 'Palliative sedation therapy does not hasten death: results from a prospective multicentre study'. *Ann Oncol* 20(7):1163–9.

Maltoni, M., Miccinesi, G., Morino, P., Scarpi, E., Bulli, F., Martini, F., Canzani, F., Dall'agata, M., Paci, E. and Amadori, D. (2012a) 'Prospective observational Italian study on palliative sedation in two hospice settings: differences in casemixes and clinical care'. *Support Care Cancer* 20(11):2829–36.

Maltoni, M., Scarpi, E., Rosati, M., Derni, S., Fabbri, L., Martini, F., Amadori, D. and Nanni, O. (2012b) 'Palliative sedation in end-of-life care and survival: a systematic review' *J Clin Oncol* 30(12):1378–83.

Mangan, J. (1949) 'An historical analysis of the principle of double effect'. *Theological Studies* 10:41.

Marker, R.L. (2011) 'End-of-life decisions and double effect: how can this be wrong when it feels so right?'. *National Catholic Bioethics Quarterly* 11(1):99–119.

Marquis, D.B. (1991) 'Four versions of double effect', *J Med Philos* 16(5):515–44.

Mashour, G.A. (ed.) (2010) *Consciousness, Awareness, and Anesthesia*. Cambridge University Press.

Massie, M.J., Holland, J. and Glass, E. (1983) 'Delirium in terminally ill cancer patients'. *Am J Psychiatry* 140(8):1048–50.

Materstvedt, L.J. (2012) 'Intention, procedure, outcome and personhood in palliative sedation and euthanasia'. *BMJ Support Palliat Care* 2(1):9–11.

Materstvedt, L., Clark, D., Ellershaw, J., Førde, R., Gravgaard, A.-M., Müller-Busch, H., Sales J. and Rapin, C.-H. (2003) 'Euthanasia and physician-assisted suicide: a view from an EAPC Ethics Task Force'. *Palliat Med* 17(2):97–101.

Mattson, R.H. (1996) 'Parenteral antiepileptic/anticonvulsant drugs'. *Neurology* 46(6 Suppl 1):S8–13.

Mazer, M.A., Alligood, C.M. and Wu, Q. (2011) 'The infusion of opioids during terminal withdrawal of mechanical ventilation in the medical intensive care unit'. *J Pain Symptom Manage* 42(1):44–51.

McKeage, K. and Perry, C.M. (2003) 'Propofol: a review of its use in intensive care sedation of adults'. *CNS Drugs* 17(4):235–72.

McLean, S. (2007) *Assisted Dying: Reflections on the Need for Law Reform*. Oxford: Routledge/Cavendish.

McMillian, W.D., Taylor, S. and Lat, I. (2011) 'Sedation, analgesia, and delirium in the critically ill patient'. *J Pharm Pract* 24(1):27–34.

McNamara, P., Minton, M. and Twycross, R.G. (1991) 'Use of midazolam in palliative care'. *Palliat Med* 5(3):244–9.

MCPCIL (Marie Curie Palliative Care Institute Liverpool) (2009). *National Care of the Dying Audit – Hospitals (NCDAH) Round 2: Generic Report 2008/2009*. Liverpool: MCPCIL.

MCPCIL (Marie Curie Palliative Care Institute Liverpool) (2010) *LCP Supporting Information. Medication Guidance Examples*. Available at www.liv.ac.uk/media/livacuk/mcpcil/migrated-files/liverpool-care-pathway/updatedlcppdfs/LCP_Medication_Guidance_Document_-_April_2010.pdf (last accessed 24 April 2013).

McWilliams, K., Keeley, P.W. and Waterhouse, E.T. (2010) 'Propofol for terminal sedation in palliative care: a systematic review'. *J Palliat Med* 13(1):73–6.

Meierkord, H., Boon, P., Engelsen, B., Göcke, K., Shorvon, S., Tinuper, P. and Holtkamp, M. (European Federation of Neurological Societies) (2010) 'EFNS guideline on the management of status epilepticus in adults'. *Eur J Neurol* 17(3):348–55.

Menten, J. (2010) *Cancer Pain: Interdisciplinary and Comprehensive Management*. Saarbrücken: Lambert Academic Publishing.

Mercadante, S., De Conno, F. and Ripamonti, C. (1995) 'Propofol in terminal care'. *J Pain Symptom Manage* 10(8):639–42.

Mercadante, S., Ferrera, P., Girelli, D. and Casuccio, A. (2005) 'Patients' and relatives' perceptions about intravenous and subcutaneous hydration'. *J Pain Symptom Manage* 30(4):354–8.

Mercadante, S., Intravaia, G., Villari, P., Ferrera, P., David, F. and Casuccio, A. (2009) 'Controlled sedation for refractory symptoms in dying patients'. *J Pain Symptom Manage* 37(5):771–9.

Mercadante, S., Valle, A., Porzio, G., Costanzo, B.V., Fusco, F., Aielli, F., Adile, C., Fara, B. and Casuccio, A. (Home Care – Italy (HOCAI) Group) (2011) 'How do cancer patients receiving palliative care at home die? A descriptive study'. *J Pain Symptom Manage* 42(5):702–9.

Meyer, J.M. (2007) 'Antipsychotic safety and efficacy concerns'. *J Clin Psychiatry* 68(Suppl 14):20–6.

Miccinesi, G., Rietjens, J.A.C., Deliens, L., Paci, E., Bosshard, G., Nilstun, T., Norup, M. and van der Wal, G. (EURELD Consortium) (2006) 'Continuous deep sedation: physicians' experiences in six European countries'. *J Pain Symptom Manage* 31(2):122–9.

Mino, J.C. and Lert, F. (2003) 'Le travail invisible des équipes de soutien et conseil en soins palliatifs à domicile'. *Sci Soc Santé* 2(1):35–54.

Mission d'évaluation de la loi n° 2005-370 du 22 avril 2005 relative aux droits des malades et à la fin de vie (2008) 'Rapport d'information fait au nom de la mission d'évaluation de la loi n° 2005-370 du 22 avril 2005 relative aux droits des malades et à la fin de vie, Tome I: Rapport'. Report No. 1287. Paris: Assemblée Nationale.

Mission d'information sur l'accompagnement de la fin de vie. (2004) 'Rapport fait au nom de la mission d'information sur l'accompagnement de la fin de vie, Tome I: Rapport'. Report No. 1708. Paris: Assemblée Nationale.

Miyashita, M., Morita, T., Shima, Y., Kimura, R., Takahashi, M. and Adachi, I. (2008) 'Nurse views of the adequacy of decision making and nurse distress regarding artificial hydration for terminally ill cancer patients: a nationwide survey'. *Am J Hosp Palliat Med* 24(6):463–9.

Morita, T. (2004a) 'Palliative sedation to relieve psycho-existential suffering of terminally ill cancer patients'. *J Pain Symptom Manage* 28(5):445–50.

Morita, T. (2004b) 'Differences in physician-reported practice in palliative sedation therapy'. *Support Care Cancer* 12(8):584–92.

Morita, T., Inoue, S. and Chihara, S. (1996) 'Sedation for symptom control in Japan: the importance of intermittent use and communication with family members'. *J Pain Symptom Manage* 12(1):32–8.

Morita, T., Tsunoda, J., Inoue, S. and Chihara, S. (1999) 'Do hospice clinicians sedate patients intending to hasten death?'. *J Palliat Care* 15(3):20–3.

Morita, T., Tsunoda, J., Inoue, S. and Chihara, S. (2000) 'Terminal sedation for existential distress'. *Am J Hosp Palliat Care* 17(3):189–95.

Morita, T., Tsunoda, J., Inoue S. and Chihara, S. (2001a) 'Effects of high dose opioids and sedatives on survival in terminally ill cancer patients'. *J Pain Symptom Manage* 21(4):282–9.

Morita, T., Tsunoda, J., Inoue, S., Chihara, S. and Oka, K. (2001b) 'Communication Capacity Scale and Agitation Distress Scale to measure the severity of delirium in terminally ill cancer patients: a validation study'. *Palliat Med* 15(3):197–206.

Morita, T., Tsuneto, S. and Shima, Y. (2001c) 'Proposed definitions for terminal sedation'. *Lancet* 358(9278):335–6.

Morita, T., Akechi, T., Sugawara, Y., Chihara, S. and Uchitomi, Y. (2002a) 'Practices and attitudes of Japanese oncologists and palliative care physicians concerning terminal sedation: a nationwide survey'. *J Clin Oncol* 20(3):758–64.

Morita, T., Tsuneto, S. and Shima, Y. (2002b) 'Definition of sedation for symptom relief: a systematic literature review and a proposal of operational criteria'. *J Pain Symptom Manage* 24(4):447–53.

Morita, T., Tei, Y. and Inoue, S. (2003a) 'Correlation of the dose of midazolam for symptom control with administration periods: the possibility of tolerance'. *J Pain Symptom Manage* 25(4):369–75.

Morita, T., Tei, Y. and Inoue, S. (2003b) 'Impaired communication capacity and agitated delirium in the final week of terminally ill cancer patients: prevalence and identification of research focus'. *J Pain Symptom Manage* 26(3):827–34.

Morita, T., Ikenaga, M., Adachi, I., Narabayashi, I., Kizawa, Y., Honke, Y., Kohara, H., Mukaiyama, T., Akechi, T., Kurihara, Y. and Uchitomi, Y. (Japan Pain, Rehabilitation, Palliative Medicine and Psycho-Oncology Study Group) (2004a) 'Concerns of family members of patients receiving palliative sedation therapy'. *Support Care Cancer* 12(12):885–9.

Morita, T., Ikenaga, M., Adachi, I., Narabayashi, I., Kizawa, Y., Honke, Y., Kohara, H., Mukaiyama, T., Akechi, T. and Uchitomi, Y. (Japan Pain, Rehabilitation, Palliative Medicine and Psycho-Oncology Study Group) (2004b) 'Family experience with palliative sedation therapy for terminally ill cancer patients'. *J Pain Symptom Manage* 28(6):557–65.

Morita, T., Miyashita, M., Kimura, R., Adachi, I. and Shima, Y. (2004c) 'Emotional burden of nurses in palliative sedation therapy'. *Palliat Med* 18(6):550–7.

Morita, T., Bito, S., Kurihara, Y. and Uchitomi, Y. (2005a) 'Development of a clinical guideline for palliative sedation therapy using the Delphi method'. *J Palliat Med* 8(4):716–29.

Morita, T., Chinone, Y., Ikenaga, M., Miyoshi, M., Nakaho, T., Nishitateno, K., Sakonji, M., Shima, Y., Suenaga, K., Takigawa, C., Kohara, H., Tani, K., Kawamura, Y., Matsubara, T., Watanabe, A., Yagi, Y., Sasaki, T., Higuchi, A., Kimura, H., Abo, H., Ozawa, T., Kizawa, Y. and Uchitomi, Y. (Japan Pain, Rehabilitation, Palliative Medicine and Psycho-Oncology Study Group) (2005b) 'Ethical validity of palliative sedation therapy: a multicenter, prospective, observational study conducted on specialized palliative care units in Japan'. *J Pain Symptom Manag* 30(4):308–19.

Morita, T., Chinone, Y., Ikenaga, M., Miyoshi, M., Nakaho, T., Nishitateno, K., Sakonji, M., Shima, Y., Suenaga, K., Takigawa, C., Kohara, H., Tani, K., Kawamura, Y., Matsubara, T., Watanabe, A., Yagi, Y., Sasaki, T., Higuchi, A., Kimura, H., Abo, H., Ozawa, T., Kizawa, Y. and Uchitomi, Y. (Japan Pain, Rehabilitation, Palliative Medicine and Psycho-Oncology Study Group) (2005c) 'Efficacy and safety of palliative sedation therapy: a multicenter, prospective, observational study conducted on specialized palliative care units in Japan'. *J Pain Symptom Manage* 30(4):320–8.

Morita, T., Hyodo, I., Yoshimi, T., Ikenaga, M., Tamura, Y., Yoshizawa, A., Shimada, A., Akechi, T., Miyashita, M. and Adachi, I. (2005d) 'Association between hydration volume and symptoms in terminally ill cancer patients with abdominal malignancies'. *Ann Oncol* 16(4):640–7.

Moyle, J. (1995) 'The use of propofol in palliative medicine'. *J Pain Symptom Manage* 10(8):643–6.

Muller-Busch, H.C., Andres, I. and Jehser, T. (2003) 'Sedation in palliative care – a critical analysis of 7 years experience'. *BMC Palliat Care* 2(1):2.

Muller-Busch, H.C., Oduncu, F.S., Woskanjan, S. and Klaschik, E. (2004) 'Attitudes on euthanasia, physician-assisted suicide and terminal sedation – a survey of the members of the German Association for Palliative Medicine'. *Med Health Care Philos* 7(3):333–9.

Mullock, A. (2012) 'Compromising on assisted suicide: is "turning a blind eye" ethical?'. *Clin Ethics* 7(1):17–23.

Murray, S.A., Boyd, K. and Sheikh, A. (2005) 'Palliative care in chronic illness'. *BMJ* 330(7492):611–12.

Murray, S.A., Boyd, K. and Byock, I. (2008) 'Continuous deep sedation in patients nearing death'. *BMJ* 336(7648):781–2.

Nambisan, V. (2012) 'Providing evidence of intention when giving palliative sedation'. *Eur J Palliat Care* 19(2):93–6.

Navigante, A.H., Cerchietti, L.C., Castro, M.A., Lutteral, M.A. and Cabalar, M.E. (2006) 'Midazolam as adjunct therapy to morphine in the alleviation of severe dyspnea perception in patients with advanced cancer'. *J Pain Symptom Manage* 31(1):38–47.

Navigante, A.H., Castro, M.A. and Cerchietti, L.C. (2010) 'Morphine versus midazolam as upfront therapy to control dyspnea perception in cancer patients while its underlying cause is sought or treated'. *J Pain Symptom Manage* 39(5):820–30.

Nemeroff, C.B. (2003) 'The role of GABA in the pathophysiology and treatment of anxiety disorders'. *Psychopharmacol Bull* 37(4):133–46.

Noreika, V., Jylhänkangas, L., Móró, L., Valli, K., Kaskinoro, K., Aantaa, R., Scheinin, H. and Revonsuo, A. (2011) 'Consciousness lost and found: subjective experiences in an unresponsive state'. *Brain Cogn* 77:327–34.

Oderberg, D.S. (2004) 'The ethics of co-operation in wrongdoing', in O'Hear, A. (ed.), *Modern Moral Philosophy*. Cambridge University Press, pp. 203–28.

Ojeda Martín, M., Navarro Marrero, M.A. and Gómez Sancho, M. (1997) 'Sedación y enfermo oncológico terminal'. *Med Pal (Madrid)* 4:101–7.

O'Neill, J. and Fountain, A. (1999) 'Levomepromazine (methotrimeprazine) and the last 48 hours'. *Hosp Med* 60(8):564–7.

Onwuteaka-Philipsen, B.D., Brinkman-Stoppelenburg, A., Penning, C., de Jong-Krul, G.J., van Delden, J.J. and van der Heide, A. (2012) 'Trends in end-of-life practices before and after the enactment of the euthanasia law in the Netherlands from 1990 to 2010: a repeated cross-sectional survey'. *Lancet* 380(9845):908–15.

Orentlicher, D. (1994a) 'The influence of a professional organization on physician behaviour'. *Albany Law Rev* 57(3):583–605.

Orentlicher, D. (1994b) 'The limitations of legislation'. *Maryland Law Review* 53:1255–1305.

Orentlicher, D. (1997a) 'The Supreme Court and terminal sedation: rejecting assisted suicide, embracing euthanasia'. *Hastings Constit Law Q* 24(4):947–68.

Orentlicher, D. (1997b) 'The Supreme Court and physician-assisted suicide – rejecting assisted suicide but embracing euthanasia'. *N Engl J Med* 337(17):1236–9.

Orentlicher, D. (2001) *Matters of Life and Death: Making Moral Theory Work in Medical Ethics and the Law*. Princeton University Press.

Orentlicher, D., Bobinski, M.A. and Hall, M.A. (2008) *Bioethics and Public Health Law*, 2nd edn. New York: Aspen Publishers.

Otlowski, M. (2000) *Voluntary Euthanasia and the Common Law*. Oxford University Press.

Palmer, H. (1957) 'Dr. Adams' trial for murder'. *Crim L R* 365–7.

Papal allocution to The International Congress on Life-Sustaining Treatment and Vegetative State: Scientific Advances and Ethical Dilemmas (2004) *Origins* 33:737–40.

Patel, B., Gorawara-Bhat, R., Levine, S. and Shega, J.W. (2012) 'Nurses' attitudes and experiences surrounding palliative sedation: components for developing policy for nursing professionals'. *J Palliat Med* 15(4):432–7.

Patel, S.B. and Kress, J.P. (2012) 'Sedation and analgesia in the mechanically ventilated patient'. *Am J Respir Crit Care Med* 185(5):486–97.

Pattinson, S. (2006) *Medical Law and Ethics*. London: Sweet & Maxwell.

Peruselli, C., Di Giulio, P., Toscani, F., Gallucci, M., Brunelli, C., Costantini, M., Tamburini, M., Paci, E., Miccinesi, G., Addington-Hall, J.M. and

Higginson, I.J. (1999) 'Home palliative care for terminal cancer patients: a survey on the final week of life'. *Palliat Med* 13(3):233–41.

Pinna, M.Á.C., Correas, M.Á.S., Posadas, R.S., Prado, M.E.A., Márquez, M. del P.R., Rojas, J.A.E, Martín, T.G., de Ayala, C.L. and López, M.P.V. (Sociedad Española de Cuidados Paliativos) (2005) *Sedación en Cuidados Paliativos*, available at www.secpal.com/guiasm/index.php?acc=see_guia&id_guia=8 (last accessed 24 April 2013).

Pitre, T.M. (2009) 'Palliative sedation at the end of life: uses and abuses'. *The Linacre Quarterly* 76(4):390–407.

Pope John Paul II (1993) *'Veritatis Splendor'*. Encyclical Letter, Vatican City: Vatican. Available at www.vatican.va/holy_father/john_paul_ii/encyclicals/documents/hf_jp-ii_enc_06081993_veritatis-splendor_en.html (last accessed 24 April 2013).

Pope John Paul II (1995) *'Evangelium Vitae'*. Encyclical letter, Vatican City: Vatican, paragraph 65. Available at www.vatican.va/holy_father/john_paul_ii/encyclicals/documents/hf_jp-ii_enc_25031995_evangelium-vitae_en.html (last accessed 24 April 2013).

Pope Pius XII (1957) *Discurso Del Santo Padre Pío Xii Sobre Las Implicaciones Religiosas Y Morales De La Analgesia*, Sunday 24 February 1957. Available at www.vatican.va/holy_father/pius_xii/speeches/1957/documents/hf_p-xii_spe_19570224_anestesiologia_sp.html (last accessed 24 April 2013).

Porta-Sales, J. (2001) 'Sedation and terminal care'. *Eur J Palliat Care* 8(3):97–100.

Porta-Sales, J. (2003) 'Sedación al final de la vida: aspectos clínico y éticos'. *Rev Esp Geriatr Gerontol* 38(Suppl 3):44–52.

Porta-Sales, J. (2008) 'Sedación palliativa', in Porta-Sales, J., Gómez-Batiste, X. and Tuca, A. (eds.), *Manual de Control de síntomas en pacientes con cáncer avanzado y Terminal*, 2nd edn. Madrid: Arán Ediciones, pp. 325–6.

Porta-Sales, J., Català-Ylla Boré, E. and Estibaliz Gil, A. (1999) 'Estudio multicéntrico catalano-balear sobre sedación terminal en Cuidados Paliativos'. *Med Pal (Madrid)* 6:153–8.

Porta-Sales, J., Nuñez Olarte, J.M., Altisent Trota, R., Aguilar, G., Loncan Vidal, P., Muños Sánchez, Novellas Aguirre de Cárcer, A., Rivas Flores, J., Rodeles del Pozo, R., Vilches Aguirre, Y. and Sanz Ortiz, J. (Comité de Ética de la Sociedad Española de Cuidados Paliativos -SECPAL) (2002) 'Aspectos éticos de la sedación en Cuidados Paliativos'. *Med Pal (Madrid)* 9:41–6.

Porzio, G., Aielli, F., Verna, L., Micolucci, G., Aloisi, P. and Ficorella, C. (2009) 'Efficacy and safety of deep, continuous palliative sedation at home: a retrospective, single-institution study'. *Support Care Cancer* 18(1):77–81.

Price, D. (1997) 'Euthanasia, pain relief and double effect'. *Legal Studies* 17(2):323–42.

Prommer, E.E. (2011) 'Dexmedetomidine: does it have potential in palliative medicine?'. *Am J Hosp Palliat Care* 28(4):276–83.

Prommer, E.E. (2012) 'Ketamine for pain: an update of uses in palliative care'. *J Palliat Med* 15(4):474–83.

Quill, T. (1993) 'The ambiguity of clinical intentions'. *N Engl J Med* 329(14):1039–40.

Quill, T.E. (1997) 'Rule of double effect: a critique of its role in end of life decision making'. *N Engl J Med* 337(24):1768–71.

Quill, T.E. (2004) 'Dying and decision making – evolution of end-of-life options'. *N Engl J Med* 350(20):2029–32.

Quill, T. and Arnold, R.M. (2008) 'Evaluating requests for hastened death #156'. *J Palliat Med* 11(8):1151–2.

Quill, T. and Arnold, R.M. (2009) *Evaluating Requests for Hastened Death. Fast Facts and Concepts #156*. Milwaukee: EPERC. Available at www.eperc. mcw.edu/FastFactsIndex/ff_156.htm (last accessed 29 April 2013).

Quill, T. and Brody, H. (1996) 'Physician recommendations and patient autonomy: finding a balance between physician power and patient choice'. *Ann Intern Med* 125(9):763–9.

Quill, T.E. and Byock, I.R. (2000) 'Responding to intractable terminal suffering: the role of terminal sedation and voluntary refusal of food and fluids. ACP-ASIM End-of-Life Care Consensus Panel. American College of Physicians-American Society of Internal Medicine'. *Ann Intern Med* 132(5):408–14.

Quill, T.E., Dresser, R. and Brock, D.W. (1997a) 'The rule of double effect – a critique of its role in end-of-life decision making'. *N Engl J Med* 337(24):1768–71.

Quill, T.E., Lo, B. and Brock, D.W. (1997b) 'Palliative options of last resort: a comparison of voluntarily stopping eating and drinking, terminal sedation, physician-assisted suicide, and voluntary active euthanasia'. *JAMA* 278(23):2099–104.

Quill, T., Lee, B. and Nunn, S. (2000) 'Palliative treatments of last resort: choosing the least harmful alternative'. *Ann Intern Med* 132(6):488–93.

Quill, T.E., Lo, B. and Brock, D. (2004) 'Palliative options of last resort', in Tännsjö, T. (ed.), *Terminal Sedation: Euthanasia in Disguise?* Dordrecht: Kluwer Academic Publishers.

Quill, T.E., Lo, B., Brock, D.W. and Meisel, A. (2009) 'Last-resort options for palliative sedation'. *Ann Intern Med* 151(6):421–4.

Quill, T.E., Holloway, R.G., Shah, M.S., Caprio, T.V., Olden, A.M. and Storey, C.P. (2010) *Primer of Palliative Care*, 5th edn. Glenview: AAHPM, pp. 139–50.

Quinn, W. (1993) 'Actions, intentions, and consequences: the doctrine of double effect', in Quinn, W., *Morality and Action*. Cambridge University Press, pp.173–93.

Rachels, J. (1986) *The End of Life: Euthanasia and Morality*. Oxford University Press.

Rachels, J. (1997) *Can Ethics Provide Answers and Other Essays in Moral Philosophy*. Lanham, MD: Rowman & Littlefield Publishers, Inc.

Radha Krishna, L.K., Poulose, V.J. and Goh, C. (2012) 'The use of midazolam and haloperidol in cancer patients at the end of life'. *Singapore Med J* 53(1):62–6.

Rady, M.Y. and Verheijde, J.L. (2010) 'Continuous deep sedation until death: palliation or physician-assisted death?'. *Am J Hosp Palliat Care* 27(3):205–14.

Rady, M.Y. and Verheijde, J.L. (2012) 'Distress from voluntary refusal of food and fluids to hasten death: what is the role of continuous deep sedation?'. *J Med Ethics* 38(8):510–12.

Raijmakers, N.J.H., van Zuylen, L., Costantini, M., Caraceni, A., Clark, J.B., De Simone, G., Lundquist, G., Voltz, R., Ellershaw, J.E. and van der Heide, A. (2012) 'Issue and needs in end of life decision making: an international modified Delphi study'. *Palliat Med* 26(7):947–53.

Ramsay, M.A., Savege, T.M., Simpson, B.R. and Goodwin, R. (1974) 'Controlled sedation with alphaxalone-alphadolone'. *BMJ* 2(5920):656–9.

Raus, K., Sterckx, S. and Mortier, F. (2011) 'Is continuous sedation at the end of life an ethically preferable alternative to physician-assisted suicide?'. *Am J Bioeth* 11(6):32–40.

Raus, K., Sterckx, S. and Mortier, F. (2012) 'Continuous deep sedation at the end of life and the "natural death" hypothesis'. *Bioethics* 26(6):329–36.

Regnard, C. (2007) 'Double effect is a myth leading a double life'. *BMJ* 334(7591):440.

Reid, C., Gooberman-Hill, R. and Hanks, G. (2008) 'Opioid analgesics for cancer pain: symptom control for the living or comfort for the dying? A qualitative study to investigate the factors influencing the decision to accept morphine for pain caused by cancer'. *Ann Oncol* 19(1):44–8.

Reuzel, R.P., Hasselaar, G.J., Vissers, K.C., van der Wilt, G.J., Groenewoud, J.M. and Crul, B.J. (2008) 'Inappropriateness of using opioids for end-stage palliative sedation: a Dutch study'. *Palliat Med* 22(5):641–6.

Rietjens, J.A.C. (2006) *Medical decision-making at the end of life.* Ph.D. thesis, Rotterdam: Erasmus University. Available at http://repub.eur.nl/res/pub/7309/060201_Rietjens-JAC.pdf (last accessed 24 April 2013).

Rietjens, J.A.C., van der Heide, A., Vrakking, A.M., Onwuteaka-Philipsen, B.D., van der Maas, P.J. and van der Wal, G. (2004) 'Physician reports of terminal sedation without hydration or nutrition for patients nearing death in the Netherlands'. *Ann Intern Med* 141(3):178–85.

Rietjens, J.A.C., van Delden, J.J.M., van der Heide, A., Vrakking, A.M., Onwuteaka-Philipsen, B.D., van der Maas, P.J. and van der Wal, G. (2006) 'Terminal sedation and euthanasia: a comparison of clinical practices'. *Arch Intern Med* 166(7):749–53.

Rietjens, J.A., Hauser, J., van der Heide, A. and Emanuel, L. (2007) 'Having a difficult time leaving: experiences and attitudes of nurses with palliative sedation'. *Palliat Med* 21(7):643–9.

Rietjens, J., van Delden, J., Onwuteaka-Philipsen, B., Buiting, H., van der Maas, P. and van der Heide, A. (2008a) 'Continuous deep sedation for patients nearing death in the Netherlands: descriptive study'. *BMJ* 336(7648):810–14.

Rietjens, J.A., van Zuylen L., van Veluw, H., van der Wijk, L., van der Heide, A. and van der Rijt, C.C. (2008b) 'Palliative sedation in a specialized unit for acute palliative care in a cancer hospital: comparing patients dying with and without palliative sedation'. *J Pain Symptom Manage* 36(3):228–34.

Rietjens, J.A.C., Buiting, H.M., Pasman, H.R.W., van der Maas, P.J., van Delden, J.J.M. and van der Heide, A. (2009a) 'Deciding about continuous deep sedation: physicians' perspectives: a focus group study'. *Palliat Med* 23(5):410–17.

Rietjens, J.A., van Delden, J.J., Deliens, L. and van der Heide, A. (2009b) 'Re: Palliative sedation: the need for a descriptive definition'. *J Pain Symptom Manage* 37(3): e10–11; author reply e11–12.

Rietjens, J.A., van der Maas, P.J., Onwuteaka-Philipsen, B.D., van Delden, J.J. and van der Heide, A. (2009c) 'Two decades of research on euthanasia from the Netherlands. What have we learnt and what questions remain?'. *J Bioeth Inq* 6(3):271–83

Rietjens, J.A., Voorhees, J.R., van der Heide, A. and Drickamer, MA. (2012) 'Approaches to suffering at the end of life: the use of sedation in the USA and Netherlands'. *J Med Ethics*, published online 14 September 2012; doi: 10.1136/medethics-2012-100561.

Rinaldi, S. and De Gaudio, A.R. (2006) 'Sedation monitoring in ICU'. *Curr Anaesth Crit Care* 17:305.

Ritchie, J. and Spencer, L. (1994) 'Qualitative data analysis for applied policy research. Analyzing qualitative data', in Bryman, A. and Burgess, R. (eds.), *Analysing Quantitative Data*. London: Routledge, pp. 173–94.

Rousseau, P. (2001) 'Existential suffering and palliative sedation: a brief commentary with a proposal for clinical guidelines'. *Am J Hosp Palliat Care* 18(3):151–3.

Rousseau, P. (2004) 'Palliative sedation in the management of refractory symptoms'. *J Support Oncol* 2(2):181–6.

Rousseau, P. (2005a) 'Existential distress and palliative sedation'. *Anesth Analg* 101(2):611–12.

Rousseau, P. (2005b) 'Palliative sedation in the control of refractory symptoms'. *J Palliat Med* 8(1):10–12.

Royal College of Physicians and British Society of Gastroenterology (2010) *Oral Feeding Difficulties and Dilemmas: A Guide to Practical Care, Particularly Towards the End of Life*. London: Royal College of Physicians.

Salacz, M.E. and Weissman, D.E. (2005) 'Controlled sedation for refractory suffering: part I'. *J Palliat Med* 8(1):136–7.

Sanft, T., Hauser, J., Rosielle, D., Weissman, D., Elsayem, A., Zhukovsky, D. and Coyle, N. (2009) 'Physical pain and emotional suffering: the case for palliative sedation'. *J Pain* 10(3):238–42.

Saunders, C.M. (1958) 'Dying of cancer'. *St Thomas Hospital Gazette* 56(2):37–47.

Saunders, C.M. (1960) 'Management of patients in the terminal stage', in Raven, R. (ed.), *Cancer*, Vol. 6. London: Butterworth and Company, pp. 403–17.

Saunders, C. (1965) 'The last stages of life'. *Am J Nurs* 65(3):70–5.

Saunders, C.M. (1967) *The Management of Terminal Illness*. London: Hospital Medicine Publications.

Schildmann, J., Hoetzel, J., Mueller-Busch, C. and Vollmann, J. (2010) 'End-of-life practices in palliative care: a cross sectional survey of physician members of the German Society for Palliative Medicine'. *Palliat Med* 24(8):820–7.

Schuman-Olivier, Z., Brendel, D.H., Forstein M. and Price, B.H. (2008) 'The use of palliative sedation for existential distress: a psychiatric perspective'. *Harv Rev Psychiatry* 16(6):339–51.

Seale, C. (2000) 'Changing patterns of death and dying'. *Soc Sci Med* 51(6):917–30.

Seale, C. (2006) 'National survey of end-of-life decisions made by UK medical practitioners'. *Palliat Med* 20(1):3–10.

Seale, C. (2009) 'End-of-life decisions in the UK involving medical practitioners'. *Palliat Med* 23(3):198–204.

Seale, C. (2010) 'Continuous deep sedation in medical practice: a descriptive study'. *J Pain Symptom Manage* 39(1):44–53.

Selling, J.A. (1980) 'The problem of reinterpreting the principle of double effect'. *Louvain Studies* 8:47–62.

Sepulveda, C., Marlin, A. and Ullrich, A. (2002) 'Palliative care: the World Health Organization's global perspective'. *J Pain Symptom Manage* 24(2):91–6.

Sessler, C.N., Gosnell, M.S., Grap, M.J., Brophy, G.M., O'Neal, P.V., Keane, K.A., Tesoro, E.P. and Elswick, R.K. (2002) 'The Richmond Agitation-Sedation Scale: validity and reliability in adult intensive care unit patients'. *Am J Respir Crit Care Med* 166(10):1338–44.

Seymour, J.E., Janssens, R. and Broeckaert, B. (2007) 'Relieving suffering at the end of life: practitioners' perspectives on palliative sedation from three European countries'. *Soc Sci Med* 64(8):1679–91.

Seymour, J., Rietjens, J., Brown, J., Van der Heide, A., Sterckx, S. and Deliens, L. (UNBIASED Study Team) (2011) 'The perspectives of clinical staff and bereaved informal care-givers on the use of continuous sedation until death for cancer patients: The study protocol of the UNBIASED study'. *BMC Palliat Care* 10:5.

Shafer, S.L. and Stanski, D.R. (2008) 'Defining depth of anesthesia', in Jürgen Schüttler, J. and Schwilden, H. (eds.), *Modern Anesthetics: Handbook of Experimental Pharmacology*. Berlin-Heidelberg: Springer-Verlag, pp. 409–23.

Shaiova, L. (1998) 'Case presentation: "terminal sedation" and existential distress'. *J Pain Symptom Manage* 16(6):403–4.

Sheldon, T. (2003) '"Terminal sedation" different from euthanasia, Dutch ministers agree'. *BMJ* 327(7413):465.

Sheldon, T. (2007) 'Incidence of euthanasia in the Netherlands falls as that of palliative sedation rises'. *BMJ* 334(7603):1075.

Shepherd, L. (2006) 'In respect of people living in a permanent vegetative state – and allowing them to die'. *Health Matrix* 16(2):631–91.

Shukry, M. and Miller, J.A. (2010) 'Update on dexmedetomidine: use in non-intubated patients requiring sedation for surgical procedures'. *Ther Clin Risk Manag* 6:111–21.

Simon, A., Kar, M., Hinz, J. and Beck, D. (2007) 'Attitudes towards terminal sedation: an empirical survey among experts in the field of medical ethics'. *BMC Palliat Care* 6:4.

Singer, P. (1993) *Practical Ethics*, 2nd edn. Cambridge University Press.

Singer, P. (1995) *Rethinking Life and Death. The Collapse of our Traditional Ethics.* Oxford University Press.

Singer, P. (2003) 'Voluntary euthanasia: a utilitarian perspective'. *Bioethics* 17(5–6):526–41.

Sluijters, B. and Biesaart, M.C.I.H. (2005) *De geneeskundige behandeling.* Deventer: Kluwer.

Sneyd, J.R. (1999) 'Propofol and epilepsy'. *Br J Anaesth* 82(2):168–9.

Somerville, M. (2001) *Death Talk: The Case against Euthanasia and Physician-Assisted Suicide.* Montreal: McGill-Queen's University Press.

Spielthenner, G. (2008) 'The principle of double effect as a guide for medical decision-making'. *Med Health Care Philos* 11(4):465–73.

Steinhauser, K.E., Christakis, N.A., Clipp, E.C., McNeilly, M., McIntyre, L. and Tulsky, J.A. (2000) 'Factors considered important at the end of life by patients, family, physicians, and other care providers'. *JAMA* 284(19):2476–82.

Stephenson, J. (2012) 'The Liverpool Care Pathway'. *Triple Helix Winter* 14–5.

Stevenson, C.L. (1944) *Ethics and Language.* New Haven: Yale University Press.

Stewart, C. (2007) 'Recent developments'. *J Bioethic Inq* 4(3):169–70.

Stirling, L.C., Kurowska, A. and Tookman, A. (1999) 'The use of phenobarbitone in the management of agitation and seizures at the end of life'. *J Pain Symptom Manage* 17(5):363–8.

Stone, P., Phillips, C., Spruyt, O. and Waight, C. (1997) 'A comparison of the use of sedatives in a hospital support team and in a hospice'. *Palliat Med* 11(2):140–4.

Sulmasy, D.P. (2000) 'Voluntary euthanasia is unethical', in Torr, J.D. (ed.), *Euthanasia Opposing Viewpoints.* San Diego: David L. Bender, pp. 24–32.

Sulmasy, D.P. and Pellegrino, E.D. (1999) 'The rule of double effect: clearing up the double talk'. *Arch Intern Med* 159(6):545–50.

Sulmasy, D.P., Curlin, F., Brungardt, G.S. and Cavanaugh, T. (2010) 'Justifying different levels of palliative sedation'. *Ann Intern Med* 152(5):332–3.

Support Principal Investigators. (1995) 'A controlled trial to improve care for seriously ill hospitalized patients: the study to understand prognoses and preferences for outcomes and risks of treatments (SUPPORT)'. *JAMA* 274(20):1591–8.

Swart, S.J., Brinkkemper, T., Rietjens, J.A., Blanker, M.H., van Zuylen, L., Ribbe, M., Zuurmond, W.W. van der Heide, A. and Perez, R.S. (2010) 'Physicians' and nurses' experiences with continuous palliative sedation in the Netherlands'. *Arch Intern Med* 170(14):1271–4.

Swart, S.J., Rietjens, J.A., Brinkkemper, T., van Zuylen, L., Van Burg-Verhage, W.A., Zuurmond, W.W., Ribbe, M.W., Blanker, M.H., Perez, R.S. and van der Heide, A. (2011) 'Palliatieve sedatie na introductie KNMG-richtlijn'. *Ned Tijdschr Geneeskd* 155:A2857.

Swart, S.J., Rietjens, J.A., van Zuylen, L., Zuurmond, W.W., Perez, R.S., van der Maas, P.J., van Delden, J.J. and van der Heide, A. (2012a) 'Continuous palliative sedation for cancer and noncancer patients'. *J Pain Symptom Manage* 43(2):172–81.

Swart, S.J., van der Heide, A., van Zuylen, L., Perez, R., Zuurmond, W.W., van der Maas, P.J. and van Delden, J. (2012b) 'Continuous palliative sedation: more than a response to physical suffering'. Submitted for publication.

Swart, S.J., van der Heide, A., van Zuylen, L., Perez, R.S., Zuurmond, W.W., van der Maas, P.J., van Delden, J.J. and Rietjens, J.A. (2012c) 'Considerations of physicians about the depth of palliative sedation at the end of life'. *CMAJ* 184(7):E360–6.

Swart, S.J., van der Heide, A., van Zuylen, L., Perez, R.S.G.M., Zuurmond, W.W.A., van der Maas, P.J., van Delden, J.J.M. and Rietjens, J.A.C. (2012d) 'Continuous palliative sedation: a medical response to a medical problem?'. Submitted for publication.

Sykes, N. and Thorns, A. (2003a) 'Sedative use in the last week of life and the implications for end-of-life decision making'. *Arch Intern Med* 163(3):341–4.

Sykes, N. and Thorns, A. (2003b) 'The use of opioids and sedatives at the end of life'. *Lancet Oncol* 4(5):312–18.

Tan, G. and Irwin, M.G. (2010) 'Recent advances in using propofol by non-anesthesiologists'. *F1000 Med Rep* 2:79.

Tännsjö, T. (ed.) (2004a) *Terminal Sedation: Euthanasia in Disguise?* Dordrecht: Kluwer Academic Publishers.

Tännsjö, T. (2004b) 'Terminal sedation: a substitute for euthanasia?', in Tännsjö, T. (ed.), *Terminal Sedation: Euthanasia in Disguise?* Dordrecht: Kluwer Academic Publishers, pp. 15–30.

Taylor, B.R. and McCann, R.M. (2005) 'Controlled sedation for physical and existential suffering?'. *J Palliat Med* 8(1):144–7.

Teasdale, G. and Jennett, B. (1974) 'Assessment of coma and impaired consciousness. A practical scale'. *The Lancet* 2(7872):81–4.

Ten Have, H.A.M.J. and Welie, J.V.M. (1992). 'Euthanasia: normal medical practice?' *Hastings Cent Rep* March-April:34–8.

Thouvenin, D. (2008). 'Audition de Mme la Professeure Dominique Thouvenin, Université Paris 7-Diderot (Procès-verbal de la séance du 15 juillet 2008)', in Mission d'évaluation de la loi n° 2005-370 du 22 avril 2005 relative aux droits des malades et à la fin de vie, 'Rapport d'information fait au nom de la mission d'évaluation de la loi n° 2005-370 du 22 avril 2005 relative aux droits des malades et à la fin de vie, Tome II: Auditions'. Report No. 1287. Paris: Assemblée Nationale.

Tolstoy, L.L. (1886) *The Death of Ivan Ilych* (translated by Maude, L. and Maude, A.), available at www.ccel.org/ccel/tolstoy/ivan.txt (last accessed 24 April 2013).

Toscani, F., Di Giulio, P., Brunelli, C., Miccinesi, G. and Laquintana, D. (End-of-Life Observatory Group) (2005) 'How people die in hospital general wards: a descriptive study'. *J Pain Symptom Manage* 30(1):33–40.

Treloar, A.J. (2008a) 'Continuous deep sedation: Dutch research reflects problems with the Liverpool care pathway'. *BMJ* 336(7650):905.

Treloar, A.J. (2008b) 'LCP concerns – clarifications and an apology'. *BMJ Rapid Response* to *BMJ* 336:781–2 (published 6 May 2008). Available at www.bmj.com/content/336/7648/781/tab=responses (last accessed 24 April 2013).

Truog, R.D., Berde, C.B., Mitchell, C. and Grier, H.E. (1992) 'Barbiturates in the care of the terminally ill'. *N Engl J Med* 327(23):1678–82.

Turner, K., Chye, R., Aggarwal, G., Philip, J., Skeels, A. and Lickiss, J.N. (1996) 'Dignity in dying: a preliminary study of patients in the last three days of life'. *J Palliat Care* 12(2):7–13.

Twycross, R.G. and Black I. (1997) 'The use of low dose levomepromazine (methotrimeprazine) in the management of nausea and vomiting'. *Prog Pall Care* 5(2):49–53.

Twycross, R.G. and Lack, S.A. (1986) 'Nausea and vomiting', in Twycross, R.G. and Lack, S.A. (eds.), *Control of Alimentary Symptoms in Far Advanced Cancer*. Edinburgh: Churchill Livingstone, pp. 175–97.

Ursea, R., Feng, M.T., Zhou, M., Lien, V. and Loeb, R. (2011) 'Pain perception in sequential cataract surgery: comparison of first and second procedures'. *J Cataract Refract Surg* 37(6):1009–14.

US Veterans Health Administration (National Ethics Committee) (2007) 'The ethics of palliative sedation as a therapy of last resort'. *Am J Hosp Palliat Med* 23(6):483–91.

Van Deijck, R.H., Krijnsen, P.J., Hasselaar, J.G., Verhagen, S.C., Vissers, K.C. and Koopmans, R.T. (2010) 'The practice of continuous palliative sedation in elderly patients: a nationwide explorative study among Dutch nursing home physicians'. *J Am Geriatr Soc* 58(9):1671–8.

van Delden, J. (2004) 'Terminal sedation: different practices, different evaluations', in Tännsjö, T. (ed.), *Terminal Sedation: Euthanasia in Disguise?* Dordrecht: Kluwer Academic Publishers.

van Delden, J.J. (2007) 'Terminal sedation: source of a restless ethical debate'. *J Med Ethics* 33(4):187–8.

van Delden, J.J.M., van der Heide, A., van de Vathorst, S., Weyers, H. and van Tol, D.G. (2011) *Kennis en opvattingen van publiek en professionals over medische besluitvorming en behandeling rond het einde van het leven. Het KOPPEL-onderzoek*. The Hague: ZONMW.

van den Beuken-van Everdingen, M.H.J., de Rijke, J.M., Kessels, A.G., Schouten, H.C. and Patijn, J. (2007) 'Prevalence of pain in patients with cancer: a systematic review of the last 40 years'. *Ann Oncol* 18(9):1437–49.

Van den Block, L., Deschepper, R., Bilsen, J., Bossuyt, N., Van Casteren, V. and Deliens, L. (2009) 'Euthanasia and other end-of-life decisions: a mortality follow-back study in Belgium'. *BMC Public Health* 9:79.

van der Heide, A., Deliens, L., Faisst, K., Nilstun, T., Norup, M., Paci, E., van der Wal, G. and van der Maas, P.J. (EURELD Consortium) (2003) 'End-of-life decision-making in six European countries: descriptive study'. *Lancet* 362(9381):345–50.

van der Heide, A., Onwuteaka-Philipsen, B., Rurup, M.L., Buiting, H., van Delden, J.J., Hanssen-de Wolf, J.E., Janssen, A.G.J.M., Pasman, H.R.W., Rietjens, J., Prins, C.J.M., Deerenberg, I., Gevers, J.K.M., van der Maas, P.J. and van der Wal, G. (2007) 'End-of-life practices in the Netherlands under the Euthanasia Act'. *N Engl J Med* 356(19):1957–65.

van der Wal, G., van der Heide, A., Onwuteaka-Philipsen, B.D. and van der Maas, P.J. (2003) *Medische besluitvorming aan het einde van het leven. De praktijk en de toetsingsprocedure euthanasie*. Utrecht: De Tijdstroom.

van Dooren, S., van Veluw, H.T., van Zuylen, L., Rietjens, J.A., Passchier, J. and van der Rijt, C.C. (2009) 'Exploration of concerns of relatives during continuous palliative sedation of their family members with cancer'. *J Pain Symptom Manage* 38(3):452–9.

Vella-Brincat, J. and Macleod, A.D. (2004) 'Haloperidol in palliative care'. *Palliat Med* 18(3):195–201.

Venke Gran, S. and Miller, J. (2008) 'Norwegian nurses' thoughts and feelings regarding the ethics of palliative sedation'. *Int J Palliat Nurs* 14(11):532–8.

Ventafridda, V., Ripamonti, C., De Conno, F., Tamburini M. and Cassileth, B. (1990) 'Symptom prevalence and control during cancer patients' last days of life'. *J Palliative Care* 6(3):7–11.

Verhagen, E.H., Hesselman, G.M., Besseen, T.C. and de Graeff, A. (2005) 'Palliateve sedatie'. *Ned Tijdschr Geneeskd* 149:458–61.

Verkerk, M., van Wijlick, E., Legemaate, J. and de Graeff, A. (2007) 'A national guideline for palliative sedation in the Netherlands'. *J Pain Symptom Manage* 34(6):666–70.

Vilà Santasuana, A., Celorrio Jiménez, N., Sanz Salvador, X., Martínez Montauti, J., Díez-Cascón Menéndez, E. and Puig Rossell, C. (2008) 'The final week of life in an acute care hospital: review of 401 consecutive patients' [in Spanish]. *Rev Esp Geriatr Gerontol* 43(5):284–90.

Wahidi, M.M., Jain, P., Jantz, M., Lee, P., Mackensen, G.B., Barbour, S.Y., Lamb, C. and Silvestri, G.A. (2011) 'American College of Chest Physicians consensus statement on the use of topical anesthesia, analgesia, and sedation during flexible bronchoscopy in adult patients'. *Chest* 140(5):1342–50.

Walder, B., Tramèr, M.R. and Seeck, M. (2002) 'Seizure-like phenomena and propofol: a systematic review'. *Neurology* 58(9):1327–32.

Walling, A.M., Asch, S.M., Lorenz, K.A., Roth, C.P., Barry, T., Kahn, K.L. and Wenger, N.S. (2010) 'The quality of care provided to hospitalized patients at the end of life'. *Arch Intern Med* 170(12):1057–63.

Walshe, C. and Luker, K.A. (2010) 'District nurses' role in palliative care provision: a realist review'. *Int J Nurs Stud* 47(9):1167–83.

Walton, O. and Weinstein, S.M. (2002) 'Sedation for comfort at end of life'. *Curr Pain Headache Rep* 6(3):197–201.

Watson, J., Hockley, J. and Dewar, B. (2006) 'Barriers to implementing an integrated care pathway for the last days of life in nursing homes'. *Int J Palliat Nurs* 12(5):234–40.

Wein, S. (2000) 'Sedation in the imminently dying patient'. *Oncology (Williston Park)* 14(4):585–92.

White, P.F., Way, W.L. and Trevor, A.J. (1982) 'Ketamine – its pharmacology and therapeutic uses'. *Anesthesiology* 56(2):119–36.

Wildiers, H. and Menten, J. (2002) 'Death rattle: prevalence, prevention and treatment'. *J Pain Symptom Manage* 23(4):310–7.

Wildiers, H., Dhaenekint, C., Demeulenaere, P., Clement, P.M., Desmet, M., Van Nuffelen, R., Gielen, J., Van Droogenbroeck, E., Geurs, F., Lobelle, J.P. and Menten, J. (Flemish Federation of Palliative Care) (2009) 'Atropine, hyoscine butylbromide, or scopolamine are equally effective for the treatment of death rattle in terminal care'. *J Pain Symptom Manage* 38(1):124–33.

Williams, G. (2001) 'The principle of double effect and terminal sedation'. *Med Law Rev* 9(1):41–53.

Wilson, M.P., Pepper, D., Currier, G.W., Holloman, G.H. Jr and Feifel, D. (2012) 'The Psychopharmacology of Agitation: Consensus Statement of the American Association for Emergency Psychiatry Project BETA Psychopharmacology Workgroup'. *West J Emerg Med* 13(1):26–34.

Wolf, P. (2011) 'Acute drug administration in epilepsy: a review'. *CNS Neurosci Ther* 17(5):442–8.

World Health Organisation (1986) *Cancer Pain Relief.* Geneva: WHO.

Xyrichis, A. and Lowton, K. (2008) 'What fosters or prevents interprofessional teamworking in primary and community care? A literature review'. *Int J Nurs Stud* 45(1):140–53.

Yamagishi, A., Morita, T., Miyashita, M., Ichikawa, T., Akizuki, N., Shirahige, Y., Akiyama, M. and Eguchi, K. (2012) 'Providing palliative care for cancer patients: the views and exposure of community general practitioners and district nurses in Japan'. *J Pain Symptom Manage* 43(1):59–67.

Zinn, C. and Moriarty, D. (2012) 'Nurses' perceptions of palliative sedation in a Scottish hospice'. *J Hospice Palliat Nurs* 14(5):358–64.

LAWS

Belgium – Wet van 14 juni 2002 betreffende palliatieve zorg (Act on Palliative Care). *Belgisch Staatsblad* 26 October 2002.

Belgium – Article 403 Penal Code of 8 June 1867. *Belgisch Staatsblad* 9 June 1867.

Belgium – Wet van 22 augustus 2002 betreffende de rechten van de patiënt (Act on Patients' Rights). *Belgisch Staatsblad* 26 September 2002.

England – Mental Capacity Act 2005.

France – Loi n° 2005-370 du 22 avril 2005 relative aux droits des malades et à la fin de vie. (Law of 22 April 2005 relating to the rights of invalids at the end of life). *Journal Officiel* 23 April 2005, 59: 7089.

France – Code de la Santé Publique (Law on Public Health).

France – Code de Déontologie Médicale (Code of Medical Ethics).

Germany – *Strafgesetzbuch* (Criminal Law).

Germany – *Grundgesetz* (Fundamental Law).

Luxembourg – Loi du 16 mars 2009 relative aux soins palliatifs, à la directive anticipée et à l'accompagnement en fin de vie et modifiant 1. le Code de la sécurité sociale; 2. la loi modifiée du 16 avril 1979 fixant le statut général des fonctionnaires de l'Etat; 3. la loi modifiée du 24 décembre 1985 fixant le statut général des fonctionnaires communaux; 4. le Code du travail. *Journal Officiel du Grand-Duché de Luxembourg*, 16 March 2009, 610.

The Netherlands – Article 7:465 of the Civil Code.

The Netherlands – Medical Treatment Contracts Act. Law passed 17 November 1994 and effective 1 April 1995.

COURT CASES

CANADA

Rodriguez v. *British Columbia*, 1993 *CarswellBC* 228 (Supreme Court of Canada 1993).

EUROPE

Case of Pretty v. *the United Kingdom (Application No. 2346/02)* (2002) 35 *EHRR* 1 (European Court of Human Rights 2002).

GERMANY

'Dolantin', *NJW* 1997:807 (Bundesgerichtshof– German Supreme Court 1996).

20 W 224/98, *NJW* 1998:2747–9 (Oberlandesgericht Frankfurt am Main – Higher Regional Court, Frankfurt 1988).

2 StR 454/09 (Bundesgerichtshof II Strafsenats – Supreme Court, 2nd Criminal Division 2010). Available at www.ethikzentrum.de/downloads/bgh-2010–06–25.pdf (last accessed 24 April 2013).

UK

Airedale NHS Trust v. *Bland* [1993] 2 *WLR* 316, [1993] *AC* 789 (House of Lords 1993).

R v. *Adams* [1957] *Crim LR* 365.

R (on the application of Purdy) v. *Director of Public Prosecutions* [2009] *UKHL* 45 (House of Lords 2009).

R (on the application of Tony Nicklinson) v. *Ministry of Justice* [2012] *EWHC* 2381 (Admin) (High Court 2012).

R v. *Woollin* [1998] 4 *All ER* 103, [1998] 3 *WLR* 382 (House of Lords 1998).

Re A (Children) (Conjoined Twins: Surgical Separation) [2000] *EWCA* Civ 254, [2000] 4 *All ER* 961 (Court of Appeal 2000).

Re B (Adult: Refusal of Medical Treatment) [2002] 2 *All ER* 449 (Court of Appeal).

W v. *M and S and A NHS Primary Care Trust* [2011] *EWHC* 2443 (High Court 2001).

USA

Vacco v. *Quill*, 521 U.S. 793 (US Supreme Court 1997).

Washington v. *Glucksberg*, 521 U.S. 702 (US Supreme Court 1997).

Index

Books in the series

Marcus Radetzki, Marian Radetzki, Niklas Juth
Genes and Insurance: Ethical, Legal and Economic Issues

Ruth Macklin
Double Standards in Medical Research in Developing Countries

Donna Dickenson
Property in the Body: Feminist Perspectives

Matti Häyry, Ruth Chadwick, Vilhjálmur Árnason, Gardar Árnason
The Ethics and Governance of Human Genetic Databases: European Perspectives

Ken Mason
The Troubled Pregnancy: Legal Wrongs and Rights in Reproduction

Daniel Sperling
Posthumous Interests: Legal and Ethical Perspectives

Keith Syrett
Law, Legitimacy and the Rationing of Health Care

Alastair Maclean
Autonomy, Informed Consent and the Law: A Relational Change

Heather Widdows, Caroline Mullen
The Governance of Genetic Information: Who Decides?

David Price
Human Tissue in Transplantation and Research

Matti Häyry
Rationality and the Genetic Challenge: Making People Better?

Mary Donnelly
Healthcare Decision-Making and the Law: Autonomy, Capacity and the Limits of Liberalism

Anne-Maree Farrell, David Price and Muireann Quigley
Organ Shortage: Ethics, Law and Pragmatism

Sara Fovargue
Xenotransplantation and Risk: Regulating a Developing Biotechnology

John Coggon
What Makes Health Public?: A Critical Evaluation of Moral, Legal, and Political Claims in Public Health

Mark Taylor
Genetic Data and the Law: A Critical Perspective on Privacy Protection